# What Readers are Saying about This Edition

"A must-have for any operations and contact center leader. This book leads the way for brands to benefit in a constantly changing world that requires reinvention to succeed with your customers."

**JOSE VASQUEZ-MENDEZ**

*Vice President, Customer Service United Kingdom, American Express*

"Brad Cleveland knows more about customer relationships than anyone on the planet. This is a book that no business with customers can do without, meaning no business at all can do without."

**ALAN WEISS, Ph.D.**

*Author,* Million Dollar Consulting *and* The Consulting Bible

"*Call Center Management On Fast Forward* provides foundational information — critical to contact center success — and new information about other customer contact channels. A must-read for anyone connected with this industry."

**JOAN SCAZZARO**

*Director of Customer Service/Inside Sales, Bright House Networks*

"Embracing change and welding it to proven fundamentals are in short, what Brad is about. This new edition will deliver what you need to keep up with the ocean of customer centricity and ride the waves that will define the next phase of 'great.'"

**TODD HIXON**

*Operations Manager, Intuit APD*

"This book is an excellent resource on how you can build a framework to remain dynamic, ensure long-term success, and deliver a consistent customer experience. A must read for all levels of contact center management."

**GLENN GEMMILL**

*VP, Customer Care Center, Coca-Cola Refreshments*

"In this new version of our industry's best-selling book, Brad Cleveland provides insightful knowledge into call center operations ... I strongly recommend it."

**KJ CHEONG**

*President of CIRC, Korea*

# What Readers Have Said About Prior Editions

(Names and titles are as they appeared at the time.)

"You will be able to re-read this book several times as your call centre evolves, each time learning new methods and tips ..."

**DEAN YARDLEY**

*Strategic Innovations Manager, British Airways*

"Get it! Read it! Highlight it! Keep it on top of your desk! Read it again and again and again! Share the knowledge with everyone who needs to understand and value the contact center as the 'front door to the customer.'"

**PHYLLIS BATSON**

*Vice President, Customer Contact, Exelon – Energy Delivery*

"Whether you are a seasoned customer service professional or new to the contact center industry, *Call Center Management on Fast Forward* is a 'must read' to learn the keys to providing real value to your customers and organization."

**LISA SUSIN**

*Director, Michigan Customer Care Center, Blue Cross Blue Shield of Michigan*

"This book is a classic. It's a must read for professionals who wish to improve their service quality, achieve process efficiency and reduce operational cost."

**LI JIAN**

*Director, Customer Service, Bank of China*

"This new version provides current customer management strategies that capture the essence of effectively serving today's more discerning and ever more demanding customer!"

**DOMINICK KEENAGHAN**

*President, INSIGHTS, Dubai*

"This book is required reading for turning your centers into high performing strategic assets. You cannot achieve excellence in your centers until you clearly understand this book's content."

**TODD ARNOLD**

*Group Vice President, Customer Service, Duke Energy*

"Whether you're a small or large call center, this is the 'Complete Guide' to call center management. Learn key ingredients to building a successful call center or refresh your mind on maintaining the right mix for success."

**LEE BARONA**

*Director, Call Center, American Diabetes Association*

"This book provides clear, easy-to-understand insight into a complex subject."

**MALLIKARJUNA RAO**

*Assistant Vice President – Service Delivery, Idea Cellular Ltd., India*

"From cost center to profit center? Brad Cleveland leads the way; again and again."

**HENK VERBOOY**

*Chief Editor, CCM Magazine, The Netherlands*

"As a new call center director, the first edition of *Call Center Management on Fast Forward* was my roadmap. Simply put, this new expanded edition is — once again — a 'must read' to understand the basic challenges in a modern call center."

**MICHELLE FOLLETTE**

*Director, Portland Customer Contact Center, PacifiCorp*

"These are the building blocks of knowledge and key insights that anyone in call centers needs — and can — relate to!"

**BRETT FRAZER**

*Regional Customer Service Manager, Customer Service and Support, Asia Pacific Region, Microsoft*

"Well done, easy to read and recommended content for any contact center employee."

**BOOK BOOKER**

*Senior Vice President, SunTrust Online Business and Technology Solutions, SunTrust Banks, Inc.*

"This is an outstanding book that provides the necessary tools for managers to effectively manage their day-to-day operations and understand the strategy behind the tasks …"

**JEAN A. KOSTELANSKY**

*Director, Physician Services, Northwestern Memorial Hospital*

THIRD EDITION

# CALL CENTER
# MANAGEMENT
# ▶▶ON FAST FORWARD

## succeeding in the new era
## of customer relationships

## BRAD CLEVELAND

THIRD EDITION

# CALL CENTER MANAGEMENT
## ▶▶ON FAST FORWARD

UBM

*ICMI* Press

succeeding in the new era
of customer relationships

## BRAD CLEVELAND

Published by:
ICMI, a registered trademark of UBM
121 South Tejon Street, Suite 1100
Colorado Springs CO 80903 USA
www.icmi.com
+1 800-672-6177
+1 719-268-0328

ISBN 978-0-9854611-0-2

This book is dedicated to Kirsten and Grace.

# Table of Contents

# Acknowledgements

I'm grateful beyond words to so many who have contributed to my understanding of call centers and to the contents of this book.

Some are no longer with us. My friend, the late Phil Ahsley of Qantas Airways, always had a beef with the way we Americans spell "center," and he spoiled me with (many) first-class seats to Australia for my work there over the years. And others — colleagues and friends who made their mark on our profession. You are missed.

I am so appreciative of the team who have worked on this edition. Layne Holley was our editor and did a terrific job of polishing the manuscript, along with contributing several of the case studies. Michael Blair, who designed the first edition of the book fifteen years ago, provided his incredible talents to this project as designer-in-chief. And Tiffany LaReau — who lent her extensive expertise in forecasting and reporting to the last edition — turned to the design of the charts and graphs this time, giving the book a newfound elegance and visual appeal. Thanks to each of you for your time, professionalism and sense of humor through this project.

Our review team for the project contributed extensively and added insight this book would not otherwise have: Thank you Jean Bave Kerwin, Laura Grimes, Rose Polchin, Paul Pope, Linda Riggs, and Gina Szabo. I'd also like to thank those who provided review comments and testimonials to this edition: Stephen Blayone, KJ Cheong, Glenn Gemmill, Todd Hixson, Mary Ann Monroe, Tony Sandonato, Matt Sartori, Joan Scazzaro, Jose Vasquez-Mendez, Annie Woo, and Missy Zacks. And a big thanks to our *proofer extraordinaire*, David Levy, and to Christina Hammarberg for her research and proofing contributions.

Many others have contributed either directly to the first or second editions or to my understanding of this industry and where it's going. Their work has helped make this book possible: Todd Arnold, Gerry Barber, Fredia Barry, Lori Bocklund, Kelly Brickley, Keith Dawson, Bill Durr, John Fahrnkopf, Donna Fluss, Rebecca Gibson, Günter Greff, Linda Harden,

Debbie Harne, Susan Hash, Cheryl Odee Helm, Ellen Herndon, Ted Hopton, Cliff Hurst, Dominick Keenaghan, Dee Kohler, Greg Levin, the late Macklin Martin, Julia Mayben (my coauthor for the first version), Jay Minnucci, Tim Montgomery, Dale Mullen, Mary Murcott, George Nichols, Daniel Ord, Michael Pace, Bill Price, Marty Prunty, Dan Rickwalder, Marilyn Saulnier, Becky Simpson, Paul Smedley, Laurie Solomon, Ann-Marie Stagg, Michael Stalker, Paul Stockford, Alan Vaughan, Henk Verbooy, George Walther, Houdong Wang, Alan Weiss, and Stella Yang.

A big thank you to Tara Gibb and the entire ICMI team for encouraging and supporting this project! It's been an honor to work alongside each of you, and to see the work you are doing to build the next-generation ICMI.

Gordon MacPherson Jr. — my friend, founder of ICMI, and business partner in the early days of the company — is as creative as ever and has been enjoying "retirement" since 1996 (which, in his case, means producing historical documentaries, traveling, volunteering for a zillion different things ...). If you see something in the book that *really* makes sense, Gordon probably came up with it years ago.

I'd like to extend a special thanks to my parents, Doug and Annie Cleveland, for their ongoing encouragement (happy 50th this year!). My father was instrumental in developing my early interest in communications.

Most of all, I want to thank my two favorite people in the whole wide world, my wife Kirsten and daughter Grace. You make it all worthwhile and I love you both!

Brad Cleveland
Sun Valley, ID

# Foreword

*Call Center Management on Fast Forward: Succeeding in the New Era of Customer Relationships* is a clear voice with an unconfusing message: To successfully lead and manage, you need a good understanding of today's unique customer contact environment and an effective planning and management framework.

This message was true when telephone operators used cord switchboards and when inbound agents at catalog companies used pen and paper to capture order information. It is just as true today, as contact center managers incorporate new contact channels, social interactions, mobile-based services, virtual call centers, and quality and performance issues that impact the entire organization. And it will continue to be true in the future as call centers increasingly heed the demands of customers to provide a continuously improving and expanding array of choices for how those customers will be served.

This book outlines principles that you can use and trust. They are not passing fads. For example, service level and queuing theory are not abstract concepts; they are material facts that can be learned. The behavior of humans relating to queuing is sometimes fickle and difficult to predict, but the resources it will take to consistently achieve a specific level of service is a matter of mathematics. And the underpinnings of quality and customer satisfaction are well known. A comprehension of service level, queuing and quality makes it easy to understand customer contact processes in any industry and rationalizes key decisions and crucially important budgets.

The truly wise understand that rapid and lasting learning comes from choosing well your instructors and texts. The best will not waste your time or go off on tangents. They will present their information in a way that makes it easy to learn and retain.

So ... you must be truly wise because you have this book in your hands. Brad Cleveland has made a career of learning everything vital to customer management and presenting it with sparkle and conviction. He has paid the price in time, effort and miles to know what's really happening, and he is the acknowledged leader in this field.

Brad and the ICMI team have put together a book that belongs on the shelf of every call center manager — as well as every senior level executive who oversees customer service operations. Turn the page now for the good stuff. You'll see what I mean!

Gordon F. MacPherson, Jr.
Annapolis, Maryland
January, 2012

*Gordon MacPherson, Jr. was founder and first president of ICMI (now UBM's International Customer Management Institute). One of the industry's most influential early thinkers, Gordon launched the first publications, events and educational programs for call center managers. Gordon's formative work helped to shape many of the terms and practices in use worldwide today. He retired from the industry in 1996 and lives in Annapolis, Md.*

# Introduction

One of my first jobs — which I worked part time while I began college — was for an interconnect company that supplied telecommunications and data systems. I was the lowest-ranking person on the team, and one of my primary responsibilities was to install communications cable. This was often underneath floors, through tight, dark spaces with spider webs, scalding hot utility pipes, and creatures that would scurry just out of flashlight range. There's a popular expression of starting one's career on the "ground floor." There were many of those days I just wanted to work my way up to the ground floor...

But I had some great mentors and, with their help and encouragement, began to acquire a palpable sense of excitement and appreciation for the burgeoning new communications era that I was a small part of. I could only imagine the opportunities those high capacity lines were opening up — ours was becoming, in the words of a common cliché at the time, a "wired world" (actually, we're more of a "wireless world" today, but the point certainly stands). Indeed, the most significant developments to date have been those used by organizations to improve their services: the invention of 800 number (toll-free) service and ACD routing systems in the late 1960s and early 1970s; the introduction of workforce management capabilities and computer telephony integration in the 1980s; Web browsers and Internet-based services in the 1990s; and more recently, the amazing developments in multimedia, cloud-based capabilities, analytics and so much more.

We are now, however, seeing a major and fundamental shift: For the first time, developments on the customers' side of the equation — the meteoric rise of smartphones, social media, broadband and mobility — are the most significant factors driving customer expectations and services. Given what is happening, I'm convinced we'll see more change in the next five years than we've seen in the past two decades. We can harness and leverage the trends to our benefit, or we can get tumbled by them. We're entering the new era of customer relationships.

It's been 15 years (wow, 15!) since the first edition of this book was introduced. The response surpassed our highest expectations, and we were excited and grateful to see the book reach so many corners of the world. It became evident that it was benefiting from a much larger trend, as organizations everywhere were building their customer contact services and reaching out for management practices that could help. Almost 10 years (and something like 18 printings) later, we decided it was time for a major revision; the second edition hit the shelves in late 2006/early 2007. (My nine-year-old daughter would see a trend here: "Ten years, five years ... Dad, the next one is due in 2.5 years ...")

As we've worked on this latest edition, two seemingly contradictory observations continue to come to mind. One is how much the call center environment is changing. Interactions increasingly involve multiple channels and serve customers that are connected, savvy about their options and diverse in their needs and expectations. The latest-generation contact center is integrated with other business functions at a much deeper level, both in serving customers and in listening to and acting on their input, in order to improve products, services and processes. It is an engine for handling customer interactions, yes, but is potentially much more. It can facilitate customer communities, serve as a hub of information for internal stakeholders, and be a powerful force in innovation, marketing and furthering the organization's brand reputation.

For all the exciting developments, though, the other observation that continues to amaze me is how little the core management principles have changed. The fundamentals are intact and are arguably more important than ever. You've got to have a clear strategic plan; establish supporting objectives; get the right resources in the right places at the right times, doing the right things; and, build an organizationwide focus on delivering services. Otherwise, today's time-driven, multichannel environment will quickly overwhelm your best efforts.

So... if you've read either of the first two editions, you'll see things that are familiar. Though this was a significant ground-level and up rewrite, we didn't try to change the unchangeable, those principles that are tried and true. But you'll find much that's new and updated, from incorporating new ways of serving customers, e.g., through social media, to the ever-expanding role of what contact centers do and how they deliver strategic value.

I am amazed to think back to those days in crawl spaces and consider what's happened in the realm of customer communications since then. Customer interaction will be a powerful force in shaping our future. We are all pioneers in defining and establishing the next generation of service, and I'm excited to be part of this opportunity with you!

Brad Cleveland

Visit the website for *Call Center Management on Fast Forward* to meet the author, see videos, interact, ask questions and learn more about the book! **www.icmi.com/fastforward**

# Part One:
# The New Era of Customer Relationships

## CHAPTER 1:
## Familiar Challenges, New Opportunities

## CHAPTER 2:
## The Blueprint — Your Customer Access Strategy

## CHAPTER 3:
## The Driving Forces in Customer Contact Centers

---

*To succeed in today's fast-evolving environment, you must understand the landscape: empowered customers, more types of interactions, increasing complexity, and the heightened impact of customer service on the organization's results and brand reputation. To those who make the effort to acquire the right professional skills and knowledge, leadership and management opportunities are significant.*

---

# CHAPTER 1:
# Familiar Challenges, New Opportunities

*If you wait for tomorrow, tomorrow comes.*
*If you don't wait for tomorrow, tomorrow comes.*

**AFRICAN PROVERB**

One of my favorite historic hotels is Hotel Monaco, in Washington, D.C. Its ultra-high ceilings, classic architecture, and the whimsical services intrigue me — they often place fishbowls with live goldfish (aptly named George Washington or Abraham Lincoln) in guest rooms. What I'm most drawn to, though, is the history. This is the site of the city's original post office and where inventor Samuel B. Morse opened and operated the first public telegraph office in the United States.

Telegraph enabled the transmission of Morse code (you know, *di-di-di-dit di-dit*), which began to drastically change communication — and, in many ways, the world. Messages that took ships weeks or land carriers days were relayed in seconds. You get a sense of the awe that this new capability inspired in the words of the first transmission Morse sent on May 24, 1844: "What hath God wrought." The message is out of the book of Numbers (written around 1400 B.C.), chosen for Morse by Annie Ellsworth, daughter of U.S. Patent Office Commissioner Henry Ellsworth. It wasn't exactly understated. I believe she, Morse and others present that day got a glimpse into an astonishing future (and I can only imagine their wonderment had they lived to see the communication capabilities we carry around in our purses and pockets today).

The immediacy of telegraph would help inspire more powerful advancements in transportation and communication. By the turn of the century, steam-driven locomotives could whisk you across a continent in a matter of days. Henry Ford's "horseless carriages," which the French called automobiles, could take you across a large town in a fraction of an hour. And in 1903, two Dayton, Ohio brothers, Wilbur and Orville Wright, built a machine that could fly. Speed was becoming a potent economic and social currency.

It was against this backdrop that the telephone, invented in 1876, was quickly becoming part of the fabric of society. And unlike the telegraph, it required no special training — its ease of use and accessibility to the public led to rapid growth (a parallel we see today in mobile apps and social media platforms). As fast as an airplane could fly between two points, the telephone could "get you there" even faster. "By the wondrous agency of electricity, speech flashes through space and, swift as lightning, bears tidings of good and evil," wrote French artist Pierre Puvis de Chavannes in a caption to one of his famous murals. Historian John Brooks described the impact of the telephone on life in the first decade of the 1900s this way: "In city and country alike, the telephone was creating a new habit of mind — a habit of tenseness and alertness, of demanding and expecting immediate results, whether in business, love or other forms of social interaction."

But fast-growing demand in both transportation and communication services — they have fed, not displaced, each other from the beginning — was creating enormous new challenges. Whether it was roads, rails, runways or relay circuits, the pressure was on to get capacity in place. And business and government leaders struggled to understand how these new capabilities would change customer behavior and their impact on the economy.

## The First Call Centers?

As the subscriber base grew, telephone companies in particular were contending with a vexing resource-planning problem. Automated central offices hadn't yet been invented, so human operators were required to establish connections for callers. The big question was, how many operators are required? Too few, and long waits would be unacceptable to customers. But too many would be inefficient and would drive up costs.

Further complicating the issue, the work seemed to occur randomly, driven by the myriad of motivations individuals had for placing calls. It was one thing to get physical infrastructure in place. But it was a different challenge altogether to get dynamic calling demand accurately matched up with the correct number of human operators — day in, day out, morning, noon and night. And service that was slow or unavailable was quickly becoming unacceptable to a public that had thoroughly embraced this new means of communication.

In the years that followed, many bright people would grapple with these and related resource management challenges. One of the first was A.K. Erlang, an engineer with the Copenhagen Telephone Company in Denmark, who, in 1917, developed the queuing formula Erlang C. The formula is widely used in today's call centers to calculate staffing requirements. Others who followed Erlang worked on disciplined forecasting techniques, scheduling methodologies, measurements and objectives, and systems and software that enabled the vast range of capabilities now available. Each advancement contributed, directly or indirectly, to those that followed.

## Today's Contact Centers

A century later, as speed and innovation have reached levels unimaginable to our industry's forefathers, there are unmistakable similarities in the challenges and opportunities we face. Even as we struggle through economic turbulence, we are witnessing significant breakthroughs in communication — from social networks that connect us in new and powerful ways to multimedia capabilities that can put us face-to-face from opposite ends of the globe. Brooks' description of the early 1900s is just as fitting today:

Communication technologies have fed a habit of demanding and expecting immediate results.

If you manage a modern call center, there is a particularly familiar ring to the demands the early telephone switchboard centers faced. Accurately matching resources to demand in a dynamic, always-changing environment is an ever-present challenge. Forecasting the workload, getting the right people and other resources in place at the right times, developing accurate budgets, meeting customer demands — these continue to be key objectives.

What call centers do, however, and the value they can deliver to organizations has evolved significantly. They have become strategic assets, powerful hubs of communication that encompass many potential channels. They enable customers to reach the information and services they need, and provide organizations with a powerful means to listen to and act on customer input. (Note: I alternate between the terms call, contact, transaction and interaction throughout the book. The terms caller and customer are

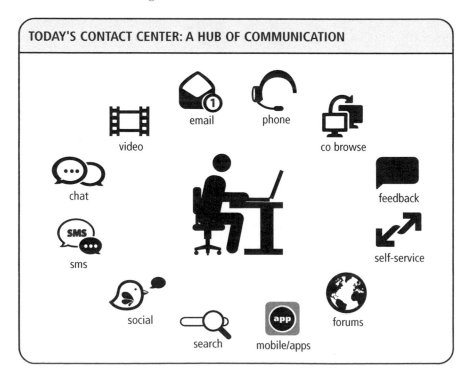

TODAY'S CONTACT CENTER: A HUB OF COMMUNICATION

video · email · phone · co browse · chat · feedback · sms · self-service · social · search · mobile/apps · forums

also used interchangeably, as are call center and contact center. See the discussion What Should You Call It? in Chapter 2.)

The latest-generation contact centers are the engines organizations depend on not only to handle interactions with customers but also to listen to and engage in external communities. They are taking on more of a "level two" role, handling issues not resolved through self-service and communities. And they are integrated with other business functions at a much deeper level, enabling the organization to better understand and improve products, services and processes. Contact centers, and the management methodologies that guide them, are bringing order to what would otherwise be an enormous, asymmetrical challenge in serving customers.

# A Definition for Contact Center Management

The International Customer Management Institute (ICMI) developed a definition of contact center management that has stood the test of time and is as applicable today as ever: "Contact center management is the art of having the right number of properly skilled people and supporting resources in place at the right times to handle an accurately forecasted workload, at service level and with quality." This definition can be boiled down to two major objectives: 1) Get the right resources in place at the right times, and 2) do the right things. Let's take an introductory look at each.

---

*Contact center management is the art of having the right number of properly skilled people and supporting resources in place at the right times to handle an accurately forecasted workload, at service level and with quality.*

---

## THE RIGHT RESOURCES IN THE RIGHT PLACE AT THE RIGHT TIMES

The ability for contact centers to deliver the right services at the right times didn't happen overnight. In terms of meeting service level objectives, the profession has evolved through three primary stages:

**1. SEAT-OF-THE-PANTS MANAGEMENT** — very little consideration of service level in planning.

**2. SERVICE LEVEL AWARENESS** — an effort to maintain good service levels, but only a vague correlation to them in planning.

**3. CORRELATING SERVICE LEVEL TO THE ORGANIZATION'S MISSION** — choosing appropriate service level objectives and provisioning the resources to achieve them on a real-time basis.

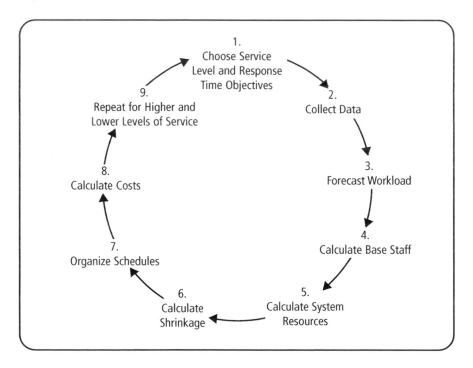

Individual organizations tend to evolve through the same general stages. They often start out with underdeveloped resource plans, and then move towards a more professional approach to management.

To deliver consistent, high levels of service, you need a thoughtful strategy that defines how you will interact with customers — we'll look at the importance of developing and maintaining an effective "customer access strategy" in Chapter 2. Then, you will need a systematic planning and management process, which can be summarized in nine steps:

**1. CHOOSE SERVICE LEVEL AND RESPONSE TIME OBJECTIVES.** These fundamental objectives set parameters for the two major types of interactions: those that must be handled right away (requiring a service level objective), and those that can be handled at a later time (requiring a response time objective). We'll explore these types of interactions in detail in Chapter 4.

**2. COLLECT DATA.** You will need information from many places. Today's contact center systems are important sources of planning data, telling you much about the interactions you're handling. But much of the information you need comes from beyond the contact center's walls — e.g., what marketing is doing, how customer preferences are changing, conversations and trends in social channels, competitive activity that may have an impact on your workload, and relevant developments in the economy. We'll discuss this important step in Chapter 5.

**3. FORECAST WORKLOAD.** Workload forecasts must include each of the components of customer contacts: average talk time, average after-call work (wrap-up), and volume. (Or just handling time and volume for contacts that don't have separate talk and wrap-up requirements, such as social or email). A good forecast predicts these components accurately for future time periods, usually down to a half hour. Forecasts should encompass all types of contacts — phone, email, chat, social interactions, SMS, et al., and your plans should also account for any related work that will require contact center resources. We'll discuss forecasting in Chapter 6.

**4. CALCULATE BASE STAFF.** Most developed contact centers use Erlang C or variations of it to calculate staffing requirements. Erlang C is the base formula used in virtually all workforce management systems. But capabilities such as skills-based routing and complex network environments present challenges that may require computer simulation and modeling. We'll explore these issues in Chapter 7.

**5. CALCULATE SYSTEM RESOURCES.** Staffing and system resource issues are inextricably associated and must be calculated together. We will summarize this step in Chapter 7.

**6. CALCULATE SHRINKAGE.** Rostered staff factor and shrinkage are terms that relate to an important step in planning: You've got to be realistic and account for breaks, absenteeism, training, work not directly part of handling customer interactions, and all of the other considerations that occupy agent time. We'll take a look at this important step in Chapter 8.

**7. ORGANIZE SCHEDULES.** Schedules are essentially forecasts of who needs to be where and when. They should lead to getting the right people in the right places at the right times. We will discuss this process in Chapter 8.

**8. CALCULATE COSTS.** This step projects costs for the resources required to meet service and quality objectives. We will cover budget issues throughout Parts Two, Three and Four.

**9. REPEAT FOR HIGHER AND LOWER LEVELS OF SERVICE.** Preparing budgets around different levels of service provides an understanding of cost trade-offs, which is invaluable in budgeting decisions. We will discuss this step in Chapter 10.

In sum, the best-managed contact centers do a good job of resource planning and management, and have built processes that are systematic, collaborative and accurate. But of course, meeting your service level objectives is just an enabler — a ticket to proceed. The real value comes from what you do with interactions once the connections are made.

## DOING THE RIGHT THINGS

Doing the right things means creating value for your customers and for your organization. Customer contact centers have the potential to create value on three distinct levels:

**LEVEL 1: EFFICIENCY.** Because contact centers pool information, people and technology resources, they are a highly efficient means of delivering service. Appropriate forecasts, accurate staffing and schedules, and effective real-time management complement and further the center's inherent efficiencies. And these disciplines retain their importance, even as an ever-expanding array of contact channels become part of the mix. These subjects are covered in Parts Two and Three of the book.

**LEVEL 2: CUSTOMER SATISFACTION AND LOYALTY.** In recent years, research has begun to reveal the powerful connection between high levels of satisfaction and profitability. And given today's powerful social communities and the opportunity for customers to share experiences, every interaction must be viewed as an event that can have an impact, positive or negative, on the organization's brand reputation.

**LEVEL 3: STRATEGIC VALUE.** The contact center is the customer's moment of truth, shaping how they perceive and will interact with the organization in the future. But there's far more to it — in the course of handling interactions and capturing customer input, the contact center can become a powerful source of intelligence (based on customer data and insight), helping business units across the board improve products, services and processes.

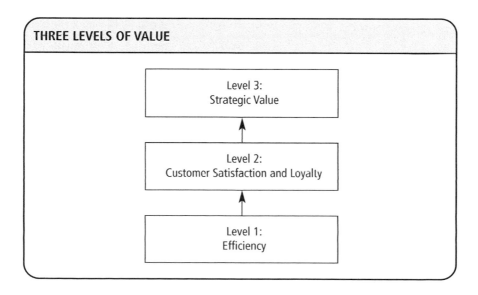

**THREE LEVELS OF VALUE**

Level 3:
Strategic Value

Level 2:
Customer Satisfaction and Loyalty

Level 1:
Efficiency

Every day, more organizations are transitioning their centers from a rote focus on efficiency to better harnessing their strategic potential. Having a greater business impact requires objectives and measures that support organizationwide contributions. It is essential to take inventory of job roles, technologies, processes and organizational design, and align them to deliver maximum value on all three levels. These subjects will be covered throughout Parts Four and Five of the book.

## Will the Fundamentals Change?

Today's always-on, connected world is changing the nature of how products and services are sold, delivered and supported. Many managers are justifiably wondering where these developments are taking us: Do the fundamentals of contact center planning and management still apply?

Short answer: Yes! Let's say you want to incorporate new interactions through social platforms (which will be covered, in context, throughout the book). Once you get started, and begin identifying and pulling in the work, you will need to establish appropriate service level objectives (Step 1). You will begin to cultivate processes for collecting necessary information (Step 2). And ... yes ... you will need to begin forecasting the workload (Step 3). That will enable you to calculate staff and system resources required (Steps 4 and 5). You can then account for shrinkage and organize schedules (Steps 6 and 7). Next, with resources defined, you can analyze costs, compare them with other service levels and (everybody's favorite) put budgets together (Steps 8 and 9). All the while, you will develop services and processes that ensure you're delivering consistent quality, boosting customer satisfaction and capturing input and insight. If you have integrated new types of work in the past, this effort should, in many ways, feel familiar.

Or, how about communicating with customers by video? Does that change things? Beyond appropriate processes and the help of enabling technologies (and the need for agents to look and dress the part!), the management approach will be much the same. The principles of getting the *right people and supporting resources in the right place at the right times, doing the right things* will never become obsolete. In short, effective, step-by-step planning and management will be as important as ever in the foreseeable future.

---

*The stakes for your organization are higher than ever.*

---

So, how is contact center management changing? An obvious answer is that there are new types of interactions, and agents proficient in handling existing workloads are not inherently comfortable with or ready for new channels. Customers will often initiate the service process through search or by seeking information in online communities — making the contacts that reach the center that much more complex and demanding. Job roles are evolving, and agents, analysts and managers are expected to know and do more. Senior managers are requiring better visibility on what the contact center is doing and the returns on those investments. And in a theme that runs throughout the book, contact centers are becoming powerful strategic assets; the stakes for your organization and brand reputation are higher than ever. Call it *call center management on fast forward!*

But if you learn well the underlying principles of effective contact center management, and know how to apply them, your skills and knowledge will be in high demand. You will be ready for the changes and developments ahead.

## From Back Room to Boardroom

Well-run customer contact operations have become a major factor in customer retention, competitiveness and the ability for organizations to adapt to changing markets. To managers who successfully meet the challenges, the opportunities for advancement are significant. Contact center management — once in the category of "mystical arts" or a little-under-

**SKILLS AND KNOWLEDGE REQUIREMENTS**

- Leadership and management
- Communication — writing, speaking and interpersonal
- Project management
- Performance assessments
- Quantitative analysis
- Customer behavior
- Cultural aptitude
- Random workload arrival
- Workload forecasting
- Queuing theory and statistical competency
- Staffing and scheduling
- Communication norms, i.e., by channel
- Technology basics
- Organizational behavior
- Ergonomics and workplace environment
- Industry vocabulary

stood supporting function — is emerging as a thriving, important and increasingly recognized profession.

An important step to meeting the challenges ahead is recognizing that you are in a bona fide profession — one that is constantly advancing. Treat it as such. That means staying in tune with the growing body of industry knowledge. It means making a commitment to personal growth and development. It requires developing a network of other professionals and resources that you can count on. In short, you have to invest the time and effort necessary for confidence and success.

Whatever your background or level of experience, I hope that this book helps you in that effort. This is an exciting time of development. Thanks for coming along!

# CHAPTER 2:
# The Blueprint —
# Your Customer Access Strategy

*If one does not know to which port one is sailing, no wind is favorable.*

**SENECA**

It could be that you have just a few people in a small department or company handling interactions with customers (internal or external). You're investigating call center management — what's it about and can it help? On the other hand, you might have thousands of agents working across multiple sites around the globe. You're looking for refinement to ensure your organization is benefiting from the latest practices.

In either case, or in any case in the span between, you need a plan — *a customer access strategy* — to guide your organization's direction and decisions. As a part of that effort, you will need to review your customers' expectations often to ensure that your plan reflects their needs and realities.

But before we explore those topics, let's answer that most basic question: *What is a contact center?*

## What Is a Contact Center?

A prerequisite to developing an effective customer access strategy is to decide that you need a call center (contact center) — or, perhaps to acknowledge that you may already have one but haven't recognized it as

**15**

such! To hurdle this initial step, it's worthwhile to review what a contact center is and does, and to identify the characteristics that define all such environments.

ICMI defines contact center as: "A coordinated system of people, processes, technologies and strategies that provides access to information, resources and expertise, through appropriate channels of communication, enabling interactions that create value for the customer and organization." Yes, it's an involved definition — but contact centers are involved operations.

---

*A contact center is a coordinated system of people, processes, technologies and strategies that provides access to information, resources, and expertise, through appropriate channels of communication, enabling interactions that create value for the customer and organization.*

---

It's often easier to explain what a contact center does than to try to define it. And diverse examples are everywhere. For example, many hospitals have launched (or partnered with an outside supplier to provide) contact center services in recent years — and referred to them variously as consumer health lines, ask-a-nurse numbers, resource centers, and similar. They are often staffed by registered nurses and other healthcare professionals. Many are open 24x7, offering a range of services — from assessing medical symptoms and recommended courses of action, to getting physician referrals, resolving insurance questions and even signing up for wellness classes.

These resource centers are a great idea, and when done right, are incredibly valuable to the medical centers and the communities they serve. You can imagine the rationale that management teams think through before the launch: Customers (patients) have thousands of questions. They contact different departments looking for answers, often reaching the wrong places. The professionals in those areas don't have the time, training or know-how to handle many of the inquiries that they get. In many cases, the employees fielding the contacts don't know where to send patients for the information they need, so they direct them to other units or back to a main switchboard.

Then someone begins to ponder a solution. *Hey ... what if we had a way to handle all of these issues? We could train qualified people and give them access to the information they will need, from symptom-based references to class schedules. We'll hire nurses to address the medical-related questions. And we'll put in a system for documenting each contact and logging critical data, such as symptoms described and advice provided. We'll put in processes for coordinating with the rest of the institution so that the information we have is up to date and accurate.*

One day ... *voilà*, a contact center is born! And it shares the basic characteristics common to all contact centers (see sidebar).

## COMMON CHARACTERISTICS OF CONTACT CENTERS

- Interactions with customers are handled by a group of people, not a specific person.
- Agents are cross-trained to handle a variety of contact types.
- The customer workload is distributed based on agent availability and/or specific skills.
- Agents have access to information on the organization's products, services, policies, and other resources they will need to handle contacts.
- Reports provide leadership with information on the quantity and nature of contacts handled, services delivered, service levels, customer information, and other data that can be used for forecasting and planning, as well as product and service improvements.

Interestingly, there are a lot of people running call centers who don't know they are ... well, running call centers. They know they handle lots of interactions, and that they need the right people available at the right times or the queue gets out of control and customers quickly become unhappy. And they realize that somehow they need to predict how many contacts they are going to get, when they are going to happen, and the agents and supporting resources needed to handle them.

One fortunate day, they will be searching the Web or talking to a supplier or colleague, and they'll learn that call center management is a bona fide modern profession supported by a world of resources. They will begin to find books, conferences and professional membership organizations made up of other people who also run call centers. They will realize — with great relief and a growing sense of excitement — *they are not alone!*

A similar discovery process can happen within organizations that already have contact centers. For example, handling customer communication through social channels may start out in the marketing department. Soon enough, those involved find themselves handling interactions that are more in the realm of customer service and support. They begin to detect workload patterns, adjust staffing levels as they can, and explore measures and management disciplines that can help. In short, their monitoring, planning and activities begin to morph into something like the operations of a contact center. The wise among them will, at this point, sit down with the broader organization and map out a unified customer access strategy that involves and leverages normal customer support operations.

(There's also a different ilk of managers — a stubborn lot who run call center-like environments but refuse to acknowledge them as such. "We're not that. No-sirrreeee," they say. "We're different!" I'm not referring to those who simply reject the terms "call center" or "contact center" — no problem there. I'm thinking of those who miss out on the benefits that forecasting, staffing, scheduling and other disciplined management practices could bring to their operations because they're purportedly something different. I don't care if you staff astronauts to take support calls from space — if you're in a contact-center-like environment, and need to match the organization's know-how with real-time customer requirements, then, by all means, put today's proven management methodologies to work! Everybody wins.)

## WHAT SHOULD YOU CALL IT?

As organizations continue to transition centers dominated by telephone calls into multichannel operations handling email, social, chat, click-to-talk, and other types of contacts, many have justifiably questioned the use of the term "call center." Examples of alternatives include:

- Contact center
- Interaction center
- Customer care center
- Customer support center
- Customer communications center
- Customer services center
- Sales and service center
- Technical support center
- Help desk
- Information line

At present, the popular business and consumer press is widely using the term call center, while many inside the industry prefer one of the alternatives, especially contact center or (when applicable) technical support center.

There are also terms specific to vertical industries, such as reservations center (travel), hotline (emergency services) and trading desk (financial services). And some organizations use specific or branded names for their centers or the teams that staff them — e.g., the Zappos Customer Loyalty Team (Zappos.com), askAAMC (Anne Arundel Medical Center), and Apple Care (the term Apple uses for its overall customer support approach, and also branded as part of the primary contact number, 800-APL-CARE).

It's common to hear consultants, suppliers and practitioners speak of transitioning a call center into a contact center (a distinction I don't make in this book). They usually draw differentiation in the variety of channels handled, the importance of the center to the organization, and how it has progressed on a maturity continuum, e.g., from focusing primarily on operational metrics to measures more aligned with customer experience. My concern is that this can encourage one-upmanship and the invention

*(continued next page)*

of yet more terms to illustrate a progression beyond contact center.

It's also worth noting that, for the kind of multichannel experience we're trying to describe, "call" is linguistically more accurate and has richer historical meaning than "contact." The original meaning of the term call, long before the telephone was invented, was "to visit." I'd visit your village; you'd visit my business. It was even used in a romantic context: "I hear George has been calling on Martha for several months now." Today, our customers are visiting us through a wide range of contact alternatives.

Ideally, we would have stayed with the term call center as a profession, and built it out to a place where the person in the next airline seat has at least a clue what we do. But I've decided this is not my battle to fight — not to the point of distraction. Perhaps like you, I tend to use contact center with industry insiders and call center (at least as a starting place) with those outside the profession. Readers of prior editions will notice I include contact center much more frequently in this version of the book, in deference to common usage. And I alternate, with no intended difference implied.

Beyond the terms, there is a very positive and ultimately more important development place: Business executives are gaining a better understanding and appreciation for what these operations do and how important they are to organizations and the customers they serve. That's what really matters.

(Oh, and we're not alone. Terms abound out there, sometimes with nuanced meaning — a point I've considered when I've turned off my phone/cell/mobile on the plane/aircraft/flight and thought about it.)

In short, contact centers enable customers to access the resources they need on a real-time basis. The best deliver these services effectively, while boosting customer satisfaction and helping to improve the larger organization's products, services and processes. But that doesn't just happen. It requires an up-to-date, effective customer access strategy.

# Developing a Customer Access Strategy

A customer access strategy can be defined as "a framework — a set of standards, guidelines and processes — describing the means by which customers and the organization can interact and are enabled to access the information, services and expertise needed."

---

*A customer access strategy is a framework — a set of standards, guidelines and processes — describing the means by which customers and the organization can interact and are enabled to access the information, services and expertise needed.*

---

At some point in developing customer contact services, the need for an overall plan becomes obvious. Not only have management activities multiplied, the interrelated nature of decisions has implications for existing organizational structure and personnel responsibilities, as well as on the allocation of resources, human and otherwise. Every decision must be viewed in terms of its impact on others and on overall results and direction.

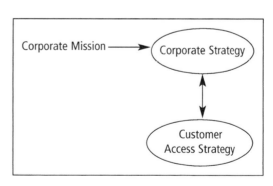

It's also important to note that developments on the customers' end — smartphones, broadband, social media and mobility — are driving the most significant progress in expectations and service. It's essential to revisit your customer access strategy often enough to keep it current, or it will fall out of alignment with what your customers need and how they choose to interact.

As with corporate strategy, a customer access strategy can take many different forms. But the most effective plans cover, in one way or another, these essential components.

**CUSTOMER SEGMENTS:** This part of the plan should define how customers and prospects are segmented (e.g., by geography, volume of business, level of service purchased, unique requirements) and how the organization will serve each. Customer segmentation generally comes from the organization's marketing strategy, but given the operational realities and practical tradeoffs of serving different segments appropriately, contact center managers are increasingly involved in this process. You may also want to summarize guidelines for how the organization communicates with customers and ensures coordination across units (e.g., informing the contact center of marketing campaigns). As you put a pencil to this part of the plan, think through who your customers and prospects are, how they access services now, how they prefer to communicate, the sites and communities they tend to use, and where are they discussing your services, company, market and competitors.

> **COMPONENTS OF A CUSTOMER ACCESS STRATEGY**
>
> - Customer Segments
> - Types of Interactions
> - Access Channels/Communities
> - Hours of Operation
> - Service Level and Response Time Objectives
> - Routing Methodology
> - People/Technology Resources Required
> - Information Required
> - Analysis, Improvement
> - Guidelines for Deploying New Services

**TYPES OF INTERACTIONS:** This step anticipates and identifies the major types of interactions that will occur — e.g., placing orders, changing orders, inquiries, technical support, providing feedback and reviews, etc. Each type of interaction should be analyzed for opportunities to build value and improve customer satisfaction and loyalty.

**ACCESS CHANNELS/COMMUNITIES:** This step — where strategy

## WHAT DOES A CUSTOMER ACCESS STRATEGY LOOK LIKE?

Customer access strategies are like business plans in that some are well documented and others exist only in pieces and in the heads of various managers. Too often, the latter is the case.

But there are standout examples of plans that are effective and up to date. A wireless carrier that I have worked with has a well-organized customer access strategy. It consists of a cleanly designed home page, the centerpiece, which provides links to each of the individual components. The links access files (databases, documents, etc.) that make up the different parts of their plan, such as customer segments, access numbers and addresses, routing diagrams, agent groups, hours of operation, service level objectives, and so forth. There are also links within these areas that allow you to logically move to others — but the home page will always get you back to the main directory. The plan could be printed, but would be many pages, given the detail of numbers, routing diagrams, etc., and is readily accessed by the team through a secure online resource.

The most impressive aspect of the plan is that it lists who is responsible for keeping the overall plan current, and the individuals who have ownership over various components: marketing (customer segments), IT/telecom (routing schematics) and others. Each document has an "updated on ___" date. The plan is current, and they don't make major decisions without referring to it.

really begins to hit home for contact centers — identifies all of the possible communication channels (phone, social, chat, email, SMS, IVR, customer communities, fax, kiosk, video, face-to-face, mail, self-service … the lot) along with corresponding telephone numbers, URLs, IVR menus, email addresses, shipping addresses, etc.

**HOURS OF OPERATION:** This part of your strategy settles on appropriate hours of operation, which are often different for different contact channels or types of interactions. Generally, self-service applications will always be available. On the other hand, while some agent-assisted services may be available 24x7, others have more limited hours; for example, you might reach a utility for a gas leak at all hours but not for general customer service. Today's customers are often described as being "always on" or "always connected" (not literally true, of course, but the point is a good one). The impact that has on the approach you take in assigning resources depends on the nature and importance of the issues being discussed, and service and brand implications of providing timely input.

**SERVICE LEVEL AND RESPONSE TIME OBJECTIVES:** This step summarizes the organization's service level and response time objectives (see Chapter 4). Different objectives are often appropriate for different types of interactions, contact channels, and customer segments.

**ROUTING METHODOLOGY:** This part of the plan covers how — by customer, type of interaction and access channel — each contact is going to be routed and distributed. While these terms have inbound connotations, this also applies to outbound; for example, when the organization originates the contact, through which agent group or system will the contact be made?

**PEOPLE/TECHNOLOGY RESOURCES REQUIRED:** This step transitions from "getting the interaction to the right place at the right time" to "doing the right things." Which agents or systems will be required for each customer segment and contact type?

**INFORMATION REQUIRED:** What information on customers, products and services will need to be accessible to agents and customers? What information should be captured during interactions? How will the organization meet applicable privacy or reporting requirements?

**ANALYSIS/IMPROVEMENT:** This step defines how the information captured and produced during contacts will be used to better understand customers and to improve products, services and processes. You may also want to summarize major performance objectives and how the contact center's value and contributions will be measured.

**GUIDELINES FOR DEPLOYING NEW SERVICES:** Finally, the plan should provide guidance on deploying new services, including technology architecture (corporate standards and technology migration plans) and investment guidelines (priorities and plans for operational and capital expenditures). This step should also describe who will keep the customer access strategy current as services evolve — e.g., who has overall responsibility, how often the plan will be updated, and who has ownership of individual components.

Your customer access strategy will help you formulate answers to many important questions. For example:

- How should your contact center be organized? How should agent groups be structured?
- What kinds of skills and knowledge will your agents, supervisors and managers need? How should your hiring and training practices support these requirements?
- What system capabilities best support your strategy? Do you have what you need in-house or will you need to build, buy or contract for required technologies?
- What kinds of processes best support your plans? Where should they be refined or restructured?
- Is it feasible or advisable to outsource some services? (If so, the customer access strategy is still the responsibility of the client organization.) What capabilities must the partner have to support the organization's requirements?
- Are internal plans and budgets in alignment?
- Can the customer access strategy help shape the organization's overall strategy, e.g., by helping to differentiate the organization's services?

## SOCIAL MEDIA: CONNECT, ENGAGE, AND THRIVE

Customer service and support is one of the most expansive, fast-developing and dynamic aspects of the social phenomenon. Many executives know their organizations should be tuned into social channels. But there's nothing like seeing these conversations in real time.

I recall an executive who works with an automobile manufacturer telling

## SOCIAL MEDIA: CHANNEL OR STRATEGY?

Terms related to social media are quickly evolving, and must be used and interpreted in context. For example, I'm often asked for advice on shaping a "social strategy." It's an important question — but without further definition, can be overly vague. Social media is a vast and ever-expanding array of platforms, tools and capabilities. It would be like referring to "Internet strategy" when the Web was gaining traction in the 1990s. There are implications for marketing, collaboration, production, HR, design, publicity, and much more.

Similarly, many in the profession, myself included, use the term "channel" for social media in the context of services and support. That's accurate when we consider the fact that social media is a means for the customer to contact or interact with the organization (and vice versa) and the related work must be forecasted and appropriate staffing made. On the other hand, it's arguably more than "just" a channel. Consider the one-to-many nature of service delivery; networking properties; the ability for a community of others with common interests to collaborate and share; and, the believability of friends' advice and recommendations over advertising. Whereas an email or a phone call is self-contained, most social conversations inherently reach others — and in that sense, go beyond the confines of a traditional communications channel.

This area of management is evolving quickly, and terms will be added and clarified. It's no problem to use any of them as they are, as long as they are expanded and explained as needed.

of standing behind a computer with several others on her team as the organization "flipped the switch" on a new social media listening tool. The conversations — blogs, tweets, Facebook posts, feedback sites — began scrolling across the screen: comments about the company's products, services, policies and brand — good and (more often) not so good. She described the urge to sit down and begin responding right then and there. *And to think they hadn't been.* It was like putting on a snorkel mask and jumping off a boat into the Caribbean — a whole new world became visible.

By listening to and learning from conversations across social sites, you can determine where you'll be most effective. You can't be everywhere at once, so most begin by looking for leverage. With the one-to-many nature of social interactions, you can often prevent similar contacts from other customers, another opportunity for call deflection. As you get better at identifying and handling interactions, you will be positioned to evolve into a more sophisticated approach, geared around criteria such as a customer's influence, root cause analysis, and marketplace opportunities.

Yes, there are risks in handling social interactions. A large audience is potentially watching, and once these conversations are out there, they are recorded, will exist forever, and can be easily found through search. But it's important to remember that there is an even greater risk to your brand and reputation by not being there. Ignoring customers, being deafeningly silent, is the worst kind of reflection on your service and organization.

Kip Wetzel, Senior Director of Social Media Services for Comcast Communications, sums up well the rationale for delivering services through social channels: "Our customers were there; that's why we felt like we needed to be there as well." Bill Gerth, a Comcast agent handling social interactions, put it this way: "Every brand right now is being talked about ... when you look at the dialog between you and the customer that starts with "I hate you" and ends with "Let's get a cup of coffee," I would say you made a pretty good impact. (See Service Level is Key to Comcast's Social Support, Chapter 4.)

## Make It Yours!

What access channels should be opened up? How can you encourage customers to use the most suitable alternatives? How many menu selections should the IVR present? These are common questions, and the fact is, beyond applying the sound management principles we'll be looking at throughout the book, these decisions are yours to make. My overarching advice: Make your customer access strategy uniquely yours — do what's best for your customers and your organization.

Evolving technologies and creative applications are enabling organizations to expand their access alternatives and boost their brands. Some examples include:

- Intuit's Accounting Professional Division developed a vibrant customer community, accessible from directly within their accounting software programs (see sidebar).
- 1800FLOWERS (1800flowers.com) is the company name, phone number, primary URL, and (you guessed it) address for Twitter, Facebook, and other channels.
- Amtrak's (Amtrak.com) speech recognition system named "Julie" (the voice of Julie Seitter, a voice-recording professional) books thousands of reservations a day and has become something of an industry legend.
- BlueCross BlueShield of South Carolina has been an early adopter of click-to-talk functionality (see sidebar, Chapter 16).
- Telematics capabilities are opening up opportunities for automobile companies and their partners to deliver an ever-expanding range of content and services to drivers, such as navigation, remote diagnostics, stolen vehicle tracking, and automatic crash response (General Motors aired a successful, long-running advertising campaign featuring recorded emergency calls through its OnStar service).
- The National Cancer Institute in the U.S. is using Facebook to reach out to families, individually, who are battling disease, need support or are looking for information and help (see Chapter 13).
- Companies that include HP, Dell, and others delivering technical support have boosted customer satisfaction and reduced call times through co-browse capabilities.
- Thousands of new apps for tablet computers and smartphones are enabling customers to access relevant services, support and communities (one of my favorite examples is an app USAA pioneered that allows its banking customers to take pictures of their checks with their phones and submit the images for immediate deposit).

## INTUIT'S USER COMMUNITIES BOOST SERVICE AND SUPPORT

Intuit — a $3.85 billion per year software company that develops financial and tax preparation software and related services for small businesses, accountants, and individuals — depends on close to 6,000 agents across the company to support customers. The Accounting Professional Division (APD), which scales to around 700 agents to support the group's customer base of tax and accounting professionals, got an idea from a sister division: Why not create a community of customers to help each other?

To give adoption of the strategy a boost, developers embedded into the firm's software the capability for customers to directly click into online forums and related services. As questions are posted, a content aggregator pings all related sources to deliver relevant and contextual information. New answers, which can come from the user community or Intuit agents, are prioritized, searchable, and archived.

As the service has taken off, APD has identified three "all stars" classes: those customers who answer many questions throughout the forums, accountant all stars who address questions in areas focused on accountants, and employee all stars who moderate and drive resolutions for unanswered questions within the forums.

While Intuit employees moderate the community, 94% of answers come from the community itself, according to Derrick Moore, APD Support & Service Strategic Planning & Execution Leader. This has led to a reduction in overall volume of 14% during busy season. An added benefit is that customers can discuss questions beyond the software, e.g., those related to tax advice, a topic that is off-limits for Intuit employees.

Moore summarizes the four primary ingredients to success: in-product access, relevant and contextual answers, the many-to-many advantage of social community, and content that is archived and searchable. According to Moore, the service has boosted customer loyalty, had a positive impact on workload, and encouraged the use of self-service, chat, and (especially) peer-to-peer support. And Todd Hixson, Operations Manager for APD, points to a significant added benefit for contact center employees: "The community has changed our agents' lives — they are no longer answer givers, but are problem solvers."

These are just some of the many examples I could cite. Observe the companies you most enjoy doing business with, and you'll notice the best deliver services that complement their brand and culture.

Given the many ways to interact, another notable trend is to create an easy-to-find online listing of access alternatives. Do a search on "how to contact [Schwab, KLM, Apple]" and you'll see good examples of company pages that list all of the ways to reach the organization. (For companies that make their numbers harder to find, a search will usually pull up other sources — blogs, customer communities, and sites such as gethuman.com — that list contact numbers, provide tips for navigating difficult IVR menus or, when the company is perceived to be purposely hard-to-reach, contact information for executives or administrative offices.) From landing pages that list contact alternatives, some organizations provide templates for entering product numbers, serial numbers or customer information that leads to more accurate routing and customized services.

---

*The best plans go awry when customers get frustrated and begin making incorrect IVR choices, dialing numbers intended for other customer needs, contacting administration offices or sending unfavorable messages through social channels.*

---

A final note, one on ensuring your customer access strategy works as intended: Be sure to provide an acceptable base level of service (through good resource planning, a topic of later chapters) so that you aren't encouraging customers to use access alternatives not ideally suited to the situation. The best plans go awry when customers get frustrated and begin making incorrect IVR choices, dialing numbers intended for other customer needs (e.g., service calls going to sales numbers), contacting administration offices or sending unfavorable messages through social channels. This is a sign that customers are trying to cope with what they see as weaknesses or failures in service delivery. As a rule, delivering a basic level of good service to all customers is a pre-requisite to providing more customized levels of service for specific needs.

This is an exciting season of development that is opening up opportunities for virtually any organization to differentiate their services. Be bold in going in the direction that builds your brand and meets your customers' expectations — a topic we'll turn to next.

## Evolving Customer Expectations

Customer demands are constantly evolving because improvements in service reset their expectations at new levels. While customers initially appreciate better services, they quickly get used to, expect and demand them. Further, the experiences that customers have with any organization — not just yours or others in your vertical sector — help shape their perceptions. In short, service leaders in virtually any line of business are raising the bar for every organization.

Fortunately, zeroing in on customer expectations is not the hit-or-miss proposition it may seem. ICMI has followed this issue for more than two decades and has found 10 customer expectations that consistently emerge from customer feedback and surveys.

**10 KEY CUSTOMER EXPECTATIONS**

1. Be accessible
2. Treat me courteously
3. Be responsive to what I need and want
4. Do what I ask promptly
5. Provide well-trained and informed employees
6. Tell me what to expect
7. Meet your commitments and keep your promises
8. Do it right the first time
9. Follow up
10. Be socially responsible and ethical

The real challenge, of course, is in defining what these expectations mean. There was a time when *being accessible* simply meant having a call center, a toll-free number and reasonably well-trained agents. Today, many access alternatives and the expectation that they will work well together — e.g., that information and services will be consistent across apps, agents and channels — have become the norm. Appropriate service level and response time objectives, easy-to-use self-service capabilities, and the customers' ability to reach the right agents through the desired channels are important aspects of accessibility. And technologies continue to evolve: Developments in Web-based services, social and mobile apps, speech recognition and other capabilities (see Chapter 16) continue to push the meaning of accessibility.

While *courtesy* used to refer primarily to the way agents handled calls, the definition today is much more systems- and process-dependent. Don't make customers repeat the same information. Don't transfer them around. And don't make them go over their account history again. Simple steps can go a long way, such as programming IVR menus that are intuitive to use and that allow callers to opt out. Another issue we continue to see in customer surveys: "Put your phone number where I can find it when I need it!" Clearly listing contact alternatives on your website (see discussion on customer access strategy, above), as well as on billing statements, products, product guides, etc., conveys that you care and are committed to delivering high levels of service.

Definitions of *responsiveness and promptness* are also evolving. Consider email response times, which have seen significant revisions in recent years — from several days, to 24 hours, to a matter of hours in many organizations (see Chapter 4). Some organizations are staffing for customer email like they do inbound phone calls and handling them as they arrive. Similarly, a small but growing minority of organizations are queuing and handling time-sensitive social interactions as they occur.

Another common expectation is to *provide well-trained and informed employees* — a major focus in many organizations. With multiple means of contact, the immediacy and brand implications of social channels, and better-informed customers who come from diverse backgrounds and generations, this is as challenging and important as ever. Leading contact centers are making great strides in upgrading recruiting and hiring practices, educating agents and managers, and implementing the necessary tools and processes.

*Tell me what to expect. Meet your commitments and keep your promises. Do it right the first time. Follow up.* These issues are inextricably interrelated and require that people, processes and technologies work in sync. For example, automated replies to electronic messages can help to establish response time expectations. Complementing the automated replies are forecasts, schedules, tools and training that ensure contacts reach the right agents at the right times and are handled appropriately. Similarly, commitments that agents make must be backed up by people, processes and technologies across departments to ensure that orders, deliveries, account changes, etc., are handled as promised. Consumers seem to live by the mantra "trust, but verify" — they'll trust your organization (and usually send more business your way) if you hold up your end of the bargain.

If you need to be rescued from a burning building, press 1.
If you've been kidnapped by an evil genius and are being held
in his secret volcano lair, press 2 ..."

Created by Carl Nelson | Caption by Jairo Baylon

*Be socially responsible and ethical.* Lapses, or even perceived lapses, in ethics or social responsibility quickly make the rounds in feedback and customer communities. Watchdog groups have established numerous websites and blogs, and consumers can monitor activities and quickly sound alarms. Corporate ethics and responsibility concern the entire organization, but the contact center, as a hub of communication internally and externally, tends to be at the center of these issues, which can develop quickly.

In short, knowing your customers and anticipating their expectations is essential to developing an effective customer access strategy. Yes, it's a challenge. But truly understanding your customers is what can most separate you from competitors in an economy where products and services can otherwise so quickly be replicated.

How do you make the most of changing customer expectations and ensure that they are being built into your plans and direction? The following are some important rules of the road:

- First, ensure that your management team thoroughly understands the 10 basic customer expectations. Post them prominently. And make a habit of considering them when making decisions. (I know of an organization that had its managers literally memorize the list.)
- Don't guess at how you're doing. Rather than create services based on what your team "believes" customers expect, get your information from the source. Listen through social channels, during interactions with agents, and through surveys that are frequent and detailed enough to provide input on how you're doing for each of the 10 expectations.
- That said, remember Steve Jobs' advice — customers don't usually know what they want until you show it to them. If you want to differentiate through service, by definition, you'll need to go beyond industry norms.
- Build cross-functional teams to ensure a common focus on serving customers. The contact center cannot single-handedly meet and exceed expectations — that takes the organization's combined infor-

mation, support, processes, products and services. It takes a team. (This reality does, however, highlight the contact center's potential to disseminate customer input and intelligence throughout the organization — see Chapter 13.)

- Finally, ensure that evolving customer expectations form the context in which you develop your customer access strategy. They should drive everything from how you segment customers to what channels you make available, service level objectives, hours of operation, right through the list.

Clearly, developing an effective customer access strategy is not something you throw together during an afternoon team brainstorm (though that can certainly give the creative part a push!). It takes leadership, persistence and participation from across the organization. It involves documentation. It's hard work and, in many ways, detailed work.

But the payoffs are compelling. From a customer's perspective, a good strategy will result in simplified access, consistent services, ease of use and a high degree of convenience and satisfaction. From the organization's perspective, the benefits translate into lower overall costs, increased capacity, higher customer retention and a framework that guides developments.

## Points to Remember

- Contact centers in today's environment must be accessible, handle increasingly complex interactions, meet customer expectations, support organizationwide initiatives and deliver a healthy return on investments.
- Meeting these challenges requires an effective customer access strategy, which is a blueprint that guides contact center developments and decisions. Your customer access strategy should be appropriate for your organization and customers, and should reflect your organization's unique brand and personality.
- Customer expectations are constantly evolving because improvements in

service shift customer demands and because the experiences that customers have with any organization influences their expectations.

- Ten customer expectations consistently emerge from customer feedback and surveys. Defining what these expectations mean and building a customer access strategy around them is an important and ongoing process.

# CHAPTER 3:
# The Driving Forces in
# Customer Contact Centers

*Calls bunch up!*

**GORDON F. MACPHERSON, JR.**

---

N ewcomers to contact centers are often surprised at how different they are compared with other types of customer service and support environments.

*"The workload is volatile."*

*"Timing is so critical."*

*"I think customers sometimes picture us sitting around in the break room!"*

Indeed, contact centers operate in a unique environment. The workload *does* change from moment to moment. And when customers don't know how long the queue is, they often become impatient much more quickly than in settings where they can "see" the line and the progress they are making.

In any center that handles contacts initiated by

> **THREE DRIVING FORCES**
>
> - Workload Arrival: Smooth, Random or Peaked?
> - The Queue: Visible or Invisible?
> - The Seven Factors of Customer Tolerance

customers (versus *only* outbound), three major forces are at work: random or peaked workload arrival; customers' perception of the queue, be it

**EXPERIENCING A CONTACT CENTER FOR THE FIRST TIME**

Those who have never been in a contact center, and see this dynamic for the first time — phone calls entering the queue, social messages lighting up screens, et al. — are usually surprised and astounded at how fast moving and real-time the environment is. Common reaction: "*Wow!*"

Everyone has experienced the fragile balance between resources and demand — expressways that ebb and flow, airports that struggle to stay on schedule as weather moves through, the immediate and pleasant impact on the wait when a busy market opens more checkout counters. But seeing this dynamic in a contact center is nothing short of an eye-opening experience.

Executives in other areas quickly see the importance of keeping systems humming, developing good cross-functional communication, and ensuring that the call center has the staff and support it needs. More importantly, a deeper appreciation for randomly arriving workloads begins to take hold. Nope, this is not an assembly line or a stack of documents to process. You cannot slow it down or speed it up. You've got to be there as the workload arrives.

visible or invisible to them; and caller tolerance. These "driving forces" help explain why the contact center environment is so unique.

Understanding them is a prerequisite to making good decisions on everything from staffing and scheduling requirements to establishing the right performance objectives.

## Customer Workload — Smooth, Random or Peaked?

If you've spent more than just a few minutes in contact center, you've discovered a dominant fact of life: contacts arrive *as they please*. They certainly do not arrive in anything resembling an even, orderly flow.

## RANDOM ARRIVAL

Customer contacts arrive randomly in most contact centers most of the time. Take a look at a monitor or a readerboard on the wall. Watch the dynamics. In comes a call. Then one, two more ... there's another. And two, three, four more ... Exactly when calls arrive from moment to moment is the result of decisions made by customers who are motivated by a myriad of individual needs and conditions. Put another way, *calls bunch up!*

The figure illustrates two possible scenarios of how 50 contacts might arrive. The input for the chart came from a statistical table of random numbers.

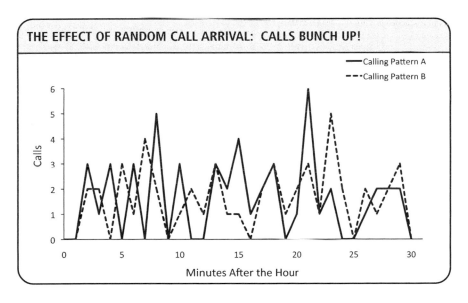

However, there is an important distinction between random call arrival and predictable call arrival patterns. Virtually all centers — even those of the more volatile type, such as emergency services centers — have distinctive calling patterns, which are usually detectable down to at least a half-hour. You can predict that you will get around, say, 240 calls next Tuesday between 11 a.m. and 11:30 a.m. What you can't predict with any precision is how many of those calls are going to arrive in the first minute, the second minute and so forth.

Consider another example. If you manage an ice cream stand, you can, with some analysis and practice, predict the number of customers and sales based on the day of week, time of day, promotions, etc. Saturday afternoons during the summer months will be busy, but traffic will be light on mid-week mornings. You could also predict the traffic before and after promotions that you run and events in the community, such as baseball games. But you wouldn't be able to predict the moment-by-moment arrival of customers.

---

### WHAT INCREMENT (INTERVAL) SHOULD YOU USE FOR PLANNING?

Given variations in the workload throughout the day, contact center forecasts and resource calculations must be based on specific increments, not daily averages. (Increments, also called intervals, are the smallest units of time reflected in reports.) Typical reporting increments include:

**30 minutes.** Thirty-minute increments are common because they provide an adequate level of detail and accuracy for many centers without burying them in unnecessary detail.

**15 minutes.** Large contact centers (e.g., those approaching or exceeding 100 agents in an agent group) often pick up additional accuracy by planning around 15-minute increments.

**60 minutes.** Contact centers that handle long calls (e.g., when the length of the interaction approaches or exceeds 30 minutes) often establish report increments and staff calculations around hours.

**10 minutes or less.** Peaked traffic, which is a surge beyond random variation within a half hour, requires reports and staffing calculations at 5- or 10-minute increments.

---

There are several important implications to random workload arrival. First, staffing must be calculated by using either a queuing formula that takes random arrival into account or a computer simulation program that accurately models this phenomenon (see Chapter 7). Other approaches almost always lead to inaccurate staffing calculations. And unfortunately, it's not just staffing that will be off. Because staffing affects the load the network and systems must carry, miscalculated staff inherently leads to miscalculated system and network resources.

Second, centers that handle customer-initiated (inbound) contacts operate in a "demand-chasing" environment. At any given time, there are either more calls than staff to handle them or more staff than calls. That means contact centers must augment good forecasting and staffing plans with real-time management (Chapter 11). A solid understanding of random arrival is necessary to avoid overreacting to normal variation in traffic arrival and underreacting to bona fide trends.

Third, performance objectives and standards must take random workload arrival into account. For example, a standard of "N widgets per day" makes no sense in an environment where the workload arrives randomly (see Chapter 14). Unless the queue is always backed up and service is lousy, your agents will spend a portion of their day just waiting for calls to arrive.

## SMOOTH AND PEAKED TRAFFIC

In addition to random or "normal" traffic, there are two other general types of workload: "smooth" and "peaked." Telecommunications traffic engineers have assigned statistical "variance-to-mean" ratios to designate each type of traffic, but essentially, the patterns for each look like those in the figure Three Types of Workload Arrival.

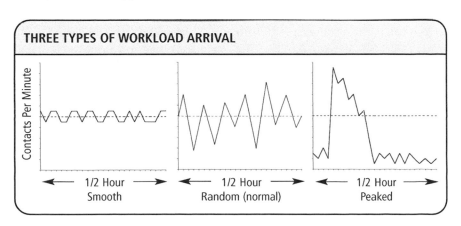

**THREE TYPES OF WORKLOAD ARRIVAL**

Contacts Per Minute

← 1/2 Hour →
Smooth

← 1/2 Hour →
Random (normal)

← 1/2 Hour →
Peaked

Smooth traffic is virtually nonexistent in centers handling incoming contacts, but can apply in outbound environments. For example, a group of people may be assigned to make outbound calls (e.g., for surveys, political interests, non-profit donations, etc.), one after another, for the duration of their shift. In that case, staffing requirements can be based on a units-of-output approach common in many manufacturing and service settings, and the number of trunks (telecommunications circuits) required will be equal to the number of agents placing the calls.

Another type of call arrival — peaked traffic — is a reality in some centers. Many of us use the term "peak" in a general sense when referring to contact center workload: What's your peak time of year? Peak day of the week? Peak time of day? But the term "peaked traffic" specifically refers to a surge of traffic beyond random variation. It is a spike within a short period of time.

Television and radio ads will often generate peaked traffic. For example, QVC, Inc. gets a surge of calls when new products are advertised on its home-shopping channel. Disaster relief and humanitarian organizations, such as the Red Cross and World Vision, get peaked traffic when their television or radio ads are aired, as do mobile phone providers when they send SMS messages to a large portion of their subscribers. And because of the proliferation of always-on Internet services, email promotions that are sent in batches can also generate an initial surge of contacts (as well as traffic that will arrive in subsequent hours and days). The (typically) large centers that handle peaked traffic can go from zero to hundreds of contacts a minute, almost instantly. (As newcomers often point out, seeing this dynamic for the first time is enough to boost your heart rate.)

It is important to correctly distinguish between random and peaked traffic. When catalog companies send out thousands of new catalogs by mail or send email offers to their lists, they begin getting calls associated with the promotion. But that's not peaked call arrival. It's random arrival, but at a much higher level than recent history. Similarly, a utility that has a power outage will get a lot of calls until the problem is fixed. But other than the few minutes following the outage, calls will arrive randomly, albeit at a much higher level than usual.

The key question is this: Is there a surge of calls that come and go within less than a half hour? If the surge lasts longer than a half hour, it's probably random call arrival for staffing purposes.

## RANDOMLY ARRIVING PEAKED TRAFFIC

Some centers experience workload arrival that is a hybrid between random and peaked traffic. Emergency services centers will get calls immediately following a traffic accident. In the past, call volume for a single event would amount to a handful of calls. Now, with the widespread use of mobile phones, they get flooded with calls reporting the same accident. And many centers have learned that news in a social world travels fast — news stories, blogs, press releases and trending topics in social communities can quickly generate customer contacts. These are examples of "randomly arriving peaked traffic."

The distinction between random and peaked traffic is important. To correctly calculate staffing needs (see Chapter 7), you need to know what type of traffic you're going to get. Traffic arrival type also helps dictate what type of real-time management strategies you deploy, which will be covered in Chapter 11.

# The Queue: Visible or Invisible?

Queue comes from the word cue, a term from Old French that means "line of waiting people." It is common in everyday British English (less so in North America, where "line" is typical) and appears frequently in call center terminology. (*Too frequently*, says the cynical customer!)

Yep, queues are a fact of life in contact centers. After all, answering every call at once would be about as practical for many centers as it would be for airlines to check in every passenger at one time. But an important difference between a contact center and the lines at an airline counter, grocery store or sports arena is that callers usually can't see how long the queue is and the progress they are making in it.

The top row of faces in the figure Visible or Invisible Queue, reflects a queue that the customers can see. Few would choose to wait in line so, as they enter the queue, the first face represents them. As they move forward, the subsequent faces illustrate their progress. The final face reflects the fact that they "made it." They are at the counter, hearing the sweet words, How may I help you?

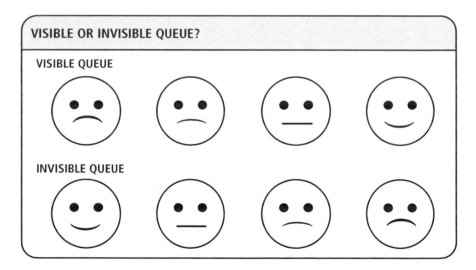

**VISIBLE OR INVISIBLE QUEUE?**

VISIBLE QUEUE

INVISIBLE QUEUE

The second row of faces represents a setting where customers are ignorant of the queue they are entering. "Ignorance is bliss," and expectations are initially high. But after some amount of waiting, say 10 or 15 seconds of ringing, they begin to doubt that they are going to get right through (second face). The third face illustrates the transition from doubt to mild frustration. By now, they have probably heard the first delay announcement and it confirms that they are in a queue.

The fourth face represents callers who, from their perspective, have waited too long. Often, the first thing they do when they reach an agent is tell him or her about the miserable experience they just had. That's a bad situation because it lengthens call-handling time, which will back up the queue even more (and may cause even more callers to unload on your agents once their calls are answered).

There's another phenomenon that kicks in here. Callers who have waited a long time in queue tend to "dig in their heels" as they attempt to squeeze all the value out of the call that they can. Customers seeking technical support are a classic example: "Geesh, I waited this long to get through, I'd better go over a few more things while I have you."

## VISIBLE QUEUE

Software company WordPerfect (now part of Corel Corporation) pioneered the "visible queue" in the mid-1980s. They set up their system to enable live "queue jockeys" to make announcements of expected hold times to incoming callers. They could also play music and deliver announcements to keep callers entertained and informed while they waited in queue:

*Thank you for calling WordPerfect. If you're calling for assistance with Version 2, there are nine of you in queue, and if you just joined us, it looks like the wait is just over three minutes. If you are calling for Version 3, there are 18 callers in queue. But we've got more staff there this morning, and it looks like your wait will be about two minutes. Now, here's Kenny G, from his latest album ...*

WordPerfect discovered that callers who abandon a visible queue do so at the beginning. Callers who decide to wait generally do so until they reach an agent.

Many contact center managers keep a diligent eye on how many customers abandon (give up on a phone call, chat, or similar, while waiting for an agent). But *when* callers abandon is an important consideration, as well. If they are abandoning early on because they are making an informed choice, that's a different story than waiting for what seems like forever in an invisible queue, then hanging up in frustration.

What the queue jockey never said, but what was implicit in the message, was something like:

*Thanks for calling. If you're going to abandon, would you kindly do so now, before you get frustrated, drive up our costs and clog up the queue only to abandon before we get to you anyway?*

Other software companies, including Microsoft, soon followed WordPerfect's lead. The feedback from callers was overwhelmingly positive. But having real-time, live queue jockeys is impractical for most organizations. Accordingly, automatic call distributors (ACDs) that could "tell time" began to appear in the early 1990s. With this technology, the ACD can analyze real-time variables, make predictions and announce expected wait times to callers as they arrive. (Today's virtual queue capabilities go a step further, enabling callers to hang up and receive a callback when an agent becomes available or at a later time. (See sidebar Can You Eliminate The Wait for Callers?)

It's a great feature, but there's a catch. These systems provide fairly accurate predictions in reasonably straightforward environments, especially in large agent groups. However, if you are using any form of complex, contingency-based routing, the system can outsmart itself. Some callers have found themselves actually moving backward in queue as arriving priority callers are moved to the front of the line. If predictions aren't accurate in your environment, you won't be able to use them. This is a challenge that system designers have yet to fully conquer.

There has been quite a bit of debate and study over the years around the question of how callers react to visible versus invisible queues. But I think that the discussion sometimes misses the real point: Given the choice, customers want to know what's happening, and they want alternatives (e.g., to continue to wait or receive a callback). There will come a time when we'll look back on the days when we, as callers, entered queues we knew nothing about. Predicted wait times might even be graphically displayed on mobile apps — and we'll be given choices when the queue is busy.

## Seven Factors Affecting the Customer's Tolerance

Another important driving force is "caller tolerance" or "customer tolerance." There are seven factors that affect tolerance. They influence everything from how long callers will wait in queue, how many will abandon, whether they will try alternative channels (chat, phone, social, self-service, et al.), and how they feel about the overall experience (vis-à-vis the expectations they had).

**1. DEGREE OF MOTIVATION.** How important is the interaction to customers? What are the consequences to them of not getting through? How badly do they need or want the product or service? Customers experiencing a power outage will usually wait longer to reach their utility than those with billing questions.

**2. AVAILABILITY OF SUBSTITUTES.** Even though they are highly motivated to make the call, callers who encounter difficulties may abandon if they know of another way to satisfy their need. Web-based self-service, social communities, IVR applications, walking down the street to a retail location, reading the manual — all are examples of potential substitutes. If callers are highly motivated and have no acceptable substitutes, they will generally wait a long time in queue (and will retry if they get busy signals). Even though they do not abandon, they still might be very unhappy about the experience.

**3. COMPETITION'S SERVICE LEVEL.** If it's easier for customers to

47

use competitive services or if they have a tough time reaching you, they may go elsewhere. (You'll need to consider whether competition is available in a practical sense. For example, if you are a bank and a customer has a problem with an online payment, a competitive bank is not going to be able to help in that case — although if the problem is difficult to get resolved, the customer may decide to switch banks.) It's also important to consider the availability of substitutes and that a contact center is often its own competition — callers may dial other numbers available, or they may choose incorrect routing selections in the IVR just to reach an agent ... any agent ... more quickly. The result is transferred calls, inflated reports and longer handling times.

> **THE SEVEN FACTORS OF CALLER TOLERANCE**
>
> 1. Degree of motivation
> 2. Availability of substitutes
> 3. Competition's service level
> 4. Level of expectations
> 5. Time available
> 6. Who's paying for the call
> 7. Human behavior

**4. LEVEL OF EXPECTATIONS.** The experiences callers have had with the contact center and the reputation that the organization or industry has for service (or the level of service being promoted) have a direct impact on tolerance. A 10-minute wait for tax help during filing season may be perceived as quite acceptable — but a similar wait for a shipping company that otherwise has a reputation for speedy service would be an unpleasant surprise. And, as discussed in Chapter 2, the services that customers receive from any organization, including those in industries completely different from yours, have a bearing on their expectations.

**5. TIME AVAILABLE.** How much time do customers have at the time of the contact? Doctors who call insurance providers have a well-deserved reputation for not tolerating even a modest wait (or what most of us would perceive to be a modest wait), while retirees calling the same companies may have more time or inclination to talk. Further, the widespread use of mobile phones has created many small windows of time your customers have to reach you, such as before boarding a flight or in between meetings, when long waits are unworkable and frustrating.

**6. WHO'S PAYING FOR THE CALL?** Callers are usually more tolerant when they are not paying for the call. Most organizations offer toll-free service, and in the rare cases they don't, a large percentage of callers will likely have calling plans associated with mobile and fixed lines that are priced by blocks of time, not distance. But there's a rub: If a caller's mobile phone plan is based on blocks of minutes, they can get understandably upset if the time they purchased is wasted on hold. (Virtual hold capabilities can help in this case — see discussion below.)

**7. HUMAN BEHAVIOR.** The weather, the customer's mood and the day's news all have some bearing on caller tolerance.

These seven factors are not static. They are constantly changing. Even so, it is important to have a general understanding of the factors affecting your customers' tolerance. Important questions to consider include:

- How motivated are your customers?
- How much does that vary based on the reason for the contact?
- What are their expectations?
- Do they vary based on the reason for the contact?
- What type of customer is least motivated?
- What type of customer is most motivated?
- What alternatives to contacting you do they have?
- Which alternatives would you want/not want them to use?
- Will they already have spent time seeking help (e.g., self-service, search, customer community, etc.)?
- What level of service are others in the industry providing?
- How do customers tend to rate your service at different service levels?
- What impact does meeting/not meeting expectations have on your brand?
- What is their tendency to share good or bad experiences through social channels?

**A CLASSIC CASE STUDY IN CALLER TOLERANCE**

To celebrate its 10th anniversary since privatization, British Airways launched an international phone promotion that drew millions of callers. The contest offered callers the chance to win virtually free tickets to fly round-trip on the Concorde, British Airway's legendary (and now retired) supersonic jet, if they were among the first 100 callers to reach the center once the promotion officially began.

The airline designated its Newcastle, England, call center to handle all calls during the promotion and doubled its staff. With a great deal of pomp and circumstance, the contest was kicked off on a Tuesday at 10 p.m. (Yes, 10 p.m.) To minimize the use of annoying busy signals, British Airways used a recorded message that gave callers information about the promotion and thanked them for calling. As expected, most callers who got the announcement kept trying to get through; those who reached the queue were willing to wait and abandonment was negligible. Just 25 minutes after the contest began — and over 20 million call attempts later — the promotion was over.

Thinking through your customers' situations and expectations will help you shape services that meet their needs and support the organization's objectives and reputation.

## Putting Abandonment in Perspective

In many contact centers, abandonment rate is viewed as a key measure of how adequately the center is staffed. I often get questions like, what is an acceptable rate of abandonment? What is abandonment in such and such an industry? Are there any studies on how long customers will wait? What should our service level be to keep abandonment under X percent?

The usual assumptions are: a) There must be industry standards for abandonment; and b) abandonment is a good indicator of contact center performance. But neither is true.

For one thing, abandonment is tough to forecast accurately, at least on a consistent basis. To do so would require predicting the impact of the seven factors of caller tolerance. But because the conditions that drive them are constantly changing, there are an almost unlimited number of variables that can have an impact on abandonment.

Further, abandonment can be a misleading measure of performance. The conventional wisdom is that longer queues translate into higher abandonment. But the seven factors can help to explain apparent paradoxes:

- When financial markets swing significantly, mutual funds and others in the financial sector get a surge of contacts. Even though service level may drop, abandonment also often goes down because customers have a higher degree of motivation and are willing to wait longer, if necessary.

- When utilities or cable providers have network outages, customers (though not happy about it) are generally willing to wait longer than under normal circumstances. Service level may drop, but abandonment will often be lower than usual.

- If callers encounter busy signals before they get into the queue, they will almost always wait longer if necessary. The psychology is, "At least I've made it into the system. I'd better hang in there."

- Callers who are waiting on hold may be simultaneously using the Web or other alternatives to search for relevant information; abandonment could mean they found what they needed.

While these may be obvious examples, what about the more subtle day-to-day shifts in tolerance? It can be baffling. Sometimes, when people have to wait a long time, they wait. Other times, when service level is really good, abandonment is higher than expected. If you don't believe it, construct a scatter diagram of service level versus abandonment by half hour for a few typical days. You are not likely to see an exact correlation, at least not consistently.

(I've had a few researchers contact me after earlier editions of *Call Center*

## CAN YOU ELIMINATE THE WAIT FOR CALLERS?

One way to eliminate abandonment would be to eliminate the queue. Realistically, though, answering all calls immediately would be highly impractical for most. The reason is the contact center version of the law of diminishing returns: When successive individual agents are assigned to a given call load, marginal improvements in service level that can be attributed to each additional agent will eventually decline (see Chapter 9). The table below illustrates this phenomenon.

| Input: 500 calls in half hour; 3.5-minute average handling time | | |
|---|---|---|
| Agents | Percent of Calls Answered Immediately | Percent of Calls Answered Within 20 Seconds |
| 59 | 10% | 16% |
| 60 | 24% | 35% |
| 61 | 36% | 50% |
| 62 | 47% | 62% |
| 63 | 56% | 72% |
| 64 | 64% | 79% |
| 65 | 70% | 84% |
| 66 | 76% | 88% |
| 67 | 81% | 92% |
| 68 | 85% | 94% |
| 69 | 88% | 96% |
| 70 | 91% | 97% |
| 71 | 93% | 98% |
| 72 | 94% | 98% |
| 73 | 96% | 99% |
| 74 | 97% | 99% |
| 75 | 98% | 100% |

Virtual queuing technologies (such as from Virtual Hold Technology, LucyPhone and Fonolo, or as a feature that is built into many of today's ACD systems) enable callers to hang up and receive a return call without losing their place in queue. They can also be given the option of scheduling a callback for a later time. For callers, this prevents the need to leave a voicemail or to wait on hold. For agents, there's little difference between an inbound call or a callback — the system places outbound calls and delivers connected calls to agents, much like inbound calls.

How well this approach works depends on the willingness and availability of callers to take callbacks and the resource capacity of the center to handle the calls. It can be especially useful in organizations influenced by weather, service outages and other factors beyond their control (travel, utilities, etc.). It's not for every situation — if customers are not available when return calls arrive, the ensuing message cycle can weigh on resources and caller patience. But a wide range of organizations, including Atmos Energy, Southwest Airlines, the Australian Tax Office and others, are citing favorable results, i.e., drops in abandonment and boosts in customer satisfaction. While there's no getting around the laws of nature — the realities of matching resources with demand are pervasive — this approach can provide choice and be a more palatable form of waiting.

*Management on Fast Forward* were published, insisting that abandonment can be predicted much of the time. Some are doing excellent work with mathematical tools that correlate abandonment to causal factors, and I fully support these efforts. As long as abandonment does not become the basis for resource planning, this research can provide managers with useful additional insight into the nuances of customer behavior.)

Organizations that maintain high levels of service — shipping companies or mutual funds committed to quick response — see abandonment rates of generally no more than one or two percent (see service level discussions, Chapter 4). No organization has zero abandonment for long — not unless they are answering every call immediately (something even emergency service centers don't always do). Most contact centers have a queue at least part of the time. And any time there is a queue, there is opportunity for callers to abandon.

In the final analysis, you can't control how customers will react or the myriad circumstances that influence their behavior. But you can control how accessible you are — how many agents are handling workloads, and the system resources you have. Concentrate on accurately matching resources with workload — the subject of the next five chapters — and abandonment will take care of itself.

# Points to Remember

- Contact centers handling customer-initiated contacts will either have random or peaked traffic arrival. The type of workload — smooth, random or peaked — will dictate the staffing calculations you should use.
- Callers behave differently, depending on whether the queue is visible or invisible. If possible, customers prefer to know the status of the queue.
- There are seven factors that affect customer tolerance, and the impact they have is constantly changing.
- You cannot directly control abandonment, but you can control how accessible you are. Concentrate on accurately matching resources with workload, and abandonment will take care of itself.

# Part Two:
# A Planning and Management Framework

## CHAPTER 4:
## Accessibility, a Core Value

## CHAPTER 5:
## Acquiring Necessary Data

## CHAPTER 6:
## Forecasting the Center's Workload

## CHAPTER 7:
## Determining Base Staff and
## System Resources

## CHAPTER 8:
## Successful Scheduling

---

*To effectively manage a contact center, you need a solid planning and management framework. Forecasting, staffing and scheduling activities should be collaborative, focused on customer needs and expectations, and built on appropriate service level and response time objectives.*

---

# CHAPTER 4:
# Accessibility, a Core Value

*"Your call is important to us ..."*
**TYPICAL DELAY ANNOUNCEMENT**

---

The principle of accessibility is at the heart of effective contact center management. Without service level objectives, the answers to many important questions would be left to chance. How long will customers have to wait in queue? What is the optimum level of staff and supporting resources? How busy are your agents going to be? Are you prepared to handle the response to marketing campaigns? What are your costs going to be?

Service level ties the resources you need to the results you want to achieve. It measures the degree to which you're getting contacts "in the front door" and to agents. It is a stable target for planning and budgeting. It is a unifying concept, and it is concrete.

Service level is tried and true in centers worldwide for contacts that must be handled as they occur. Inbound phone calls are a common example, and interactions that include chat, click-to-talk, time-sensitive social interactions, walk-in customers and video calls also fit into this category. Service level is as important as ever in today's multichannel environment.

Most centers are also responsible for contacts that belong in a second category — those that don't have to be handled right away. Examples include most email messages, many types of outbound calls, interactions

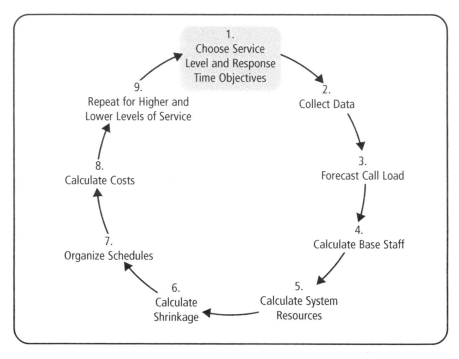

through social channels that can be deferred, faxes, postal mail, and customer voicemail. These interactions allow larger windows of time and more flexibility in terms of when the center can respond. It is important to have concrete response time objectives for these contacts and ensure that they are met through disciplined resource planning and management.

## Service Level and Response Time Defined

The term service level is often used to refer to an organization's overall responsiveness to customer contacts. (I, too, often use it to refer in a general sense to accessibility.) But, when applied to resource calculations, service level has a specific expression: "X percent of all contacts answered in Y seconds," e.g., 90 percent of calls answered within 20 seconds.

There are various alternative terms in use. Service level is sometimes referred to as telephone service factor, or TSF, which obviously sounds limited to phone calls. Some call it grade of service (GOS), although I don't

## OPERATIONALIZING SOCIAL INTERACTIONS

A notable and important trend in leading organizations is to pull social interactions into customer service and support operations. Several years ago, I wrote a blog entitled "History's Most Powerful Consumer Movement," and favorably mentioned Zappos. Within just a few hours, Derek Flores, who was part of the Zappos Customer Loyalty Team, thanked me for the post (I asked his permission to repost the exchange, to which he gladly agreed):

---

From: Derek Flores
To: Brad Cleveland
Subject: Your most recent blog post

Hello Brad,

I just read your most recent blog about "History's Most Powerful Consumer Movement," and I wanted to let you know that what you said about Zappos is great. It is great to see people recognizing us for the service we provide our customers. Zappos has always been about the very best customer service and customer experience as well as our focus on company culture! Our unique company culture allows for our Customer Loyalty Team to be happy at work and deliver that great customer service we focus so much on! An unhappy employee would never be able to deliver that kind of service!

I have shared your blog with some of my colleagues and we look forward to more Brad! Thanks again and have a great weekend!

Derek Flores
Tony's Team
Zappos.com

---

This is one of the reasons Zappos has been so successful — they have built an organization that has the capacity, the tools, the training and the empowerment to be able to respond and interact quickly. They are singularly focused on the customer at the operational level.

> Many organizations start out by handling social channels as a part of marketing, publicity, or corporate communication efforts. No problem there, and we absolutely need the skills and know-how those disciplines bring to this effort. But the sooner you are ready to pull the full range of interactions and channels into your customer service operations, the sooner you will be able to scale resources and respond as opportunities unfold.

prefer that term because it can be confused with the same term to denote the degree of blocking on a group of trunks (see Chapter 7). It can also be called accessibility and service standard.

Service level is not average speed of answer, X percent of calls answered (which is the inverse of abandonment — e.g., a 97 percent answer rate would inherently mean a 3 percent abandonment rate) or longest delayed call. When applied to staff requirements, I will stick to the definition and use of service level as it's covered in this chapter.

Response time is the related objective for contacts that don't have to be handled when they arrive, and is expressed as "100 percent response within N days/hours/minutes," e.g., handling customer email messages within 24 hours. Response time can be referred to as speed of reply or even "service level" (not to be confused with the specific definition of service level). Throughout the book, I will use response time in the specific sense described here, to refer to the level of service assigned to contacts that can be handled at a later time.

Differentiating between service level and response time is essential because base staff calculations vary for these two major categories of contacts. Service level is used in situations with randomly arriving traffic and requires Erlang C or computer simulation for determining staff requirements. Response time contacts can be held for later processing and can rely on traditional methods of staff planning used outside of contact centers. (We'll discuss staff calculations in Chapter 7.)

There is a point at which response time objectives become service level objectives. For example, some organizations have upped their response time objectives for email from 24 hours to "within the same hour." Some are going even further and handling email, social and other customer interactions as they occur, just as they do inbound phone calls. For targets of less than an hour, service level, not response time, becomes the defining objective and base staff requirements should be calculated using a service level methodology (see Chapter 7).

Some contact types are easy to categorize. For example, inbound calls or walk-in customers should usually be considered service level interactions. (Okay, someone out there is making the case that they *could* be response time, and that's true if, for example, callers opt to receive callbacks. However, they're usually service level.) Similarly, email messages from customers, as a rule, don't have to be processed when they arrive. (Exception: An email such as, "I think you should know that your home page has been hijacked.")

What about social interactions, the newcomer to contact center workloads? That depends. If a customer tweets that their power is out, it should probably be handled sooner rather than later (it's a "social – real-time" contact). On the other hand, if someone posts an involved question on how to use your software program, it can probably be deferred ("social – deferred"), allowing you time to put together an appropriate post or FAQ. (And with an active community, you will likely get some help from other customers.)

But how do you know the difference? Start by thinking through the major types of issues that come up in light of the seven factors of tolerance

> **TWO MAJOR CATEGORIES OF CONTACTS**
>
> - Those that must be handled as they occur. Performance objective: *Service Level*
> - Those that can be handled at a later time. Performance objective: *Response Time*

| CATEGORIZING CUSTOMER INTERACTIONS | | |
|---|:---:|:---:|
| | **Use Service Level** | **Use Response Time** |
| Inbound phone calls | X | |
| Outbound phone calls* | | X |
| Email* | | X |
| Social – real-time** | X | |
| Social – deferred* | | X |
| SMS | X | |
| Web chat | X | |
| Web call-me-now | X | |
| Web call-me-later | | X |
| Web click-to-talk | X | |
| Fax | | X |
| Postal mail | | X |
| Video calls | X | |
| Walk-in customers | X | |

*These contacts use response time if they can be deferred. Some may require handling when they arrive.
**Social interactions are varied, and are broadly categorized here as those that should be handled as they occur and those that can be deferred.

covered in Chapter 3 (their expectations, motivation, etc.). Do your best to put yourself in their shoes. Consider the impact on resources. And then, all of this considered, establish objectives and plans that enable you to deliver services in line with your customers' needs and your brand.

## Understanding and Using Service Level Objectives

Why service level and not percent answered, percent abandoned, average speed of answer or other alternatives? Because "X percent answered in Y seconds" gives the clearest indication of what customers experience when they attempt to reach the organization. And as we'll see in more detail in later chapters, service level is the most stable measurement of the queue.

Average speed of answer (ASA) is a close cousin of service level and is derived from the same set of data. But a big downside to using ASA is that it is often misinterpreted. Most of us tend to assume that the average lies somewhere in the middle of a set of data, or that average represents a "typical experience." Not so with ASA. It is mathematically correct, but does not represent what happens to individual callers.

ASA has its uses, so don't throw it out. For example, ASA is an important variable when calculating the load that your systems must carry (discussed in Chapter 7). Further, if service level is so bad that zero percent of calls are answered within Y seconds, ASA is a practical alternative to service level. But service level is usually a more reliable and more telling measure of what callers experience. You know exactly what happens to the percentage of customers you define. If you do use ASA reports, just remember, ASA is not a bell curve — longest waits are far beyond what those numbers suggest, and it's important to know what is really happening.

What about customers who give up on a phone call, chat, or similar contact, while waiting for an agent? As discussed in Chapter 3, looking solely at abandonment rates as a measure of whether staffing levels were appropriate can be highly misleading. The point is not to ignore abandonment. A high abandonment rate is probably a symptom of significant staffing problems. But a low abandonment rate doesn't necessarily mean everything is fine. Further, if abandonment is beyond acceptable, what are you going to do? You are going to look at instances when it's out of whack, and why. You will likely run smack into a low service level. When service level is appropriate, abandonment tends to take care of itself.

Service level also has a direct impact on channel switching, which occurs when customers begin trying different access alternatives. For example, if they encounter an extended wait, they might use self-service alternatives, try different telephone numbers or IVR menu selections (which is, technically, the same channel but a different routing alternative), switch from

## AVERAGE SPEED OF ANSWER IS MISLEADING!

Average speed of answer (ASA) reflects the amount of time callers spend in queue, waiting to reach agents. It's available from virtually any ACD. It's widely used and reported — and it's misleading.

ASA is mathematically sound, no problem there. The problem is in interpretation. Let's say you expect 250 calls in a given half hour and anticipate an average handling time of 3.5 minutes. If you want to achieve an ASA of between 10 and 15 seconds, you'll need 34 agents, which will produce an ASA of 12.7 seconds (these calculations are based on Erlang C, covered in Chapter 7).

But the following illustration gives the waiting times for individual calls in this scenario. Notice what happens. Sixty-five callers will wait 5 seconds or longer. In the next 5 seconds, 7 of those callers reach agents, so 58 callers are still waiting 10 seconds or longer. In the next 5 seconds, 6 more callers will reach agents, leaving 52 callers waiting 15 seconds or more. And so forth. There's still a caller waiting at 3 minutes. As you can see, no caller is waiting 4 minutes or more.

| | Number of Calls Still Waiting This Many Seconds: | | | | | | | | | | | | |
|---|---|---|---|---|---|---|---|---|---|---|---|---|---|
| | Immediate Answer | <5 | 10 | 15 | 20 | 30 | 40 | 50 | 60 | 90 | 120 | 180 | 240 |
| Calls | 185 | 65 | 58 | 52 | 46 | 37 | 29 | 23 | 18 | 9 | 5 | 1 | 0 |
| Scenario: 250 calls in half hour 34 agents required | 3.5-minute average handling time ASA predicted to be 12.7 seconds | | | | | | | | | | | | |

So, the contact center reports an ASA of 12.7 seconds and everything's dandy — other than for an unhappy customer or two who say they waited "several minutes" to get through. "C'mon," you say. "ASA is less than 15 seconds! Surely no one waited over 30 seconds, tops!" Take a deeper look, though, and the real story becomes clear.

chat to phone or vice-versa, send a targeted message to the company through a social channel, or throw up their hands and send a message to the world at large via social media (Twitter message: *Have been waiting on hold for 20 minutes now to reach @XYZco. #Fail!*). Or, they might try simultaneous (parallel) contacts and see which generates a response first.

All of this brings up a very important point: Different callers have different experiences with your contact center, even if they are part of the same set of data measured by service level, ASA and other reports. Why? Random workload arrival. Because of this reality, you will need an understanding of what happens to different callers. At a high level, service level is the single best measure of these queue experiences. In later chapters, we'll also look at other measures that will fill the gaps.

> **SERVICE LEVEL:**
>
> - Provides a link between resources and results
> - Affects customer goodwill and word of mouth
> - Affects abandoned (lost) calls
> - Affects channel switching and simultaneous contacts
> - Affects agent burnout and errors
> - Focuses planning and budgets

## How Systems Calculate Service Level

There are a number of ways your systems can be set up to calculate service level. (My thanks to consultant Cheryl Odee Helm for providing a summary for the first edition of this book.) You will need to know which is being used since each handles abandoned calls somewhat differently. Here are some common formulas for calculating service level:

**1. (CALLS ANSWERED IN Y SECONDS + CALLS ABANDONED IN Y SECONDS) ÷ (TOTAL CALLS ANSWERED + TOTAL CALLS ABANDONED).** This calculation takes all calls into consideration and is generally a good alternative. Calls that abandon before the objective positively affect service level.

**2. CALLS ANSWERED IN Y SECONDS ÷ TOTAL CALLS ANSWERED.** This alternative only considers answered calls and is not a good reflection of all activity. Outsourcers being measured on abandonment like it, because it prevents being marked down twice. But all things equal, given that abandonment is entirely ignored, I do not recommend this calculation.

**3. CALLS ANSWERED IN Y SECONDS ÷ (TOTAL CALLS ANSWERED + TOTAL CALLS ABANDONED).** This alternative tends to be the least popular among many contact center managers because all calls that abandon negatively affect service level, even those that abandon before the objective. It's a favorite of some, though. As consultant Laura Grimes puts it, "It's the high road calculation; it gives me an edge over other methods in building a business case for agents."

**4. CALLS ANSWERED IN Y SECONDS ÷ (TOTAL CALLS ANSWERED + CALLS ABANDONED AFTER Y SECONDS).** With this calculation, abandoned calls only have a negative impact on service level if they happen after the Y seconds specified. Calls that abandon before the objective do not affect service level. Consequently, this is a way to avoid getting "penalized" by callers who abandon quickly without ignoring abandoned calls altogether. All things considered, this is a good approach.

Whatever approach you settle on, use it consistently and ensure others understand the assumptions you are making. That's what is most important. (And if you're in a multisite operation, or have a mix of internal and outsourced services, by all means, use the same formula!)

## Giving Service Level Teeth

For service level to have meaning, it must be interpreted in light of blockage, or calls that aren't getting through. Any time a portion of callers are getting busies, whether the busies are generated by the system or are a result of a limited number of staff and trunks during a busy time of day, the reports only tell you what is happening to the calls that get through. In fact,

## WAIT — THAT'S CHEATING!

I once did some consulting work for a center handling calls for a large utility. They had two people, referred to as "traffic controllers," who monitored the queue and helped facilitate staffing adjustments as necessary.

I also learned they had a few tricks up their sleeves. For example, if service level began to slip, they would take blocks of queued calls and put them into a holding pattern, allowing calls just entering the system to go right to agents. As the queue settled down, they would release the calls from the holding pattern and allow them to reach agents. (It was akin to putting aircraft over a busy airport into a holding pattern and allowing newer arrivals to land first.) In this way, they could literally control their service level results — or at least how they *appeared in reports*.

*Ouch!* My subtle comment to their management team: "That's cheating!" The happy ending is that they acknowledged it, stopped the practice, and (though the reports looked worse for awhile) were able to make meaningful adjustments to staffing levels. It was a good reminder: Without clear values and a strong focus on customers, there are many ways to manipulate reports.

you can make reports such as service level and average speed of answer look as good as you want them to by limiting the calls that get through or manipulating order of answer (see sidebar).

You must also view service level over an appropriate time frame. Daily service level reports often conceal important information. Service level can take a big hit in the morning, but if you have staff handling every call immediately much of the afternoon, the daily report will look okay. The level of service from callers' perspectives is a different story.

Further, managers who are held accountable for daily reports may have an incentive to manage inappropriately. If the morning was rough, they may keep agents on the phones through the afternoon when the call load drops, just to make the reports look better. That's a waste of valuable time and resources, and it doesn't help callers who encountered poor service earlier in the day.

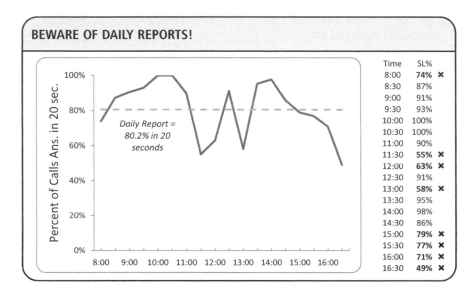

**BEWARE OF DAILY REPORTS!**

| Time | SL% | |
|------|-----|---|
| 8:00 | 74% | ✖ |
| 8:30 | 87% | |
| 9:00 | 91% | |
| 9:30 | 93% | |
| 10:00 | 100% | |
| 10:30 | 100% | |
| 11:00 | 90% | |
| 11:30 | 55% | ✖ |
| 12:00 | 63% | ✖ |
| 12:30 | 91% | |
| 13:00 | 58% | ✖ |
| 13:30 | 95% | |
| 14:00 | 98% | |
| 14:30 | 86% | |
| 15:00 | 79% | ✖ |
| 15:30 | 77% | ✖ |
| 16:00 | 71% | ✖ |
| 16:30 | 49% | ✖ |

Daily Report = 80.2% in 20 seconds

If daily reports are potentially misleading, monthly averages for service level are virtually meaningless. They simply don't reflect the day-by-day, half-hour-by-half-hour realities. Monthly reports that aggregate data remain an all-too-common way to summarize activity to senior management (we'll look at better alternatives in Chapter 10).

## Choosing Service Level Objectives

The number of staff you need to handle contacts and the schedules you produce should flow from your service level objective. Imagine that, in a half-hour period, you're going to receive 50 calls that last an average of three minutes. If you have only two people to answer the calls, the delay time for most callers will be long, and you'll probably have high abandonment. As you add people, delay times will drop.

How many people should you add? Enough to reduce the queue to an acceptable level for you and your callers. In other words, the answer to that question becomes your service level target, and you won't be able to achieve your target without the correct level of resources.

There is generally no "industry standard" service level that you can hang your hat on. (There are some exceptions, e.g., service levels for many utilities are regulated.) The optimum service level is affected by a host of factors, including the value of the contact, fully loaded labor costs, telecommunications costs, customer tolerances, the organization's unique customer access strategy and the desire and commitment to differentiate through service. An industry standard would have to be based on organizations having the same values for these things.

**WHY THERE IS NO INDUSTRY STANDARD SERVICE LEVEL**

- The value of an interaction
- Labor costs
- Telecommunications costs
- The seven factors of customer tolerance
- The organization's unique customer access strategy
- The organization's desire to differentiate products or services by the level of service provided

The correct service level for your organization is the one that (in no specific order):

- Meets customers' needs and expectations
- Keeps abandonment at acceptable levels
- Minimizes agent burnout and errors
- Minimizes expenses
- Maximizes revenue
- Supports the organization's mission and brand
- Is understood and supported by senior management

From a practical sense, no one service level would fit all situations affecting how long customers will wait. Consider the factors of caller tolerance: How motivated are customers to reach you? What is the availability of substitutes for various access alternatives? What is your competition's service level? What are your customers' expectations based on their past experiences? How much time do they have? What are the conditions at the locations from which they are calling?

There are essentially five approaches you can use to determine your service level objective, though all require some subjectivity and judgment. One is to listen to customer feedback gathered through conversations with agents, customer surveys, in focus groups, and in comments and ratings provided through social channels. You will also want to think through the seven factors of caller tolerance (see Chapter 3).

While it's always a good idea to know what your customers expect, random call arrival means that different customers have different experiences with your contact center. Even for a relatively modest service level such as 80 percent answered in 60 seconds, more than half of the callers will get an immediate answer. Some, though, will wait in queue for 3 to 5 minutes, assuming no overflow or other contingency (we'll cover how to make these calculations in Chapter 7). As a result, many in that set of callers would say that your service level is great, while a handful would tell you that it is poor.

> **ALTERNATIVES FOR CHOOSING A SERVICE LEVEL OBJECTIVE**
>
> - Listen to the voice of the customer
> - Go with a "middle of the road" objective, e.g., 80/20
> - Relate to competition — match or go higher/lower
> - Adjust to minimize abandonment
> - Use a combined approach

Some managers use a variation of a typical customer survey. They have taken samples of individual callers and then compared the responses with actual wait times of those calls. The results are interesting. In many customer service environments, waits of up to 60 to 90 seconds are generally okay with callers. But beyond about 90 seconds, callers' view of reality can become rather skewed, and their moods can sour. Those who wait three minutes in queue may say they waited 4 or 5. Those who wait 5 minutes will often tell you they waited something like 8 or 10 minutes. Of course, answers will vary based on the type of organization and the seven factors

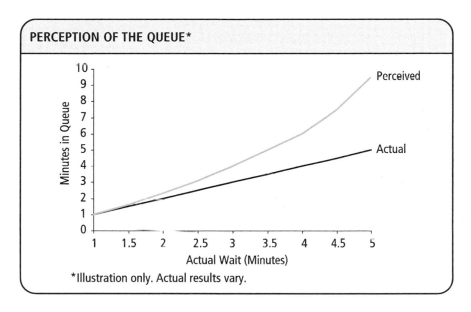

**PERCEPTION OF THE QUEUE***

Minutes in Queue

Perceived

Actual

Actual Wait (Minutes)

*Illustration only. Actual results vary.

affecting caller tolerance. But the issue remains: At some point, perception deteriorates beyond reality.

Another popular approach is to choose a "middle-of-the-road" service level objective, such as 80 percent answered in 20 seconds. The 80/20 objective was once published in ACD manuals as an industry standard. In reality, it never was, but many early call centers used this target. The objective 80/20 is still fairly common because for many contact centers it is a reasonable balance between callers' expectations and the practicality of having enough staff to meet the objective. It may or may not be right for you.

A third alternative for choosing a service level objective is to benchmark competitors or organizations similar to yours, or to use industry surveys that relay what others are doing. Just keep in mind that the results reported by others and what they are actually achieving may be two very different things. I once worked with three different insurance companies with the same stated service level objective, 80 percent answered in 30 seconds. But the results they were achieving (and how they were measuring them) were very different.

A fourth method is to choose a service level objective by, essentially, ask-

## INCREMENTAL REVENUE ANALYSIS EXAMPLE

| Phone Agents | 25 | 26 | 27 | 28 | 29 | 30 |
|---|---|---|---|---|---|---|
| Rostered Staff (Agents x 1.3) | 32.5 | 33.8 | 35.1 | 36.4 | 37.7 | 39.0 |
| Calls Ans. In 20 sec. | 45% | 62% | 74% | 83% | 89% | 93% |
| Assumed % Lost Calls | 26.0% | 12.5% | 6.5% | 3.5% | 2.0% | 1.5% |
| Assumed % Calls Lost Forever | 7.80% | 3.75% | 1.95% | 1.05% | 0.60% | 0.45% |
| Trunk Hours | 29.1 | 24.3 | 22.3 | 21.3 | 20.8 | 20.5 |
| Eventual Calls Handled | 369 | 385 | 392 | 396 | 398 | 398 |
| Gross Revenue Avg. per Call $22.25 | $ 8,210 | $ 8,566 | $ 8,722 | $ 8,811 | $ 8,856 | $ 8,856 |
| Labor Cost $15 per hour | $ 488 | $ 507 | $ 527 | $ 546 | $ 566 | $ 585 |
| Toll-free Trunk Cost 5¢ per minute | $ 87 | $ 73 | $ 67 | $ 64 | $ 62 | $ 62 |
| Net Revenue | $ 7,635 | $ 7,986 | $ 8,128 | $ 8,201 | $ 8,228 | $ 8,209 |
| Incremental Revenue | - | $ 351 | $ 142 | $ 73 | $ 27 | $ (-19) |

Sample Assumptions:
3 minute talk time
30 second After Call Work
30 minutes of calls = 200
Rostered Staff Factor = 1.3x

**Optimum**

ing, how low can you go without losing callers? This assumes that a higher level of service means lower abandonment and vice versa. A big flaw with this approach, however, is that abandonment levels and service levels don't always correlate. It's dangerous to assume that as long as callers don't abandon, service level is acceptable. As discussed in Chapter 3, abandonment will fluctuate as the seven factors of caller tolerance change. As a result, it is difficult to forecast, and choosing a service level around abandonment is

| EXAMPLE SERVICE LEVEL OBJECTIVES | |
|---|---|
| **General Comparisons** | **Service Levels**<br>**(X percent answer / Y seconds)** |
| Emergency services | 100/0 |
| Service level objectives that are "high" | 90/20, 85/15, 90/15 |
| Service level objectives that are "moderate" | 80/20, 80/30, 90/60 |
| Service level objectives that are "modest" | 70/60, 80/120, 80/300 |

building on the proverbial foundation of "shifting sand."

Incremental revenue analysis is a variation of this approach and is a more formal methodology to determine the potential impact of abandonment on overall costs. This approach has been traditionally applied in revenue-generating environments — e.g., reservation centers, catalog companies, or humanitarian organizations that depend on contributions — where calls have a measurable value. It's difficult to apply in centers where the value of calls is difficult to measure, such as customer service centers and help desks.

To use this approach, you attach a cost to abandoned calls and make assumptions around how many calls you would lose for various service levels. The theory is you should continue to add agents and trunks as long as they produce positive incremental (marginal, additional) revenue (value) after paying for their own costs (see example).

Incremental revenue analysis can be valuable when used in conjunction with other approaches, as long as the assumptions (e.g., the uncertainties of predicting abandonment) are understood and communicated to others in the budgeting process. Nevertheless, don't let the scientific look of this approach mislead you — it requires some pretty serious guesswork.

A fifth, and overall best, approach to choosing service level is an iterative process that combines the strengths of each of these methods. See where you are, run some calculations, consider what others are doing and (especially) your unique brand, and assess what callers are saying and how

## THE QUICK VERSION OF CHOOSING A SERVICE LEVEL OBJECTIVE

I often hear, "Okay, the analysis is fine, but let's get to the point: What should our service level objective be?"

Fair enough. If you're in a competitive industry, such as retail, shipping, or mutual funds, and want to be on the high end of the scale, 90/20 is fairly common. Others go for 85/15 or 90/15. If you hit these targets fairly consistently, your abandonment rate will likely be around 1 percent or 2 percent.

Going for the middle of the road? 80/20 is common. That's what a lot of banks, insurance companies and travel reservation centers shoot for. Still popular as mid-range service levels are 80/30 and 90/60. Hit these objectives consistently, and you'll generally see abandonment rates of 3 percent or 4 percent.

Want a service level that is more modest? Targets more common with many technical support centers and government organizations are 70/60, 80/120 or even 80/300. Abandonment can climb to 10 percent, 15 percent or higher. But hold your judgment — some of these organizations do a great job of hitting these objectives consistently, a lesson many with more lofty goals could use.

Of course, just throwing out numbers like this can be dangerous. There are exceptions to the norm in any industry; for example, technical support operations that charge for support, or that serve internal customers who have time-sensitive requirements, usually maintain comparably high service levels. Also, interpret these numbers with common sense. If you are an emergency services center, you will target 100/0. On the other end of the scale, there are centers for which 80/300 is a dream. I once worked with a center that was blocking over 70 percent of its calls, yet still losing a large portion of those that got through due to excruciatingly long waits (they've since dramatically turned things around).

Finally, remember that it's not just how high your objectives are, but *how consistently you hit them*. If your service level objective is 90/20, but you base your performance on daily or monthly summaries, you might be getting walloped midmornings when a lot of your customers are calling. If you really want to see how you're doing and what realistic targets might be, produce some service level graphs like those shown in Chapter 8.

they are reacting. In that sense, choosing a service level happens further down the line in the planning process. You need a forecast in order to calculate staff, schedules, etc. So this step initially has to happen in parallel with others.

Whichever combination of methods you choose, you will have more success managing your center just by having a service level target on which to base your planning. Showing senior management what kind of service can be bought for a specific amount of funding is an excellent way to involve them in this decision and to get buy-in from the beginning.

## Realistic Targets, Taken Seriously

If your operation is chronically missing your target, it may be an indication of a fundamental misconception about the importance of service level. You'll need to focus on a service level objective that your center can realistically achieve. Once you know your center's true capabilities, you must be able to back up your objectives with the right amount of resources. Service level should not be a "goal," something that is nice to strive for. An airline doesn't have the "goal" of reaching Toronto when the plane takes off from Denver. It's a concrete objective, supported by adequate resources (fuel, pilots, navigation equipment, etc.).

**SERVICE LEVEL OBJECTIVES SHOULD BE:**

- Realistic
- Understood
- Taken seriously
- Adequately funded

Why is it that some contact centers don't get the resources they need? Sometimes it's because the money isn't available. Or maybe management at the top believes that it's possible to achieve the service level target with the current level of resources, thinking all that is needed is a little improvement in efficiency. Or maybe the contact center manager has failed to educate senior management on the link between service level and budget.

Service levels that are impossible to hit are particularly difficult for man-

## SERVICE LEVEL IS KEY TO COMCAST'S SOCIAL SUPPORT

Cable giant Comcast Corporation has been much maligned in the past for providing poor service, a perspective that reached a low point in 2007. On August 17, a customer, 75-year-old Mona Shaw, took a hammer to the computer and telephone equipment in a Comcast facility in Manassas, Va., following a series of problems that, according to her, included a missed installation, service outage, endless IVR menus and, finally, a two-hour wait for a manager at the local office, only to then learn he had left for the day. The incident earned her a $345 fine, a restraining order to stay away from the office — and widespread notoriety as the story went viral. (ABC's *Good Morning America* entitled their story, "Cable Rage Pushes Granny Over the Edge.")

Since then, Comcast has made significant progress in improving services across the board. As a part of that effort, the Comcast Cares Digital Team, launched by Frank Eliason, former Customer Service Manager, began delivering services through social channels, including Twitter. "Five years ago, I would not have told you that Twitter would be a force in political change," reflects Guy Kawasaki, a social media pioneer and former Chief Evangelist at Apple, in a recent video that profiles the service. "Who would have predicted that, much less, enabling Comcast to provide technical support when someone's cable modem is not working."

All such service initiatives ultimately depend on blocking and tackling: getting the right resources in place at the right times, doing the right things. For Comcast, that includes responding to Twitter messages as they occur — in contact center terms, planning for and handling them as service-level-type interactions. "If you catch that tweet, and respond and fix that problem, you've saved the customer," observes Kawasaki.

"We do strive to reply to customers as soon as they tweet," says Melissa Mendoza, Social Media Customer Service Specialist. "If we can give a response within a minute, I mean, that's giving great service. Let me have this one chance to make it right and I can make you a lover of Comcast."

Kip Wetzel, who leads the company's innovative social media services, puts it this way: "We're given almost a second chance here. And social

> media not only lets us form a bond with those people, but maybe transform them from a dissenter into someone who is a promoter."

agers whose job success and salary are tied to meeting the objectives. When senior management hands down an objective without backing it up with adequate resources, these managers are set up for failure.

Part of taking a service level objective seriously means getting the buy-in of everyone who is involved in achieving it. To reach your target, agents, supervisors, managers and those with supporting roles should know what the service level objective is, why it was set where it is, and whether or not it is being met. A value system that people do not understand will have little or no impact.

A contact center that is serious about service level objectives will ensure that hitting them is a priority. But you can't forget work that is not immediately part of service level, such as non-phone work, correspondence, research and similar. If this work is not handled in a reasonable amount of time, customers will contact the organization again, and downstream activities will reach a standstill. Consequently, to maintain consistent and appropriate levels of service, you will also need to establish corresponding response time objectives.

# Understanding and Using Response Time Objectives

Response time is the equivalent of service level for contacts that don't have to be handled when they arrive. Response time, like service level, becomes the critical link between the resources you need and the results you want to achieve.

## VARIATIONS ON RESPONSE TIME

There are often several components to the organization's response. The most common are:

**AUTOMATED REPLY:** This is a system-generated response that automatically sends a reply to the customer acknowledging that a message they sent was received and informing them of when to expect a response. This establishes appropriate expectations and minimizes phone calls or other additional contacts inquiring about the status of the original message.

**AGENT-ASSISTED RESPONSE:** This refers to the response the customer receives when the transaction is actually handled by an agent. The time that elapses between the customer's original message and the contact center's response is measured as response time.

**RESOLUTION:** This is a measure of when the problem or issue is actually resolved and is used in environments where the contact center's initial response may not fully resolve the issue. For example, in a technical support environment, additional research may be necessary; the problem is "resolved" when the matter is handled to completion and the case is closed.

Additionally, there are two primary types of response time, scheduled and rolling. Scheduled response time, like a dry-cleaning service, is geared around blocks of time. For example, you may commit to handle all

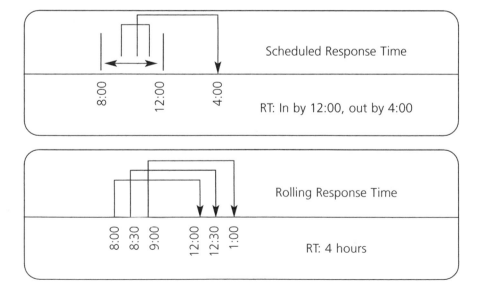

messages received up to noon by 4 p.m., and to respond to messages received between noon and 5 p.m. by 10 a.m. the next day.

Rolling response time is hinged on the specific time each message arrives. Strictly applied, if you establish a four-hour response time, a customer who sends a message at 9:03 a.m. should get a response by no later than 1:03 p.m., and one who sends a message at 9:12 a.m. should receive a response by no later than 1:12 p.m.

## CHOOSING RESPONSE TIME OBJECTIVES

Choosing response time objectives involves considering many of the same questions you analyzed when establishing an appropriate service level, such as the seven factors affecting customer tolerance.

Today, many contact centers are establishing straightforward, 24-hour scheduled response time objectives (or a close variation, such as by end of next business day). But some have raised the bar and set objectives of several hours or less as the norm. A small but growing number of centers are handling what used to be response-time type contacts, such as email, as they do inbound calls (queuing them and handling them as they arrive), in which case service level, rather than response time objectives, apply.

| EXAMPLE RESPONSE TIME OBJECTIVES* | | |
|---|---|---|
| | **Common** | **High End of Range** |
| Customer email | Within 24 hours | Within 1 to 4 hours |
| Customer voicemail | Within 24 hours | Within 1 to 4 hours |
| Social – deferred** | Within 24 hours | Within 1 to 4 hours |
| Postal mail | Processed within one week | Processed within one to two business days |

\* These should be considered examples only; according to industry surveys, there is a wide disparity in response time objectives.
\** This refers to social interactions that do not require immediate response.

An important step in establishing response time objectives is to relay to customers what your objectives are. That means telling them up front what they can expect. Otherwise, what started out as an email or inquiry on your company's Facebook page may turn into a call: "I'm calling to check up on a question I have. I haven't heard from you yet, and am wondering ..."

## INTERNAL COMMUNICATIONS

In some cases, meeting response time objectives for customers requires various internal resources to be available in a timely manner. Don't leave this to chance. Create a plan with your group that establishes agreed-upon internal service level and response time standards.

For example, the agreement should stipulate levels of priorities and appropriate responses for internal email — i.e., urgent messages (requiring an immediate response), routine messages (requiring a response time of, say, the same day) and informational messages only (requiring no response).

Instant messaging, wikis, Internet forums, and a growing variety of internal social networking and collaboration tools are becoming pervasive and valuable for communication. But you'll need to talk through expectations and get agreement on when and how they will best be used. Ditto for internal phone calls, voicemail messages and other channels of communication. Coming up with an agreement, even just an informal understanding, will go a long way toward meeting customer expectations and preventing unnecessary stress among colleagues.

As we will discuss in Chapter 13, one useful way to identify the resources required to handle an interaction is to chart the handling process step by step. This will identify weak links and help to identify where internal standards are necessary, ensuring that customers are getting the response time promised.

# The Link to Quality

When you talk about being accessible, someone is bound to bring up an important point: You can achieve your service level objectives regularly and, at the same time, be creating waste, extra work and low quality.

Sure, you can rush through those calls in queue, and service level will improve while quality suffers. You can have fast service even though your agents misunderstand customer requests, enter data incorrectly, relay the wrong information to customers, make them mad, miss opportunities to capture valuable feedback, and unnecessarily cause repeat contacts.

But longer-term, service level and quality are inextricably associated with, and complementary to, each other. You cannot have one without the other. What if data is not entered correctly? What if the caller does not have confidence the call was handled correctly? What if you did not capture useful information from the transaction? These problems contribute to repeat calls, escalation of calls, complaints to higher management and unfavorable reviews and comments in social channels. The problems also entail callbacks and rework, further reducing service level.

Just as service level and quality are linked, so, too, are quality and response time. For example, if customers don't get a reply to an email as quickly as expected, or don't receive the correct or expected response, they may send another. Or, they may send the same message through multiple channels. This can be the start of a similar cycle.

A poor service level will steal away productivity. As service deteriorates, more and more callers will express their frustration when their calls are answered. Your agents will have to spend valuable time apologizing, which means they will not be able to answer as many calls as they would if service were better. Your costs will go up.

But that is just the beginning. The interactions also get longer because agents will eventually pace themselves differently. If they can't get a "breather" between contacts because the "in-between" time no longer exists, they may start taking their breathers while they're on calls as a survival mechanism. When service level initially starts to slip, agents often try to clear up the queue. If this proves to be a futile effort, they eventually settle in for the long term. Handling time goes up. If this condition continues, employee morale will sink. Turnover and burnout will go up. So will recruitment and training costs.

"At this time, we'd like to remind you
to eat and drink at regular intervals.
Thank you for continuing to hold."

© Randy Glasbergen | Reprinted with permission

Somewhere along the way, quality begins to suffer, which has a further negative impact on service level. When your agents are overworked due to constant congestion in the queue, they become less accurate and can become less "customer friendly." Callers are telling them in no uncertain terms about the tough time they had getting through. And agents make more mistakes. These mistakes contribute to repeat contacts, duplicate messages through alternative channels, escalation of calls and complaints to higher management, call backs to customers, etc., all of which drive service level down further. It's an unfortunate and costly cycle.

---

*The contact center can have a positive impact on the entire organization's workload, productivity and quality.*

---

Service level against quality? Nope. Service level and quality go hand in hand. In the end, they must be viewed in the context of a much larger objective: customer satisfaction and strategic value. Consider the positive impact on the organization's workload when the contact center helps other service and production areas pinpoint quality problems, develop more focused marketing campaigns or customer communication, or improve the usability and acceptance of self-service systems. At that level, the contact center can have a positive impact on the entire organization's workload, productivity and quality. (We'll look at these issues in Chapter 13.)

Service level and response time objectives are enablers. Nothing happens unless contacts get to the right places at the right times. In the chapters to follow, we will cover the planning steps required to meet the service level and response time objectives you have established. These activities will include forecasting, staffing, scheduling and budgeting. But none of these later steps are possible without first establishing appropriate targets.

# Points to Remember

- Service level is the performance objective for contacts that must be handled as they occur, such as inbound calls and time-sensitive social interactions. Response time is the performance objective for contacts that can be handled at a later time, such as customer email.
- Staffing, system resources, scheduling and budgeting are all hinged upon your service level and response time objectives.
- Choosing service level and response time objectives is not an exact science, and you may need to adjust your targets as you determine required resources and calculate costs in later planning steps.
- Service level and response time objectives are not at odds with quality. Good quality improves service levels by minimizing repeat contacts, channel hopping, and waste and rework. And good service levels create the environment in which quality can thrive.

# CHAPTER 5:
# Acquiring Necessary Data

*We're drowning in information and starving for knowledge.*

**RUTHERFORD D. ROGERS**

Collecting the data you need for effective contact center management is a critical but often undervalued activity in the planning process. To many, collecting data sounds mechanical, a humdrum step on the path to

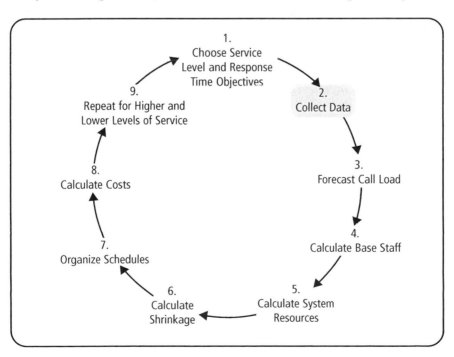

bigger and better things.

*Au contraire!* Too often, inaccurate forecasts, variable quality and unpredictable costs stem from a lack of good information. Acquiring the data that you need will take you to distant corners of your organization and into the farthest reaches of the external environment. It's one of the most involved, politically charged and outwardly focused aspects of successfully managing a customer contact center.

## Sources of Data

The information necessary for effective planning and management comes from many different places. Consider the systems, departments and external sources of information that a customer support operation for, say, a financial services organization would turn to (listed in no specific order):

- Customer information systems
- ACD systems
- Quality monitoring/recording systems
- Workforce management/optimization systems
- Social monitoring tools
- Analytics systems
- Web servers
- CRM applications
- Email servers
- Imaging servers
- Fax servers
- Dialers
- Knowledge management tools
- IVR/voice processing systems
- Telecommunications network
- Vendors/suppliers
- Marketing department

- Legal department
- Upper management
- Human resources department
- Employees
- Customers
- Product development
- Regulatory bodies
- Economic reports
- Competitive information
- The media

Lots of information! Contact center systems alone crank out reports with a vengeance. In fact, it's all too easy to get buried in information. And data does little good unless it becomes usable, actionable knowledge.

In today's world, the external environment changes so rapidly that past history is not as good a predictor of future activity as it once was. This is why having more data from more systems hasn't inherently translated into better-managed centers, and why human know-how and experience are as important as ever in managing these information-intensive environments.

---

*Past history is not as good a predictor of future activity as it once was. This is why having more data from more systems hasn't inherently translated into better-managed centers, and why human know-how and experience are as important as ever.*

---

## Diverse Requirements

For an appreciation of the diverse information requirements in today's customer contact environment, consider how job titles and responsibilities are evolving. As recently as a decade ago, "call center manager" was the usual title for those who ran these operations. Often, the same person or team (depending on the size of the center) would do the recruiting, hiring, coaching, training, systems troubleshooting and about everything else that goes into running the center. Forward-thinking managers would make time to do basic forecasting, staffing and scheduling. "Be proactive, not reactive" was the oft-repeated management admonition.

Today, many additional job roles and responsibilities have emerged, each requiring different types of information from different sources, and with a unique combination of both "push" and "pull" requirements (see sidebar). In larger centers, job roles can include forecasting analysts, training managers, quality specialists, knowledge managers, reporting analysts, finance managers, traffic controllers, coaching and monitoring supervisors, real-time coordinators and professionals with a host of other titles and positions. If you run a small contact center, you probably wear many of these hats — but they are increasingly specialized hats, nonetheless!

Given the need for specialized roles, along with the numerous variables affecting the contact center's workload, it's easy to understand why many organizations that were previously successful at developing accurate forecasts and plans are now finding these requirements more challenging. The process for acquiring, interpreting and using the data has become almost as important as the data itself. Those who view the data collection step as little more than a rote, mechanical process are asking for trouble!

### PUSH AND PULL REQUIREMENTS

Information requirements can be broadly categorized as either "push" or "pull."

**PUSH:** The information needs to be delivered as soon as it becomes available (e.g., workload trends that impact real-time resource requirements).

**PULL:** The information is stored and is accessible as needed (e.g., HR data on tenure by recruiting source).

**IDENTIFYING THE INFORMATION YOU NEED**

A great way to identify gaps in getting and using the data you'll need for resource planning is to create a flow chart of the nine-step planning process and the data required for each step. The chart should identify:

- The information you need for each step
- The form it should take
- Where it comes from
- Who or what produces it
- When you need it
- How and when it fits into the planning process

This exercise will identify missing links in your data collection activities and lead to ideas for developing a more integrated, collaborative approach. For best results, you'll need to update the chart fairly regularly (I usually suggest semi-annually at a minimum). A similar approach can be used for other aspects of management, such as quality improvement.

# Building Cross-Functional Processes

Identifying the information you need begins with a clear customer access strategy. Your customer access strategy will help to define such things as customer segments, agent group structure, service level objectives, the information needed for handling contacts, etc. (see Chapter 2). These issues will, in turn, help reveal specific data requirements.

Many centers have charged a person or a group of people with essential planning responsibilities, i.e., forecasting, staffing and scheduling. As a part of their job, they are given the task of collecting information required for these activities. But if they don't get the cross-functional input they need, they are set up for failure. The organizations that do the best job of planning have developed cross-functional teams that are an integral part of the planning and management process.

Cross-functional planning groups can take many forms. For example:

- Georgia Power set up an agent liaison team to facilitate information exchange between the contact center and other departments; typical tasks for an agent liaison include participating in meetings in other areas, reporting contact center activities and exploring ways to achieve overall goals.

- Mountain America Credit Union's contact center implemented a similar initiative with their public relations team — made up entirely of contact center agents who communicate the center's activities to other areas of the business and stay abreast of those divisions' objectives to ensure that cross-functional projects and processes are successful.

- Capital One's "war room" enables customer service agents and representatives from other areas to share customer input and then identify operational improvements. It is part of a comprehensive voice of the customer initiative that has improved cus-

**FACTORS AFFECTING CONTACT CENTER WORKLOADS**

- Changes in products and services
- New products and services
- Revenue growth (or decline)
- Marketing activities
- Social trending topics
- Website revisions (content or structure)
- Technology changes (internal and external)
- Evolving customer demographics
- Competitor activities
- Mergers and acquisitions
- Changes in laws and regulations
- Customer experience levels
- Agent experience levels
- New product rollouts
- Customer relationship initiatives
- Reorganizations
- Quality improvement initiatives
- Publicity
- New suppliers and business partners
- Human resources policies
- Cost-cutting or growth initiatives
- Economic trends
- Media activities

tomer satisfaction scores by 46 percent — and earned the company awards from J.D. Power, ICMI and others.

- Retailer and catalog company Eddie Bauer pioneered an interdepartmental forecasting team some years ago that directly involves representatives from marketing and other business units in the forecasting process; many organizations have since established similar integrated planning initiatives.

Customer "listening posts" — which often consist of a regular (typically, weekly) meeting with representatives from departments throughout the organization who review customer input and implications for projects and processes — have become popular. And given the many diverse aspects of good planning, some organizations have established a dedicated planning manager position whose primary function is to enhance cross-functional communication within the organization, and to use the shared information to drive better forecasts and plans. Whatever the specific approach, better cross-functional communication depends on a commitment from the contact center management team to reach out and better understand other areas.

Internal social networking capabilities can dramatically boost collaboration on customer-focused issues (e.g., service and product improvements). Popular use of Facebook, Twitter and LinkedIn, on a personal level, have trained people to think in social terms, and bring those skills to internal initiatives. Beyond information sharing, these platforms can facilitate cross-functional relationships and build the contact center's stature, which encourages even more collaboration. (Note that these activities are especially critical if an outsource partner is handling some or all of the customer contacts. High-quality, cost-effective services are absolutely dependent on good cross-functional, cross-organizational planning.)

## Better Reporting Tools

New developments in contact center reporting are creating opportuni-

## HOT TOPIC'S "DAILY HUDDLE"

Fashion retailer Hot Topic won first place in an ICMI video contest for a creative portrayal of their "secret to service success," a daily communications huddle. In it, they compare the daily meeting, which keeps employees up to date, to the ingredients of a gourmet meal:

- Main ingredient (lasagna noodles): Important information, such as current sales, and information that helps customers find great deals and contribute to the bottom line.
- Meat: Critical events of the day, such as trends and special scheduling needs.
- Ricotta: Tech updates, including Web or system upgrades, and details on future technology projects.
- Sauce: Product knowledge, including music, fashion and the latest trends.
- Mozzarella: Company info, i.e., daily sales plans or future business ventures.
- Salad: Team feedback, the opportunity for reps to voice their opinions, e.g., on processes, new technology, and customer feedback.
- Dessert: Recognition, the many reasons to recognize the team, including customer compliments, peer recognition, excellent performance, and "just being a Hot Topic rock star."

Now, that's a recipe worth sharing!

ties for more closely integrating activities, getting a handle on what customers are experiencing, and anticipating key trends. But good results don't happen just because new information is available. The mandate for contact center managers is to identify both the opportunities and the potential problems that information-generating systems present, and to develop appropriate plans and guidance.

One of the key benefits of ACD, workforce optimization, quality monitoring, CRM, and other systems prevalent in contact centers has always been their ability to produce reports — lots of them. In the past, reporting was system-specific and based primarily on parameters defined by the suppliers.

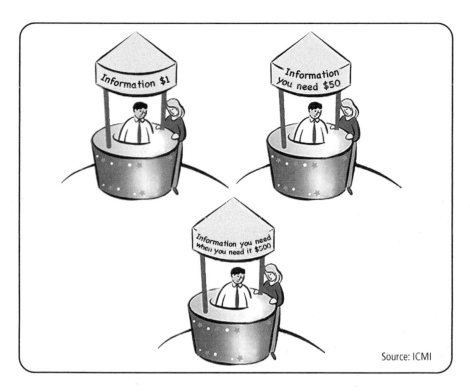

Source: ICMI

Today's systems are characterized by open standards and interfaces that allow reporting and integration across an organization (and beyond, to include service partners, suppliers and others). In many cases, anyone who is part of the organization's information systems can view, extract, print and store real-time and historical information (as allowed by system administrators). This trend has been enormously helpful in raising the contact center's profile internally, especially where management teams have actively identified information that would be helpful to colleagues across the organization, and have enabled them to access and understand it.

Most systems also have the capability to export data to a variety of formats. This allows anyone with some programming ability to develop custom reports that combine information from multiple systems. The result has been reports and analysis that give a much more "three-dimensional" view of customer interactions — i.e., you can correlate details such as contact types, channels, quality scores and contact trends to customer demographics, marketing campaigns, sales, customer satisfaction, buying histories and other relevant information.

Another highly useful development is the ability to model and test different scenarios. Examples include:

- Quality monitoring, text and speech analytics, and performance management tools can use what were disparate historical observations and identify causal factors, trends and probable outcomes given different sets of variables.
- IVR and ACD programming modules are often represented graphically, and even managers with limited programming know-how can design and test alternative call-handling routines.
- Workforce optimization tools have greatly improved in their ability to model and test alternative staffing, scheduling and budget scenarios.

These forward-looking capabilities are major improvements over relying primarily on historical reports to identify problems and improvement opportunities.

| Old Reporting Environment | New Reporting Environment |
|---|---|
| Proprietary | Exportable to other formats and systems |
| Defined by system manufacturers | User-definable |
| Limited data storage | Large storage capacity |
| System-specific | Integrated reports from a variety of systems |
| Limited graphing | Expansive graphing capabilities |
| Limited number of users | Accessible across the network and (in many cases) remotely |

## New Responsibilities

Emerging information capabilities are creating challenges that necessitate informed and active leadership. For example, the rapid market penetration of contact center systems has brought computer and communications monitoring technologies to tens of thousands of organizations. But it's still somewhat uncommon for the use of these capabilities to be preceded by training on how to establish appropriate policies and practices. In many cases, supervisors have been left to implement technologies with potentially enormous legal, quality and productivity implications. And within organizations with multiple sites, policies and practices often differ between locations.

A related challenge is the balance between service and privacy, and the uneasiness many customers feel about the sheer quantity of information that is being captured, shared, integrated with other data, and used for management and marketing purposes. And employees can feel much the same: "The computer watches me all the time; it never blinks." These issues require sound and up-to-date policies on customer privacy, data protection, internal monitoring practices and good communication with all involved. (See Chapter 14 for more on monitoring and related issues.)

Some managers have also assumed, perhaps in part due to overly aggressive promises from some supplier representatives, that new systems can practically "run the business." And yet, an understanding of underlying processes and a supporting culture are necessary for these capabilities to reach their potential. For example, workforce management systems don't coordinate with marketing, watch economic reports, or define how the organization should be structured. Quality monitoring systems can't define quality or strategic value for your operation. Real-time management information can't compel agents to want to be in the right place at the right times. The rich information provided by reporting, analytics and collaboration tools doesn't inherently bring business units together to create better products, services and customer experiences. As capable as today's systems are, they require effective leadership and clear direction.

In short, using information effectively is as important and challenging as ever. Ensuring that those in your center are getting and judiciously using the right information at the right times for the right purposes is a key leadership responsibility and an important enabler to running an effective customer contact operation.

## Revisit and Refine This Step

Data collection is a planning step that you'll need to continually reassess and improve. Don't leave it to chance! Regularly revisit the issue of how you are using information and why. Which information is relevant? How do you want the information formatted and presented? Who should have access to what? How will the information be used?

And remember to keep your eye on the prize. The purpose of information is to support key activities of the contact center that, in turn, further the principles and mission of the organization. To that end, we'll look at the specific information you'll need in chapters to follow.

## Points to Remember

- The data required for contact center planning and management comes from numerous internal and external sources.
- Acquiring and using the information you need must be a collaborative, cross-functional effort.
- Develop a flowchart of the information required for each of the key aspects of contact center planning and management; this will help to identify weak or missing links and point to collaboration opportunities.
- Continually review and improve your information systems and processes to ensure that they are supporting your most important objectives.

# CHAPTER 6:
# Forecasting the Center's Workload

*If you don't know where you're going, you'll wind up someplace else.*
**YOGI BERRA**

Matching resources with the workload is a critical step in managing a contact center effectively. This responsibility goes to the heart of contact center management: "having the right number of properly skilled people and supporting resources in place at the right times to handle an accurately forecasted workload, at service level and with quality."

Here's the scoop: If the forecast is not reasonably accurate, the rest of the planning process will be off the mark. The forecast is the basis for determining staffing needs and requirements for other resources, such as how many workstations are required and how many lines are necessary. It provides the foundation for:

- Calculating base staff required to meet your service level and response time objectives
- Calculating trunking and system requirements
- Minimizing abandoned and blocked calls
- Organizing accurate, workable schedules
- Predicting future staffing and network costs
- Meeting customer expectations
- Establishing an environment in which quality service can be provided

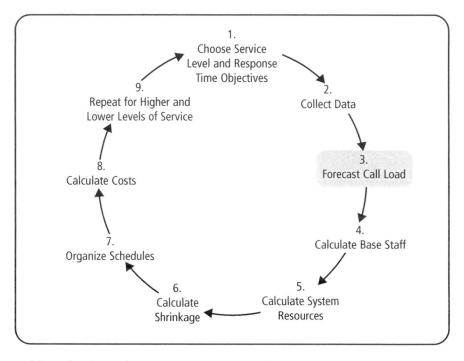

Note that I use the most common type of traffic in contact centers today — randomly arriving inbound calls — to cover basic forecasting principles. Once we've walked through the basics, we'll discuss considerations for other types of contacts.

## Art and Science

Forecasting is the proverbial mix of art and science. It begins with predicting how many contacts you are going to get in a future period, usually a year. To do that, you look at historical data to determine patterns that reflect when people contact you, and you consider possible trends that will affect traffic patterns. You then take that information and break it into the contacts that will be coming to you in different months, weeks of the month, days of the week, and half hours of the day — or even five minutes of the half hour, if you are forecasting peaked traffic. Next, you factor in the handling times of the interactions. Finally, you modify results based on conditions not reflected in historical data.

In the contact center environment, longer-term forecasts look out a year and beyond. They are used to estimate future annual budgets, establish long-term hiring plans and define future system needs. Shorter-term forecasts project workload out to three months. They are necessary for organizing and adjusting scheduling requirements, anticipating seasonal staffing needs, planning for holidays, and determining imminent hiring requirements. Weekly, daily and intraday forecasts are short-term tactical forecasts used to tighten up schedules and adjust priorities around current conditions and near-term events.

How far out you forecast will depend on the purpose of the forecast. Regardless, the basic principles and concepts are similar.

## Essential Data

The basic historical data you need for forecasting includes how many contacts you have received in the past, when they arrived and how long they took to handle. Four key terms reflect this activity:

- **TALK TIME** is everything from "hello" to "goodbye." In other words, it's the time callers are connected with agents. Anything that happens during talk time — such as putting the caller on hold to make an outbound call, confer with a supervisor or access an internal help desk — should be included in this measurement.

- **AFTER-CALL WORK** (also referred to as "wrap-up" or "not ready") is the time agents spend completing transactions after saying goodbye to callers. Legitimate after-call work should immediately follow talk time.

- **AVERAGE HANDLING TIME** (AHT) is average talk time plus average after-call work.

- **CALL LOAD** is the volume of contacts coupled with how long they last. More specifically, it is volume x (average talk time + average after-call work), for a given period of time.

These terms are used primarily for phone calls, but differ for other types of contacts. We'll discuss variations as we consider other media, in this chapter and in Chapter 7. In the end, you'll need projections for workload that encompass every channel (volume multiplied by average handling time); and, you'll need to develop your forecasts with all channels in mind, given their impact on each other.

---

**CLEAN THE DATA!**

It's important to "clean" the data you use to forecast future resource requirements. Too often, we see managers take data from systems and use it for forecasting and planning without giving it a second thought. But what if the IVR was down for an hour? What if a reporting system malfunctioned for part of a morning? What if a relevant news story hit the wires? (I was working with the management team of a credit card company one afternoon, when Oprah Winfrey featured a guest who encouraged viewers to call their financial institutions and negotiate interest rates. Talk about lighting up the monitors!) What about other variables that will, or will not, repeat and that need to be either included in or backed out of the numbers? In these cases, appropriate adjustments that reflect what's likely to continue will ensure that you are building forecasts on a solid foundation.

---

## OFFERED CALLS

The historical data you use in forecasting should reflect "offered calls" discounted for multiple attempts from individual callers. Offered calls include all of the attempts your customers make to reach you. There are three possibilities for offered calls: They can get busy signals; they can be answered by the system, but abandon before reaching an agent; or they can successfully reach an agent.

There has been a lot of debate around the term "offered call." Some define it as a call that reaches the ACD. Many ACDs utilize that definition,

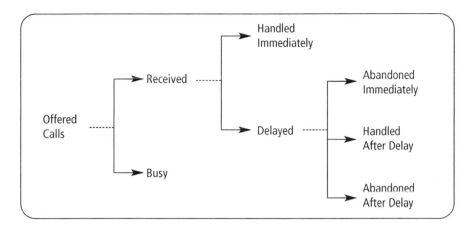

and have report columns labeled "offered calls" that reflect answered calls (those that reach agents) and abandoned calls. However, the traditional definition of offered call — and the one I'll stick with here — is any attempt a customer makes to reach you, even if they never reach the ACD (for instance, they get a busy signal in the network).

## ABANDONED CALLS

Acquiring data on abandoned calls is usually straightforward. Virtually every ACD provides reports on abandonments down to specific increments of time. The seven factors of customer tolerance (see Chapter 3) will influence how long a queue callers will tolerate, how many will abandon and how many will call back if they abandon.

Many managers count abandoned calls "one for one." The usual logic is that the forecast is based on half hour data and callers who abandon are not likely to call back within the half hour. To the degree that callers who abandon do, in fact, call back and get through to agents, they will be counted more than once in the data. Consequently, some managers use either "educated guesses" or, in some cases, hard data made possible by automatic number identification (ANI) reports (alternatively referred to as calling line identification, CLI) to discount a portion of the abandoned calls.

Without good data, you run the risk of discounting calls too deeply, which will lead to forecasts that underestimate demand. Consequently, I generally recommend that you include most (70 percent or more) abandoned calls in the data, unless you have specific reports or surveys you can use as a guide. This may lead to forecasts that overstate demand; however, forecasts that underestimate the workload will likely lead to insufficient staffing and abandoned calls, which will perpetuate the problem.

## BUSY SIGNALS

Busy signals are far less common today than they once were. Even on an individual level, voicemail and call waiting have all but eliminated busy signals. So, there's far less cultural acceptance of them. But they still can and do happen, and when they do, they wreak havoc on reports. The age-old question is, for every 100 busy signals, was that 100 people who tried to reach you once, or one persistent soul who tried 100 times? Of course, the answer is usually somewhere in between. Studies have shown that even when callers have other options, they will generally retry at least once or twice when they get a busy signal. So busy signals should almost always be discounted. The question is, how much?

Callers will encounter busy signals either when you don't have enough physical capacity to handle the calls or when you've programmed your ACD system to reject calls from entering the queue if the wait backs up beyond a threshold you define. Consequently, data on busy signals may come from your ACD, local telephone company, long-distance provider or all of the above.

Virtually all ACDs have a report called "all trunks busy" (ATB). This will tell you how much of the time and how many times all of the trunks in a specific group were 100 percent occupied. But it won't tell you how many attempts callers made to reach you when all trunks were busy, nor how many callers were represented by those attempts.

If your ACD can dynamically generate busy signals based on real-time circumstances, it will likely provide a report on how many calls received busies. Likewise, you can often obtain basic reports from your local and long-distance providers that give data on how many times busies were generated, for specific time periods. However, these basic reports won't tell you how many individuals are represented by those attempts, unless you can capture callers' numbers and run a sort to identify multiple attempts.

Some network carriers provide more advanced reports that can help solve the retrial mystery. These reports provide actual retrial rates (average number of attempts per individual caller), down to the specific days or increments of time that you specify. They can also be helpful if you are considering adjusting operating hours, as they will provide volumes on traffic you receive after your center is closed. (One caveat: If your customer base includes large organizations, contacts from different individuals can look like repeat calls from the same number.)

Alternatives to retrial reports can include customer surveys, answering all calls for a short period (even if by voicemail) to determine true demand and variations of judgment (guessing). Naturally, it's best to have hard data. But whatever information is available, be sure to question the rules of thumb, which generally state that callers will retry an average of three to five times. Like abandoned calls, retries are determined by the seven factors affecting caller tolerance — and three to five attempts may be off the mark for your scenarios.

Whatever the level of reports you can get, your forecast should, as accurately as possible, reflect the number of individuals attempting to reach you. If you count every busy signal and abandoned call, the forecast will overestimate true demand. If you ignore busy signals and abandoned calls, your forecast will underestimate demand.

## WHAT ABOUT IVRS AND ROUTING CONTINGENCIES?

Many organizations use interactive voice response units (IVRs) to provide customers with self-service options and to help route calls. Additionally, contingency-based routing alternatives can mean that calls start out in one place and end up in another depending on real-time circumstances.

Consequently, callers may make several hops and be counted by multi-

> ## UNDERSTANDING AGENT GROUPS
>
> An agent group (also called a split, gate, queue or skills group) shares a common set of skills and knowledge, handles a specified mix of contacts (e.g., service, sales, billing or technical support) and/or channels (e.g., phone, email, social, et al.) and may comprise hundreds of agents across multiple sites. Supervisory groups and teams are often subsets of agent groups.
>
> Agent groups are the building blocks of contact center structure. If you have one group of 100 agents handling all contacts, you will have one forecast and one set of schedules. If you have 10 groups of 10 agents, you'll need 10 sets of forecasts and schedules — one for each unique agent group. In other words, planning must be specific enough to ensure that you get the right number of properly skilled people and supporting resources in place at the right times, for each agent group.

ple systems before reaching an agent. While it is important to predict the workload that will be handled by your network and systems so that you can engineer them correctly, you'll need a forecast specific to each agent group for staffing purposes. In other words, count and forecast the contacts that reach each individual agent group, whatever the path that got them there.

## PROPORTIONS

The fundamental information you need for forecasting includes the three components of call load: talk time, after-call work and volume (or their variations for other contact channels). From this data, proportions can be derived. If you received 1,000 calls for the day, and 60 came in between 10:00 and 10:30, that half hour's proportion would be 6 percent or .06 (60/1,000). Proportions are used to project patterns into the future.

This is information your ACD and/or workforce management system should be collecting now and forever. Building on this essential half-hour data, you will accumulate necessary daily, weekly and monthly data. Whatever you do, don't throw data away. You'll never know when you will

| | Contacts | Prop. | Average Talk Time | Average Work Time | Average Hndl. Time |
|---|---|---|---|---|---|
| 08:00-08:30 | | | | | |
| 08:30-09:00 | | | | | |
| 09:00-09:30 | | | | | |
| 09:30-10:00 | | | | | |
| 10:00-10:30 | | | | | |
| 10:30-11:00 | | | | | |
| 11:00-11:30 | | | | | |
| 11:30-12:00 | | | | | |
| 12:00-12:30 | | | | | |
| 12:30-13:00 | | | The Fundamental Quantitative Information Necessary For Forecasting | | |
| 13:00-13:30 | | | | | |
| 13:30-14:00 | | | | | |
| 14:00-14:30 | | | | | |
| 14:30-15:00 | | | | | |
| 15:00-15:30 | | | | | |
| 15:30-16:00 | | | | | |
| 16:00-16:30 | | | | | |
| 16:30-17:00 | | | | | |
| 17:00-17:30 | | | | | |
| 17:30-18:00 | | | | | |
| Totals/Avgs | | | | | |

need information about that campaign from several years ago. "Hey, how did customers react that time we ..."

## REPEATING PATTERNS

Virtually all centers handling customer-initiated contacts notice at least three dominant patterns.

**MONTH OF YEAR OR SEASONALITY.** The graph, "Monthly Calls Offered," illustrates data from a financial services company. Notice that the most recent year is at a higher plane, but looks similar to the patterns in previous years. Even if your organization is going through dramatic changes, you will usually detect seasonality in your call arrival patterns. Three years of data will provide a good reading on these patterns; if you have additional history, even better. If you don't have three years of data, use what you have; even one year will often reflect what is likely to continue.

**105**

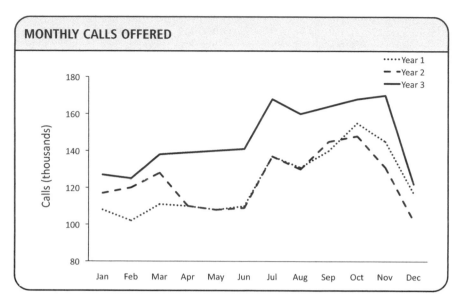

**DAY OF WEEK.** The graph, "Calls by Day of Week," is from a telecommunications company. The first week reflects a holiday on a Monday. The contact center was open, but, of course, callers were behaving differently than usual. Consequently, that following Tuesday gets more calls than normal, illustrating the "pent-up demand" that is common after holidays.

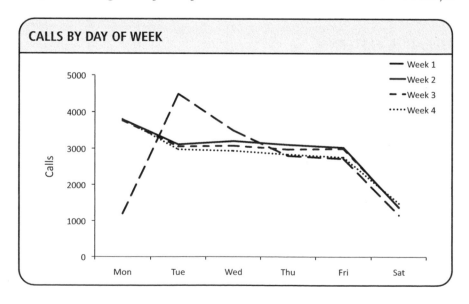

Otherwise, the pattern is highly predictable from one week to the next. (Holiday weeks are predictable, as well, if you have some history of similar holidays.) As the example shows, as few as four or five weeks' worth of history can reveal this pattern.

**HALF HOUR OF DAY.** The data for the graph Half-Hourly Calls Offered is from a bank. Notice the system outage? That kind of exception from the norm tends to really stick out. And it raises an important point: Exceptions need to be pulled out of the data or they will throw off predictions. A week or two's worth of data will often be enough to identify this pattern.

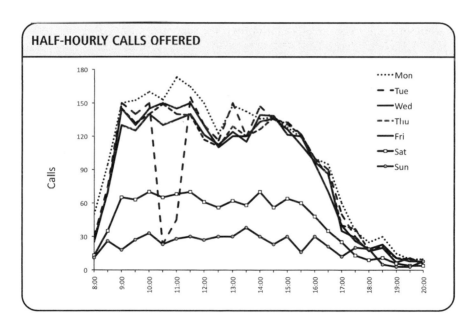

HALF-HOURLY CALLS OFFERED

You may have other patterns, as well. For example, if you send out statements to your customers on the 5th and 20th of each month, you'll notice day-of-month patterns. And marketing campaigns will create their own traffic patterns.

Individuals call for a myriad of reasons, but become part of highly predictable patterns. It's pretty amazing, actually. (Whoever said that forecasting was *boring*?!)

So, one of the most essential steps in forecasting is to look at your data and identify the patterns that exist. Even if you are using forecasting software, it is still important to graph the "raw" patterns so you can identify exceptions.

## Breaking Down a Forecast

OK, grab that double tall breve latte, and let's go through a basic approach that illustrates how to break down a forecast. This example starts with longer-term patterns and works its way down to specific half-hour increments. The steps involved include:

### BREAKING DOWN A FORECAST

| | |
|---|---|
| 720,000 | Current year's calls |
| x 1.12 | add 12% (proportion) |
| 806,400 | Forecasted annual calls |
| x .071 | January proportion |
| 57,254 | January calls |
| ÷ 31 | Operation days - January |
| 1,847 | Average calls per day |
| x 1.469 | Monday's index factor |
| 2,713 | Monday's calls |
| x .055 | 10:00 to 10:30 proportion |
| 149 | Forecasted calls 10:00-10:30 |

Notes:

1. Determine operation days by counting the days the contact center will be open.
2. Calculate day-of-week index factors by dividing average day-of-week into the specific day's proportion.

JANUARY

| S | M | T | W | T | F | S |
|---|---|---|---|---|---|---|
| | | 1 | 2 | 3 | 4 | 5 |
| 6 | 7 | 8 | 9 | 10 | 11 | 12 |
| 13 | 14 | 15 | 16 | 17 | 18 | 19 |
| 20 | 21 | 22 | 23 | 24 | 25 | 26 |
| 27 | 28 | 29 | 30 | 31 | | |

| Example: | DOW Prop. | | Avg. Prop. | | Index Factor |
|---|---|---|---|---|---|
| Monday | .210 | ÷ | .143 | = | 1.469 |
| Tuesday | .170 | ÷ | .143 | = | 1.189 |
| Wednesday | .165 | ÷ | .143 | = | 1.154 |
| Thursday | .165 | ÷ | .143 | = | 1.154 |
| Friday | .150 | ÷ | .143 | = | 1.049 |
| Saturday | .095 | ÷ | .143 | = | .664 |
| Sunday | .045 | ÷ | .143 | = | .315 |

1. Obtain the number of calls received in the past 12 months; 720,000 in this example.

2. Multiply the year's calls by 1.12 to reflect 12 percent expected growth. Factoring in growth at this level assumes that contacts will increase propor-

tionally to previous years' patterns. If growth will instead be concentrated around marketing campaigns or other events that don't necessarily happen at the same time from year to year, you should factor it in at a more specific level, such as monthly or weekly.

3. Multiply the estimated calls in the year you are forecasting by January's proportion, 7.1 percent. This percentage comes from history and is the typical proportion of the year's calls that January receives.

4. Divide the number of operation days in the month into the estimated monthly calls. This yields average calls per day. In this example, the center is open every day of the month.

5. Adjust average calls per day, using the appropriate daily index factor. The first column in the index factor calculation gives the proportion of the week's transactions that typically arrive each day. For example, Monday normally gets 21 percent of the week's traffic; Tuesday gets 17 percent and so forth.

The next column reflects the proportion of a week that an operation day represents. For example, if you're open seven days a week, each day is 1/7, or 14.3 percent of a week. If your center is open five days, each day is 1/5, or 20 percent of a week. A day in a six-day workweek is 16.7 percent of the week.

The final column is the result of dividing the first column by the second column. These index factors are then multiplied against the average calls per day to estimate traffic by the specific day of week. In this example, Monday's index factor, 1.469, is multiplied against 1,847.

6. The final step is to multiply the predicted calls for each day of the week by each half hour's proportion. In this example, the half hour 10:00 to 10:30 will get a projected 149 calls.

This process must take a lot of time, right? Actually, once you establish a system and an approach, it won't take nearly as much time as you may think. You will get better at it with practice. And forecasting software or, even spreadsheets, can take much of the labor out of it. And for the time you do invest, remember that forecasting is one of the most high-leverage activities in the planning process. You'll spend a lot more time "putting out fires" later on if you don't have a good forecast.

Keep in mind, this is a basic approach and there are many possible refinements — e.g., to account for calendar variations, intra-month trends or other variables — that may improve accuracy. But if you are pulling out the exceptions and working with good data, going through this type of process provides a good foundation on which to build. You will still need to blend in judgment, coordinate with marketing, etc. (see upcoming discussions). After all, past history doesn't always reflect what's going to happen in the future.

You may also need to incorporate other patterns into the forecast. For example, if you send out billing statements twice a month, that activity will generate traffic when the bills begin to arrive. But the percent increase caused by these events will also fall into predictable patterns, and you can adjust accordingly. You may need to calculate day-of-month index factors, a process similar to deriving day-of-week index factors.

## HOLIDAY WEEKS

Holiday weeks will require their own index factors. But the pattern for one week with a holiday on a Monday will often be similar to another week in the year with a holiday on a Monday. Holidays that fall on various days

| Examples of Calculating Day-of-Week Index Factors For Week With A Holiday (divide proportion by average proportion) | | | |
|---|---|---|---|
| | Prop. | Avg. Prop. | Index Factor |
| Monday | 0 | 0 | 0 |
| Tuesday | .290 | .167 | 1.737 |
| Wednesday | .240 | .167 | 1.437 |
| Thursday | .175 | .167 | 1.048 |
| Friday | .155 | .167 | 0.928 |
| Saturday | .095 | .167 | 0.569 |
| Sunday | .045 | .167 | 0.269 |

of the week are another reason to hang on to your historical data.

## INTRADAY FORECASTS

Intraday or intraweek forecasts are quick and easy to produce, and are often quite accurate. Typically, short-term forecasts are more accurate than long-term forecasts.

The approach works like this: At some point in the morning, say just after 10:30 a.m., you begin to realize that this is not a typical day. Your reports indicate that you have received 402 calls so far, which may be more or fewer than originally expected. Either way, you divide the usual proportion of the day's calls that you would expect by 10:30 — 18 percent in this case — into 402 (18 percent came from looking at traffic patterns on previous days and calculating half-hourly proportions). Bingo, you now know that if the trend continues, you can expect to receive 2,233 calls for the day.

---

**INTRADAY FORECASTING**

|  |  |
|---:|:---|
| 402 | Calls received by 10:30 a.m. |
| ÷ .18 | Usual proportion of calls by 10:30 a.m. |
| 2,233 | Revised forecast for day |
| x .066 | 3:30 - 4:00 p.m. proportion |
| 147 | Intraday forecast for 3:30 - 4:00 p.m. |

---

Next, you can break down the revised daily forecast into the remaining half hours by multiplying historical half-hourly proportions by 2,233. For example, since you would normally expect to get 6.6 percent of a day's calls between 3:30 and 4:00 p.m., you can expect 147 calls during that half hour.

The assumption behind intraday forecasting is that the morning will set the tone for the afternoon. However, if you are a utility getting swamped with calls in the morning due to a major power outage, this will be a bad assumption. When the outage is fixed, the calls will go away. In many cases, though, intraday forecasting is a useful and accurate tool. You can use similar logic to create an intraweek forecast.

---

### INTRAWEEK FORECASTING

|  |  |
|---|---|
| 3,050 | Calls received on Monday |
| ÷ .23 | Usual proportion of calls by Monday |
| 13,261 | Revised calls forecast for week |
| x .17 | Friday's proportion |
| 2,254 | Intraweek forecast for Friday |

## SALES FORECASTS

Some contact centers use sales forecasts to verify or improve their call load forecasts. To use this methodology, you need to know the average sales value in the contact center and the conversion factor (the number of received calls that result in a sale compared to the total calls received). The conversion factor can be expressed as a whole number or as a proportion. For example, if it takes five calls on average to make a sale, then the expected number of calls would be sales times five (i.e., 5 x 1,000 = 5,000). Alternatively, you could divide one by five to get a proportion and then divide the number of sales expected by that proportion (i.e., 1,000 ÷ .20 = 5,000).

### HOW WILL NEXT YEAR BE DIFFERENT? — SALES

|  | Jan | Feb | Mar | Apr | May | June | July | Aug | Sept | Oct | Nov | Dec | Total or Avg |
|---|---|---|---|---|---|---|---|---|---|---|---|---|---|
| A. Projected Revenue | __ | __ | __ | __ | __ | __ | __ | __ | __ | __ | __ | __ | __ |
| B. Average Sale Value | __ | __ | __ | __ | __ | __ | __ | __ | __ | __ | __ | __ | __ |
| C. No. of Sales (A ÷ B) | __ | __ | __ | __ | __ | __ | __ | __ | __ | __ | __ | __ | __ |
| D. Conversion Factor 1 ÷ (orders ÷ calls) | __ | __ | __ | __ | __ | __ | __ | __ | __ | __ | __ | __ | __ |
| E. Projected Calls (C x D) | __ | __ | __ | __ | __ | __ | __ | __ | __ | __ | __ | __ | __ |

The subject of sales forecasting is complex and you will need the input and collaboration of the marketing professionals in your organization. With their help, a sales forecast can provide a good sanity check to ensure that the contact center is able to handle the load from marketing efforts.

## DIRECT MARKETING CAMPAIGNS

Organizations that run direct marketing campaigns often utilize response rates to forecast call load. Usually there is a taper-down effect, where volume is relatively high in the initial days of a campaign and then tapers down over time.

One of the things that makes this tricky is that there are often overlapping campaigns going on at any given time. Another is deciding what constitutes an order — is it a single call from a customer or each item ordered? You will need to decide on definitions and stick to them.

---

**HOW WILL NEXT YEAR BE DIFFERENT? — SALES**

A. Target Audience Size _____

B. Overall Response Rate (orders ÷ target audience) _____

| | Day 1 | Day 2 | Day 3 | Day 4 | Day 5 | Day 6 | Day 7 | Day 8 | Day 9 | Day 10 | Day 11 | Day 12 | Day 13 | Day 14 |
|---|---|---|---|---|---|---|---|---|---|---|---|---|---|---|
| C. Percent Orders by Day | | | | | | | | | | | | | | |
| D. Projected Orders (A x B x C) | | | | | | | | | | | | | | |
| E. Conversion Factor 1 ÷ (orders ÷ calls) | | | | | | | | | | | | | | |
| F. Number of Calls (D x E) | | | | | | | | | | | | | | |

---

## PEAKED ARRIVAL

In many ways, underlying forecasting principles are similar for both random and peaked traffic. But one big difference is in the level of detail required in your reports. While half-hour reports are sufficient for random call arrival, you will need historical reports down to more specific increments of time (five- or 10-minute segments) in order to adequately forecast and staff for peaked traffic.

The other big difference is that the specific targeted promotions you are delivering — television or radio ads, for example — will dramatically influence response. That's true for any kind of marketing, of course, but because of concentrated workload arrivals, the impact on contact center resources is that much greater. The audience you are reaching (numbers and demographics), the products and services being offered, the channels you are making available, and the effectiveness of the ads themselves will drive how many contacts you get, the nature of the interactions, and how concentrated they are within a specific timeframe. Identifying primary drivers and correlating them to response is key.

You'll also want to take the steps you can to influence when the work will come in so that you're ready to handle it. For example, you may have a choice between running television ads at precise times, or receiving discounts to run them anytime within a larger block of time (as the network's programming needs dictate). Ad-buy savings can quickly evaporate when you weigh the costs of having staff standing by. These decisions should be made collaboratively (including marketing, the contact center and the media partner), with the total picture in mind.

## OTHER CHANNELS

There are some notable differences in forecasting phone calls and other types of contacts. As you probably know instinctively, the basic workload terms, "talk time" and "after-call work," don't make as much sense for email or social interactions — "handling time" is a better fit. The series of exchanges with a customer over a short period of time (the back and forth that takes place in a chat or social dialog) is often referred to as a session (chat) or conversation (social). You'll need to anticipate the number of customer sessions or conversations, the time it takes to handle them and, given their back-and-forth nature, the number of customers an agent can simultaneously handle (see Chapter 7).

The social environment, in particular, is a vast and complex ecosystem. When anticipating staffing requirements in a customer service setting, think more along the lines of forecasting the weather. *Partly cloudy this morning, with a warming trend this afternoon.* You won't always get it right. But look out as far as possible, think through as many variables as feasible, and observe patterns and how they are developing. In the end, dress for any kind of weather (meaning, build flexibility and scalability into your staffing plans).

---

*The social environment, in particular, is a vast and complex ecosystem. When anticipating staffing requirements in a customer service setting, think more along the lines of forecasting the weather ... and dress for any kind of weather (meaning, build flexibility and scalability into your staffing plans).*

---

Social monitoring tools — which range from free to high-end and can be standalone or integrated into existing contact center systems — enable you to make sense of what's being said about your company, products and services. They can help you identify top influencers, prominent opinions, where conversations are taking place and which are having the most impact on the perception of your brand. You can then establish criteria for when and how to engage and determine what needs to be included in the workload that is delivered to your agents.

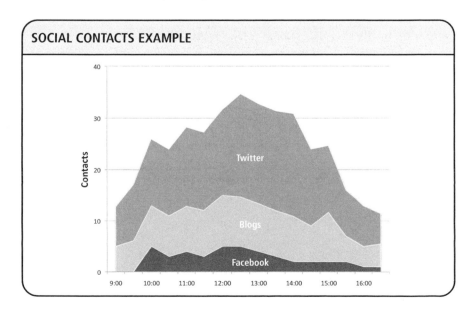

**SOCIAL CONTACTS EXAMPLE**

The good news is that underlying patterns almost always exist. Yes, social trending topics and posts that quickly multiply can create unique staffing challenges. But being responsive in their early stages can help head off what would be repetitive contacts. In short, the same basic principles apply: Look for patterns, consider the variables, and use what you're seeing to project future workload. You will also need to blend in appropriate judgment (see below).

## AVERAGE HANDLING TIME

Many of us have a habit of referring to the volume of contacts as the only criterion in the workload: "How many contacts did you handle last year? How about yesterday? How about this morning?" Equally important, though, is average handling time, which, when coupled with volume, makes up call load. It is call load that matters. Volume alone is relatively meaningless.

As with call volume, average talk time and average after-call work usually fall into predictable, repeating patterns. Similarly, the basic forecasting approach involves utilizing historical reports along with a measure of good judgment. You begin by looking at the average handling time for a recent

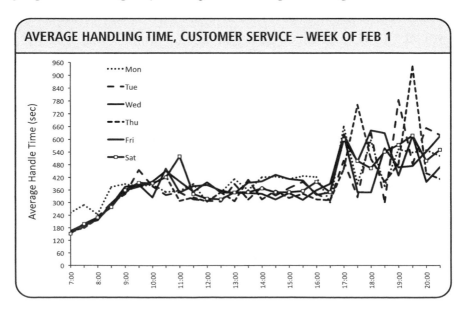

AVERAGE HANDLING TIME, CUSTOMER SERVICE – WEEK OF FEB 1

week, broken down by half-hour increments. If the week is "typical," the data represented by this pattern is what will likely continue.

The graph of average handling time is from a mobile phone company. Their average handling time went up in the evenings, and was far more variable, for several reasons. First, they let agents bid on shifts based on seniority. Most agents, when given the choice, prefer to start and quit earlier in the day, so they had a higher concentration of new agents (and, probably, less experienced supervisors) assigned to the evening shift. That's not necessarily a bad approach, but it will impact average handling time and must be reflected in the forecast.

Second, they did not have a good definition for after-call work, and much of it was getting postponed until late in the day. Third, their call mix changed throughout the day and calls got relatively longer in the evening.

Average handling time, like call volume, must be incorporated into planning by the half hour. Assuming the same average handling time all day for forecasting purposes will not reflect the environment accurately.

Some relatively simple analysis can go a long way toward tightening up your projections. Here are a few important prerequisites for getting this part of your forecast right:

**1. LOOK FOR PATTERNS.** For each answer group, identify how average talk time and average after-call work vary. You may also discover patterns by day of the week, season of the year, billing cycles and marketing campaigns. For a deeper look at average handling time, make separate graphs for average talk time and average after-call work. This will reveal the patterns for each. You will need these reports when calculating system resources, which will be discussed in Chapter 7.

**2. TRAIN YOUR AGENTS TO USE WORK MODES CONSISTENT-LY.** Each agent has an impact on the components of handling time (talk time and after-call work) and, therefore, on the data that will be used in forecasting and planning for future call loads. When the queue is building, it can be tempting to postpone after-call work that should be done at the time of the call. This skews reports, causes planning problems and may lead to increased errors. An important and ongoing training issue is to define ahead of time what type of work should follow calls and what type of work can wait.

**3. IDENTIFY THE AVERAGE HANDLING TIME FOR DIFFERENT CALL TYPES.** This presupposes that you have defined and categorized calls by type, that you are accurately tracking calls based on the categories, and that you have the reporting capability to link average handling time to the categories. A Pareto chart is often the best way to represent this data.

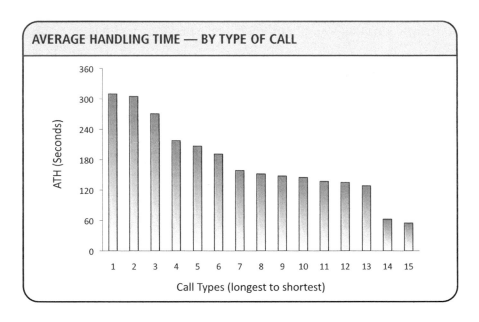

**AVERAGE HANDLING TIME — BY TYPE OF CALL**

ATH (Seconds)

Call Types (longest to shortest)

You can use this information in a number of ways. For example, when you are forecasting an increase or decrease of a specific type of call, you will be able to project the impact on average handling time. A marketing campaign will generate certain types of calls. A new Web-based service or mobile app will likely reduce some types of calls agents handle (and may increase others). In each case, you'll be equipped to estimate average handling time.

**4. ASSESS THE IMPACT OF NEW AGENTS, LANGUAGES HANDLED, AND PROCESS CHANGES.** Less-experienced agents often require more time to handle contacts as they learn how to deal with process-

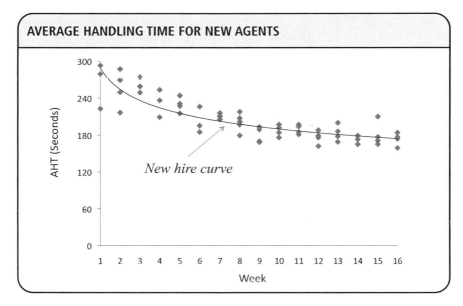

AVERAGE HANDLING TIME FOR NEW AGENTS

*New hire curve*

es, systems, cultures and callers. Further, some languages require more time than others (for example, French takes somewhat longer than German, and Spanish requires more time than English).

Compare average handling time to the experience levels of your agents, languages handled, etc. Doing this will enable you to estimate the impact of these variables on AHT, and will be useful in establishing realistic expectations.

These same steps are recommended, regardless of contact channel. For example, look for patterns in the social contacts you are handling, ensure agents are using work modes consistently, identify the handling time for different kinds of contacts, and assess the impact of new agents and process changes on handling time.

## Beyond the Basics

The major categories of quantitative forecasting include "time-series" and "explanatory" approaches. The examples in this chapter are fairly basic, and more advanced alternatives within each category exist. I'll introduce a

## SOFTWARE AND SERVICES FOR ADVANCED FORECASTING

If you're in an organization or industry going through significant changes, or if your center handles contacts generated by television commercials or overlapping direct marketing campaigns, the simple time-series and explanatory techniques used in most workforce management systems or user-defined spreadsheets may not cut it. Fortunately, there are alternatives.

For example, standalone business forecasting software packages — such as those from SAS, ForecastPro and others — include a wide range of forecasting methodologies. These programs enable you to build in multiple events and variables, and produce forecasts based on different models. By comparing forecasts, you can identify the best methodology for your environment. Since one approach may work better than others for specific types of events, you can change models as circumstances dictate. You may need an analyst to spearhead this effort, but more accurate forecasts (and therefore, better staffing plans and schedules) often provide a solid return on the investment.

You may also want to explore outside services. For example, forecasting services offered by consultants can provide forecasts based on advanced methodologies for centers that need transitional or ongoing help. Similar services exist in other fields, e.g., financial and sales forecasting, and this alternative is becoming more common and accessible in the contact center environment.

few of them here to give you an idea of the breadth of possibilities.

Time-series forecasting methods include simple or "naive" rules (e.g., the forecast equals last year's same month, plus 12 percent), decomposition, simple time-series and advanced time-series methods. The governing assumption behind time-series forecasting is that past data will reflect trends that will continue into the future. Time-series methodologies are common in workforce management software. Most time-series forecasts are reasonably accurate when projecting out three months or less.

Explanatory forecasting methods include simple regression analysis, multiple regression analysis, econometric models and multivariate methods. Explanatory forecasting essentially attempts to reveal a linkage between two or more variables. For example, if you manage an ice cream shop, you could statistically correlate the weather (e.g., outside temperature) to ice cream sales. In a contact center, you might correlate a price increase to the impact on calling volumes.

Advanced time-series and explanatory forecasting methods go beyond the scope of this book. In fact, you can spend a couple of college semesters — make that a career — learning about forecasting. If you would like more information, we recommend *Principles of Forecasting — A Handbook for Researchers and Practitioners* (Jay Scott Armstrong, Editor), which includes contributions from experts on a wide range of forecasting topics and references to other useful sources.

## Blending in Judgment

So far, we've looked at quantitative forecasting — in other words, how to use hard data in your forecasting process. Judgmental forecasting goes beyond purely statistical techniques and encompasses what people *think* is going to happen. It is in the realm of intuition, interdepartmental committees, market research and executive opinion.

Many things, from politics to personal agendas, can influence judgmental forecasting. However, some judgment is inherent in virtually all forms of forecasting. And a degree of good judgment can significantly improve accuracy. The trick is to combine quantitative and judgmental approaches effectively, and to be aware of the limitations of each.

The worksheet, "Blending in Judgment," illustrates one way of applying common sense and a logical approach to judgmental forecasting. In a customer service environment, the number of contacts is often primarily a function of the total number of customers or constituents in the organization's universe. It is possible to project calls based on historical data, utilizing the relationships between calling volume and total customers (calls per

---

**BLENDING IN JUDGMENT**

|  | May 1 | May 8 | May 15 | May 22 | May 29 | June 5 | June 12 | June 19 |
|---|---|---|---|---|---|---|---|---|
| A. Projected Customers | ___ | ___ | ___ | ___ | ___ | ___ | ___ | ___ |
| B. Calls per Customer | ___ | ___ | ___ | ___ | ___ | ___ | ___ | ___ |
| C. Base Calls (A x B) | ___ | ___ | ___ | ___ | ___ | ___ | ___ | ___ |
| D. Activity Level Change | | | | | | | | |
| 1. New Customers | ___ | ___ | ___ | ___ | ___ | ___ | ___ | ___ |
| 2. Media Attention | ___ | ___ | ___ | ___ | ___ | ___ | ___ | ___ |
| 3. Advertising | ___ | ___ | ___ | ___ | ___ | ___ | ___ | ___ |
| 4. New Rate Structure | ___ | ___ | ___ | ___ | ___ | ___ | ___ | ___ |
| 5. New Terms & Conditions | ___ | | | | | | | |
| 6. New Service Procedures | ___ | | | CONTACTS (+ OR -) | | | ___ | ___ |
| 7. New Information Required | ___ | ___ | ___ | ___ | ___ | ___ | ___ | ___ |
| 8. New Product Introduction | ___ | ___ | ___ | ___ | ___ | ___ | ___ | ___ |
| 9. General Activity Level | ___ | ___ | ___ | ___ | ___ | ___ | ___ | ___ |
| 10. Product Performance | ___ | ___ | ___ | ___ | ___ | ___ | ___ | ___ |
| 11. Competitors' Actions | ___ | ___ | ___ | ___ | ___ | ___ | ___ | ___ |
| 12. Other | ___ | ___ | ___ | ___ | ___ | ___ | ___ | ___ |
| E. Total (add 1 through 12) | ___ | ___ | ___ | ___ | ___ | ___ | ___ | ___ |
| **F. Projected Calls (C + E)** | ___ | ___ | ___ | ___ | ___ | ___ | ___ | ___ |

---

customer). To the degree that the future repeats the past, this forecast will be accurate.

Part D of the form is where judgment plays a significant role. In this section, you customize the forecast by adding or reducing contacts, based on information you develop from your own and others' input. For some of these factors, you may have some hard data that you can use. For others, you'll be making more of an "educated guess."

The factors in Part D are only examples, derived from the following list. You will need to create your own list specific to your environment. For example, in a support center for broken-down or stranded vehicles, weather would be a key influence on call load.

You will need a routine mechanism or forum for blending judgment into the forecast. A fairly common approach in contact centers is a weekly forecasting meeting. These meetings typically include members of the scheduling department and a representation of supervisors and managers from the center and other departments. The meeting will typically last only 30 or 45 minutes. It often works like this:

- The person in charge of the meeting prepares an agenda of items to be discussed.
- The scheduling person (or team) prepares the quantitative forecast before the meeting.
- During the meeting, the attendees discuss issues that may influence the forecast, such as those in Part D of the worksheet. Each participant brings a unique perspective to the process.
- As each issue is discussed, the forecast is adjusted up or down, based on what the group believes will happen.

The collaborative approach is most effective when key team members who are accountable for staffing take an active role in forecasting (in large contact centers, they can be rotated through this process). The forecast not only improves as a result of their perspective, but they gain an understanding of the factors that contribute to staffing. As a result, they more effectively lead their teams.

## Measuring Accuracy — Strive for Five

How accurate should your forecast be? Large agent groups (100 or more agents) generally see relatively stable call patterns and should strive for plus or minus 5 percent (or better) of call load down to specific intervals. Small groups (15 or fewer agents) often have more volatile patterns and should shoot for plus or minus 10 percent. Those in-between should strive for something close to 5 percent.

This is not to suggest you can't do better. On the other hand, if you're just getting started with, say, a small group handling social interactions, being within 200% might be a pretty good start! But don't give up. Make this aspect of planning a priority. Be relentless in your focus until you begin to get your arms around it. Forecasting impacts everything to follow — staffing calculations, schedules and budgets, and, ultimately, the services you deliver.

### MEASURING FORECAST ACCURACY

| | | Call Volume | | | |
|---|---|---|---|---|---|
| | | Forecast | Actual | Difference | Percent* |
| 8:30 | 9:00 | 342 | 291 | 51 | 17.5% |
| 9:00 | 9:30 | 399 | 343 | 56 | 16.3% |
| 9:30 | 10:00 | 461 | 499 | -38 | -7.6% |
| 10:00 | 10:30 | 511 | 582 | -71 | -12.2% |
| 10:30 | 11:00 | 576 | 649 | -73 | -11.2% |
| 11:00 | 11:30 | 605 | 578 | 27 | 4.7% |
| 11:30 | 12:00 | 572 | 513 | 59 | 11.5% |
| 12:00 | 12:30 | 505 | 412 | 93 | 22.6% |
| 12:30 | 1:00 | 456 | 540 | -84 | -15.6% |
| | | **4427** | **4407** | **20** | **0.5%** |

The accuracy of forecasting must be measured here …

Not here!

* Variance of forecast to actual

Note: This example illustrates volume only; for an even more accurate assessment, apply this same approach to call load (volume X AHT).

When measuring accuracy, it's essential to look at intervals rather than an average over a day or more. One way to assess how you're doing by interval without producing mounds of detail is to create a table that summarizes the percent of intervals that fall within various ranges of accuracy. You determine the thresholds, and you can tighten them down the road as forecasts become more accurate.

### FORECAST ACCURACY BY INTERVAL

| Accurate Within: | Percent of Intervals |
|---|---|
| 5% or less | 11% |
| 5.1% to 10% | 11% |
| 10.1% to 15% | 33% |
| 15.1% to 20% | 33% |
| Over 20% | 11% |

You can summarize a week, month, year or more in this way, and still provide meaningful data. This approach isn't perfect; for example, it doesn't tell you which intervals were most important. But it's a lot better than most cumulative summaries, and will get your team focused on intervals and on moving the numbers in the right direction.

## Common Forecasting Problems

Over the years, the team at ICMI has investigated why some contact centers have accurate forecasts and others don't. Ten common problems tend to consistently emerge, and they are summarized here (in no specific order). In centers with inaccurate forecasts, usually two or three of these issues are most prevalent. The good news? You can avoid these problems, and the remedies in most cases are fairly obvious.

**1. NO SYSTEMATIC PROCESS IN PLACE.** There are often two erroneous beliefs that some managers use to justify the absence of a systematic forecasting process. Some say, "Our environment is too unpredictable. We're growing; we're adding contact channels; we're introducing new products; you can't predict social interactions ... there is no way we can expect to produce an accurate forecast." However, there are many centers in highly volatile environments that do a respectable job of forecasting.

Others aren't convinced that forecasting is worth the time. Yep, it takes time — but not nearly as much as some imagine. Further, a good forecast will save a lot of time later on.

**2. AN ASSUMPTION THAT "THE FORECASTING SOFTWARE KNOWS BEST."** If you have forecasting software or a workforce management system, don't just relinquish decisions to the program, assuming that it knows best. The software doesn't know what the marketing department is about to do, or that average handling time will be affected by changes you are making to your systems. And if you have busy signals, you will also need to ensure that the system incorporates adjusted offered calls, not just calls received by the ACD system.

Further, it is important to understand the assumptions your forecasting software is making. Some of the techniques it will utilize are user-definable. For example, you can program the system to give more weight to recent historical data, or you can tell it to ignore data that varies beyond X percent of the norm. It's a great idea to have the supplier provide a flow chart of the methodology the system is using and decision points where your input is necessary.

**3. NOT FORECASTING AT THE AGENT GROUP LEVEL.** Even a perfect forecast of the aggregate call load will be of limited use if you route calls to specialized groups. If you have a group of Mandarin-speaking agents handling services A, B and C, you will need to forecast calls from Mandarin-speaking callers who need help with those services.

**4. THE FORECAST IS TAKEN LIGHTLY.** If the forecast has been wildly inaccurate in the past or if no one understands the assumptions used in the process, it will not be given the prominence it needs in the planning steps to follow.

**5. EVENTS THAT SHOULD BE EXCEPTIONS BECOME A PART OF THE FORECAST.** Utilities tend to get lots of calls when storms knock out power, the financial industry gets swamped when confusing tax changes are implemented, and many centers have, on at least one occasion, dealt with calls from an unannounced marketing campaign. (Have your agents ever had to sheepishly ask a caller, "Um, what does the ad say we are offering?")

Those preparing the forecast have to be aware of the root causes of contacts in order to make a good judgment on what is likely to continue (and therefore should be built into the forecast) versus the exceptions.

**6. ONGOING COMMUNICATION WITH OTHER DEPARTMENTS DOESN'T EXIST.** Most of what happens in a contact center is caused by something going on outside the center. The forecast is doomed if strong ties with other departments don't exist.

**7. PLANNING IS DONE AROUND GOALS, NOT REALITY.** If staffing is based on a handling time of four minutes when actual handling

## ONE DAY, A LONG TIME AGO

As a new call centre manager many years ago, I recall the "pain" of having to deal with a "rogue" product manager who routinely bombarded my inbound/outbound centre with direct marketing campaigns, without giving my team (or me) any advance warning. The product manager, who we'll call Theresa, had dropped three such campaigns on us the previous month and as you might expect, the results were not pretty: Stressed out agents, angry customers, and a nightmare for our workforce management team, who were valiantly trying to improve our forecasts.

When the fourth "mystery" campaign hit the following week, I had Bob, our technology manager, reroute the 1-800 number to Theresa's direct extension. In less than 10 minutes, I got a call from a distraught Theresa: "What the heck is going on with the 1-800 campaign? How am I supposed to handle these calls?" My reply: "Now you know how we feel!"

Things got better quickly. I explained that launching campaigns without properly preparing the contact centre was not only stressful for our agents, it also reduced the success of the campaigns and potentially damaged our brand in the eyes of our customers.

I'm older and wiser now, and NO, I don't recommend trying this approach in your own centre. It can get you fired! It was, admittedly, the result of both my inexperience and Theresa's in this area. But it's a story I tell today because it reinforces the importance something I've since stressed for many years, that of developing strong relationships across the organization. Educate and engage. We're all in this together.

By Gina Szabo, SMI Inc. and ICMI Senior Certified Associate, Toronto, Canada

time is more like seven minutes, the resulting staff calculations and schedules will be based on a pipe dream. Maybe improved training, streamlined procedures and better systems would move things in that direction. But ignoring reality in the planning process is no way to achieve better results or build confidence in the forecast.

**8. NO ONE IS ACCOUNTABLE.** As vital as a good forecast is, often there is no one who spearheads the effort. Someone needs to be responsible for bringing the various types of input together, ensuring that it is integrated into the forecast, and investigating which assumptions were off when the forecast is not accurate.

**9. AGENTS ARE MIXING FLEXIBLE ACTIVITIES INTO WORK MODES.** If agents are not using work modes consistently, especially after-call work, then accurate forecasting will be elusive.

**10. NOT MAKING THE CONNECTION WITH STAFFING.** Forecasts mean nothing unless they are tied to staff and system resources required. That is the subject of Chapter 7.

## Look Back and Adjust

Organizations that produce accurate forecasts are not necessarily those that have the most stable environments. Rather, they have a group of people (or an individual) who have made accurate forecasting a priority. They have taken responsibility, established good ties across departments, pulled in the data required, and established a forecasting process they are continually improving. They set accuracy goals and monitor progress. And they continue to work on and improve the assumptions they are making when looking ahead. In short, they consider accurate forecasting to be mission-critical.

Forecasting takes practice. You will never learn all there is to know about it — but you'll get better at it. One of the most important steps you can take to improve accuracy is to compare your forecasts with actual results and then ask, "Why?"

## Points to Remember

- Forecasting is a blend of art and science, and it incorporates both quantitative and judgmental approaches.

- The forecast should accurately predict all possible components of handling contacts: talk time, after-call work, and volume (or equivalent variations for non-phone interactions). Volume alone is meaningless.
- The forecast should reflect adjusted offered calls or the individuals who try to reach you.
- There are numerous quantitative forecasting methodologies. Time-series forecasting is popular for contact centers.
- You need mechanisms, such as a collaborative weekly meeting, to blend good judgment into your forecasts.
- You need a workload forecast for each agent group.
- Accurate forecasts provide a solid foundation for the planning steps that follow.

# CHAPTER 7:
# Determining Base Staff
# and System Resources

*Having the right number of properly skilled people and supporting resources*
*in place at the right times ...*

**ICMI**

The key to achieving service level and response time objectives ultimately comes down to having the right people in the right place at the
right times, supported by sufficient system resources. With a reasonably
accurate forecast, base staff calculations are usually straightforward.

However, there are two caveats to getting this part of planning right: 1)
You will need to use the right methodology in your calculations; and 2)
trunking (the lines or bandwidth capacity you need) should be calculated
with an understanding of staffing requirements because staffing impacts
delay, which affects the load that systems and networks must carry.

In this chapter, we'll dispel some common myths about staffing and
trunking. We'll go through the mechanics of correct calculations and
explore how chat, social, long calls and other types of contacts impact
requirements. We'll contrast traditional (switched) trunks and VoIP-based
services. And we'll review important definitions and measurements related
to this aspect of planning.

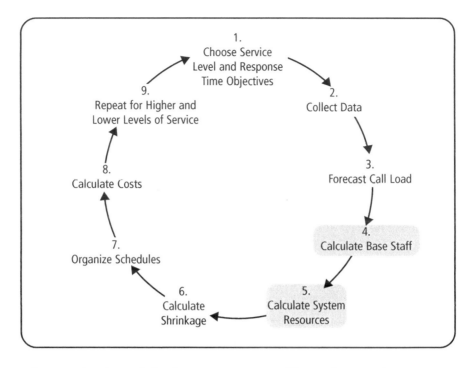

## The Relationship between Staff and Trunks

If, about now, you are thanking your lucky stars that you have an IT/telecom department to worry about system issues, and, frankly, never wanted to know about trunks and certainly not any *relationship* between staff and trunks ... I do understand. But stick with me on this. Understanding the underlying dynamics is important, and will serve you for a career, even if you're not the one doing the calculations.

Let's first look at a few basic definitions. We'll consider them in a plain, traditional context (e.g., a trunk as a line required to carry a conversation). When interpreting the diagram, Definitions You Must Understand Precisely, assume inbound calls entering a "straight-in" environment, where callers dial a number and are routed directly to the agent group. This example assumes no IVR ("Press or say one for ...").

- **DELAY:** Delay is everything from when the trunk is seized to the point at which the caller is connected to an agent.

- **AGENT LOAD:** Agent load includes the two components of handling time — talk time and after-call work.
- **TRUNK LOAD:** Trunk load includes all aspects of the interaction other than after-call work, which does not require a circuit. The "caller's load" is the same as the trunk load, other than the short time it takes for the network to route the call to the contact center.

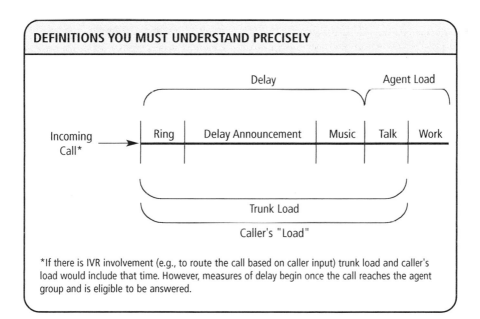

**DEFINITIONS YOU MUST UNDERSTAND PRECISELY**

*If there is IVR involvement (e.g., to route the call based on caller input) trunk load and caller's load would include that time. However, measures of delay begin once the call reaches the agent group and is eligible to be answered.

Notice that agent load and trunk load both include talk time. However, trunk load carries the delay, which is not a direct part of the agent load. And the agents handle after-call work, which is not carried by the trunks.

This realization leads to two important considerations when calculating staff and trunks:

**1. STAFF SHOULD BE CALCULATED IN CONJUNCTION WITH TRUNKS.** The more staff handling a given call load, the less delay callers will experience. In other words, staffing impacts delay; therefore, it directly impacts how many trunks are required. There is no way to know base trunking needs without knowing how many staff will be handling the projected call load.

**2. THERE IS NO SINGLE STAFF-TO-TRUNK RATIO YOU CAN COUNT ON.** You may hear rules of thumb such as that you need 1.5 trunks per agent (15 trunks for every 10 agents). However, there is no such ratio that can be universally applied. The reasons? For one, after-call work, which occupies agents but doesn't require trunks, is different from one contact center to the next. Second, caller tolerances vary widely among organizations, as influenced by the seven factors affecting tolerance (Chapter 3). If you have a high service level, the trunks will carry little delay. If your service level is low, the trunks will have to carry more delay and, consequently, you will need more capacity.

There's a better way to determine resources: Calculate staff, then calculate trunking capacity the right way. Whatever the ratios turn out to be, that is what will work for you.

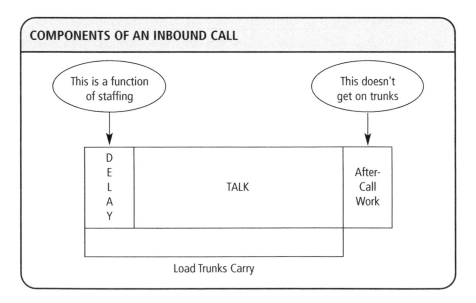

INTEGRATE BUDGETS

Despite the inextricable relationship between staff and trunks, contact centers traditionally have paid for these resources out of different budgets. Unfortunately, that will cause inaccurate budget projections and could lead to what the late quality guru W. Edwards Deming called "sub-optimizing," where one aspect of the operation is optimized in a vacuum while overall costs and performance suffer. Staff and trunks are a classic example of the need to look at the big picture.

## "Wrong" Ways to Calculate Staff

To calculate how many agents you need, why not use this formula? Take the average handling time of a call (average talk time + average after-call work) and multiply it by the number of calls forecasted. Then, divide the result by 1,800 seconds (the total seconds in a half hour). You may even build in extra time, such as an added 10 percent or 20 percent, assuming agents will actually need a breather now and then.

Or what about this formula? Determine the actual average calls per agent in a group. Then, divide that into the number of calls forecasted. Or use target objectives, as in "our agents ought to be able to handle X calls per half hour; therefore ..."

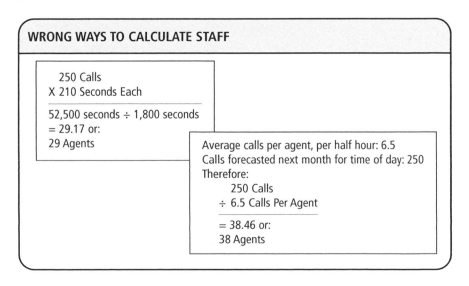

**WRONG WAYS TO CALCULATE STAFF**

250 Calls
X 210 Seconds Each

52,500 seconds ÷ 1,800 seconds
= 29.17 or:
29 Agents

Average calls per agent, per half hour: 6.5
Calls forecasted next month for time of day: 250
Therefore:
250 Calls
÷ 6.5 Calls Per Agent

= 38.46 or:
38 Agents

These methods may sound logical, and some managers use them. Unfortunately, they are dead wrong. They do not relate the outcome to a target service level. Further, they are based on moving targets. The average group productivity (contacts that the group can handle) is not a constant factor. Instead, it is continually fluctuating because it is heavily influenced by vacillating call loads and the service level objective. But the biggest problem is that these approaches ignore a fundamental driving force in centers that handle customer-initiated interactions: *Calls bunch up!* (See Chapter 3.)

The following figure illustrates a possible queuing situation. (It's not as complicated as it first looks!)

| SIMULATION OF QUEUING SITUATION | | | | | |
|---|---|---|---|---|---|
| Arrival | | One Agent Case | | Two Agents Case | |
| (1) Arrival number | (2) Time of arrival | (3) Time call is answered | (4) Waiting time (min.) | (5) Time call is answered | (6) Waiting time (min.) |
| 1 | 0:04.3 | 0:04.3 | 0 | 0:04.3 | 0 |
| 2 | 0:04.4 | 0:07.3 | 2.9 | 0:04.4 | 0 |
| 3 | 0:15.7 | 0:15.7 | 0 | 0:15.7 | 0 |
| 4 | 0:17.3 | 0:18.7 | 1.4 | 0:17.3 | 0 |
| 5 | 0:21.1 | 0:21.7 | 0.6 | 0:21.1 | 0 |
| 6 | 0:22.1 | 0:24.7 | 2.6 | 0:22.1 | 0 |
| 7 | 0:25.4 | 0:27.7 | 2.3 | 0:25.4 | 0 |
| 8 | 0:26.3 | 0:30.7 | 4.4 | 0:26.3 | 0 |
| 9 | 0:27.4 | 0:33.7 | 6.3 | 0:28.4 | 1.0 |
| 10 | 0:27.5 | 0:36.7 | 9.2 | 0:29.3 | 1.8 |
| | Average Delay: | | 2.97 | | .28 |

In this scenario, 10 calls arrive in a half hour, and each call is assumed to last three minutes. The second column shows when each of the 10 calls arrives. The third column gives the time each call is answered, and column four is the waiting time (the difference between when a call arrives and when it is answered).

For example, call number two arrives 4.4 minutes into the half hour, but has to wait 2.9 minutes before being answered because the first call is still in progress. With one agent, the waiting times build throughout the half-hour and beyond, and service is poor. With two agents, it's a different story; service is much better and waiting times are minimal.

If sorting out staffing for random call arrival is this involved with two agents, imagine a scenario with 15 agents. Or 115! The point is, if you want to determine staffing correctly, you need the right tools. You need a method that takes the usual randomness of call arrival into consideration. That means using the Erlang C formula (or a variation of it) or computer simulation.

## Staffing the "Right" Way

As introduced in the first chapter, the widely used Erlang C formula was developed in 1917 by A.K. Erlang, a Danish engineer with the Copenhagen Telephone Company. Erlang C can be used to determine resources in just about any situation where people might wait in queue for service — whether it is at a ticket counter, a bank of elevators or concessions in a stadium. Erlang C (or variations of it) is currently built into virtually all of the commercially available workforce management software packages.

(If you go to Copenhagen, Denmark, you can visit an interesting display on A.K. Erlang's life and work, in the building in which he used to work. I've been there. At the time, I was the *only* one there … Okay, so it's not up there with the popularity of the Little Mermaid statue just yet.)

Erlang C calculates predicted waiting times (delay) based on three things: the number of servers (agents); the number of people waiting to be served (callers); and the average amount of time it takes to serve each person. It can also predict the resources required to keep waiting times within targeted limits, and that's why it is useful for contact centers.

As with any mathematical formula, Erlang C has built-in assumptions that don't perfectly reflect real-world circumstances. For one, it assumes that "lost calls are delayed." In plain English, that means that the formula

**137**

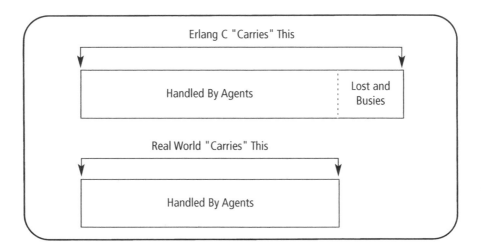

assumes that calls are queued. No problem with that. The problem is, it assumes that callers have infinite patience — they will wait as long as necessary to reach an agent and nobody will abandon. *Oops!*

Erlang C also assumes that you have infinite trunking and system capacity or that nobody will get a busy signal. But busies can and do happen. *Oops again!*

The result, in a nutshell, is that Erlang C may overestimate the staff you really need. If some of your callers abandon or get busy signals, your agents

## VARIATIONS ON ERLANG C

Many workforce management vendors use traffic engineering formulas that are modifications of traditional queuing formulas. For example, Pipkins developed the "Merlang" formula, a modification of A.K. Erlang's original work, which can adjust for busies, abandoned calls and variations in agent group structure. And Michael Hills, PhD, created the Hills B formula, which "is designed to overcome 'deficiencies' associated with the use of Erlang C and other classic queuing models." Says Dr. Hills, "Erlang C is fatalistic and can overestimate required staff by 20 percent. No formula is perfect, but we have built-in assumptions that better model the real environment."

| ADVANTAGES OF ERLANG C | DISADVANTAGES OF ERLANG C |
|---|---|
| • Assumes random arrival and that contacts go into queue if an agent is not immediately available.<br>• Is accurate at good service levels, where abandoned calls and busy signals are minimal.<br>• Is easy and quick to use, and is available in software programs from a wide variety of sources.<br>• Illustrates resource tradeoffs well (e.g., when service level goes up, occupancy goes down).<br>• Is the basis for staffing calculations in most workforce management programs. | • Assumes no abandoned calls or busy signals.<br>• Assumes "steady-state" arrival, or that traffic does not increase or decrease beyond random fluctuation within the time period.<br>• Assumes you have a fixed number of staff handling calls throughout the time period.<br>• Assumes that all agents within a group can handle the contacts presented to the group.<br>• Calculations assume no calls in queue from the prior half hour (unless the user or workforce management system makes this adjustment). |

won't have to handle all of the calls Erlang C is including in its calculations. For a given level of staff, Erlang C predicts that conditions will be worse than they really are. Erlang C also assumes that you have the same level of staff on the phones the entire half hour. In reality, if service level starts taking a nosedive, you may be able to add reinforcements on short notice. All things considered, Erlang C overstates how bad things will be for poor service levels.

So then why is Erlang C so popular? As you might guess, there are defensible reasons to use it. For one, it's a planning tool, and most contact centers are planning to have good service levels. Erlang C is fairly accurate for good service levels — and when service level is decent, you should theoretically have little in the way of lost calls or busy signals. If you do have a lot of calls disappearing or getting busy signals, it's probably because *you don't have enough staff* to handle the load. In that case, who's worried about over-staffing? As your staffing more accurately reflects the workload demand, Erlang C will inherently become more accurate.

Further, if you adjust for abandoned calls and busy signals, and retry rates turn out to be higher than you estimate, you could wind up underes-timating staff. (And frankly there's a little industry secret ... *shhh* ... some managers have decided that a little over-calculation as a safety net isn't such a bad thing. They figure that they fail to get full effective use of their already authorized headcount anyway, due to staff turnover and the time it takes to hire and train replacements.)

Finally, from a practical sense, many staffing and scheduling programs do, in fact, use Erlang C as just part of their approach (an important part, to be sure), and enable you to adjust variables as you see fit. Just be certain to have the supplier review with you the assumptions being made — your CFO will probably ask you the same thing.

Erlang C is designed for straightforward environments, like sales calls going here and technical support calls going there. But the realities of

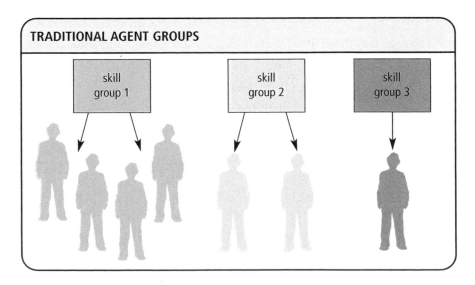

**TRADITIONAL AGENT GROUPS**

skill group 1

skill group 2

skill group 3

| ADVANTAGES OF COMPUTER SIMULATION | DISADVANTAGES OF COMPUTER SIMULATION |
|---|---|
| <ul><li>Can be programmed to assume a wide variety of variables, including overlapping agent groups and skills-based routing.</li><li>The assumptions can include lost calls and busy signals.</li><li>Variables can often be labeled to use the terminology of your systems.</li><li>Results may cover a wide range of outcomes and include additional analysis (such as impact on costs).</li><li>Results may be more credible to decision makers who are not familiar with alternative queuing formulas.</li></ul> | <ul><li>Takes time to set up and use.</li><li>Requires a relatively advanced user.</li><li>Is often a standalone tool that is not integrated with forecasting and staffing modules.</li><li>Does not tell you what to do (it instead illustrates what will happen based on variables you input).</li><li>Is more expensive than standalone Erlang C programs or entry-level staffing and scheduling packages.</li></ul> |

today are not so straightforward. You may have complex routing contingencies in place, such as agent groups that overlap, skills-based routing and complex network interflow.

Enter computer simulation. What staffing simulation does for contact centers is comparable to what flight simulators do for aircraft manufacturers. Boeing, Airbus and other suppliers spend a lot of time simulating their new designs. And they do fail — on computer. By the time the real thing is produced, they know the ins and outs of good design.

Similarly, you can use simulation to zero in on the resources your contact center needs without making too many real mistakes in your live environment. There are various simulation packages available (some designed specifically for contact centers and some more generic), and workforce management systems are increasingly providing simulation modules within their applications.

But computer simulation has some downsides, too. For one thing, simulation by itself is designed for modeling, design and verification, and is generally not meant to be a forecasting and scheduling tool. As a result, if you want the time-saving benefits of software, you will still need a forecasting and scheduling system.

Second, simulation software takes more time and expertise to set up and use than Erlang C. Like a flight simulator, you have to run it over and over to identify potential results. That is a phenomenon of its added flexibility, and the time spent will be time saved if you have a complex environment that requires a simulator's perspective. But it takes more effort and know-how to enter and test variables and interpret the results.

So, what should you use? For fairly straightforward environments with good service levels, Erlang C or variations of it will likely be sufficient. And even if you have a more complex environment, there is something to be said for a combination of Erlang C, intuition and experience. But if you really want to understand requirements in the most complex settings — maybe you're using skills-based routing extensively or have a complex network with many call-handling variables in play — no formula will ever beat simulation.

Just remember, no method can perfectly predict outcomes, at least not consistently. As much science as may be involved, it's inexact and must be augmented with common sense and resource plans that are at least somewhat flexible.

## Basic Staffing

One of the advantages of using Erlang C is that it is a great educational tool, and it illustrates queue dynamics and resource tradeoffs well. So, that's what I'll be using here to outline basic staffing requirements and tradeoffs in a contact center setting.

---

**ERLANG C**

$$P\,(>0) = \cfrac{\cfrac{A^N}{N!}\quad\cfrac{N}{N-A}}{\displaystyle\sum_{x=0}^{N-1}\cfrac{A^X}{x!} + \cfrac{A^N}{N!}\,\cfrac{N}{N-A}}$$

Where    A = total traffic offered in erlangs
              N = number of servers in a full availability group
              P(>0) = probability of delay greater than 0
              P = probability of loss — Poisson formula

For most of us, Erlang C in its raw form is unwieldy at best and totally unusable at worst. That's what prompted various sources to publish Erlang C tables before computer-based programs came along. But using an Erlang C table wasn't that easy either because you had to take factors from the table, multiply them against the "holding time" and so on, to get usable answers. And using an Erlang C table was anything but self-evident if you wanted to relate staffing to service level. For all the complexities of a modern contact center, we can count our blessings for much better tools!

(Note: In the examples to follow I am using QueueView, a low-cost program provided by ICMI. Other free and low-cost staffing calculators are available from a wide variety of sources — online, as apps, as stand-alone programs, and as modules within workforce management programs.)

Erlang C requires you to input four variables:

- **AVERAGE TALK TIME, IN SECONDS.** Input the projected average for the future half hour you are analyzing.
- **AVERAGE AFTER-CALL WORK, IN SECONDS.** Input the projected average for the future half hour you are analyzing.
- **NUMBER OF CALLS.** Input the projected volume for the future half hour you are analyzing.
- **SERVICE LEVEL OBJECTIVE, IN SECONDS.** If your service level objective is to answer 90 percent of calls in 20 seconds, you will input

20 seconds. If it's 80 percent in 15 seconds, plug in 15 seconds. In other words, the program needs the Y seconds in the definition, "X percent of calls answered in Y seconds."

Input the numbers and *voilà*! The output provides a wealth of information and insight into the dynamics of contact center queues (see table, Erlang C for Contact Centers — Staffing Module). Probably the first column you'll look at is labeled "SL," which is service level. That's the X percent to be answered in the Y seconds you input. In the first row, the number 24 means that you'll answer 24 percent of the calls in 20 seconds. The next row is 45 percent, meaning 45 percent answered in 20 seconds.

## ERLANG C FOR CONTACT CENTERS — STAFFING MODULE

Average talk time in seconds: 180
Calls per half hour: 250

Average after-call work in seconds: 30
Service level in seconds: 20

| Agents | P(O) | ASA | DLYDLY | Q1 | Q2 | SL | OCC | TKLD |
|--------|------|-----|--------|----|----|------|------|------|
| 30 | 83% | 209 | 252 | 29 | 35 | 24% | 97% | 54.0 |
| 31 | 65% | 75 | 115 | 10 | 16 | 45% | 94% | 35.4 |
| 32 | 51% | 38 | 74 | 5 | 10 | 61% | 91% | 30.2 |
| 33 | 39% | 21 | 55 | 3 | 8 | 73% | 88% | 28.0 |
| 34 | 29% | 13 | 43 | 2 | 6 | 82% | 86% | 26.8 |
| 35 | 22% | 8 | 36 | 1 | 5 | 88% | 83% | 26.1 |
| 36 | 16% | 5 | 31 | 1 | 4 | 92% | 81% | 25.7 |
| 37 | 11% | 3 | 27 | 0 | 4 | 95% | 79% | 25.4 |
| 38 | 8% | 2 | 24 | 0 | 3 | 97% | 77% | 25.3 |
| 39 | 6% | 1 | 21 | 0 | 3 | 98% | 75% | 25.2 |
| 40 | 4% | 1 | 19 | 0 | 3 | 99% | 73% | 25.1 |
| 41 | 3% | 1 | 18 | 0 | 3 | 99% | 71% | 25.1 |
| 42 | 2% | 0 | 16 | 0 | 2 | 100% | 69% | 25.0 |

Source: ICMI's QueueView Staffing Calculator

Let's say your objective is to answer 80 percent of calls in 20 seconds. Keep going down the rows and ... hey, where's 80 percent? The answers go from 73 percent to 82 percent, but where's 80 percent? You guessed it — the program is calculating staff required, and people come in "whole numbers," so some rounding is involved. Since 82 percent meets your standard, that's the row you would then concentrate on.

Next, glancing across that row, you can see that you need 34 agents (first column), average speed of answer will be 13 seconds (third column), etc. In other words, each column provides insight and information into the service level you choose.

Here's what the column headings stand for:

- **AGENTS:** Number of agents required to be plugged in and available to handle contacts. In this example, 34 agents will achieve a service level of 82 percent answered in 20 seconds.
- **P(0):** Probability of a delay greater than zero seconds. In other words, the probability of not getting an immediate answer. In this example, about 29 percent of calls will be delayed. That means 71 percent of callers won't be delayed, but instead will go right to an agent.
- **ASA:** Average speed of answer. With 34 agents handling calls, ASA will be 13 seconds. ASA is the average delay of all calls, including the ones that aren't delayed at all. In this example, 250 calls are included in the calculation. (See discussion on why ASA is often misinterpreted, Chapter 4.)
- **DLYDLY:** Average delay of delayed calls. This is the average delay only of those calls that are delayed — 43 seconds, in this example. DLYDLY is a better reflection than ASA of what's actually happening to the calls that end up in queue. But keep in mind, it's still an average. Some calls wait five seconds and others may wait several minutes. If calls end up in queue any amount of time, they will be included in the calculation.
- **Q1:** Average number of calls in queue at any time, including times when there is no queue. The label is somewhat of a misnomer, because Q1 incorporates all calls into the calculation, including those that don't end up in queue. However, this column makes a useful contrast to the next, Q2.
- **Q2:** Average number of calls in queue when all agents are busy or when there is a queue. In the example, an average of six calls are in queue, when there is a queue. Again, this is an average, and some of

the time there will be more than six calls in queue, some of the time less. But this figure can provide useful guidance for what to look for when monitoring real-time information, and can also be useful for determining overflow parameters.

- **SL:** Service level, the percentage of calls that will be answered in the number of seconds you specify — 82 percent in 20 seconds, here.

- **OCC:** Percent agent occupancy. The percentage of time agents will spend handling calls, including talk time and after-call work. The balance of time, they are available and waiting for calls. In the example, occupancy will be 86 percent. Notice the tradeoff: When service level goes up, occupancy goes down. We will discuss this dynamic in Chapter 9.

- **TKLD:** This column is the hours (erlangs) of trunk traffic, which is the product of (talk time + average speed of answer) x number of calls in an hour. Since Erlang B, bandwidth calculators and other alternatives used for determining trunks often require input in hours, these numbers can be readily used as is. The actual traffic carried by trunks in a half hour will, in each row, be half of what is given.

The mechanics of staffing are easy enough. Plug in your numbers and you get some answers. *Cool.* However, the interpretation takes a bit of thought and application.

A good question to ask for any service level is, "What happens to the calls that don't get answered in Y seconds?" Programs that calculate delay can be very useful in answering this question. (The following is also part of ICMI's QueueView program.)

As you can see, 34 agents will result in a service level of 82 percent of calls answered in 20 seconds. But here we get additional insight into what happens to individual calls. Sixty-five callers will wait five seconds or longer. In the next five seconds, seven of those callers reach agents, so only 58 callers are waiting 10 seconds or longer. In the next five seconds, six more callers will reach agents, leaving only 52 callers waiting 15 seconds or more. At this service level, one caller is still waiting three minutes or more

## ERLANG C FOR CONTACT CENTERS — DELAY MODULE

Average talk time in seconds: 180          Average after-call work in seconds: 30
Calls per half hour: 250                        Service level in seconds: 20

|←——————— Number of callers waiting longer than x seconds ———————→|

| Agents | SL% | 5 | 10 | 15 | 20 | 30 | 40 | 50 | 60 | 90 | 120 | 180 | 240 |
|---|---|---|---|---|---|---|---|---|---|---|---|---|---|
| 30 | 24 | 203 | 199 | 195 | 191 | 184 | 177 | 170 | 163 | 145 | 129 | 101 | 80 |
| 31 | 45 | 156 | 149 | 143 | 137 | 126 | 115 | 105 | 97 | 74 | 57 | 34 | 20 |
| 32 | 61 | 118 | 111 | 104 | 97 | 85 | 74 | 65 | 56 | 38 | 25 | 11 | 5 |
| 33 | 73 | 89 | 81 | 74 | 67 | 56 | 47 | 39 | 32 | 19 | 11 | 4 | 1 |
| 34 | 82 | 65 | 58 | 52 | 46 | 37 | 29 | 23 | 18 | 9 | 5 | 1 | 0 |
| 35 | 88 | 47 | 41 | 36 | 31 | 24 | 18 | 14 | 10 | 4 | 2 | 0 | 0 |
| 36 | 92 | 34 | 29 | 24 | 21 | 15 | 11 | 8 | 6 | 2 | 1 | 0 | 0 |
| 37 | 95 | 24 | 20 | 16 | 14 | 9 | 6 | 4 | 3 | 1 | 0 | 0 | 0 |
| 38 | 97 | 16 | 13 | 11 | 9 | 6 | 4 | 2 | 2 | 0 | 0 | 0 | 0 |
| 39 | 98 | 11 | 9 | 7 | 5 | 3 | 2 | 1 | 1 | 0 | 0 | 0 | 0 |
| 40 | 99 | 7 | 6 | 4 | 3 | 2 | 1 | 1 | 0 | 0 | 0 | 0 | 0 |
| 41 | 99 | 5 | 4 | 3 | 2 | 1 | 1 | 0 | 0 | 0 | 0 | 0 | 0 |
| 42 | 100 | 3 | 2 | 2 | 1 | 1 | 0 | 0 | 0 | 0 | 0 | 0 | 0 |

Source: ICMI's QueueView Staffing Calculator

(Murphy's Law: That's the chairman of the board testing your service).

Note an important implication of delay: Because of random call arrival, different callers have different experiences even though they called during the same half hour and even though the call center may be hitting its target service level. (Some centers attempt to set two service levels for the same queue, e.g., to handle 80 percent of calls in 20 seconds and the rest within 60 seconds. As you can see here, that is not possible — 80/20 and 100/60 are distinctly different service levels, and therefore require different staffing levels to achieve.) What's the worst case that your organization is willing to tolerate? That becomes a key question when exploring these tradeoffs.

If you have never used an Erlang C program, we recommend that you get one and experiment with it. You will learn more about staffing dynamics and tradeoffs in an hour or two than it once took someone years of using tables or — heaven forbid — the raw formula to learn.

So far, you have calculated staff required to handle a specified mix of inbound contacts that must be handled when they arrive, for one half hour of the day. You will also need to calculate base staff for each half hour of the day and for every unique group of agents — sales, customer service and other types of groups you have. In Step 6 of the planning and management process, we will discuss how to factor in breaks, absenteeism and non-phone activities so that the schedule (Step 7) reflects the total staff you need.

## RESPONSE TIME CONTACTS

Recall the two major categories of contacts defined in Chapter 4: those that must be handled when they arrive and those that can be handled at a later time. Staffing for interactions that must be handled when they arrive — defined by service level — should be calculated using Erlang C or computer simulation.

Calculating staff requirements for a workload that does not have to be handled at the time it arrives is generally based on the centuries-old "units-of-output" approach. Here's the logic: If you get 60 email messages that have an average handling time of four minutes, that's four hours of work. One agent working non-stop could handle the load in four hours. If you need to complete the transactions within two hours, you will need a minimum of two agents working over a period of two hours. So, as with service level and inbound telephone calls, the email workload and response time objective dictate staff requirements. Accordingly, the basic formula for

---

**BASIC RESPONSE TIME FORMULA**

$$\frac{\text{Volume}}{(\text{RT} \div \text{AHT})} = \text{Agents}$$

Volume = Number of contacts to be handled
RT = Response time
AHT = Average handling time

---

calculating the minimum staff required is as shown.

Volume is the quantity of interactions you must handle, AHT is the average amount of time it takes agents to handle them (the equivalent of average talk time and average after-call work for inbound phone calls), and response time is the time you have to respond to customers after receiving their messages. Using the formula, you could handle the 60 messages previously mentioned in two hours with two agents: $60 \div (120 \div 4) = 2$.

There are several things to keep in mind:

- You can slice and dice base staff schedules many ways to achieve your objectives. In fact, in the example, you could have 60 agents rush in and handle all 60 transactions just before the promised response time and still meet your objective. What you are really doing is looking for an efficient way to distribute the workload across your schedules within the promised response time.

- The basic response time formula assumes a "static" amount of work to be completed — in other words, that you have a defined amount of work that has already arrived and is waiting to be processed. However, email and other contacts that can be deferred arrive throughout the day in patterns that are often similar to phone traffic. With 24-hour response time objectives, projected workload can simply be built into the following day's staffing requirements. But if you have more aggressive response time objectives, you'll need to look at both on-hand workload and projections by interval to determine staffing requirements.

- When response time objectives are less than an hour, traffic engineers generally recommend using Erlang C or computer simulation to calculate base staff. This would be a queuing and service level scenario, like inbound phone calls.

- Breaks, absenteeism and other activities that keep agents from the work need to be added to base staff calculations (a step we'll cover in the next chapter).

**149**

- An "efficiency factor" acknowledges that agents cannot handle one transaction after another with no "breathing" time in between. For example, if you want to build in an efficiency factor with a ceiling of 90 percent, divide base staff calculations by .9 to determine if additional agents are required.

In short, meeting response time objectives requires:

- Setting response time objectives.
- Forecasting these interactions, within timeframes specific enough to calculate base staff required.
- Calculating base staff needed.
- Factoring in breaks and other activities that will take staff away from the work.
- Factoring these staffing needs into overall schedules.

## OUTBOUND CONTACTS

There are three general types of outbound contacts. Each has implications for staffing requirements:

**1. OUTBOUND THAT IS A PART OF THE INBOUND WORKLOAD.** For example, calls to an emergency roadside service from stranded customers often involve outbound calls to arrange towing or repair services. Whether these outbound contacts happen during calls from customers or immediately following the calls as part of after-call work, they should be considered part of handling time. As such, they are inherently included in base-staff requirements for the inbound call load.

**2. OUTBOUND CONTACTS THAT ARE SCHEDULED.** In many cases, outbound calls to customers or prospects can be scheduled based on factors such as convenience to customers, highest probability of making successful connections, etc. Within these blocks of time, outbound contacts can be generated and handled one after another. Base-staff requirements can be calculated using traditional response time calculations; for example, a minimum of five agents would be required to handle 20 hours' worth of calls in four hours time. As with other response time calculations, a reasonable efficiency factor should also be included in the assumptions.

**3. OUTBOUND CONTACTS THAT ARE NEITHER A PART OF RANDOMLY ARRIVING INBOUND LOAD NOR SCHEDULED.** In every contact center, there are at least some outbound calls to colleagues or customers that are neither part of the inbound load nor specifically scheduled. If significant enough to merit consideration in resource requirements, they can be reflected in Step 6, covered in the next chapter.

# Staffing for Non-Traditional Groups

Today's environment is often characterized by a variety of contact channels and routing alternatives. You may be utilizing skills-based routing, overlapping agent groups, sophisticated network environments and other configurations that go beyond simple agent groups. Your environment will dictate the staffing methodology that will yield the best results.

### SKILLS-BASED ROUTING

Available in ACD routing systems since the early 1990s, skills-based routing is a powerful capability designed to match each caller with the agent who has the skill set best suited to handle the call on a real-time basis. It has been a boon to the efficiency and quality of services provided by centers that, by nature, have overlapping groups or complex routing contingencies. And variations of skills-based routing are also working their way into multimedia queuing environments. But to be effective, skills-based routing must be managed well. In this environment, Erlang C's assumption of traditional agent groups no longer fits, but computer simulation can help fill the gap.

The basic requirements for skills-based routing include:

- Identify and define the skills required for each call type.
- Identify and define individual agent skills.
- Prioritize agent skills, based on individual competency levels.
- Devise and program an appropriate routing plan into the ACD.

**151**

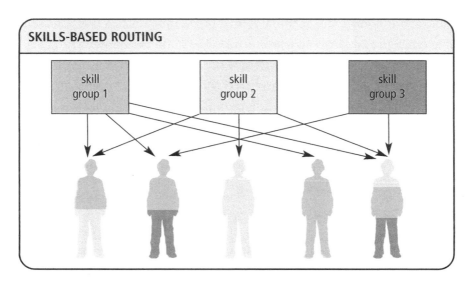

Although specific programming approaches vary by system, you will essentially create two "maps" when you set up your ACD for skills-based routing. One will specify the types of calls to be handled and the other will identify the skills available by agent. As an example, the maps for a technical support center handling calls across Europe might look like this:

## MAP 1

English-speaking callers who need assistance with Internet access.
English-speaking callers who need assistance with printers.
English-speaking callers who need assistance with storage devices.
English-speaking callers who need assistance with PCs.

French-speaking callers who need assistance with Internet access.
French-speaking callers who need assistance with printers.
French-speaking callers who need assistance with storage devices.
French-speaking callers who need assistance with PCs.

German-speaking callers who need assistance with Internet access.
German-speaking callers who need assistance with printers.

German-speaking callers who need assistance with storage devices.
German-speaking callers who need assistance with PCs.

And so on. The second map might look like this:

## MAP 2

**TOM** — Speaks English, Dutch and French. Trained on Internet access and printers.

**ANGELIQUE** — Speaks French and Italian. Trained on printers, PCs and storage devices.

**ERIK** — Speaks Swedish, French and English. Trained on Internet access and PCs.

**MARIA** — Speaks Spanish, Italian and French. Trained on printers and storage devices.

Consider a simple case that illustrates the basic steps in staffing for skills-based routing. Assume you have two languages to handle — English and Spanish. And let's say that you have four call types to handle — orders and technical support calls in each language. The agent skills can be illustrated as shown.

Next, let's assume that your plan is to route calls to the least-skilled agent

## AGENT SKILLS

| Caller Types (Based upon IVR menu selections) | Agent | Agent | Agent | Agent | Agent | Agent | Agent | Agent | Agent |
|---|---|---|---|---|---|---|---|---|---|
| Orders – English | X | X | | | | | | X | X |
| Orders – Spanish | | | | X | | X | | X | X |
| Tech Support – English | | X | X | | X | | | | X |
| Tech Support – Spanish | | | X | | | | X | X | X |

who can handle the call because you want to preserve your more experienced or skilled agents for less common or more complex calls. Consequently, the routing plan would appear as shown.

## ROUTING PLAN

| Call-Routing Hierarchy | Order-English | Order-Spanish | Tech Support English | Tech Support Spanish |
|---|---|---|---|---|
| Skill Choice 1 | Agent Type 1 | Agent Type 4 | Agent Type 5 | Agent Type 7 |
| Skill Choice 2 | Agent Type 2 | Agent Type 8 | Agent Type 2 | Agent Type 6 |
| Skill Choice 3 | Agent Type 8 | Agent Type 6 | Agent Type 3 | Agent Type 3 |
| Skill Choice 4 | Agent Type 9 | Agent Type 9 | Agent Type 9 | Agent Type 9 |

You set up the simulator the same way you program the maps into your ACD. You tell it what types of calls you are going to get and the skills of your group. You also plug in the same data required by Erlang C: volume of each type of contact you expect and corresponding talk time and work time estimates. Additionally, you can specify caller tolerance levels by type of call, trunking configurations and other conditions.

We used this data to run three different scenarios, all using the same call load and service level objective:

- Conventional ACD groups (one group for each call type)
- Skills-based routing
- Universal agents (a fully cross-trained group)

As the results in the table indicate, skills-based routing is more efficient than separate, segmented groups. Also note that universal agents, where each agent is fully cross-trained and speaks both languages, is the most efficient arrangement.

In general, skills-based routing works best in environments that have small groups where multiple skills are required. It can also help to quickly

## RESULTS OF EACH ROUTING SCENARIO

| Time Period | Separate Groups by Language and Call Type | Skills-Based Routing Scenario | Universal Agents |
|---|---|---|---|
| 9:00-9:30 | 30 | 27 | 24 |
| 9:30-10:00 | 43 | 41 | 39 |
| 10:00-10:30 | 64 | 62 | 59 |
| 10:30-11:00 | 58 | 56 | 52 |
| 11:00-11:30 | 44 | 41 | 40 |
| 11:30-12:00 | 31 | 28 | 27 |

integrate new agents into call handling, by sending only certain calls to them. And it has the potential to improve efficiency by matching callers with "just the right agent."

Skills-based routing has some disadvantages, though. In application, it seems to be Murphy's Law that the agent with just the right skill is on break at the wrong time. Mapping out skills and programming routing scenarios is one thing; getting people in the right place at the right times can be quite another. Small, specialized groups are tough to manage, and they can eliminate the efficiencies of pooling (a principle I'll cover in detail in Chapter 9) common to conventional agent groups.

Further, routing and resource planning become more complex. Be prepared to run enough simulations to learn what's workable in your environment. You also need to develop contingency plans for when the call load of a specific call type is greater than expected, or when you don't have the specialized staff you planned for (e.g., because of unplanned absences). And get used to an irony — the most skilled agent may be the most idle, given the usual intent to route calls to agents with the minimum qualifying skills to handle them (as in the example).

Skills-based routing is a powerful capability. But it must be managed well. That means going through the planning process diligently. You'll need a good forecast and solid staff calculations. Also, remember to work toward pooled groups, to the degree that your circumstances allow. All

## TROUBLESHOOTING SKILLS-BASED ROUTING

Skills-based routing ... Intelligent. Flexible. Real-time. The perfect answer to that proverbial contact center challenge of getting the right call to the right place at the right time. At least, that's the way it's supposed to work. But in too many cases, skills-based routing also has created difficult new challenges that have obviated potential benefits. Here are five of the most common problems:

**Staff shrinkage.** Breaks, lunch, meetings, projects, research, training, absenteeism ... you know the story. These things are particularly vexing in a skills-based routing environment where you are trying to get calls to just the right agents. There's no substitute for realistically planning and budgeting for the things that keep agents from the phones (a subject we'll cover in Chapter 8).

**Inaccurate forecasts.** The inability to forecast accurately for specific types of skill requirements is the Achilles' heel of the powerful simulation tools available — and of skills-based routing in general. To anticipate staffing needs, you first need to know how many Spanish-speaking callers you're going to get between 10:00 and 10:30, how the call mix will change throughout the day for the expert group handling call types A, B and C, and when your Mandarin Chinese-speaking agents will go on break. Accurate forecasting at this level of specificity takes time and effort, but it's well worth it. If you're struggling with it, consider combining skills to form more manageable groups.

**Inaccurate base staff calculations.** Whatever staffing method you use (Erlang C, a variation of it, or simulation), a certain amount of trial and error and a healthy dose of intuition and experience are necessary to accurately model the environment. You will need to run through quite a few (sometimes dozens of) "what-if" scenarios to get it right.

**Poor assumptions and rationale.** Skills-based routing works best in environments that require many skills and have many possible combinations of skill sets. It can also help to quickly integrate new agents by initially routing only simple calls or calls of a predefined nature to them. What it can't do is compensate for poor planning, inadequate training or poorly designed information systems. Keep it as simple as possible, and

> remember that skills-based routing depends on — rather than compensates for — accurate planning and good processes.
> **No routing manager/coordinator.** If all of this sounds time-consuming, that's because it is. Even relatively small contact centers have learned through tough, practical experience that it often takes the equivalent of a full-time person to keep skills-based routing running smoothly. Projecting requirements, assessing current capabilities, updating system programming and adjusting staffing plans and schedules to accommodate evolving circumstances are ongoing activities.

things being equal, an environment with proficient, cross-trained agents will be the most efficient.

## NETWORK ENVIRONMENTS

Networked environments, like skills-based routing, can introduce complex contingencies into staffing calculations. The method you use for calculating staff will depend on the type of networked environment you have.

Generally, your calls will be routed in one of three ways:

**1. PERCENT ALLOCATION.** This traditional approach has become less common with the introduction of more sophisticated alternatives. Where it still exists, routing is set up to allocate calls among sites according to thresholds you define. For example, you may program 40 percent of your calls to be routed to one site, 35 percent of the calls to go to a second site, and the balance, 25 percent, to go to a third site.

Erlang C will generally provide good results in this environment. Even if you change call allocation throughout the day based on evolving circumstances, Erlang C will be an effective planning tool. As with ACD groups in a single site, you will forecast the call load you anticipate and run Erlang C calculations for each site.

**2. NETWORK INTERFLOW.** Networks that are designed to interflow calls are a step up from straight percent allocation. In this type of environment, calls initially presented to one site can be simultaneously queued at other sites, based on thresholds you define. As circumstances allow, calls can then be sent from an original site to a secondary site.

Contingencies will vary based on how you program the network. The criteria that determine how calls are interflowed can run the gamut, from availability at each site to the types of calls you are handling. For example, you might immediately send high-priority calls to available agents in any site, but queue lower-priority calls longer for intended agent groups. Given the variables, simulation can help to model and test the environment under different conditions.

**3. VIRTUAL OR CLOUD-BASED CONTACT CENTER.** In a true virtual environment — becoming more common as network services advance, cloud-based capabilities inherently enable distributed contact centers, and costs of running traffic over distances fades — each call is routed to the first available agent (or longest-waiting agent). Other routing and queuing contingencies (such as skills-based routing) notwithstanding, this environment represents a traditional agent group regardless of where agents are (at home, across campus, or on the other side of the world), and Erlang C will generally produce accurate calculations.

## LONG CALLS

Long calls pose another staffing challenge. Thirty-minute reporting periods provide an adequate level of detail and accuracy for most contact centers. However, some centers, particularly those in help desk environments, handle calls that are complex enough that average handling time approaches or exceeds 30 minutes.

When long calls are not distributed as Erlang C anticipates, they may violate the assumptions of the formula. Compounding the problem is the fact that some ACDs count calls in the period in which they begin, but report average handling time in the period in which they end. Consequently, reported averages can be skewed.

If your AHT approaches 30 minutes, you may need to adjust your default reporting interval to an hour versus a half hour. Most Erlang C programs will allow you to define the interval you want to examine. Alternatively, you can program a simulator to model the mix of contacts you are handling. If, on the other hand, long calls are not common, but they do occasionally occur, you will need to adjust your statistics (remove them from assumptions) before using your historical data.

You will also need to consider how you manage long calls. Most technical support environments have established a second tier of support to handle long and/or complex calls. You will need to manage the service level for both tiers, or it will tend to suffer in both. But when managed well, this approach can ensure that long calls don't tie up the primary group and cause erratic service levels.

## PEAKED TRAFFIC

Peaked traffic, as discussed in Chapter 3, is a surge beyond random variation within a half hour, which poses a unique staffing challenge. For the purposes of this discussion, there are two types of peaked traffic — the type you can plan for and those incidents that are impossible to predict.

The calls that utilities get just after a major power outage will surge far beyond normal random variation. Similarly, if a national news program unexpectedly provides your telephone number to the viewing audience as part of its story, you will get unannounced peaked traffic — and it will be quite an experience!

The problem is, you can't predict these events, and you're probably not willing to staff up for them just in case they happen. So staffing for unexpected peaks falls more in the category of real-time management or disaster recovery planning.

On the other hand, peaked traffic that you are expecting belongs squarely in the realm of normal, ongoing planning. Forecasting, staffing and scheduling to meet a specified service level still apply. However, planning must happen at much more detailed periods of time, often in 5- or 10-minute increments. For a given service level, peaked traffic requires more staff than random traffic, and agents will have a lower occupancy over a half-hour period.

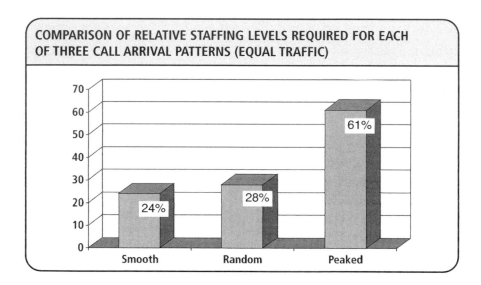

**COMPARISON OF RELATIVE STAFFING LEVELS REQUIRED FOR EACH OF THREE CALL ARRIVAL PATTERNS (EQUAL TRAFFIC)**

Most centers use Erlang C to calculate base staff for predicted peaks. If you expect 200 calls in a 5-minute span, that's the equivalent of 1,200 calls in a half hour. If you use an Erlang C program based on half-hour data, you will assume 1,200 calls for the calculations. Alternatively, some staffing programs allow you to specify the timeframe you choose, and can accommodate short intervals.

But common sense is required. If you have 75 people to handle the 200 calls, and the calls come in at virtually the same time, you know that the first 75 are going to be answered immediately. The next 75 are going to have to wait, and the average wait will be similar to the average handling time of the first 75 calls. The last 50 calls will have to wait something like two times the average handling time of the calls.

The situation can be similar to a bus dropping people off in front of a sports arena. Those reaching the gates first get quick service. For others, service levels can be dramatically different, depending on where they end up in the line. Consequently, how peaked the traffic is (how concentrated it is within a small period of time) will dramatically impact service level.

## WEB CHAT

Web chat is a service-level-oriented contact, and the essential planning steps apply. You can determine the most conservative (highest) estimate of agents you'll need by assuming that each agent can interact with only one customer at a time, then using Erlang C or simulation to calculate staff requirements based on the usual input — number of contacts, average session transaction time (the equivalent of AHT), and your service level objective. However, this will overestimate actual requirements in many cases; between workflow-routing options and technology possibilities, there really is no "one-size-fits-all" approach. Good service will depend on a few decisions you'll need to make, such as the number of customers an agent can handle at once.

Let's review some important terms. The following are definitions that we use and recommend. (Note that depending on the application, the roles may be reversed — the agent may make an initial request to a customer browsing the organization's website.)

**SESSION:** The whole of the interaction, from hello to goodbye.

**EXCHANGE:** A part of a session that begins with an inquiry from the customer and concludes with a response from the agent.

**SESSION RESPONSE TIME:** The time it takes the organization to respond to the initial request for a session from the customer.

**EXCHANGE RESPONSE TIME:** The time that elapses between the customer sending a question or comment and the delivery of the agent's response.

**CUSTOMER RESPONSE TIME:** The time it takes the customer to read an agent's reply and send a response.

**EXCHANGE HANDLE TIME:** The time it takes for the agent to prepare and deliver a response during an exchange.

**SESSION HANDLE TIME:** The cumulative total of the exchange handle times for the session.

**SESSION TRANSACTION TIME:** The time elapsed from the beginning of the initial exchange to close-out.

**CLOSE-OUT:** The moment in time when the session is considered to be complete.

While some organizations use chat extensively, it makes up a relatively small portion of the contact workload for many others. If you're just starting out, you'll need to answer a fundamental question: When do you move from "educated guessing" to staffing approaches that are more scientific? After all, if you only need one or two agents handling chat, advanced mathematical approaches won't yield any more accuracy than common sense.

ICMI recommends that a sensible threshold is five — when you need five or more agents handling chat at any one time, a more disciplined approach will begin to pay off. (This is also a sensible threshold for social and other types of interactions.)

Another key decision is around the number of simultaneous sessions you allow agents to handle. Some systems can be configured to enable 16 or more simultaneous sessions per agent — which, of course, is impractical from a human standpoint in most cases. The number of maximum concurrent sessions you allow will impact response times, customer satisfaction, accuracy, and employee morale. Our advice to those just starting out: Go with no more than two or three until you get a better read on what's possible and get the kinks worked out of the system.

To determine how far beyond one session at a time you can move, basic math comes in handy. Let's assume that you set the maximum number of concurrent sessions at five. It's simple and valuable to develop worst-case estimates. Here's the formula: Multiply the maximum number of concurrent sessions you expect by the average exchange handle time. The result will give you an idea of what could happen (worst case) to customer wait

---

**THE REPORTING CHALLENGE**

Although multiple concurrent chat sessions can improve productivity, they can also make reporting more difficult. Consider again the example of five concurrent sessions, where all five customers initiate an exchange at the same time. The last customer served will have to wait 6.25 minutes for a response — but most of that time was spent on other exchanges with other customers. The reporting challenge is accounting for these variables.

For example, when a customer initiates an exchange, the reporting system must note how many concurrent exchanges are already in queue for that agent in order to determine the exchange handle time. The customer who is fourth in line will wait a total of five minutes for a response. Divide that wait time by the number of exchanges in queue, and you'll come up with the exchange handle time of 1.25 minutes (5 ÷ 4). But you can see that reporting must account for many variables.

In short, these are issues you'll need to review with your technology provider. How does the system make these calculations and what do the reports produced really mean?

---

times. For example, if five customers initiate an exchange at the same time, and the average exchange handle time is 1.25 minutes, the last customer in line will have to wait 6.25 minutes for a response (5 x 1.25). This scenario won't happen often. But if and when it does, the delay would be well beyond the expectations of most customers. So, five concurrent sessions would be too high for an organization focused on delivering high levels of service.

Another decision you must make is when an agent will receive a session. If a customer's initial request is immediately delivered to an agent, you can send an automated, personalized greeting from that agent to the customer. If you decide to wait on routing, you will need to deliver either a blank text-chat box or one with a generic greeting. Here's the staffing tradeoff: If you provide the more personalized approach, you will need to live with the chance that you may be tying up an agent too early — some customers will

**163**

request a chat session but then never initiate the exchange, and the agent will be left waiting for a question that never comes. Given this possibility, you will probably want to allow relatively more concurrent sessions per agent than in a scenario where an agent is selected only after an exchange is initiated.

You will also need to define when a session ends. Often, the point of close-out is clear — but sometimes it's not. For example, customers may get what they need and ignore further attempts at communication; they may step away from their computers; or they might head off to competitors' websites. (Chat is often perceived to be less personal than phone calls, and customers may apply different rules of courtesy.) While your agent waits for a response, the session is considered active. So you'll need to decide on procedures to try to re-engage the customer, and when the agent can, in effect, "give up" and close the session. Staffing implication: The longer the threshold until close-out, the more time the agent will spend waiting for an exchange that may never occur; accordingly, a long threshold would suggest you can allow a relatively higher number of concurrent sessions per agent.

In short, staffing for chat revolves more around questions of workflow and technology application than on mathematical calculations. As volumes rise, you'll need to make decisions in each of these areas that are right for your organization and customers.

## SOCIAL INTERACTIONS AND SMS

For staffing purposes, there are different types of social interactions, each requiring a specific approach to resource planning. Here are some common variations:

**1. SOCIAL INTERACTIONS — REAL TIME, WITH SINGLE RESPONSE.** In this setting, the organization handles interactions through social channels as they occur, with one response generally being sufficient. Typical examples include responding to customers with numbers they can contact, specific email addresses, or links to online resources that provide necessary information. These are service-level-type interactions, and the staffing approach is like that for inbound phone calls.

**2. SOCIAL INTERACTIONS — REAL TIME, WITH MULTIPLE EXCHANGES.** In this case, the organization strives to handle interactions when they are initiated, and the dialog often involves multiple back-and-forth messages. Once engaged, customers may continue to ask questions or seek clarification. These are service-level-type contacts with staffing considerations like those of chat.

**3. SOCIAL INTERACTIONS — DEFERRED.** This approach involves addressing inquires or issues that do not require an immediate response. Common examples include responding to general inquiries posted on the organization's Facebook page, or sending responses, FAQ documents, or relevant links that address questions posted in forums. In this scenario, staffing is response time oriented, like that for email or outbound contacts that are scheduled.

**4. INTERNAL INTERACTIONS.** As with other types of internal communication (instant messaging, phone calls, email, etc.), the impact of internal collaboration on staffing requirements must be considered in context. If dialog is necessitated by and happens while handling customer interactions, the time required should be reflected realistically in the average handling time associated with those contacts. On the other hand, internal communication that is not directly associated with handling customer contacts (e.g., it's for internal projects or, simply, the everyday communication that is part of a normal work environment) should at least be accounted for in overall schedule requirements (see Chapter 8).

Note that different systems will deliver social interactions to agents in different ways. For example, some present social interactions in email-like format. That's fine. Just remember, it's not email in the usual sense, and staffing requirements should be driven by whether the work needs to happen at the time and whether it involves multiple exchanges.

### SERVICE LEVEL IN NON-PHONE CHANNELS

Contact center professionals often liken the time it takes for customers to receive a reply to a non-phone contact to what service level means to inbound phone calls. But there is an important difference: Speed-of-answer statistics associated with phone calls are based on *when the call reaches the agent*. But speed-of-response for other kinds of contacts — e.g., chat, social, SMS, email — is based on *when the customer receives a reply*, which can only happen after the agent actually handles the inquiry.

Is this distinction important? That depends. For email — where response time is typically measured in hours or days — it doesn't matter much. But chat and social interactions that need to take place as they arise are a different matter. Response time is measured in seconds or minutes, and the time required for the agent to craft the reply must be taken into account. We've seen cases where well-intentioned executives set a response time target for exchanges of one minute or less when it takes longer than that to create the right reply! That's a recipe for disaster (or, at the least, for missed targets). It is up to the management team to establish workable objectives supported by the right level of resources.

Considerations for SMS messages (those that involve agents) are similar — do they occur at the time of initial inquiry (requiring a service level approach) or can they happen later (response time)? And, are they generally handled in one response (like a phone call) or do they require some back-and-forth (like chat)?

*Whew!* It's a lot to think about. And multimedia queues, depending on how you use them, can include any combination of these channels and contact types. Given the variables and increasing variety in today's workloads, you and your team have a lot coming at you. It's enough to make the Little Mermaid want to jump back into the water.

But take heart: Getting staffing right is something you get better at with practice. And it goes to the heart of what contact centers have always excelled at: matching up supply and demand in real time. Remember that when all is said and done, success is more important than perfection.

# Calculating Trunks

As we consider trunks and related system resources, let's start with the traditional assumption that you need a trunk (a line, a circuit) for each simultaneous conversation (we'll then look at how that might not be the case). More specifically, you need enough trunks to carry the delay that callers experience (the time from the moment calls arrive at the routing system until agents say "hello") and the conversation time (talk time), for the period you are analyzing.

The general method for calculating trunks is as follows:

1. Forecast the call load (work load) to be handled for the busiest half hour in the foreseeable future.

2. Compute the number of agents required to handle the forecasted call load at your service level objective.

3. Determine the trunk load according to the call load you will be handling and the service level you can realistically achieve. The trunk load represents how much time, in hours, callers are in queue or connected to agents over an hour.

4. Determine the number of trunks required to handle the calculated trunk load, using an appropriate formula.

Erlang B or variations of it (yep, also the work of our beloved Danish engineer) is widely used and is often available in workforce management programs or in resource calculators (including QueueView, the program that I am using for examples). There are also other alternatives you can choose from and each has built-in assumptions (see table, below).

With any of the usual formulas used for calculating trunks, you will need to specify the probability of busy signals you can live with; if you input zero, you'll need as many trunks as there are calls. But if you can tolerate even a

---

> ### ERLANG B FORMULA
>
> $$P = \frac{\dfrac{A^N}{N!}}{\displaystyle\sum_{x=0}^{N} \dfrac{A^x}{x!}}$$
>
> Where   A = total traffic in erlangs
>                N = number of trunks
>                P = grade of service

small probability of busy signals (let's say 1 percent), then the number of trunks required becomes much more realistic. In the staffing sample on page 144, 38 trunks are required to handle 26.8 hours of traffic with a 1 percent probability of busy signals.

If you have more than one trunk group, you will need to allocate the trunk load among your trunk groups before calculation. For example, if 25 percent of the traffic will arrive on a trunk group that handles local calls and the other 75 percent on a group that carries toll-free traffic, you will need trunks to handle 6.7 hours of traffic in the first group (.25 x 26.8 hours) and 20.1 hours in the second (.75 x 26.8 hours).

Today, traditional circuits are being augmented or replaced by VoIP-based services. Session Initiation Protocol (SIP) trunking, for example, is a way of converging voice and data. SIP can boost efficiency by dynamically allocating bandwidth to make use of network capacity — just as your Internet service at home carries voice, data and those Skype calls to your best friend in Singapore.

But these services have to be engineered appropriately to ensure good voice quality. Enter bandwidth calculators. They consider the load you need to carry, the level of voice compression you can live with, network architecture and protocols, and other factors to help ensure you've got sufficient bandwidth in place.

In addition to the types of trunks you have (e.g., circuit switched or SIP), there will likely be other considerations. For example, you may have an IVR

| FORMULA | ASSUMPTIONS |
|---|---|
| Erlang B | Assumes that if callers get busy signals, they go away forever, never to retry. Since some callers retry, Erlang B can underestimate trunks required. |
| Poisson | Assumes that if callers get busy signals, they keep trying until they successfully get through. Since some callers won't keep retrying, Poisson can overestimate trunks required. |
| Retrial Tables | Used less frequently by traffic engineers, but correctly assumes that some callers retry and others go away. |
| Bandwidth Calculations | More a genre of methods than a formula. Bandwidth calculators consider variables such as voice compression and coding algorithms to estimate requirements. |

that callers go through before they reach an agent (to enter their account number, route themselves, etc.). If so, the time callers spend in the IVR will have to be factored into the calculations. And if trunks are shared among different agent groups, that would also be a consideration. When all is said and done, you need adequate bandwidth to support the busiest foreseeable increments in your contact center.

There are many possible trunking scenarios that go beyond the scope of this chapter, and I highly recommend that you get the help of a competent IT/telecommunications professional to help you engineer your system. But ensure that they understand the relationship between trunks and staff. And make sure that staffing and trunking are coordinated activities, both in calculations and in your budgets.

Remember the fundamental concept, which always holds true: Staffing affects trunking and related system requirements. Delay is key — the fewer people you have for a given call load, the more network and system capacity you'll need.

---

**THE IMPACT OF SERVICE LEVEL ON TRUNK LOAD**

Load trunks carry when service level is met:

| Delay | Talk |
|-------|------|

Load trunks carry when service level is below objective:

| Delay | Talk |
|-------|------|

---

# Points to Remember

- Staffing and trunking are inextricably related. The fewer people you have for a given call load, the more network and system capacity you'll need.
- The Erlang C formula is commonly used for calculating base staff and is easy to use and widely available. Computer simulation is more difficult to use than Erlang C, but can more accurately model complex environments.
- Social interactions, email, chat, SMS, outbound calls and other kinds of contacts require staffing approaches appropriate to the unique characteristics of each.
- No staffing methodology is perfect, and it is important to understand the assumptions each makes and to blend in a good dose of common sense.
- Base staff calculations tell you how many agents you need to handle the workload at the service level and response time targets you've set. But many things can keep agents away from the work, and Steps 6 and 7 — covered in the next chapter — incorporate these activities so that schedules are realistic and reflect total staffing needs.

# CHAPTER 8:
# Successful Scheduling

*Where are they?*

ANONYMOUS CALL CENTER MANAGER

A ccurate scheduling is more challenging than ever, and a number of trends have contributed to the complexity. At the top of the list: Today's contact centers support a broader range of products and services than they did in the past. A close second is that self-service technology and search (which enables customers to quickly locate information, forums and other resources) have enabled many issues to be automated or resolved *before they reach the center*, meaning that those contacts that do make the trip are increasingly

**CONSEQUENCES OF BEING OVERSTAFFED**

- Unnecessarily high staffing costs
- Underutilization of agents
- Boredom of agents
- Loss of credibility in budgeting

**CONSEQUENCES OF BEING UNDERSTAFFED**

- Unhappy customers
- Abandoned calls
- Longer calls
- Additional or simultaneous contacts
- More errors and rework
- Higher telephone network usage and costs
- Staff stress and burnout
- Impact on brand reputation

**171**

varied and demanding. And, of course, contact centers are handling a growing range of channels.

The irony is that the very forces that are making scheduling increasingly difficult in many centers have created an environment in which accurate scheduling is paramount. It's an unenviable tradeoff: Get your schedules right or brace for chaos.

Fortunately, the core objective of scheduling — get the right people and supporting resources in the right place at the right times — hasn't changed. Nor have the principles driving the process: correctly identifying and categorizing the different types of activities; making accurate base staff calculations; anticipating shrinkage requirements; using scheduling alternatives that provide necessary flexibility; and ensuring that things go as planned (through effective schedule adherence, for example).

From one perspective, a schedule is a high-level forecast. It incorporates all of the planning steps discussed in previous chapters and predicts who

*"Thank you for calling. Currently our agents are either:*
- *On a break*
- *At lunch*
- *Checking their Facebook page*
- *Making calls*
- *In a meeting*
- *Helping a colleague*
- *Downloading a new app*
- *In the restroom*
- *Working on a project*
- *Rebooting their computer*
- *Checking Twitter*
- *Researching something*
- *Out sick*
- *On vacation*
- *In a coaching session*
- *Catching up with internal email*
- *Getting supplies*
- *Updating their LinkedIn profile*
- *Showing visitors around the center*
- *Stuck in after-call work*
- *In training*
- *Assisting other customers*
*Thank you for your patience, and please continue to hold ... "*

needs to be where, doing what and when. It is also a "game plan," designed specifically for agents to follow (though like any plan, it may need to be revisited as the game unfolds).

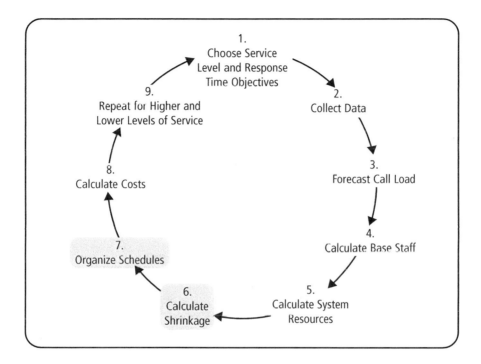

## The Scheduling Challenge

Before we head into the next two planning steps, let's take stock of where you are in the planning process. You chose service level and response time objectives (Step 1), acquired the necessary planning data (Step 2), and forecasted the workload associated with the various types of work you must handle (Step 3). You then calculated base staff and trunks required (Steps 4 and 5).

At this point, if you graph out half-hour staffing requirements for any day of the week, you will see that you need different levels of agents every half hour. And, you'll need different levels of staff for each day of the week and different seasons of the year. Scheduling for an average half hour of the day, average day of the week or average month of the year will mean being either overstaffed or understaffed much of the time. Consequently, schedules need to reflect the workload as it changes throughout the day, week and year.

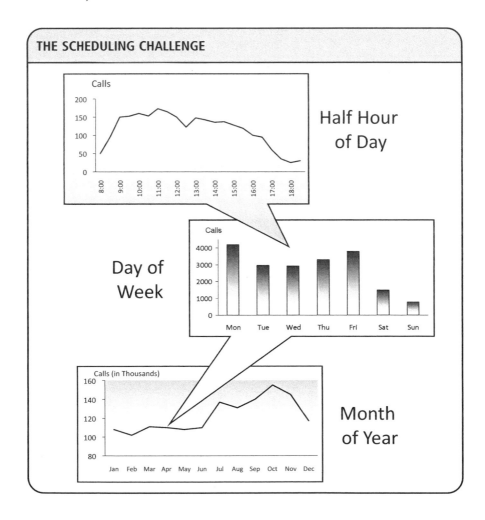

Effective scheduling depends on both longer-term budgets and short-term execution. You'll need a big enough bucket of resources to work with — in other words, do you have the staff you need to put schedules together that match the workload? We'll cover longer-term staff planning and budgeting in Chapter 10. Short-term execution is at the other end of the spectrum. You can accurately forecast the workload, know how many people you need and schedule accordingly, yet still miss your service level and response time objectives by a long shot because your agents aren't in the right places at the right times. We'll look at schedule adherence in Chapter 14.

## ACCOUNTING FOR SHRINKAGE

Have you ever looked at a supervisor monitor or conducted a headcount on the floor and wondered, "Where is everybody?" I have a hunch that every contact center manager has asked that question at one time or another! Part of the answer is schedule adherence. But another part is realistically anticipating the things that can occupy agents' time.

Rostered staff factor (RSF), alternatively called an "overlay," is a numerical factor that leads to the minimum staff needed on schedule over and above base staff required to achieve your service level and response time objectives. It is calculated after base staffing is determined and before schedules are organized.

RSF is a form of forecasting. The major assumption is that the proportion of staff off the phones will be similar to what is happening now. In other words, if one person is on break in a group of 10, 10 people will be on break in a group of 100. An illustration of how to calculate RSF is shown in the table. (I use phone and email as examples, but the methodology applies to any of your customer contact channels, as long as base staff is calculated accurately. See Chapter 7.)

The mechanics include five steps:

**1. ENTER THE BASE STAFF REQUIRED BY HALF HOUR.** What base staff includes will depend on the structure of your groups. For example, if you have separate agent groups for different contact channels, the base staff entered represents one of those groups. You will need RSF calculations for each group. On the other hand, if you set up groups that han-

**175**

## ROSTERED STAFF FACTOR (SHRINKAGE) CALCULATIONS

| | Base Staff Required* | | Absent | Break | Training | On Schedule | Rostered Staff Factor |
|---|---|---|---|---|---|---|---|
| | Phone | Email | | | | | |
| 08:00-08:30 | 18 | 4 | 2 | 0 | 0 | 24 | 1.09 |
| 08:30-09:00 | 20 | 4 | 2 | 0 | 4 | 30 | 1.25 |
| 09:00-09:30 | 20 | 4 | 2 | 0 | 4 | 30 | 1.25 |
| 09:30-10:00 | 25 | 5 | 2 | 3 | 4 | 39 | 1.3 |
| 10:00-10:30 | 25 | 5 | 2 | 3 | 4 | 39 | 1.3 |
| 10:30-11:00 | 31 | 5 | 2 | 3 | 4 | 45 | 1.25 |

$$\text{Rostered Staff Factor} = \frac{\text{On Schedule}}{\text{Base Staff Required}}$$

* Phone and email are examples; use the channels that apply.

dle both categories of contacts, as the example shows (service level, i.e., inbound calls; and response time, i.e., customer email), base staff is first calculated for both types of work separately and then added together. You then calculate RSF for the combined group.

**2. IDENTIFY THE THINGS THAT ROUTINELY KEEP AGENTS FROM THE WORKLOAD.** The next three columns reflect the numbers of staff absent, on break and in training, as they now occur. These categories are just examples: You can include research, non-scheduled outbound calls (those that are neither part of talk time or after-call work nor otherwise included in base staff calculations) and other activities. You may also want to further subdivide the categories. For example, absenteeism can be divided into planned absenteeism, such as vacations, and unplanned absenteeism, such as sick leave.

**3. ADD BASE STAFF TO THE NUMBER OF AGENTS WHO WILL BE AWAY FROM THE WORKLOAD, FOR EACH HALF HOUR.** The "on-schedule" column is the sum of the entries in previous columns, by half hour.

**4. CALCULATE RSF.** The last column is derived by dividing the staff required on schedule by base staff required for each half hour. The propor-

## SHRINKAGE VERSUS ROSTERED STAFF FACTOR

Some use the terms rostered staff factor (RSF) and shrinkage interchangeably to refer to the reality of needing more staff on schedule than the base staff required to handle customer contacts. There's nothing wrong with that, as long as it's understood that, in that context, the terms refer to the overall concept of needing more staff on schedule than base staff required to handle the workload.

Others use the terms more specifically — nothing wrong with that either, as long as the context is understood. When differentiated — and it's subtle — shrinkage refers to how much loss (shrinkage) there is between scheduled staff and base staff, while rostered staff factor looks at how much needs to be added to base staff required to reach schedule requirements.

What's not subtle is how the calculations for each are used when they are differentiated in this way. Consider an example where base staff is 40 and 10 agents will be involved in other activities, the schedule requirement is 50 agents.

The RSF is 50/40, or 1.25
*Application: 40 x 1.25 = 50 agents*
(or)
The shrinkage (loss) = 10/50, or 20%
*Application: 40 / (1 - 20%) = 50 agents*

Uh, oh ... you can see what's coming here. Some mistakenly apply shrinkage in place of what should be RSF and end up with too few scheduled agents; others use RSF in place of what should be shrinkage and end up with too many scheduled agents.

Investment analysts often have to remind clients of a similar principle in the world of finance. If a $5,000 investment drops by 20 percent, the new balance is $4,000; $4,000 would need to grow by 25 percent (4,000 x 1.25) to again reach $5,000. Many contact center managers have found themselves in a similar education process: "Yes, scheduled staff shrinks by 20 percent, which is why we need 25 percent additional staff above base-staff requirements for that increment!"

*(continued next page)*

**177**

In that sense, RSF has some advantages — it's easier to explain. Correctly applying either method at the interval level will lead you to the same answers. However, you have to take shrinkage a step further to calculate staff required, while RSF provides requirements more directly. The RSF methodology also tends to fit nicely into the logical progression of planning, e.g., calculate staff and supporting resources (Steps 4 and 5), determine and apply RSF (Step 6), organize schedules (Step 7). Shrinkage tends to jump from schedules (Step 7) to determining loss or shrinkage (Step 6), to applying the formula to base staff (Step 5) to get back to schedule requirements (Step 7). It's a small point, but I do prefer the RSF approach when explaining these principles to others.

Shrinkage has some advantages, as well. It's the term that, more often than not, has been adapted by workforce management providers (consequently, I run into people who have been in the industry for years and have never heard of RSF). And it's used more broadly in other business settings, such as where grocers must account for inventory loss caused by damage or food expiration.

Finally, the time horizon you are considering may impact the approach you use. As described here, RSF and shrinkage are for scheduling (near and medium term) purposes. When we look at a longer planning horizon, in order to determine full-time equivalent requirements (Chapter 10), we'll use a shrinkage-like approach in the methodology. But caution is in order: Any mismatch of time — e.g., taking a calculation for shrinkage or RSF determined over a broader timeframe, and applying it to smaller increments — simply doesn't work.

There are different ways to get from point A to point B. When used correctly and in the right context, both shrinkage and RSF lead to the same answer.

tions are the mechanism you will use to project future schedule requirements.

**5. USE THE FACTORS WHEN ORGANIZING FUTURE SCHED-ULES.** The result of these calculations is a set of factors reflecting expected requirements by the half hour. You multiply them against the base staff you will need when assembling future schedules. For example, if you are putting together a schedule for four weeks from now, and you project a requirement of 32 base staff between 8:30 and 9:00, you will need to schedule 40 agents (32 x 1.25) for that half hour — plus a margin for staff that will be working on projects, in meetings, or doing anything else not included in the calculation.

## WHAT TO INCLUDE

While breaks and absenteeism should almost always be included in RSF calculations, other activities require some analysis and judgment. For example, should training be included? If training schedules frequently change and/or require differing proportions of staff, keep training out of calculations and, instead, factor it into schedules on a case-by-case basis. But if training happens in predictable proportion to the base staff required, include it. Note: After-call work is already included in base staff calculations (as part of average handling time) so it should not be included in RSF factor calculations.

In many contact centers, RSF ebbs and flows in the 1.1 to 1.5 range throughout the day, meaning that a minimum of 10 percent to 50 percent additional staff are required on schedule over those handling the workload. But don't trust rules of thumb: You will need to produce your own calculations. If activities not related to the workload are significant, RSF can be as high as 2.0, meaning that you'll need to schedule two people for each agent required. This is fairly common in some technical support environments that require more extensive offline research.

We recommend that you initially produce a table of factors for each day of the week and for each agent group you will be scheduling. Then, adjust the calculations as circumstances dictate, such as for vacation season or major changes in training schedules.

## IMPROVING ACCURACY

Larger centers will pick up some accuracy by going through this planning step in 15-minute increments. In smaller centers, half-hour periods are sufficient, but you should use numbers that are conservative. For example, if you have two people on break the first 15 minutes of the half hour, and four on break in the second half of the period, use four in the calculations.

If you calculated staff for hour increments due to long calls (as discussed in Chapter 6), you can also generally calculate RSF by hour, since scheduled breaks and lunch tend to get moved around by long calls. If you find that hours are not picking up the activity accurately, drop to half-hour increments.

If you are handling peaked traffic, you can usually use half-hour or 15-minute increments for RSF even though you calculated base staff for even shorter periods. Naturally, you will plan any activities that are flexible around the inbound peaks.

## A PREREQUISITE TO EFFECTIVE BUDGETS AND SCHEDULES

Frankly, the whole notion of rostered staff factor raises lots of questions in the budgeting process — and understandably so. You'll hear some variation of, "You mean to tell me we need to hire 42 people so we can have 30 on the phones handling calls?" (In the contact center's defense, folks in every other part of the organization also go on breaks, take vacations and handle a variety of tasks; they're just not scheduled down to the nth degree.) There is simply no substitute for illustrating what's going on and why extra staff is required. And it's a great chance to reinforce the contact center's unique, time-sensitive environment. In short, RSF calculations are valuable in communicating budget requirements effectively.

An added advantage of making this effort is that it will force you to examine these activities. Should they be happening when and to the degree that they are? Some changes may provide better coverage or make scheduling easier or more acceptable to agents. Like any aspect of plan-

**CAN YOU SKIP STEP 6?**

Why bother with RSF — Step 6 in the planning process — if you know how many staff you will need simply by adding the columns together? Better yet, why bother with any of it, if your scheduling package accounts for these sorts of things? Can you calculate base-staff requirements, then jump right into scheduling — skipping Step 6 altogether?

With scheduling software, you can, in a sense, do just that. After calculating base-staff requirements, you will begin building schedules. And yes, they will account for and include breaks, holidays, training and other variables you enter. But Step 6 is still important, for several reasons:

- Simply understanding the principle is key to understanding the spread between base-staff and schedule requirements. And you'll need to explain this issue to others in various planning and budgeting settings.
- There will be times when you'll want to model the schedule requirements for different workload scenarios, without laboring though the minutia of adding up individual shrinkage components. There's nothing that beats the speed and accuracy of having a complete set of factors.
- Because it is a ratio, RSF can be easily tracked and graphed, enabling you to see relative trends and identify improvement opportunities. That is much more difficult when looking at a full-blown schedule.

ning, examine how accurate your predictions are compared to actual results, and adjust accordingly.

After you have calculated RSF, you know your staffing requirements accurately down to specific times of day. The next challenge is to identify scheduling alternatives and parameters so that you can organize schedules that closely match staffing requirements.

## Scheduling Alternatives

Considering that staffing needs fluctuate significantly throughout the

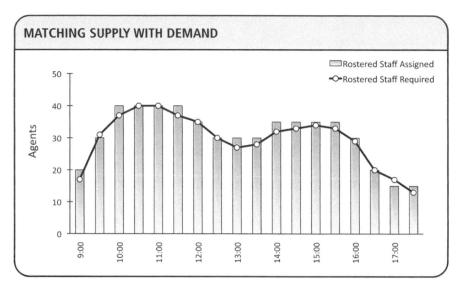

MATCHING SUPPLY WITH DEMAND

day, month and year, what can you do to ensure you have an adequate number of people in place without being overstaffed much of the time? After all, there aren't too many people who like to work half-hour shifts.

Fortunately, quite a few alternatives exist and we'll summarize many of them here. Not all will be feasible for you. This aspect of planning involves putting all options on the table, identifying the scheduling approaches that could work in your environment, and then making a decision on those that you will use.

**USE HIRING TO YOUR ADVANTAGE.** Important criteria when hiring new agents should be the hours and days they can (or can't) work.

**UTILIZE CONVENTIONAL SHIFTS.** Most organizations have a core group of agents who work a traditional five-day week with shifts during normal hours (e.g., 9 a.m. to 5 p.m.). That's just fine, assuming there are additional scheduling options to address variability in workload within and beyond these hours.

**ADJUST BREAKS, LUNCH, MEETING AND TRAINING SCHEDULES.** Even slight changes to when these activities are scheduled can mean that a few more people are handling contacts at just the right times. And that can make a big difference (see Chapter 9). This alternative is available to virtually every organization.

**STAGGER SHIFTS.** For example, one shift begins at 7 a.m., the next at 7:30 a.m., the next at 8 a.m., etc., until the center is fully staffed for the busy mid-morning traffic. This is a common and effective approach. Be sure to tweak these shifts as necessary to account for changes in workload patterns.

**OFFER CONCENTRATED SHIFTS.** Given the choice, some agents will opt to work fewer days with more hours per day, while others would rather work fewer hours in a day, even if that means a six- or seven-day workweek (see sidebar, Explore Your Options). But keep in mind that not all agents can perform at high levels throughout extended shifts.

**USE AN ENVELOPE STRATEGY.** With more types of work to handle in today's environment, many contact centers are using an "envelope" strategy (see figure). This approach recognizes that some types of work have to be handled at specific times of the day, and other types of work allow more flexibility. The idea is to move in and out of the various types of work as circumstances dictate. Collateral work provides flexibility, if it is planned and managed well.

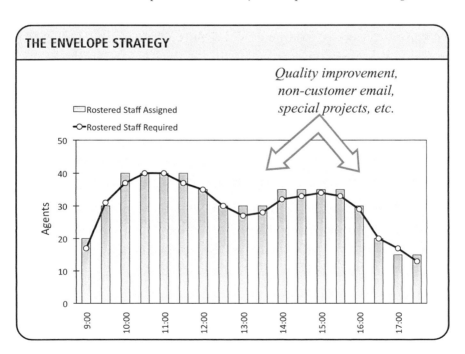

**THE ENVELOPE STRATEGY**

*Quality improvement, non-customer email, special projects, etc.*

☐ Rostered Staff Assigned
—○— Rostered Staff Required

**OFFER OVERTIME.** No additional training is required, and many agents will volunteer for the extra work. However, overtime can be expensive as an ongoing strategy and, once again, there is the question of whether or not agents can sustain high performance for the entirety of longer shifts.

**GIVE AGENTS THE OPTION TO GO HOME WITHOUT PAY.** Often referred to as LWOP (leave without pay, pronounced "el-wop"), this is a popular approach on slower days, and there are usually enough agents willing to take you up on it.

**SCHEDULE PART-TIMERS.** Some centers are prevented from using part-time help by union agreements or by practicalities, such as complex services requiring extensive training. But when available and feasible, this is a popular and common approach.

**ESTABLISH REINFORCEMENTS.** When contact-handling duties are combined with other tasks, such as correspondence, making outbound calls, or data entry, the agents assigned to these collateral duties can act as reinforcements when the workload gets heavy. Often called the "reinforcement method," this approach is a bit like being able to bring in part-timers on an as-needed basis (keep an eye on the workload being put aside so that you aren't creating downstream problems). Initially, you will need to tackle training, scheduling and cultural issues — and perhaps even those related to pay, work rules, and unions.

**CREATE A SWAT TEAM.** This approach takes the reinforcement method to the larger organization, where employees from other areas help handle customer services as needed. To implement this alternative successfully, you'll need to address training, scheduling, pay and cultural issues (see sidebar, Explore Your Options).

**ARRANGE FOR SOME AGENTS TO BE ON CALL.** Although this option is impractical for many, it can work in situations where events cannot be precisely predicted (i.e., catalog companies during the initial days of a new promotion). Typically, for it to be effective, agents must either live near the facility or (even better) be equipped to work from home.

**OFFER SPLIT SHIFTS.** Granted, split shifts — where agents work a partial shift, take part of the day off, then return later to finish their shifts — are not common. We've seen them in situations where university students are employed and work around class schedules. But don't count this alternative out in other settings. A group of full-time employees in one of MetLife's call centers once volunteered to work in the mornings and then come back for the less popular evening shift. They were happy to have the free midday time to get in a round of golf. Not a bad arrangement!

**SEND CALLS TO AN OUTSOURCER.** Today, outsourcers of all types and capabilities are available. The better among them can handle the most complex types of contacts, and many focus on specific industries, languages and contact channels. With some, the capacity to quickly ramp up as work loads dictate is a key selling point.

**COLLABORATE WITH SIMILAR ORGANIZATIONS.** Some centers have formed successful staffing alliances with other organizations. With different seasonality patterns, two centers can "lend" agents to one another to help each company effectively handle peak contact periods and minimize costs that would be incurred to hire and train temporary staff. While not a common practice, we have seen organizations from diverse industries use this staff-sharing approach successfully (see sidebar, Explore Your Options).

**SET UP A HOME-AGENT PROGRAM.** This is not a scheduling alternative per se, but it can create an environment in which unpopular shifts will be more palatable and where agents can handle contacts on short notice (see Chapter 16). Numerous organizations have successfully implemented work-at-home agent programs, benefiting not only from enhanced scheduling flexibility but also increased productivity and agent retention. Some companies have embraced "extreme telework," where the majority of staff are home agents (see sidebar, Explore Your Options).

**SACRIFICE SERVICE LEVEL FOR A PLANNED PERIOD OF TIME.** It may be unrealistic for some customer service or technical support centers to meet service level (and response time) objectives during the initial weeks of a new product introduction or during the busiest season. As a

## EXPLORE YOUR OPTIONS

Scheduling is a creative process — putting all options on the table, then implementing those that are a fit. Here are some examples:

- Vanguard, the large financial services company, helped to pioneer a "SWAT team" approach (they call it their Swiss Army), and employees up to and including the founder and CEO have been known to help handle customer interactions when the pressure is on. Similarly, People's United Bank's center in Bridgeport, Conn., has used former skilled agents (many of whom work in the company's marketing or accounting departments) to help with seasonal call spikes.
- Global investment firm AMVESCAP's Retirement Resource Center has benefited from concentrated (10 x 4) workweek shifts, where a portion of the firm's most experienced agents work from 10 a.m. to 9 p.m., four days a week. Agents' extra day off rotates so that, once a month, each person gets a free Friday and a three-day weekend. (Nobody is ever off on Monday, the center's busiest day.) The arrangement has helped in covering peaks, and in boosting the number of skilled agents on staff for the night shift.
- Organizations from diverse industries and sometimes very different businesses have created alliances where they share staff during their "counter-cyclical" peak seasons: Day Timer and Accor; John Deere and American Girl; even the Internal Revenue Service (IRS) and the Federal Emergency Management Agency (FEMA) during major disasters. With close working arrangements and the right training and approach, they can help centers cost-effectively manage peaks and valleys.
- Vegas.com, the multichannel contact center that handles customer interactions for Las Vegas' travel destination website, enables agents, many of whom work at home, to schedule their own shifts around blocks of time that match forecasted requirements. When discussing the organization's operational flexibility and multichannel capabilities, Rob Cate, Senior Director, looks ahead with confidence: "As that sort of multimedia trend continues to grow and develop in our communications cycle as a country or world, we're not only ready for it, we're experts at it."

- JetBlue, American Express, Wyndham International, and many others use at home agents (which is not a scheduling option per se, but opens up many flexible scheduling alternatives). The number of organizations that have home-agent programs has skyrocketed in recent years, enabled by advancements in technology, lower transmission and facility costs, and the flexibility these arrangements can provide (see sidebar, Chapter 15, Should You Consider Home Agents?).

result, some conscientiously "sacrifice" service level for several weeks or more and rely on customers to understand. This must be carefully planned; and, to be acceptable to customers, it must fall within the realm of their expectations. (Think of queuing for a new product or for a specific sale.)

Sometimes we hear defeatist attitudes related to staffing and scheduling: "Hey, they're going to give us what they are going to give us" (see chart Someone Who Has Given Up). But there are many scheduling alternatives available, even in relatively restrictive environments. Further, would senior management be persuaded by budgetary requests based on solid planning? The answer is usually an unequivocal "yes."

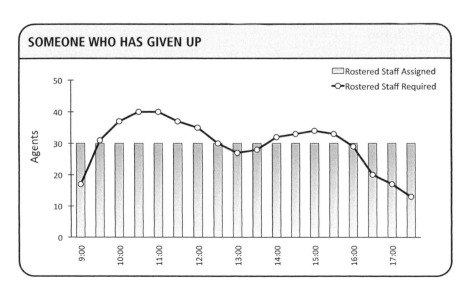

**SOMEONE WHO HAS GIVEN UP**

## Putting the Pieces Together

Scheduling is inherently an iterative process. Effective scheduling will always involve a certain amount of trial and error. As you identify scheduling alternatives, there are a number of important considerations:

**AGENT PREFERENCES.** If you involve agents in identifying scheduling possibilities up front, they will often generate ideas you didn't consider and will better accept and adhere to the schedules that are produced. Scheduling modules that provide the ability for agents to directly create, swap and adjust schedules (within established parameters) are popular with agents and workforce managers alike. And education on the implications of service level, quality and the impact of each person help enormously (see Chapter 9).

**AGENT GROUP STRUCTURE AND CHANNEL MIX.** How specialized are your skill requirements? Some centers can't say with precision where contacts go because their skills- or contingency-based routing environments are so complex. Keep your routing contingencies simple enough to manage. Similarly, what's your channel mix, and how does that (and should that) impact your agent group structure? These issues in mind, invest the time necessary to forecast, staff and schedule for the unique mix of contacts your center is handling.

**SCHEDULE HORIZON.** How far in advance will you determine schedules (the schedule horizon)? If you schedule further out, say for two or three months from now, your schedules will be less efficient. They will be locked in place, even if the workloads deviate from the forecast. But a big plus is that they will be more agreeable to your staff, who prefer to know their work schedules well in advance. On the other hand, if you use a shorter timeframe, the scheduling process will be less popular with agents, but schedules will likely be more accurate. This issue is a balancing act.

**UNION, LEGAL AND CONTRACT REQUIREMENTS.** You will need to carefully consider union, legal and any specific contractual requirements to ensure that you are scheduling within acceptable parameters.

Restrictions on part-time staff, hours worked and overtime pay will impact the alternatives you can use. If you are a union-based shop, an open, collaborative environment with union representatives — as well as educating all involved on the principles covered in Chapters 7 through 9 — can help immensely.

Scheduling software can be a big help in shuffling the pieces and generating schedules according to the parameters you establish. Conversely, it can turn out schedules that people will look at and say, "Are you kidding? There's no way we can adhere to that." So you'll need to define the rules and manage the process for best results.

As in other aspects of planning, you'll need to make sure that the software is considering all of the alternatives and parameters unique to your environment. You will also need to be realistic about agent preferences and encourage their involvement. In short, this, like other planning steps, should be a collaborative effort; and it involves a great deal more than mechanics.

## How Did It Go?

Want to really know how well scheduling is going? Make a line graph of your service level as it was during a recent week (you can also do this for response time). The following charts represent agent groups in three different contact centers (note, the hours and days of operation are different for each, as are their service level objectives). Each chart covers a specific week, and each line represents a different day.

Because these graphs display actual results by half hour, versus results for a single day or averages for a week or month, they can expose recurring problem areas. The first graph illustrates a fairly consistent service level that is centered on the organization's target of answering 85 percent of calls in 30 seconds (minus a few short-lived problem areas). You are striving for a consistent, on-target service level such as this. Yes, it looks a bit variable, but because service level is a high-level report, these graphs won't

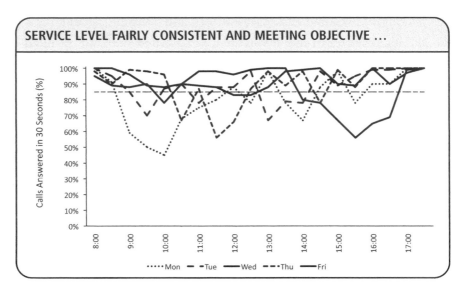

SERVICE LEVEL FAIRLY CONSISTENT AND MEETING OBJECTIVE ...

show stable, repeating patterns usually inherent to handling time or volume graphs.

The next graph illustrates a service level that ... um ... isn't so hot. You can see that service level is relatively consistent from day to day but well below the contact center's objective of answering 75 percent of calls in 20 seconds. It dips mid-morning, mid-afternoon and some around lunchtime,

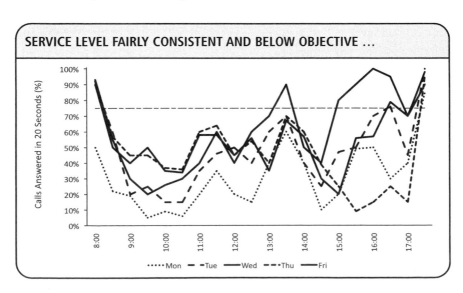

SERVICE LEVEL FAIRLY CONSISTENT AND BELOW OBJECTIVE ...

probably the result of breaks and lunch.

The afternoons are, let's put it this way, consistently inconsistent. My hunch is, customer-related or non-phone work is building up through the first part of the day and being squeezed into the afternoons, often at the expense of service level. Monday (likely the busiest day of the week) takes a beating. Service level also drops Thursday afternoon, possibly the result of meetings, training or some other activity that occupies part of the staff.

Based on these observations, you could investigate the following:

- Can breaks and lunch be adjusted to provide better coverage during the mornings and afternoons? For example, can you move lunch to a later time for some agents? Granted, you have to be reasonable — few would want to take a break at 9 a.m. or eat lunch at 3 p.m. But even slight adjustments can yield significant results.

- Is phone-related and non-phone work being forecasted and managed as well as possible? Do supervisors and agents know when to move from handling inbound calls into other types of work? Do they have real-time information on service level? Can some of the work be shifted into the evening, when service level is high?

- Are there any scheduling strategies available that would provide better coverage on Monday? Are there any activities on Monday (non-phone work, meetings, training, etc.) that can be moved to another day? Is there any way to provide better coverage Thursday afternoon (maybe not ... this may be the best time for the event that is affecting service level)?

- Are there sufficient resources to achieve the service level target, especially on Monday? Consistent results such as these can indicate that, when all is said and done, the group may be doing about as well as it can. In that case, only additional staff or a reduction of call load is going to improve results.

The next figure reveals an erratic service level that is usually below management's objective of 80 percent answered in 20 seconds. This may be an indication that the resources to meet the objective are adequate, but that they aren't in the right places at the right times.

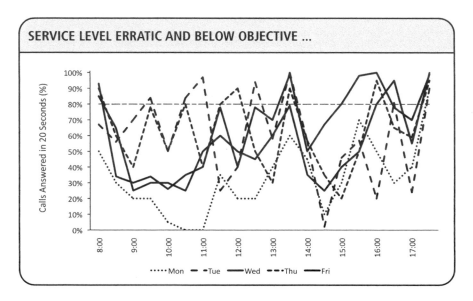

There are probably inconsistencies in how agents are handling the workload. Further, agents may not understand or have information on service level. Some of the issues to investigate include:

- Is non-phone work being forecasted and managed as well as possible? Can some of the non-phone work be moved into the evening when service level is generally better?

- Do supervisors and agents have real-time information on service level so they know when to sign off or go into other work modes versus when to "plug in" and help handle the queue?

- Do agents use the after-call work mode consistently? Do they know what constitutes after-call work, or are they mixing other activities into this mode?

- Are there scheduling strategies available to provide better coverage on Mondays?

- Is staffing adequate to achieve service level, assuming breaks, training and non-phone work are being scheduled as appropriately as possible?

## SECRETS TO BETTER SCHEDULING RESULTS

The very forces that are making scheduling difficult — more complex products and services, additional contact channels, faster pace of change, and the need for diverse agent skills — are creating an environment in which accurate scheduling is absolutely essential. Fortunately, scheduling is a process that can be learned and continuously improved. You get better at it with practice!

We've found that organizations getting the best scheduling results commonly take steps beyond the mechanics of calculating required staff and putting schedules together. Here are five of their secrets.

**1. Clarify Your Organization's Values.** This involves a dialog and set of decisions with the organization's senior-level management around key questions, which might include the following: What is the contact center's mission? How committed are you to providing good service even when the forecasts may be uncertain? What are your priorities — which activities get done first? What alternatives exist to maintain consistent service levels, from scheduling options to backup from other departments or outside help? Be ready for these discussions; they are opportunities to clarify direction and make a case for the resources and support that the contact center requires.

**2. Model Different Scenarios.** Modeling, or periodically creating test schedules with different sets of variables, can be a real eye-opener for possibilities and solutions. What's the impact of changing call-routing alternatives? Agent group structure? Schedule horizon? Training and meeting schedules? Shifts? While modeling takes time — you're basically having a person or team produce example schedules under different parameters — you'll get this investment back in multiples in the form of better decisions that come from an understanding of tradeoffs and points of leverage. (Scheduling software can be a big help in this effort, particularly in larger or more complex centers.)

**3. Ensure that All Activities Are Included.** Too often, contact centers have extra work outside of the schedule that is unaccounted for but that exacts a heavy price in psychological weight and creates fires when it's ignored

*(continued next page)*

**193**

for too long (e.g., unfinished projects, administrative work, reading updates, coaching sessions, and case work). Take an inventory of activities that is as comprehensive and specific as possible.

**4. Resolve the "Power Struggles."** If power struggle sounds a bit dramatic, you ought to see some of the challenges those in forecasting and scheduling roles have encountered: requests from other areas preempting schedules, unplanned marketing campaigns, unannounced schedule exceptions among agent teams, and unclear lines of authority between supervisors and workforce planners. These challenges are not insurmountable — unless they go unaddressed. (Educating supervisors and agents on the basics of forecasting and scheduling is an important part of the solution!)

**5. Ensure that the Process Is Simple, Flexible and Inclusive.** Effective scheduling will always involve a certain amount of trial and error. It's important to keep your routing contingencies simple enough to manage, and get people involved in helping to identify scheduling possibilities and solutions. Education on the implications of service level, quality and the impact of each person is essential (see Chapter 9).

Staffing and scheduling is an art and science that takes some time, practice and collaboration to master. As the environment becomes more complex, this step becomes more important. The results you are getting are telling, and you'll learn a lot by making the effort to compare what actually happens with what was scheduled to happen.

Scheduling is a creative process that requires support from contact center leadership, depends on ongoing communication, and is implemented only through effective collaboration throughout the center. It takes an ongoing commitment. But as a prerequisite to a stable and well-run customer-focused operation, it's worth the effort many times over.

# Points to Remember

- Scheduling is both a forecast and a game plan. It requires accurate planning and good schedule adherence.

- An important prerequisite to effective scheduling is to get your arms around all of the activities that occupy agents' time and build schedules that are realistic.

- Many scheduling alternatives exist, even in relatively restrictive environments. You should regularly reassess which alternatives are feasible in your contact center and how you can use them.

- Creating service level graphs by half hour will reveal how well schedules are matching agents to the workload and will expose recurring problem areas.

# Part Three:
# Understanding Contact Center Dynamics

### CHAPTER 9:
## How Contact Centers Behave

### CHAPTER 10:
## Communicating with Senior Management

### CHAPTER 11:
## Real-Time Management

---

*There are important fundamental principles that govern how customer contact centers behave. Understanding them is key to everything from communicating with senior management and making a case for the budget you need, to managing the center in real time.*

---

# CHAPTER 9:
# How Contact Centers Behave

*Every why hath a wherefore.*

**SHAKESPEARE, THE COMEDY OF ERRORS**

As surely as the laws of physics define the parameters for air travel, fundamental principles govern contact centers. When these principles are misunderstood or ignored, the results are often low or volatile service levels and response times, inappropriate staffing, excessive costs and unhappy customers.

Six "immutable laws" are at work in any center that handles inbound customer contacts. (Reason: Many of these laws are driven by random call

## SIX IMMUTABLE LAWS AT WORK IN CONTACT CENTERS

1. For a given call load, when service level goes up, occupancy goes down.
2. Keep improving service level and you will reach a point of diminishing returns.
3. For a given service level, larger agent groups are more efficient than smaller groups.
4. All other things being equal, pooled groups are more efficient than specialized groups.
5. For a given call load, add staff and average speed of answer will go down.
6. For a given call load, add staff and trunk load will go down.

**199**

arrival — see Chapter 3.) They are immutable (unchangeable): They always have and always will be with us. Understanding them is key to cultivating an effective planning process, setting fair standards, preparing accurate budgets, and communicating contact center activities to upper management and others across the organization.

Note that throughout this chapter, I will primarily refer to inbound phone calls when covering these principles. But the underlying dynamics apply to all types of interactions — chat, social, SMS, walk-in customers, et al. — that arrive randomly and that must be handled as they occur.

## When Service Level Goes Up, Occupancy Goes Down

As discussed in Chapter 4, service level is expressed as "X percent of calls answered in Y seconds." Occupancy is the percent of time during a half hour that those agents who are on the phones (or available to handle other types of contacts) are actually handling contacts (e.g., in talk time and after-call work). The inverse of occupancy is the time that agents spend

| Avg. Talk Time: 180 sec; Avg. Work Time: 30 sec; Calls: 250 | | | | |
|---|---|---|---|---|
| Agents | SL%<br>in 20 Sec. | ASA | Occupancy | Trunk Load<br>(in hours) |
| 30 | 24% | 208.7 | 97% | 54.0 |
| 31 | 45% | 74.7 | 94% | 35.4 |
| 32 | 61% | 37.6 | 91% | 30.2 |
| 33 | 73% | 21.3 | 88% | 28.0 |
| 34 | 82% | 12.7 | 86% | 26.8 |
| 35 | 88% | 7.8 | 83% | 26.1 |
| 36 | 92% | 4.9 | 81% | 25.7 |
| 37 | 95% | 3.1 | 79% | 25.4 |
| 38 | 97% | 1.9 | 77% | 25.3 |
| 39 | 98% | 1.2 | 75% | 25.2 |
| 40 | 99% | 0.7 | 73% | 25.1 |
| 41 | 99% | 0.5 | 71% | 25.1 |
| 42 | 100% | 0.3 | 69% | 25.0 |

waiting for calls, plugged in and available.

As the table illustrates, a service level of 80 percent of calls answered in 20 seconds (82/20, to be precise) equates to occupancy of 86 percent (given that particular call load). If service level drops to 24 percent answered in 20 seconds, occupancy goes up to 97 percent.

The relationship between occupancy and service level is often misunderstood. The incorrect logic goes something like, "If agents really dig in, service level will go up and so will their occupancy." In reality, if occupancy is high, it is because agents are taking one call after another, with little or no wait in between. Calls are stacked up in queue and service level is low. In the worst scenario, occupancy is 100 percent because service level is so low that all callers spend at least some time in queue.

When service level gets better, occupancy goes down. Therefore, average calls taken per agent will also go down. That suggests that setting standards on number of contacts handled is inherently unfair, because agents can't directly control occupancy. Further, that would conflict with an important objective: Ensure that enough agents are available to handle calls so that

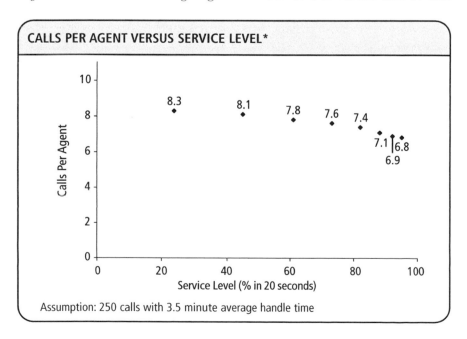

**CALLS PER AGENT VERSUS SERVICE LEVEL\***

Assumption: 250 calls with 3.5 minute average handle time

your service level objectives are achieved. (We will discuss individual performance standards in Chapter 14.)

Occupancy is driven by random call arrival and is heavily influenced by service level and group size (see the third immutable law). Managers don't exactly love this one — no one wants "unproductive" time baked into the process. However, the time that agents spend waiting for calls is sliced into 12 seconds here, two seconds there, and so on, a factor of how contacts are arriving.

In many centers, agents handle various non-phone or response-time-oriented work when the inbound call load slows down. In fact, blended environments (where agents move in and out of these types of work as circumstances dictate) make a lot of sense because no one has a perfect forecast all of the time, and schedules don't always perfectly match staff to the call load. But don't be misled. When other work is getting done, either: a) more agents are on the phones than the baseline staff necessary to handle the call load at service level, at that time; or b) the service level objective is sacrificed. In other words, don't try to force occupancy higher than what base staff calculations predict it should be.

## WHAT'S TOO HIGH?

As any agent knows, periods of high occupancy are stressful. Studies suggest that agents begin to burn out above around 90 percent occupancy if the condition lasts for an extended time, e.g., several half hours in a row (some have the threshold as low as 88 percent, others as high as 92 percent). Although most contact center managers agree, high occupancy tends to feed on itself. Taking breaks is a natural reaction, and compounds the problem.

As an example, consider this scenario. Jen, Ben and Mary are three of 32 agents plugged in and taking calls. Staffing calculations (see table above) predict that the average occupancy for the half hour for 32 agents will be 91 percent and service level will be just above 60 percent answered in 20 seconds.

Jen: *Whewww! It's call after call this morning. I need a breather! I don't have a scheduled break for a while, so I think I'll head to the water cooler and chill for a couple of minutes.*

OOPS. Now there are only 31 agents on the phone. If traffic keeps arriving at about the same clip, service level will drop and occupancy will go up, naturally.

Ben begins to ponder ... *Things sure are busy today, one call after another. And this customer sure is friendly. Wish everyone were this pleasant. I wonder what the weather is like where she is ...*

So Ben takes a little bit longer on the call, essentially taking a breather during talk time, service level drops another notch, and occupancy goes up more. Mary really begins to feel the load ...

Mary: *This call doesn't really require wrap-up, but ...*

This is the proverbial "vicious cycle." If things are chronically backed up, service level will consistently be low and occupancy will be high. The real fix, of course, goes to the fundamentals of managing a contact center — a good forecast, accurate staffing calculations and schedules that match people to the workload.

## OCCUPANCY VERSUS ADHERENCE TO SCHEDULE

Notice an important distinction that this law reveals. When adherence to schedule improves (goes up), occupancy goes down. Why? Because when agents are available to handle more calls, service level will go up. And when service level goes up, occupancy goes down. For agents, this means that if you work the schedule, you don't have to work as hard.

---

*When adherence to schedule improves (goes up), occupancy goes down.*

---

The terms adherence to schedule and occupancy are often incorrectly used interchangeably. They not only mean different things, they move in opposite directions. And as we will revisit at in Chapter 14, adherence to schedule is within the control of individuals, whereas the laws of nature outside of an individual's control determine occupancy.

## The Law of Diminishing Returns

Economists identified the law of diminishing returns many years ago as it applies to manufacturing environments, but it also can have significant impact on contact centers. It can be defined this way: When successive individual agents are assigned to a given call load, marginal improvements in service level that can be attributed to each additional agent will eventually decline.

The figure, Law of Diminishing Returns, is based on the data from the first table (based on Erlang C). It shows that 30 agents at the given call load will provide a service level of just over 23 percent in 20 seconds. Keep in mind, these numbers will not be exact — at that low of a service level, many of the calls may get cleared via busies and abandons, so Erlang C may exaggerate how bad things will be. But the exact results notwithstanding, service level will be poor.

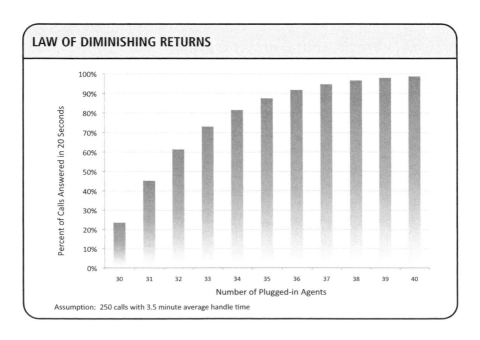

**LAW OF DIMINISHING RETURNS**

Assumption: 250 calls with 3.5 minute average handle time

With 31 agents, things improve dramatically. Service level jumps to 45 percent, a quantum improvement. Adding one more person yields another big improvement. In fact, adding only four or five people takes service level from the depths of poor service to something respectable. That means a commensurate drop in average speed of answer (ASA) and trunk load.

The same principle is true for larger groups, as the next table shows. Each person has a significant positive impact on the queue when service level is low, even in groups with hundreds of agents.

| Avg. Talk Time: 180 sec; Avg. Work Time: 30 sec; Calls: 1,000 in 1/2 hr. | | | | |
|---|---|---|---|---|
| Agents | SL% in 20 Sec. | ASA | Occupancy | Trunk Load (in hours) |
| 117 | 7% | 607 | 100% | 437.0 |
| 118 | 24% | 135 | 99% | 175.0 |
| 119 | 39% | 69 | 98% | 138.0 |
| 120 | 51% | 42 | 97% | 123.5 |
| 121 | 61% | 79 | 96% | 115.9 |
| 122 | 69% | 21 | 96% | 111.4 |
| 123 | 75% | 15 | 95% | 108.4 |
| 124 | 80% | 11 | 94% | 106.3 |
| 125 | 85% | 9 | 93% | 104.8 |
| 126 | 88% | 7 | 93% | 103.7 |
| 127 | 91% | 5 | 92% | 102.9 |
| 128 | 93% | 4 | 91% | 102.2 |
| 129 | 94% | 3 | 90% | 101.7 |
| 130 | 96% | 3 | 90% | 101.4 |
| 131 | 97% | 2 | 89% | 101.1 |
| 132 | 97% | 2 | 88% | 100.8 |
| 133 | 98% | 1 | 88% | 100.7 |

Contact center managers who struggle with a low service level will like this law because it often doesn't take many people to improve things dramatically. On the other hand, those who want to be the "best of the best" in terms of service level find that it takes a real commitment in the staffing budget. The relationship between varying levels of resources and service level should be demonstrated in the budgeting process.

Viewed from a different angle, if you have the right number of people handling contacts to begin with, but just a few of them unplug or go unavailable at an inopportune moment, things begin to back up. Think of what a stalled car blocking just one lane can quickly do to a busy expressway. This phenomenon has been referred to as "falling in the swamp."

## SWAMP-AVOIDANCE STRATEGIES

Here are some steps you can take to avoid this pitfall:

- Educate every agent on these principles and relay — directly, consistently and often — how important they are to the contact center's success. Each person matters! And what they do has an impact on customers, the organization and their peers (see sidebar, Understanding How Contact Centers Behave).
- Provide real-time queue information to agents. Readerboards from a variety of manufacturers provide current data on the queue, and most have color-coded information for easy interpretation or to make the point (red means "help!"). And information delivered to desktop and phone displays can provide detailed insight into the queue and how workloads are evolving. (Caution: Without the right education on interpretation, readerboards can send the wrong message, e.g., hurry! We'll discuss real-time management in Chapter 11 and boosting individual performance in Chapter 14.)
- Fix the basics, if necessary. If queues are predictably and consistently backed up, occupancy will be high and you will have to be sensitive to the need for more breaks, even though they add to the problem. The real fix is in improving the planning process and making an effective case for the necessary resources.

Ultimately, there is a fine line between a service level that's good for everybody (callers and agents alike) and one that snowballs out of control, zapping the productivity and fun out of the environment.

## UNDERSTANDING HOW CONTACT CENTERS BEHAVE

The central reality that shapes contact center operations is that they are dynamic in the truest sense. Because of the randomly arriving nature of customer contacts, each person has a huge impact on the organization's responsiveness. That, in turn, is an important enabler to delivering great customer experiences, boosting loyalty and contributing to successful business results.

A notable trend among the most effective contact centers is to educate their entire teams — agents, supervisors, managers and analysts, as well as colleagues from across their organizations — on contact center dynamics and the value they deliver when strong collaboration and cross-functional support is in place. ADP, American Express, USAA, Zappos, and FedEx are just a few examples of highly rated companies that have made this an ongoing priority.

Providing an understanding of how contact centers behave is a gift to those who work in or support them. It just makes good sense.

## SMALL IMPROVEMENTS, BIG RESULTS

From another perspective, the law of diminishing returns reveals why improvements to processes can yield such dramatic results. Some examples include:

- An insurance company, which upgraded its computer systems to improve response time, cut 9 seconds off average handling time. Service level went from 60 percent answered in 20 seconds to about 80 percent answered in 20 seconds during busy half hours.

- A consumer resource center for a manufacturing company improved call tracking in its database system, clarified codes and agent training on them, and assigned a small team to prepare reports for the quality assurance, marketing and consumer relations departments. While sales went up, call volume dropped by 7 percent, the result of improvements to products and better customer communication. Service level improved by 30 percent during busy half hours.

- A financial company added additional services to its existing IVR application and reduced traffic to its customer service group by around 5 percent. Service level improved by more than 15 percent during busy half hours. (Note: Improved service and access, while valuable for many reasons, doesn't always reduce the call load requiring agent assistance. We'll discuss this more in Chapter 16.)

## Larger Groups Are More Efficient

Average group productivity (contacts that a group handles) is not a constant factor. Instead, it's constantly fluctuating as the call load ebbs and flows. Even when you maintain a consistent service level through good planning and schedules, you'll find that average productivity is relatively lower at lower call volumes and relatively higher at higher call volumes. Since the number of calls is changing throughout the day, so is average group productivity.

Why? Mathematically, larger groups of agents are more efficient than smaller groups, at the same service level. Therefore, larger groups assigned to heavy mid-morning traffic will be more efficient than smaller groups handling the lighter evening load. So, calculating staff the wrong way — assuming fixed productivity at different call volumes — will be highly inaccurate (see table, The Impact of Group Size).

### THE IMPACT OF GROUP SIZE

| Calls In Half Hour | Service Level | Agents Required | Occupancy | Avg. Calls Per Agent |
|---|---|---|---|---|
| 50 | 80/20 | 9 | 65% | 5.6 |
| 100 | 80/20 | 15 | 78% | 6.7 |
| 500 | 80/20 | 65 | 90% | 7.7 |
| 1000 | 80/20 | 124 | 94% | 8.1 |

Assumption: Average Handle Time is 3.5 minutes

This is yet another reason why setting standards on the number of contacts that agents handle is an inherently unfair way to measure productivity. Attempting to compare groups or sites in a distributed environment may also be misleading (the exception would be a network that finds the longest-waiting agent, regardless of location).

Despite mathematical efficiencies, there is a point where groups become large enough that occupancy becomes too high for agents. Some managers believe that the number of agents in a single group should be limited to 125 to 150 people. However, there are plenty of centers that have much larger agent groups (the U.S. Social Security Administration, Centrelink Australia, Indian Railways, United Airlines, China Mobile and others can have hundreds or even thousands of agents in a single agent group).

A better approach than establishing a strict limit to group size is to watch occupancy and take appropriate measures when it climbs above 90 percent. For example, in the scenario on page 205, scheduling 129 plugged-in agents is recommended, even though the required service level may be exceeded.

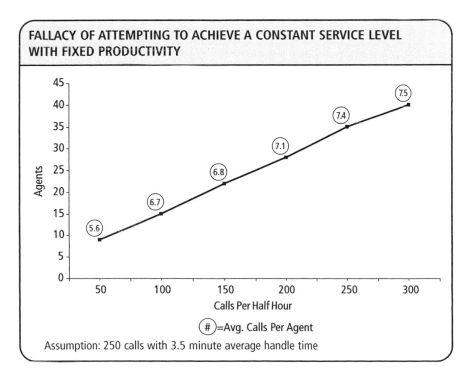

**FALLACY OF ATTEMPTING TO ACHIEVE A CONSTANT SERVICE LEVEL WITH FIXED PRODUCTIVITY**

(#)=Avg. Calls Per Agent

Assumption: 250 calls with 3.5 minute average handle time

Callers sure won't mind, and your staff will have a fighting chance at being able to function proficiently throughout their shift.

## The Powerful Pooling Principle

The powerful pooling principle is a mathematical fact based on the laws of probability and is well rooted in telecommunications engineering practice. It states: Any movement in the direction of consolidation of resources will result in improved traffic-carrying efficiency. Conversely, any movement away from consolidation of resources will result in reduced traffic-carrying efficiency. Put more simply, if you take several small, specialized agent groups, effectively cross-train them and put them into a single group, you'll have a more efficient environment.

> **THE POWERFUL POOLING PRINCIPLE**
>
> - Handle more contacts, at the same service level, with the same number of agents
> - Handle the same number of contacts, at the same service level, with fewer agents
> - Handle the same number of contacts, at a better service level, with the same number of agents

Note, again, the table on page 208, which compares service level to group size. Fifteen agents are required to provide a service level of 80/20. But only 124 agents are necessary to handle a load 10 times as large (not 150 agents, or 10 x 15).

The pooling principle should be a consideration from the highest levels of strategic planning (How many centers should you have? How should agent groups be designed?), down to more tactical decisions related to real-time adjustments or how to best invest training time and resources.

In one sense, pooling resources is at the heart of what ACDs and networks do. In fact, when ACDs first came into the market in the early 1970s, the big challenge was to get users to abandon the "clientele" approach.

A clear trend in recent years, though, is the recognition that different customers often have different needs and expectations, and that different agents with a mix of aptitudes and skills are required. Powerful capabilities, such as skills-based routing, give us the means to handle contacts based on a myriad of criteria (see Chapter 7).

Can we have specialization without foregoing the benefits of the powerful pooling principle? It depends. Skills-based routing can boost efficiency by getting calls to the agents best able to handle them. But when not managed well, when overused, the number of contingencies can multiply beyond the center's ability to understand and manage them. The interplay can become stupefying. And the whole notion of agent groups and traditional call center organization begins to erode.

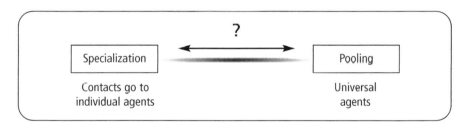

As real and pervasive as the pooling principle is, it is not an all-or-nothing proposition. There is a continuum between pooling and specialization — think of a variable rheostat rather than an on-off switch. Your objective should be to get as close to the pooled end of the spectrum as circumstances allow. Examples of supporting steps would include hiring multilingual agents, integrating new channels, such as social or chat, into existing agent groups where feasible, and improving information systems so that agents are equipped to handle as broad a range of contacts as possible.

## Add Staff, and ASA Goes Down

Anyone who has ever waited in line knows that if there were a few more tollbooths or a few more people behind the counter, the line wouldn't be so long! And when someone behind the counter gets reassigned to another matter, or goes on break, the wait increases (this happens anytime I enter a line — it's a cosmic joke on any of us who study queues).

The same principle is at work in contact centers. When more agents are plugged in and handling calls, assuming they are proficient and equipped to do so, the queue will be shorter. Fewer agents means a longer queue. This principle leads to the next immutable law.

## Add Staff, and Trunk Load Goes Down

When more agents are assigned to a given call load, trunk load (the load on the telecommunications network) goes down. The converse is also true: When fewer agents are available to handle a given call load, trunk load goes up because delay increases (see discussion on trunks, Chapter 7).

Each customer connected to your system is part of call load, whether they are talking to an agent or waiting in queue. If you have toll-free service (or any other service that charges a usage fee), you are paying for this time. Telecommunications costs are inextricably wrapped in staffing issues. If service level is continually low, the costs of network services will escalate.

See the following table for another scenario that illustrates the inherent tradeoffs between staffing levels and service level, average speed of answer,

| | Avg. Talk Time: 180 sec; Avg. Work Time: 30 sec; Calls: 350 in half hour | | | |
|---|---|---|---|---|
| **Agents** | **SL% in 20 Sec.** | **ASA (in sec.)** | **Occupancy** | **Trunk Load (Erlangs)** |
| 42 | 29% | 144 | 97% | 62.9 |
| 43 | 47% | 63 | 95% | 47.3 |
| 44 | 61% | 35 | 93% | 41.8 |
| 45 | 72% | 21 | 91% | 39.1 |
| 46 | 80% | 13 | 89% | 37.6 |
| 47 | 86% | 9 | 87% | 36.7 |
| 48 | 90% | 6 | 85% | 36.1 |
| 49 | 93% | 4 | 83% | 35.8 |
| 50 | 95% | 3 | 82% | 35.5 |
| 51 | 97% | 2 | 80% | 35.3 |
| 52 | 98% | 1 | 79% | 35.2 |

occupancy and trunk load. Recall from Chapter 7 that trunk load represents how much time in hours callers are queued up for and/or talking to agents in this group over the equivalent of an hour. Staff is calculated for a half hour's traffic, but the trunk load is converted to an hour's traffic simply because telecom managers almost universally use hour increments for engineering and management purposes.

## UNDERSTANDING TRUNK LOAD

Let's run through a trunk load calculation, just to see where these numbers come from (not to worry; it doesn't take long, and you only have to do it once to get the gist). Using the scenario in the preceding table, assume that you will have 46 agents handling calls and, therefore, will be able to achieve a service level of 80/20. Here's how the calculations produced an estimated 37.6 hours on the trunks:

- First, you can see that calls will be queued for agents an average of 13 seconds (ASA) and will be connected to agents an average of 180 seconds (average talk time), for a total of 193 seconds. The 180 seconds represents the forecast for what average talk time will likely be; the 13 seconds ASA comes from the Erlang C calculation.

- Since the table provides call volume for a half hour, multiply 350 calls by 2 to assume 700 calls in an hour.

- Since the assumed 700 calls spend an average 193 seconds queuing for and connected to agents, the trunk load in seconds is 135,100 seconds (700 calls x 193 seconds).

- Finally, since trunk load is customarily presented in erlangs — hours of traffic over the course of an hour — divide 135,100 by 3,600 (the number of seconds in an hour) and you come up with 37.6 hours, just as the output provides. To use the correct telecom lingo, you'll have the equivalent of 37.6 erlangs of traffic on the trunks for this agent group during this time period. (Note: This example does not add the time calls may spend in the IVR before arriving at the agent group.)

The big variable is average speed of answer (average delay) before calls get connected. It goes up (gets worse) with fewer agents, and goes down (gets better) with more agents. Glance through the table, and you'll see that if 50 agents are handling calls, ASA will be a projected 3 seconds. If 42 agents are handling calls, ASA will be a projected 144 seconds. In short, the number of staff you have in place determines the average delay, which is a key variable in trunk load and, therefore, in what you pay for toll-free services.

## THE IMPACT OF STAFF ON TOLL-FREE COSTS

As you can see in the following figure, telecommunications costs are inextricably wrapped up in staffing issues. All things equal, scrimping on staffing levels results in higher costs on the network. Of course, there may also be other considerations — busies and abandons (likely at low service levels), and answer delay (whereby the ACD doesn't immediately return "answer supervision" to the long-distance carrier) may lower toll-free costs. And as the telecommunications world transitions to VoIP, contracts are

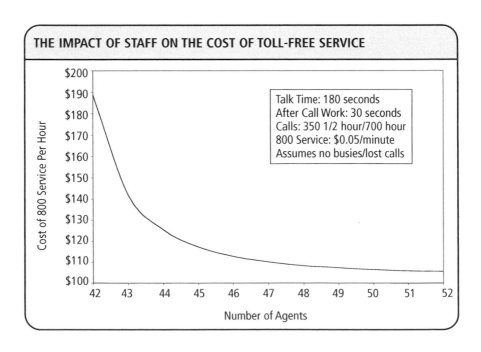

**THE IMPACT OF STAFF ON THE COST OF TOLL-FREE SERVICE**

Talk Time: 180 seconds
After Call Work: 30 seconds
Calls: 350 1/2 hour/700 hour
800 Service: $0.05/minute
Assumes no busies/lost calls

becoming less time- and distance-sensitive. Nonetheless, the tradeoff between staff and network costs is direct and predictable.

As you decide on service levels and how to allocate budgets, you should think about network costs, too. All other things being equal, if your service level is low, adding an agent will often bring total costs down because network costs drop dramatically.

Managers who see these numbers often want to calculate the point where staffing and network costs are optimized. Just remember, that's not necessarily the place to set your service level objective, as service level should also consider caller needs and expectations. Assuming your network costs are low, you'll likely need to provide better service levels than this tradeoff in isolation would indicate.

The staff versus toll free costs tradeoff used to be much more dramatic. In many parts of the world, toll-free costs are just pennies a minute. In the days when toll-free service was 15 cents, 25 cents and higher, improving service level meant huge drops in network costs, often producing savings that far surpassed the cost of adding staff. With today's lower network costs, the tradeoff is much less significant.

However, don't lose the value of the exercise. You're still likely to have expenses related to circuits, ports, IVR capacity, maintenance, taxes, etc. (One easy way to estimate your actual cost per minute is to divide total monthly network services charges by the number of minutes carried.)

Delay takes resources and it is not free. Assessing the impact on network costs underscores the importance of considering both agent and network costs together. Improving service level will save at least some money on network services; these savings should be factored into predictions of overall costs.

## THE COST OF DELAY

The direct expense of putting callers in queue is called the "cost of delay." It is expressed in terms of how much you pay for toll-free service each day (or month, hour, or half hour) just for callers to wait in queue until they reach an agent.

You may want to plot the cost of delay. It's simple. First, take the total delay for the day, as reported by your ACD, and convert that into minutes or hours. Next, multiply the minutes or hours of delay by the average per-minute or per-hour cost of your toll-free service. Then add that figure to a graph that illustrates these costs (see example).

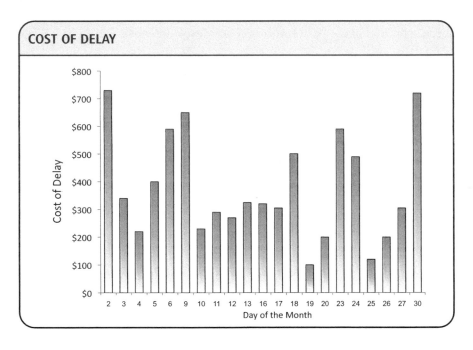

The cost of delay graph will be a reminder that poor service is not cheap. And it will catch the interest of senior managers, who will look at the graph and wonder aloud, "You mean that's what we're paying just for callers to wait? Why, we could use that money for ..."

# Points to Remember

- There are immutable laws at work in any center that handles inbound contacts.
- A common theme runs through these laws: Do a good job of matching staff with the workload or bad things will happen.
- The impetus doesn't fall solely on those who do the planning and scheduling. Designing and managing a contact center requires a big-picture perspective and the collaborative effort of all involved.
- A good understanding of these immutable laws is a prerequisite to developing an accurate planning process, setting fair objectives and standards, developing a good strategy and just about every other aspect of effective management.
- It's important that agents, senior-level managers and others who work in or support the contact center are aware of these principles.

# CHAPTER 10:
# Communicating with Senior Management

*Talk low, talk slow and don't say too much.*

**JOHN WAYNE**

Contact center managers have the responsibility of succinctly, but adequately, conveying budgetary requirements, activities and contributions to senior management. And that can be quite a balancing act! There's a whole heck of a lot going on in most contact centers, and simplified budgetary requests and summary reports can gloss over important details. Complex budgets and reports filled with pages of numbers may provide more information, but senior managers may not have the time or the expertise to read and make sense of them.

In short, conveying information and requirements effectively — cutting through the clutter of busyness — is critical to success. And just as important as the information itself is establishing good lines of communication and an understanding of how contact centers operate and how they support the organization's mission.

In this chapter, we will review the essential processes of budgeting and reporting. And we'll (hopefully!) help you find a good balance in producing and communicating critical information.

# What Senior-Level Managers Should Know About Contact Centers

To fulfill their potential, customer contact centers need commitment and involvement from the top. A prerequisite to getting necessary support is that senior-level managers understand the unique contact center environment — what they do and how they operate. Here's a list of 10 "must knows" I believe make a good starting place for taking stock of your own team's awareness; I encourage you to take inventory and look for ways to boost the understanding of them from top to bottom:

1.   **CONTACT CENTERS ARE INCREASINGLY IMPORTANT TO THE ORGANIZATION'S SUCCESS.** They are strategic assets, not clerical/administrative/backroom operations. They are hubs of communication, and vital to understanding and serving diverse customers, capturing marketplace intelligence and harnessing the voice of the customer to improve products and services.

2.   **CALLS "BUNCH UP."** In any center that handles at least some inbound work, the workflow dynamics are unique (see Chapter 3). Customers decide when and how they will contact the organization, and the resulting work will not arrive in a nice, even flow. Staffing and productivity issues must be considered in that context (Chapters 7 and 14).

3.   **THERE'S GENERALLY NO INDUSTRY STANDARD FOR ACCESSIBILITY.** No single service level or response time objective makes sense for every contact center. Different organizations will have different costs, customers and brand objectives. However, there are objectives that will make sense for your organization, ones that fit your customers' needs and your organization's brand (Chapter 4).

4.   **THERE'S A DIRECT LINK BETWEEEN RESOURCES AND RESULTS.** You may need 36 people handling contacts to achieve a service level of 90 percent answer in 20 seconds, given your customer workload. If you have only 25 people and are told to hit 90/20, that's not going to work. And "staffing on the cheap" is expensive, leading to high agent occupancy,

220

burnout and turnover, unhappy customers, poor word of mouth, and other direct and indirect costs (Chapters 7, 9 and 13).

5. **WHEN SERVICE LEVEL IMPROVES, "PRODUCTIVITY" DECLINES.** Productivity is often measured as calls handled or occupancy. (This is a perspective we question and hope to help change, in Chapter 14). As discussed in Chapter 9, when service level goes up, occupancy goes down, as does the average number of contacts handled per agent. Translation: In any center that is achieving a good service level, some agents will be waiting idle some of the time, given random call arrival (Chapter 9).

6. **YOU WILL NEED TO SCHEDULE MORE STAFF THAN BASE STAFF REQUIRED.** Schedules should realistically reflect the many things that can keep agents from handling contacts, such as training, breaks, holidays, collateral work and other diversions (see Chapter 8). In many organizations, these factors are becoming more prevalent as the increasingly complex environment requires more training and research/development time.

7. **SUMMARY REPORTS DON'T GIVE AN ACCURATE PICTURE OF WHAT'S REALLY HAPPENING.** Reports that average activity may suggest that performance is just fine, yet they may be concealing serious problem areas. Those producing and interpreting data must know what they're really looking at (see Chapters 4 and 12, and this chapter).

8. **QUALITY AND SERVICE LEVEL WORK TOGETHER.** Though they are sometimes presented as tradeoffs, service level is a prerequisite to getting contacts in and done. And better quality is the key to a better service level, by upping first-call resolution, reducing repeat contacts and picking up intelligence ("knowledge") that helps improve processes, products and services across the organization (Chapters 12, 13).

9. **CONTACT CENTERS ARE BECOMING MORE COMPLEX.** Traditional transaction-oriented centers have evolved into more dynamic and holistic operations that contribute to and require the support of departments across the organization. Social media, multimedia, multi-gen-

221

**SIDE-BY-SIDE WITH SENIOR MANAGEMENT AT BT GLOBAL**

Senior managers at many companies find out what's happening in their contact centers through memos, reports and meetings. BT Americas (now part of BT Global) established an approach that enables execs to also get the lowdown directly — through one of its center's headsets. Each year, over the course of two weeks, dozens of senior managers for the communications solutions provider travel to the company's Regional Center of Excellence in Atlanta to spend an entire day listening in on customer calls with an agent and, importantly, identify at least one critical customer issue that they must later help to resolve.

"It demonstrates BT's senior management commitment both to our customers and to our representatives," says Thom Ray, vice president of service operations for BT Americas. "It provides senior managers across BT — regardless of what specific organization they are in — the opportunity to spend an entire shift with a customer-facing person, and to listen, learn and proactively support the individual [agent with whom they are seated]." Since launching this initiative in the Atlanta center, BT has implemented numerous improvements, ranging from better workflows to enhanced customer information on agents' desktops and more dynamic call-routing processes.

erational customers, economic pressures and other trends are upping the ante (see Chapters 2 and 13).

**10. TO FULLFILL THEIR POTENTIAL, CONTACT CENTERS NEED SUPPORT FROM THE TOP.** They need commitment and involvement from senior management to ensure that they get the support and resources they need, and in turn, that they deliver the strategic value they can and must.

I am convinced that the only way to really understand the unique customer contact environment is to spend some time in it. These are issues you'll need to continually reinforce — but they tend to come to life when experienced first hand. Senior-level executives who have made the effort to understand contact center issues and processes invariably come away with better insight into evolving customer requirements and interdependencies across the larger organization.

# Principles of Effective Budgeting

Ensuring that you're getting necessary resources is an important part of enabling the contact center's strategic potential. That, of course, requires an effective budget — and a clear understanding of what the returns on those investments should be.

A budget is simply a summary of proposed or agreed-upon expenditures for a given period of time, for specified purposes. Sounds tame enough. But the process of putting a budget together is often seen as tedious, time-consuming and, some say, distracting from "more important management responsibilities." Don't forget, however, the outcome of this much-maligned process: the funding the contact center will have to accomplish its mission and potential.

Here are the essential principles we've uncovered in analyzing and working with contact centers that consistently get the right amount of funding, at the right times, for the right things:

**VIEW THE BUDGET AS MUCH MORE THAN A DOCUMENT.** Those who picture rows and columns of line items and figures when they think "budget" are missing the point. It's really a communication process that presents a larger opportunity to learn about the business and make a case that's a win for everyone (employees, customers and the business). I've seen managers spend many hours — make that many days — putting the details together, only to have their priorities swept away or diluted in a matter of minutes in the CFO's office. I've also seen powerful (and positive) budgetary agreements happen over lunch, literally on the back of a napkin. Remember, it's the effectiveness of your case, not the detail of your analysis, that matters most.

When you see the budget as an ongoing dialog, and not just a document, you spend more of your time and talent on opening channels of communication, educating decision makers and highlighting key priorities and tradeoffs. In short, you focus on ensuring that the effort in its totality creates the right results.

**ANSWER THE BIG QUESTION — WHY?** Why are we spending this money? Why does the contact center exist? Why are we spending more (or less) than last year? These answers must form the backdrop of the budgetary process. They are sometimes addressed in the communication that takes place during the process, and also may be summarized in budgetary documents. Regardless, those who are involved in preparing and approving the budget need a common understanding of the value the center contributes to the organization.

**REMEMBER TO FOCUS ON RESULTS.** Handling 2.2 million calls, achieving 90 percent first-call resolution, or hitting service level targets are not the results decision makers are looking for. They are only means to an end. As your center's objectives and focus mature from handling transactions efficiently to delivering great customer experiences, you will have a greater impact on business results — revenues, profitability, market share, word of mouth and others (see figure). Illustrating this connection focuses budgetary discussion on the things that matter most (see Chapters 12 and 13).

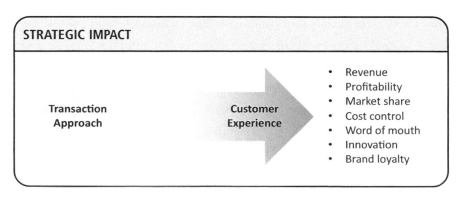

BASE THE BUDGET ON A CLEAR STRATEGY. A prerequisite to a successful budgeting process is agreement on the contact center's direction and priorities. Your customer access strategy is the framework that defines how customers will interact with your organization (see Chapter 2). By defining who your customers are, when and how they desire to reach you, the means by which you will identify, route, handle and track those contacts, and how you will leverage the information that comes from them, the customer access strategy is the de facto blueprint for the budget. Without this foundation, budgetary decisions are likely to head off in many unrelated directions and may be at odds with your organization's larger objectives.

**ENSURE THAT BUDGETING IS AN EXTENSION OF RESOURCE PLANNING.** In well-run contact centers, forecasting, staffing, scheduling and cost analysis are ongoing responsibilities. These activities should take much of the work out of the budget process, because the budget should ultimately be based on the same workload predictions.

---

*Forecasting, staffing, scheduling and cost analysis are ongoing responsibilities. These activities should take much of the work out of the budget process, because the budget should ultimately be based on the same workload predictions.*

---

There's an important principle at work here. Objectives should drive the budget, not the other way around. If your budget is based on precedent (last year's numbers), arbitrary decisions, or anything other than the objectives identified in your customer access strategy and workload predictions, you are at a disadvantage from the get-go. (You're not alone, by the way!) If that's the case, you've got a great opportunity to reshape assumptions (see figures The Right Way ... and The Wrong Way ...).

**IDENTIFY KEY TRADEOFFS.** What happens if the forecast is high? Low? What happens if you provide better levels of service? Lower levels of service? How much would you save/spend if ...? Once the budget for expected workload is established, along with recommended resources, it is

---

**THE RIGHT WAY: KEY OBJECTIVES DRIVE THE BUDGET**

- Choose service level and response time objectives
- Forecast call load (contacts)

- Calculate base staff
- Calculate system resources

- Calculate schedule shrinkage
- Organize schedules

- Calculate costs; compare to alternative service levels
- Finalize budgets

--->

---

**THE WRONG WAY: THE BUDGET DRIVES KEY OBJECTIVES**

- Determine budget

- Estimate feasible schedules and probable schedule shrinkage

- Determine staff and system capacities

- Estimate feasible service levels based on available resources

--->

---

fairly straightforward to rerun scenarios for both different workload assumptions and alternative service levels. These illustrations will contribute to good budgeting decisions and will improve the understanding others have of contact center dynamics.

**LOOK FOR OPPORTUNITIES TO MAXIMIZE CROSS-FUNCTIONAL RESOURCES.** Often, an organization's overall results can be improved by investing more in one area, to the benefit of others. Rather than focus on expenditures in a departmental vacuum, effective budgetary-thinking maximizes cross-functional resources.

For example, marketing managers might be willing to provide the contact center with budget to capture and analyze information on consumer trends and expectations, because they can save substantial money on target marketing. Legal departments are increasingly helping the center make the case for investments that will improve tracking and consistency in customer contacts. And product development budgets may be directed, in part, to the contact center for improved analysis on customer suggestions and input. These possibilities become evident to the degree that relationships exist and collaboration is in place among functional areas.

**HIGHLIGHT INVESTMENT OPPORTUNITIES.** As with many organizations in general, most contact centers are consistently searching for ways to do more with less. But there's also a place for making some high-leverage investments in sensible areas, including:

- Planning and process improvements
- Selective technology investments
- Management-level education
- Cross-sell and upsell programs
- Focused agent and supervisor coaching initiatives
- Research and development

The key is selection — to focus on those areas that are most likely to yield a high return on investment.

**PRESENT THE BUDGET FORMALLY.** This recommendation may seem odd, given the emphasis on collaboration and communication. But a formal presentation can be an important part of the process. For example, it can be the catalyst for getting all decision makers together at one time. (How many times did you answer the same questions for different people last year?) All in attendance will hear the questions and comments of the others, saving time and raising the general level of understanding more quickly. And you will be duly motivated to "have your ducks in a row."

**KEEP THE PRESENTATION SHORT AND UNCLUTTERED.** Use graphs and illustrations where possible. Provide backup material as necessary, such as actual system reports (but only as backup and not as a part of the main presentation). And sprinkle the conversation with real examples; for instance, "Sarah Johnson, a small-business owner in Seattle and a four-year customer, was one of the 4,200,000 contacts we handled last year. She called us because she was concerned that ..." Examples bring realities to life. And service tradeoffs become much more relevant when Sarah Johnson and the customers who made the 4,199,999 other contacts are at stake.

227

**ANTICIPATE AND PREPARE FOR THE "USUAL QUESTIONS."**
They have come up a jillion (give or take) times before, and they will come
up many more times in the future:

- What did we spend on the center in total last year?
- Did it accomplish what it intended to?
- What was our ROI on these investments?
- What's the contact per customer ratio? Sales per customer?
- Are new channels (e.g., social or self-service) changing the workload
  for agents? (Reducing? Increasing? Altering?)
- What's our cost per contact? Is it going down or up?
- What are you doing to reduce unnecessary contacts?
- Can we use the resources we have now to handle the expected work-
  load?

There are probably others, and you probably know what they will be in
your situation. Be ready. They are opportunities to shine. Some may be relevant, some may be less important — but having a competent grasp of the
facts will provide you with credibility throughout the process.

**ENSURE THE BUDGETING PROCESS IS HONEST AND RESPON-
SIBLE.** You should be realistic and candid about the recent past and
whether or not the contact center has been meeting its objectives. The
budget must put that in context with customer and agent satisfaction, and
with the objectives and funding being proposed. It must support the mission of the organization and dovetail with the roles and requirements of
other areas. And it must be transparent about opportunities and challenges.

Yes, effective budgeting requires some number crunching and analysis.
But above all, it requires a clear direction, good communication and a solid
understanding of the contact center's needs and strategic contributions.
This is a process that will bring your leadership, communication skills, cultural savvy and professional expertise to bear. Don't treat it as a once-a-year
event. It should be part of a continuous effort. Revisit it often and, as with
other aspects of planning, make adjustments as necessary.

## GROWTH OR CONTRACTION — PLAN ACCORDINGLY

Increasing workloads remains one of the biggest challenges facing many customer contact centers. Yes, even with the growth of social communities and self-service capabilities, many centers continue to grow. (Why? Remember that Econ 101 principle of elasticity? When you improve service, customers will use more of it!) Senior-level management will understandably need to know why these services represent a greater percentage of the organization's expenses (if they do), and where the money is going.

FRANK & ERNEST by ® Bob Thaves

Reprinted with permission.

An important principle in managing growth is to do an analysis of the likely impact of growth in advance. The objective is to avoid surprises so you aren't going into the budget process "behind the power curve."

Accurate growth projections often take the form of a document that illustrates projected costs and time frames, such as 5 percent growth in call load, 10 percent growth, 20 percent growth, and so on (up to at least double the current size if you're growing quickly). Your analysis should consider each major contact center component and answer important questions like these: When will you need additional ACD capacity (if you're structured that way, versus hosted service, for example)? More IVR ports? More space? Additional supervisors or analysts? What is the ideal lead time for each increment of growth? How long does it take to recruit, hire and train agents?

**229**

Contraction is also a planning challenge. Even as many grapple with growth, long-established centers in some vertical sectors have contracted or closed. For example, hotels and airlines have successfully encouraged a large portion of customers to use self-service systems for inquiries, bookings, check-in and upgrades. In these cases, plans and budgets must anticipate how contact centers can be scaled down as workload drops. React too slowly, and expensive and unnecessary resources drive up costs. Cut too quickly, and service will be poor.

Because the document is a projection, it won't precisely predict required resources. It's not a budget *per se*. But it will illustrate required lead times and key decision points necessary to align resources with workload. The idea is to avoid costly surprises.

## Getting Staffing Budgets Right

For many contact centers, staffing makes up between 65 and 75 percent of the budget. These figures can vary greatly depending on salaries, technology investments, cost differences by region, and other factors. But it's safe to conclude, this one slice of the budgetary pie usually trumps all other costs combined. Getting it right is a make-or-break factor in the center's efficiency and effectiveness.

Let's take a look at the basics of longer-term staff planning. As discussed in Chapter 8, effective scheduling depends on both longer-term budgets and short-term execution. You'll need a big enough bucket of resources to work with — in other words, the right number of staff on payroll (or through contracts) to put schedules together that match workload requirements. You'll also need to manage schedule adherence, a subject we'll discuss in Chapter 14.

A long-term staffing plan (sometimes called budgetary staffing plan) generally represents staffing requirements at a monthly level for the next 12 months. The goal is to accurately predict the paid hours required to handle the workload at your target service level and response time objec-

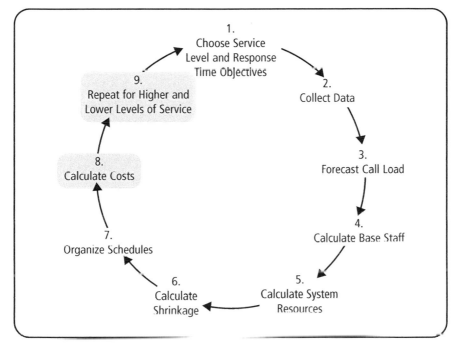

tives. The best long-term plans are set up so that they are easily adjusted and clearly demonstrate the "whys" behind budget requirements.

Projections should be based on your workload forecast and required staff, accounting for "availability factors" that keep agents from handling the work. Staff availability can be grouped into three categories:

**PRESENCE.** Is the agent working today (i.e., is he or she in the building or connected remotely)?

**UTILIZATION.** Is the agent scheduled to handle customer contacts?

**RANDOM.** Is the agent actually handling a contact?

Let's walk through a staffing example that accounts for each of these categories and leads to the number of full-time equivalents (FTEs) required to handle the workload. Here, we'll look at just 1 month, but you'll normally be projecting out for 12 months or more.

Note that throughout the example, rounding variations can produce slightly different totals and results. Also note, we'll consider two common types of work: calls and email. You can adjust the model so that it incorporates the channels you handle. (This example is provided by ICMI's consulting division.)

## BEGIN WITH WORKLOAD

The workload forecast is the primary driver of staffing needs. Workload includes the projected volume of contacts multiplied by average handling time; the result is then converted into staff hours required. Let's say your July projections for inbound and related outbound calls are as follows (we'll factor in email later):

---

### JULY WORKLOAD — CALL LOAD

| Item | Projection | Rationale |
|------|-----------|-----------|
| Call volume | 89,857 | Based on forecasts |
| AHT (sec.) | 210 | Based on forecasts. Typical since last system upgrade. |
| Workload (hours) | 5,242 | Calculation: (volume x AHT) ÷ 3,600 (sec. in an hour) |

---

So, you will have a projected 5,242 hours of workload to handle in July. (If you're remembering from Chapter 6 that average handling time often varies increment by increment — you're right. This estimate is a broad brushstroke used for longer-term staffing calculations and is based on the number you're most likely to see on average over the month. It's okay to use it this way for longer-term budgeting purposes — just don't try to base half-hour-by-half-hour staffing calculations and schedule requirements on an average!)

## IDENTIFY AVAILABILITY FACTORS

Next, you'll calculate agent availability factors, beginning with presence. The typical variables that will keep agents from working include vacations, absenteeism, leave of absence, disability, and holidays. They might be as follows for the month of July:

## AVAILABILITY: PRESENCE

| Item | Projection | | Rationale | Percent of paid time calculation |
| | In units at left | As % of paid time | | |
| --- | --- | --- | --- | --- |
| Holidays (days per agent for the month) | 1.00 | 4.35% | As per holiday calendar | 1 ÷ 23 (number of paid days in the month) |
| Disability (days per agent for the month) | 1.20 | 5.22% | Based on past history for this month | 1.20 ÷ 23 |
| Vacation (days per agent for the month) | 1.60 | 6.96% | Based on past history and vacation policy | 1.60 ÷ 23 |
| Total absence | 3.80 | 16.52% | Sum of presence factors. Presence will be 83.48% (100% - 16.52%) | 3.80 ÷ 23 |

According to the calculations, you'll lose an estimated 16.52 percent of paid hours to these factors. Agents will be at work 83.48 percent of paid hours (100% - 16.52%), or 33.39 hours out of the 40-hour workweek.

Next, you will project utilization, which includes all of the things that keep your agents from handling contacts even though they are at work — e.g., breaks, meetings, training and various projects. These variables are illustrated in the table that follows.

Note that lunch is missing from the list. Since it is not paid time, it is not included in this model. Also, the factor used for breaks is adjusted for presence (you shouldn't count breaks for agents not at work).

Consequently, if agents are not at work 16.52 percent of the time (meaning they are at work 83.48 percent of the time), then the factor would be 30 minutes (time on breaks) divided by 480 minutes (minutes in day), multiplied by 83.48 percent; the result is 5.22 percent and not the usual 6.25 percent many managers associate with breaks. Conversely, training and

## AVAILABILITY: UTILIZATION

| Item | Projection In units at left | As % of paid time | Rationale | Percent of paid time calculation |
|---|---|---|---|---|
| Breaks (minutes per day) | 30.00 | 5.22% | Per work rules | (30 minutes ÷ 480 paid minutes per day) x presence factor of 83.48% |
| Meetings (hours per month) | 3.00 | 1.36% | Three one-hour meetings per month | 3 ÷ 184 (number of paid hours in the month) x presence factor of 83.48% |
| Training (hours per month) | 2.50 | 1.36% | Required for new application training | 2.5 ÷ 184 |
| Coaching (hours per month) | 2.00 | 1.09% | Two one-hour coaching sessions per month | 2 ÷ 184 |
| Committee (hours per month) | 2.00 | 0.91% | As requested by VP of Customer Service | (2 ÷ 184) x presence factor of 83.48% |
| Total non-phone utilization (hours per week) | 3.97 | 9.93% | Out of a 40-hour week, an agent will be utilized for non-phone tasks an average 3.97 hours (40 x .0993) | The sum of all utilization categories |

coaching percentages are not adjusted by the presence factor because these activities will be rescheduled when missed due to absence.

So, you're down another 9.93 percent in total payroll hours to account for variables that keep agents off the phones. Added together, presence and utilization factors total 26.45 percent. Put another way, your projections show that agents will be scheduled to handle contacts 73.55 percent of the time (100% - 26.45%).

But you're not there yet. There's a third category of factors, which can be termed random, that also need to be included. Don't let the term trip you up — schedule adherence isn't random from a mathematical sense like random call arrival. You can, for example, cause a positive impact on schedule adherence (see Chapter 14). But while you can accurately predict the total amount of time that will go to these factors, they are random because you cannot predict the minute-to-minute impact. This inability to control the timing of these events is what separates them from activities like breaks, meetings and training.

| | Projection | | | |
|---|---|---|---|---|
| **AVAILABILITY: RANDOM FACTORS** | | | | |
| Item | In units at left | As % of paid time | Rationale | Percent of paid time calculation |
| Adjustment for adherence (90% of scheduled time on phones) | 10% | 7.36% | As per objectives and past history | 10% x scheduled rate of 73.55% |
| Adjustment for occupancy (85% of time in talk and after-call work) | 15% | 9.93% | 85% occupancy is from Erlang C calculations based on volume, handle time and service level objectives | 15% x manned percent of 66.20% |
| Total random | 6.91 | 17.29% | Out of a 40-hour week, agents will lose an average 6.91 hours to random factors | The sum of all random categories |

In the example, you will subtract adherence time from your scheduled rate of 73.55 percent because, again, you do not want to double-count time for agents not on the phones (or handling other types of contacts). Following this logic, you'll also need to remove adherence time from scheduled time when calculating occupancy so that you do not include hours lost to schedule adherence in the occupancy rate.

The expected occupancy rate is determined by running enough Erlang C calculations (based on expected volume, average handling time and service level scenarios) that you feel comfortable you've identified a "typical" occupancy rate. (Yes, if you're recalling from Chapters 7 and 9 that occupancy varies increment by increment, you're right. As with average handling time, this estimate is a broad brushstroke used for longer-term staffing calculations and is based on the number you're most likely to see over the month.)

---

**AVAILABILITY SUMMARY**

| Item | As % of Paid Time | Meaning |
|------|-------------------|---------|
| Presence factors | 16.52% | 6.61 hours per FTE per week (40 x .1652) |
| Utilization factors | 9.93% | 3.97 hours per FTE per week (40 x .0993) |
| Random factors | 17.29% | 6.92 hours per FTE per week (40 x .1729) |
| Total non-availability | 43.74% | 17.50 hours per FTE per week (40 x .4374) |
| Design factor | 56.26% | 22.50 hours per FTE per week spent handling contacts: (100% - 43.74%) x 40 |
| Rostered staff factor | 1.78 | Need 1.78 FTEs for every 40 hours of workload per week (100 ÷ 56.26) |

---

You have now identified all of the factors keeping your agents from handling the workload. Next, you can convert that into a rostered staff factor, as illustrated.

All of the factors keeping your agents from handling the workload total 43.74 percent. Consequently, agents are projected to spend 56.26 percent of their time (100% - 43.74%) actually handling contacts. This is converted into a longer-term rostered staff factor of 1.78, which is the ratio of staff needed on schedule divided by staff needed to handle the workload (100 ÷ 56.26).

**CONVERT TO FULL-TIME EQUIVALENTS (FTEs)**

Using full-time equivalents (FTEs) instead of headcount will allow you to accurately account for part-timers; so the final step in determining required staff is to convert these figures into FTEs. If a full workweek is 40 hours, 1 full-time employee working 40 hours is one FTE. Two part-time employees, working 20 hours each, would equal one FTE, as would 4 employees who work 10 hours each.

To convert the workload to FTEs, multiply the workload hours by the RSF and divide by the number of hours per month worked by a full-time employee. For example:

### FTEs REQUIRED FOR CALL LOAD

| Item | Amount |
|---|---|
| Workload hours | 5,242 |
| Staff ratio | 1.78 |
| Staff hours required (5,242 x 1.78) | 9,331 |
| Staff hours per FTE for the month | 184 |
| FTEs required (9,331 ÷ 184) | 50.71 |

Going through a similar process for non real-time work might produce the following:

### EMAIL FTEs REQUIRED

| Item | Amount |
|---|---|
| Workload Hours | 1,365 |
| Staff ratio | 1.51 |
| Staff hours required (1,365 x 1.51) | 2,061 |
| Staff hours per FTE for the month | 184 |
| FTEs required (2,061 ÷ 184) | 11.20 |

Adding phone and email FTE requirements yields a total of 61.91 FTEs, as shown.

The end result of this part of the model is the number of agents required on payroll to handle your planned workload and achieve your service level and response time objectives. Since this number often does

| TOTAL FTEs REQUIRED | |
|---|---|
| Item | Amount |
| Telephone FTEs required | 50.71 |
| Email FTEs required | 11.20 |
| Total FTEs required | 61.91 |

not match the current staffing in the center, we recommend going one step further and incorporating a staff planning component that illustrates gaps between the required and the current headcount.

The staff planning section includes current staff, turnover and new-hire information. It also factors in part-time employees and shows how close your current staff comes to your required staff. Hiring plans are often produced many months in advance (perhaps by someone outside the contact center) around general business trends. This section allows you to assess and adjust hiring plans as needed so that they match workload needs as precisely as possible. For example, before going through this final step, your hiring activity might produce the sample comparison of required FTE versus planned FTE.

| HIRING PLAN (BEFORE) | | | | | | |
|---|---|---|---|---|---|---|
| | July | Aug | Sept | Oct | Nov | Dec |
| FTEs required | 61.91 | 55.00 | 62.50 | 64.10 | 65.05 | 61.00 |
| Planned staff | | | | | | |
| Starting FTEs | 52.00 | 58.92 | 56.56 | 57.87 | 59.13 | 62.36 |
| Attrition % | 4% | 4% | 3% | 3% | 3% | 3% |
| Net FTEs | 49.92 | 56.56 | 54.87 | 56.13 | 57.36 | 60.49 |
| New-hire FTEs | 9 | 0 | 3 | 3 | 5 | 4 |
| Planned FTEs | 58.92 | 56.56 | 57.87 | 59.13 | 62.36 | 64.49 |
| FTE +/- | -2.99 | 1.56 | -4.63 | -4.97 | -2.69 | 3.49 |

In the example, there are two months (September and October) where you will be understaffed by three or more FTEs, and one (December) where you are overstaffed by more than three. Since your goal is to keep your actual staff numbers as close as possible to required numbers, you can adjust staffing plans (represented by the new-hire FTEs in the next table) to reduce the over/under. The results might be as shown.

| HIRING PLAN (AFTER) | | | | | | |
|---|---|---|---|---|---|---|
| | July | Aug | Sept | Oct | Nov | Dec |
| FTEs required | 61.91 | 55.00 | 62.50 | 64.10 | 65.05 | 61.00 |
| Planned staff | | | | | | |
| Starting FTEs | 52.00 | 58.92 | 56.56 | 60.87 | 65.08 | 63.13 |
| Attrition % | 4% | 4% | 3% | 3% | 3% | 3% |
| Net FTEs | 49.92 | 56.56 | 54.87 | 59.04 | 63.13 | 61.24 |
| New-hire FTEs | 9 | 0 | 6 | 6 | 0 | 0 |
| Planned FTEs | 58.92 | 56.56 | 60.87 | 65.08 | 63.13 | 61.24 |
| FTE +/- | -2.99 | 1.56 | -1.63 | 0.98 | -1.92 | 0.24 |

The new plan keeps every month to within three FTEs of requirements. It also reduces total hiring during the six months shown. All in all, it is a better fit to requirements.

Once the plan is created, you are set to make a case for your staffing needs. You have created a model that is fully adjustable at the workload, staffing factor and staff planning levels. It illustrates staffing needs while allowing all parties to quickly see the results of changes in any variable.

We've found that talking through the process line by line helps those who are involved understand and participate in the assumptions. As a result, they usually feel much more comfortable about how you reach requirements. There may be spirited discussion along the way about specific issues. But with line-by-line agreement (and changes that may be merited), one plus one plus three should add up to five — not four or six.

# Reporting Contact Center Activity

Reporting contact center activity to senior-level management and others in the organization can seem a daunting task. The wide variety of activities in a typical center, the reality of senior management not having the time to pore over detailed reports, and the fact that summary reports often gloss over important information, all contribute to the challenge. Consequently, many diligently prepared reports either go unread or, worse, are misunderstood.

Clearly, good communication doesn't happen just because detailed information is available. Any manager buried in system reports yet struggling to convey basic realities can testify to that fact. As with budgets, the process you establish to communicate ongoing contact center activity is as important as the information itself. The following steps can help you identify and prepare meaningful reports and ensure that they are understood.

**1. DETERMINE YOUR OBJECTIVES.** What are the objectives for the reports? In other words, what should other managers know about the contact center or the information it has acquired, and why? To find the answers, assemble a team for a working discussion. A cross-section of managers from across the organization, contact center managers, supervisors and agents should be involved. General areas of concern usually include:

- Customer satisfaction and sentiment analysis
- Quality measurements
- Contributions to other business units
- Access alternatives and workload trends
- Costs and revenues
- Queue reports (such as service level and abandonment)
- Resource utilization and requirements (e.g., staffing and scheduling needs)

From these major categories, important measurements will emerge. It's often useful to preface this exercise with a question like, "If we could wave a magic wand, what would we really want to know about our contact center?" At this stage, don't be concerned about whether or not you have the reports to support the objectives you identify. Your objectives — not the reports you happen to have — should drive this process.

**2. IDENTIFY SUPPORTING INFORMATION.** List the possible reporting alternatives under each of the objectives you identified in the first step. Include information from systems, databases, surveys, other departments and external sources.

The challenge now becomes one of selection. Stephanie Winston, author of the classic book, *The Organized Executive*, advises that a report should not simply collect facts, but serve as a judgment tool for management. To pare down the lists, Winston suggests asking a variety of questions: Is the report really necessary? What questions does it answer? Which reports would you dispense with if you had to pay for them? Could several reports be combined? Will you act on the information to effect change?

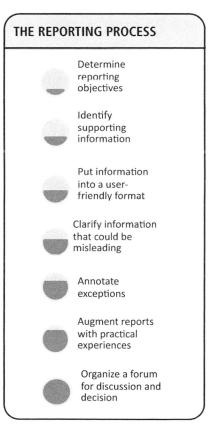

**THE REPORTING PROCESS**

- Determine reporting objectives
- Identify supporting information
- Put information into a user-friendly format
- Clarify information that could be misleading
- Annotate exceptions
- Augment reports with practical experiences
- Organize a forum for discussion and decision

**3. PUT THE INFORMATION IN A USER-FRIENDLY FORMAT.** Once you have a list of desired reports, the next step is to compile them into a simple, understandable format. This often means creating graphs of the information. For example, simple line charts can illustrate trends that would otherwise appear as hard-to-decipher numbers. Reports that rely on graphs may take more pages, but a 10-page report consisting primarily of graphs is often quicker to read and easier to comprehend than two pages of detailed numbers in rows and columns. Look for data that can be combined or contrasted to provide a more complete story (see example).

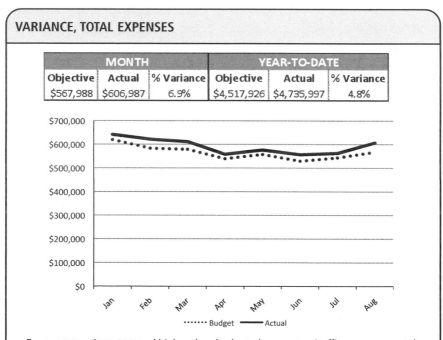

**VARIANCE, TOTAL EXPENSES**

| MONTH | | | YEAR-TO-DATE | | |
|---|---|---|---|---|---|
| Objective | Actual | % Variance | Objective | Actual | % Variance |
| $567,988 | $606,987 | 6.9% | $4,517,926 | $4,735,997 | 4.8% |

Expenses continue to trend higher than budgeted amounts. Staffing expenses at the agent level account for 88% of the variance, due to higher-than-anticipated staffing levels required to meet service level objectives. The extra staffing requirement is due to talk time at 5% higher than projections and email volumes nearly one-third higher than anticipated. The increase in talk time is largely because of additional scripting prompted by legislative factors, while the higher e-mail volume is attributable to the success of our website marketing campaign. One other variance of note is a higher-than-expected internal turnover rate, which has resulted in two more new-hire training classes this year than anticipated ($30,000 per class).

**4. CLARIFY INFORMATION THAT COULD BE MISLEADING.** As any seasoned contact center manager has learned, you can make reports show whatever you want. For example, you can prop up service level by overflowing calls to other groups, changing distribution priorities, or taking

---

**YOU'RE LOOKIN' (TOO?) GOOD ...**

Reporting the contact center in the best possible light can undermine success. There are a lot of ways to produce reports so that the center looks as productive as possible to senior management (see Chapter 4). However, if you mask serious resource deficiencies or process problems, the center is less likely to get the resources and support it needs. That, in turn, will undermine the center's ability to perform. There's also the related issue of psychology — when upper-level managers see room for improvement, they tend to feel more assured they are getting the whole story.

---

messages for later callbacks. Or you can provide overall reports or select timeframes that combine data and conceal problematic intervals. Clearly, simply providing a high-level report on service level or quality can be misleading. The reader needs more information.

**5. ANNOTATE EXCEPTIONS.** There will be points that are clearly out of the norm. Don't leave your audience guessing. Explain deviations, both what happened and why. Why did wait times go through the roof in early February? A simple footnote can provide the answer: "Power outage in Northeast; call load 40 percent higher than normal."

**6. AUGMENT REPORTS WITH PRACTICAL EXPERIENCES.** Giving recipients a report to read on what happens on Monday mornings versus bringing them into the center to observe what happens is the difference between night and day. You need to do both. Teaching key contact center dynamics to managers outside the center is necessary to create a clear understanding of how cross-functional decisions and actions link with the center's overall effectiveness. And contact center executives need a solid understanding of the concerns, challenges and objectives in other areas of the organization. This mutual understanding forms a strong and essential foundation for effective reporting and communication.

**7. ORGANIZE AN ONGOING FORUM FOR DISCUSSING AND ACTING ON THE INFORMATION.** Presenting data in a clear, concise and actionable format is a start. But reports must be followed by a forum for discussing and acting on the information. This becomes the primary opportunity to turn information into sound business decisions.

We'll pick up with a discussion of important measurements in Chapter 12, and how to use them to improve performance within the contact center and organization in Chapter 13. The key point here: Effective reporting is an ongoing communication process, not an end result.

## Points to Remember

- Senior management needs a basic knowledge of the contact center; the summary of 10 key principles covered here is good starting point.
- Anticipating the impact of growth (or contraction) of the center's workload is critical, and should be a part of the communication and budgeting process.
- The budgeting process should build credibility and clearly demonstrate important tradeoffs and decision points.
- An effective staffing budget is fully adjustable, clearly demonstrates the "whys" behind budget requirements, and enables all parties to quickly see the results of changes in any variable.
- Reporting is, in essence, communication. It happens best as part of a systematic approach that ensures that the right information is understood, delivered to the right people at the right times, and acted on.

# CHAPTER 11:
# Real-Time Management

*The pessimist complains about the wind; the optimist expects it to change;*
*the realist adjusts the sails.*

**WILLIAM ARTHUR WARD**

O K, the planning is done, the schedules are in place and — hang on to your hat — the calls are pouring in. *Uh oh, now what?*

Even with good forecasts and accurate schedules, the random arrival of customer contacts means that we inherently operate in a "demand-chasing" mode. Demand must be chased with the supply of answering capabilities. If you think about it, at any instant, there are either more contacts to be handled than resources available, or more resources than contacts. And those times they are in perfect balance (with no waiting agents and no waiting callers)? They last a fleeting moment or two, before the balance tips in one direction or the other.

Up and down, ebb and flow. Yes, the best-managed contact centers are close to the mark the vast majority of the time. But it's a dynamic, ever-changing environment.

Then there are those times planning goes off the rails. The forecast is on the low side. Customers behave differently than expected (geesh, that new app was supposed to *reduce* workload). Marketing sends an email blast without telling you. The flu is taking a toll on your team. IT is finishing up the desktop upgrade. Oh, and that group is arriving later this morning for the tour.

**245**

At the risk of stating the obvious: Unscheduled activities and unplanned absenteeism cause unexpected staffing problems. Even the most accurate contact center planning must be augmented by effective real-time management: monitoring events as they happen and making adjustments as necessary.

Real-time management should complement planning. When the planning is done, it's the moment-by-moment decisions and actions that will enable you to maintain an appropriate service level and response time. Effective real-time management includes establishing a good foundation, monitoring real-time developments and implementing a workable escalation plan.

(Note, I use customer calls in many of the examples in this chapter, but the principles apply to other contact channels. Further, the time and priority requirements of different channels present opportunities for prioritizing and triaging work, a subject we'll explore.)

# A Good Foundation

An important prerequisite to effective real-time management is to establish a good foundation before the work comes flooding in. This involves clearing up potential misconceptions among staff, putting the right tools in place, and establishing workable objectives and a good planning process. In other words, it means ensuring that you aren't *creating* many of the crises to which you are reacting.

## SERVICE LEVEL AND QUALITY

One important principle is to make sure that everybody understands the complementary relationship between service level and quality (covered in Chapters 4 and 13). Supervisors and agents sometimes see little connection between what they do here and now and what those in planning roles do. They may feel that the pressure of the moment forces them to make tough tradeoffs between seemingly competing objectives.

Although service level and quality seem to be at odds in the short-term, poor quality will force a negative impact on service level in the long-term, by contributing to repeat and escalated calls, duplicate or parallel contacts, as well as other forms of waste and rework. So, the emphasis should be on handling each customer contact correctly, regardless of how backed up the queue is.

But your team might believe they are getting mixed signals from management: "Hey, you train us to do a quality job, but then you put a lot of emphasis on achieving an efficient service level and response time objective. You put queue displays all over the place and get unhappy when service level and response time drop. What do you really want?"

---

*I have no time to hurry.*
**IGOR STRAVINSKY**

---

The real answer is: "Both!" Look at the contacts in queue, make sure that people are plugged in and in the right mode, and do what's possible to arrange flexible activities around the workload. But handle each contact right the first time, regardless of what's happening with service level and response time.

## THE IMPACT OF EACH PERSON

Everybody in the contact center needs to be aware of how much impact they each have on the queue. Remember the law of diminishing returns (covered in Chapter 9). The message, as it relates to real-time management, is clear: When the queue is backed up, each person makes a big difference!

This issue sheds light on the importance of training agents on how a queue behaves (e.g., how fast it can spin out of control) and, with cautions discussed below, providing them with real-time information so they can adjust priorities as necessary. Real-time information can be delivered via:

- Windows with queue information on desktop displays
- Supervisor monitors
- Wall- or ceiling-mounted readerboards
- Displays on telephones programmed to give queue statistics
- Mobile apps
- Don't have the latest technology? I know of a few small centers that still post regularly updated results on easels or whiteboards. (I agree, this sounds way last century, but there's something about the earthiness of it that seems to bring focus.)

Queue information must be complemented with appropriate training so that agents know what to look for and how to react. There are two things directly within the control of agents: being in the right place at the right times, and doing the right things (schedule adherence and quality, in industry terms). A backed-up queue does not mean you should change the *way you handle work*, the process necessary for handling each contact with quality. Real-time queue information must be interpreted in that context, a subject we'll look at further in this chapter, and in Chapters 12 and 14.

CURRENT DISPLAY ...

Calls Waiting:1001          Longest Holding:+99:99

ED...WE'RE DOOMED...WE'RE DOO

It is important to establish clear expectations on adherence to schedule, a subject we'll cover in Chapter 14. Many contact centers diligently track adherence factor, which is a measure of how much time agents spend plugged in and available to handle contacts. Often, it's viewed only as an issue of *how much*. Equally important, though, is *when* agents are plugged in and available to handle customer contacts. A key responsibility of supervisors and team leaders is to remove schedule roadblocks so that those on their teams can be in the right places at the right times.

## AUTO-AVAILABLE AND AUTO WRAP-UP

Most ACD systems can be programmed for either "auto-available" or "auto wrap-up." Auto-available automatically puts agents into the available mode after they complete a contact. Auto wrap-up automatically puts them into the after-call work mode.

It usually makes sense to program your system to put agents into the mode they will most often need to be in. This can save seconds here and there (which really add up over the course of a year's contacts) and minimize the need for agents to manually put themselves in and out of modes.

Some managers program their ACD to put agents into the after-call work mode for a predetermined amount of time. This is usually a bad idea. There is no way you can anticipate how much time after-call work will take for an individual contact. If your objective is to give people breaks due to a heavy workload, you are by default adding more time to each contact, further backing up the queue.

> *There is no way you can anticipate how much time after-call work will take for an individual call.*

It's a much better idea to give agents control over the mode. (There is one exception to this rule: Some older ACDs require a small window of time after a call is disconnected, i.e., a few seconds, to enable agents to put themselves into the after-call work mode.)

Another alternative you have when programming your ACD is to use a feature generally referred to as "call-forcing." This may strike you as a terribly autocratic-sounding term, but appearances aside, it's a valuable and agent-friendly capability. With this feature, calls are automatically connected to agents who are available and ready (thus, obviating the need for them to manually answer calls). Agents are notified that a call has arrived by a gentle beep (zip tone).

Studies indicate that call-forcing can cut four to six seconds off each call. And agents almost always like the feature once they get used to it. It removes what would be an extra step from the process. And, importantly, they remain in full control. If they aren't ready for the next call, they simply stay out of the available mode.

## CONSISTENCY

Another important step in building a good foundation is to ensure that agents maintain a consistent approach to handling contacts, regardless of queue conditions. Each agent has an impact on the components of workload, and therefore, on the data that will be used in forecasting and planning for future workloads. When the queue is building, it can be tempting to postpone some of the after-call work. As discussed in Chapter 6, this skews reports, causes planning problems and may lead to increased errors.

The solution is to define ahead of time which types of work should follow contacts and which types of work can be completed later. Then, train agents and supervisors accordingly.

## ACCURATE RESOURCE PLANNING

Real-time management can never make up for inadequate planning. The nine-step planning process covered in preceding chapters should be as accurate as possible. This includes:

- Establishing service level and response time objectives that everybody understands
- Accurately forecasting the workload associated with all types of contacts
- Calculating staffing requirements
- Planning for and managing activities not related to handling customer contacts
- Building schedules that match staff to the workload as closely as possible

**PERPETUATING THE PROBLEM**

Real-time management, though essential, has a serious downside. Real-time tactics that enhance supply or curb demand can also undermine the organization's ability to create accurate resource plans. These tactics — such as adjusting call-handling processes, overflowing calls to secondary groups, postponing breaks and training, or reassigning agents to unplanned work — can create skewed activity reports. They can defer essential work or training. And they often complicate future workload and schedule predictions. In short, real-time management tends to perpetuate the imbalances that created the need for reactionary measures. That doesn't mean that real-time tactics shouldn't be used, but you should employ them judiciously and be alert to their implications on planning and management.

# Monitoring Real-Time Developments

The second major principle in effective real-time management is to monitor developments and identify trends as early as possible. The key is to react appropriately to evolving conditions. Random call arrival means that, at times, it will look like you are falling behind even though you are staffed appropriately. But if you are experiencing a genuine trend, you need to move quickly. Time is of the essence.

### INTERPRETING REPORTS

Service level is "rolling" history. The ACD has to look back at least some amount of time or at some number of calls to make the calculation. Consequently, even though service level is a primary focus in planning, it is not a sensitive real-time report. (In the strictest definition, it's *not* a real-time report.)

With many ACDs, you can define how far back the system looks to provide real-time service level status. You may need to experiment some. You'll need enough of a sample that reports aren't jumpy, but it also needs to be recent enough to be valuable. Also note that "screen refresh" does not correlate to the timeframe used for calculations. Your monitors may display updated information every few seconds, but that has nothing to do with how much data your ACD uses for the calculations that require rolling history.

Service level will tell you what has already happened, given recent unique call volume, random arrival, average handling time and staff availability patterns. But it's important to realize that what is being reported is not necessarily an indication of what is about to happen.

On the other hand, the number of calls presently in queue *is* a real-time report, as is longest current wait and current agent status. Understanding the distinction between reports that are genuinely real-time and those that must incorporate some history explains apparent contradictions.

For example, service level may indicate 65 percent of calls are answered in 20 seconds, even though there are no calls in queue at the moment. Keep watching the monitor, though, and service level will begin to climb. Alternatively, service level may look high at the moment, even though an enormous volume of calls recently entered the queue. Give it a few minutes and, unless circumstances change, it will fall to the bottom of the barrel.

There will be at least several minutes delay before service level reflects the magnitude of a trend. As a result, for service level to have meaning, it must be interpreted in light of the recent past, calls in queue and current longest wait. If you focus only on service level, you could misread the situation.

Since the number of calls in queue foretells where service level is about to go (unless conditions change), it should be a primary focus, along with longest current wait. As circumstances dictate, you would then assess the state agents are in — signed off, auxiliary, handling calls, etc. — and make appropriate adjustments.

In summary, focus on real-time reports in this order:

**1. NUMBER OF CALLS IN QUEUE.** This is the real-time report most sensitive to changes and trends. Look at this first.

**2. LONGEST CURRENT WAIT (OLDEST CALL).** This is a real-time report, but it behaves like a historical report (e.g., many calls can come into the queue, but longest current wait will take some time to reflect the problem). This report gives context to number of calls in queue. For example, if there are far more calls in queue than normal, but longest current wait is modest, you are at the beginning of a downward trend. Now is the time to react.

**3. SERVICE LEVEL, AVERAGE SPEED OF ANSWER, AVERAGE TIME TO ABANDONMENT AND OTHER MEASURES OF THE QUEUE AND CALLER BEHAVIOR.** These reports provide additional context to number of calls in queue and longest current wait. For example, if service level is low, but there are few or no calls in queue, then you have hurdled the problem and service level will begin to climb. Don't sweat it.

**4. AGENT STATUS.** This real-time report indicates how many agents are available and what modes they are in. Some managers suggest that agent status should be at the top of the list. Their argument is that if agents are where they need to be, there won't be much of a queue in the first place. There is some logic in that argument. However, I generally place agent status after other reports because it can be difficult to interpret unless you know something about the queue. So what if few agents are taking calls, if few calls are coming in? In that case, you would want agents to be working on other tasks.

> **MONITORING REAL-TIME REPORTS**
>
> 1. Number of calls in queue
> 2. Longest current wait (oldest call)
> 3. Service level/average speed of answer
> 4. Agent status
> 5. Escalation plan ...

In the end, the debate on the order of reports doesn't matter much because you should monitor and interpret them together. With the right training on what real-time information means and the activity it is reporting, experienced agents and supervisors can scan and decipher these reports quickly.

**253**

**APPLE'S FAST-RESPONSE CULTURE**

Apple Inc.'s customer contact centers face a unique challenge as a result of their company's long-standing commitment to surprise product announcements. Apple's iconic former CEO, the late Steve Jobs, always garnered worldwide attention when he spoke at major events, such as the MacWorld conference, because the innovative company has always been intent on maintaining secrecy. To this day, few know in advance what new products will be introduced — and that includes customer support employees. As current CEO Tim Cook relays important announcements (as Jobs did), the news hits the wires and devoted Apple customers begin calling.

How does the contact center team cope? Beyond knowing that an announcement of some kind is coming, they rely on their finely tuned instant update process. The top-secret information is prepared by a small, but trusted team — not even the Global Training Director gets to see it. Every agent stands by, waiting for the update to be electronically delivered as the information is being made public. The contacts begin arriving and agents — armed with information they received minutes before — handle them smoothly and confidently.

It's a tremendous challenge for the contact center, but the team takes pride in rising to it. And it's a great example of anticipating and planning everything possible in advance — so that when the moment arrives, the center is ready to respond.

## DISPLAY THRESHOLDS

Some ACD and wall display systems allow you to establish various priority thresholds. For example, you can color-code information yellow when the queue begins to back up, and red when it's in bad shape. Alternatively, some ACDs, particularly older models, provide blinking lights, which can be programmed to blink more rapidly as the queue builds.

The problem is, the thresholds are often set arbitrarily. Further, agents often do not understand what is expected of them at different levels. If that's the case, real-time information will raise everybody's stress level. And your agents might feel like it's their fault that they can't clear up the queue. Proper programming and training are necessary.

Generally, the first threshold should be set for any call (one call) in queue. Agents should proceed normally, and no tactical adjustments are required. The second threshold should indicate that there are more calls in queue than the average expected for the desired service level (see "Q2" in Chapter 7). Routine adjustments, such as postponing flexible work, should be made to get the calls answered. The next threshold should indicate that there are more calls in queue than the agents can realistically handle. In this case, more involved real-time tactics (e.g., calling in reinforcements or triaging the work) are required.

You can program many of today's systems to adjust thresholds dynamically as calling loads change (10 calls in queue may be no problem during a fully staffed shift, but would be a nightmare for 2 people handling calls at 3 a.m.). The most important thing is understanding where the information comes from and what it considers, so that those interpreting it can make good decisions.

## CONSIDERING ALL CHANNELS

Ever had this happen? Someone looks at the real-time reports and everything is fine, so he or she decides to unplug and begin work on a project or take a break. Unfortunately, others have the same idea at the same time, resulting in queues that spin out of control. Interpreting real-time information when there is no queue is almost as tricky as identifying trends when there is a queue!

Consequently, most large or multisite centers have a designated "traffic control" person (or small team) that coordinates activities. The traffic controller's authority can range from making informed suggestions on priorities to flatly dictating what can and can't happen at any given time.

This responsibility should include the full range of channels. If you pull agents from email to handle inbound calls, customers who sent email messages might begin calling. There's a balance here. If you don't have coordination across systems, you could be addressing these issues twice, once by phone and again by email. In the worst case, the answers are inconsistent, creating confusion and further work.

In sum, whatever the size of your center, you will need someone with the whole field in view to monitor conditions. This person may also produce and interpret intraday forecasts (see Chapter 6) and make adjustments to system or network thresholds.

©King Features Syndicate. Reprinted with permission.

## A Workable Escalation Plan

Regardless of what channels you are supporting, you will need to make appropriate tactical adjustments as conditions change. An important principle in effective real-time management is to outline a workable escalation plan that is in place before a crisis. Most contact centers use a tiered approach.

### LEVEL 1

The first level of action involves routine, commonsense adjustments that enable you to get the contacts handled. Agent status becomes the focus, and many use a variation of the time-honored phrase "Everybody take a call!" This is generally directed toward people on the floor who are not currently handling contacts. It can also be for agents stuck in wrap-up mode.

At this level, agents make routine adjustments to work priorities. Flexible tasks are postponed. If you have agents handling contacts that are not as time-sensitive and can wait — social interactions like updating the company Facebook posts that can be deferred, email, mail, outbound calls, or data entry — they can be temporarily assigned to the calls in queue. You might also automatically overflow calls to agents in other groups (who are, of course, trained to handle the calls).

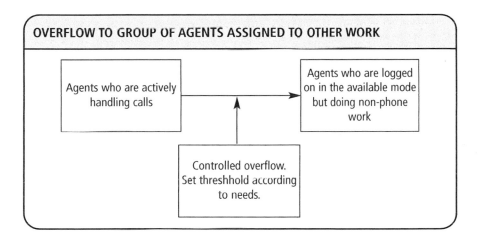

Make sure that your agents understand that speeding up their rate of speech will not help. Callers can usually sense they are rushed, and will often dig in their heels to slow things down. However, agents shouldn't go beyond what is necessary to completely satisfy the caller's stated objectives and handle the call with quality. There's a line somewhere, and common sense applies.

## LEVEL 2 AND BEYOND

If the workload still outpaces the staff required to handle it, the contact center can move on to more involved real-time alternatives. For example, it may be feasible to reassign agents from one group to another.

**EXAMPLE REAL-TIME TACTICS**

- "Everybody take a call"
- Adjust breaks
- Assist people who are stuck in talk time or wrap-up
- Assign project work and short-term training (for slack)
- Postpone or move up flexible work
- Triage channels and contacts by type
- Record appropriate system announcements
- Bring in secondary groups
- Adjust overflow or network parameters
- Reassign agents to groups that need help
- Adjust the placement of announcements
- Use supervisors wisely
- Bring in agents who are on call
- Send contacts to outsource partner
- Mobilize the SWAT team
- Adjust call-routing priorities
- Take messages for callback
- Generate controlled busy signals

Another possible Level 2 activity is to change system announcements so that they offload what would otherwise be routine calls. Utilities use messages such as, "We are aware of the power outage in the Bay Ridge area, caused by nearby construction. We hope to have power restored by 11 a.m. We apologize for the inconvenience. If you need further assistance, please stay on the line; one of our representatives will be with you momentarily."

More routinely, calls can be directed elsewhere: "Thank you for calling ABC airline. If you would like to use our automated flight arrival and departure system, please say or press ..." Some centers also give callers the ability to check the status of an order, listen to specific product information, or hear answers to commonly asked questions while they wait and without losing their place in the queue.

Sometimes, you can foster empathy with system announcements: "Due to the snowstorm hitting the East Coast, we are operating with fewer of our associates than normal. However, your call is very important to us. We apologize for the delay and will be with you just as soon as possible. Thank you for your patience." This tactic will backfire if it's overused or stretches the truth.

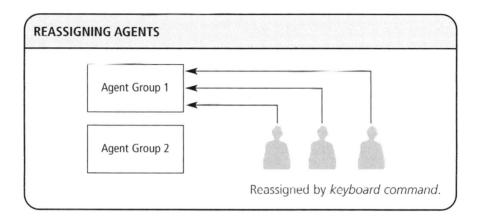

**REASSIGNING AGENTS**

Agent Group 1

Agent Group 2

Reassigned by *keyboard command.*

You might also be able to improve circumstances by changing call-routing thresholds between groups or sites. Most of today's routing systems are based on a form of "if-then" programming logic to automate this process. But there are cases that may require some adjustments. And if you have a network that sends fixed percentages of calls to various sites, you may need to adjust these thresholds.

You can also begin to triage contacts in a way that makes sense. For example, inbound calls in queue generally require priority over handling customer email or responding to customer inquiries in social forums. And you can go a step or two further by prioritizing calls by type, based on numbers dialed, routing selections, customer identification and other criteria. (Of course, caution is in order — email that sits too long turns into repeat or parallel contacts, such as additional phone calls or social posts. And outdated or insufficient FAQs may be a root cause of contacts requiring agent assistance. We'll look further at these tradeoffs in Chapter 13.)

It also may make sense for supervisors and managers to help handle customer contacts. However, this approach must be well thought-out, because if they are unavailable when agents need help, the situation could further deteriorate. Some union agreements restrict supervisors and managers from handling contacts, but if allowed, this can be an effective tactic.

Some centers take messages for later callback, a capability that is greatly facilitated by virtual queue technologies (see Chapter 4). However, this approach doesn't work well in all cases. Potential challenges include: How do you ensure that the callbacks are timely if you're busy now? What is your policy when you reach the caller's voicemail? You may have to experiment to find out whether it's workable in your environment.

Other Level 2 tactics include calling in a SWAT team or bringing in agents who are on reserve (see Chapter 8), routing some contacts to outsource partners, or adjusting the placement of announcements (see next section).

In sum, establishing an effective escalation plan involves:

- Identifying feasible real-time tactics (ahead of time)
- Determining the conditions in which each should be implemented (ahead of time)
- Monitoring conditions (real time)
- Deciding on adjustments necessary (real time)
- Coordinating and communicating changes to all involved (real time)
- Implementing the tactics (real time)
- Assessing how well the escalation plan worked (after the fact)

It is wise to "react in advance" (a term I first heard from industry executive Tim Montgomery) — that is, make adjustments ahead of time. For example, if you know by looking at workload trends that your schedules aren't matching requirements, you can make adjustments before the dust is flying.

In the example, we have more agents than needed early tomorrow morning, and fewer than required later in the morning. By planning ahead, we can schedule computer-based training and adjust some breaks to address the slack in the earlier increments. By rescheduling agents

## SCHEDULE VARIANCE, TOMORROW

| Interval | Required | Scheduled | Variance |
|---|---|---|---|
| 7:00 | 8 | 14 | 6 |
| 7:30 | 12 | 19 | 7 |
| 8:00 | 22 | 25 | 3 |
| 8:30 | 29 | 26 | (-3) |
| 9:00 | 37 | 39 | 2 |
| 9:30 | 45 | 45 | 0 |
| 10:00 | 51 | 46 | (-5) |
| 10:30 | 57 | 55 | (-2) |
| 11:00 | 56 | 51 | (-5) |
| 11:30 | 54 | 48 | (-6) |

assigned to email, we can cover the shortage later in the day.

This kind of approach makes sense. It's more limited than a perfect forecast and schedule assembled weeks in advance. But, given the realities of plans sometimes getting out of sync with workloads, it's far better than reacting as the crunch happens. And it underscores an important principle: Do everything possible, as far in advance as possible, to align your schedules with workload requirements. Even in the short term, advance planning trumps in-the-moment reaction.

## PLANNING TO REACT IN ADVANCE

| Interval | Required | Original Scheduled | Original Variance | Notes | New Scheduled | New Variance |
|---|---|---|---|---|---|---|
| 7:00 | 8 | 14 | 6 | Deliver 1 hr CBT session to 6 agents | 8 | 0 |
| 7:30 | 12 | 19 | 7 | Deliver 1 hr CBT session to 6 agents | 13 | 1 |
| 8:00 | 22 | 25 | 3 | Add 3 breaks from following interval | 22 | 0 |
| 8:30 | 29 | 26 | -3 | Move 3 breaks to previous interval | 29 | 0 |
| 9:00 | 37 | 39 | 2 | | 39 | 2 |
| 9:30 | 45 | 45 | 0 | | 45 | 0 |
| 10:00 | 51 | 46 | (-5) | Bring in 5 e-mail agents for 2 hrs | 51 | 0 |
| 10:30 | 57 | 55 | (-2) | Bring in 5 e-mail agents for 2 hrs | 60 | 3 |
| 11:00 | 56 | 51 | (-5) | Bring in 5 e-mail agents for 2 hrs | 56 | 0 |
| 11:30 | 54 | 48 | (-6) | Bring in 5 e-mail agents for 2 hrs | 53 | (-1) |

On the other end of the crunch (or unexpected slack) is an important but sometimes neglected aspect of real-time management: analyzing what happened so that you can prevent recurring problems. How well did your escalation plan work? Were the right tactics deployed? What would you do differently? This analysis will help you to fine-tune your escalation plan and improve the planning process. It is especially important if you are responding to more than two or three significant crises per week.

## THE PSYCHOLOGY OF ANNOUNCEMENTS

Most call centers provide announcements to callers who wait in queue. The first announcement recognizes callers, provides reassurance they are in the right place, and promises that the calls will be answered. Many also include the phrase, "Your call will be answered in the order in which it was received ..."

> *Due to our inability to staff appropriately, your call will be delayed ... and so will many others.*

The typical behavior of callers who abandon can provide insight into the use of delay announcements. Callers who hang up when they hear the first delay announcement are called "fast clear-downs." The customer may have dialed the wrong number or may just have changed their mind and decided to bail out when they didn't get right through to an agent.

Some centers have found that repositioning the first delay announcement can lower abandonment. For example, if the delay announcement is normally set to come on just after a caller enters a queue, moving the threshold out to provide additional rings can buy your agent group additional seconds to get to callers before they become fast clear-downs. Further, because callers don't always mentally register that they are in a

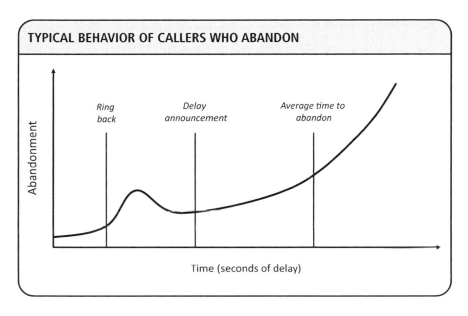

**TYPICAL BEHAVIOR OF CALLERS WHO ABANDON**

*Ring back* · *Delay announcement* · *Average time to abandon*

Abandonment

Time (seconds of delay)

queue until they hear the announcement, they may wait longer.

Will this help? Maybe. Does it solve serious staffing imbalances? Nope. You'll have to experiment to see if it has a positive impact. And keep in mind, this technique will actually increase average speed of answer and

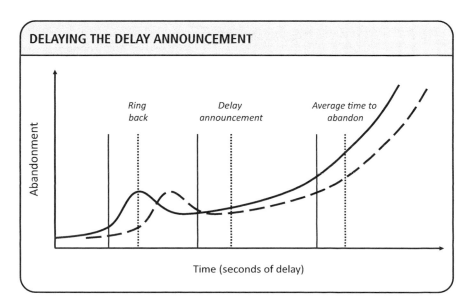

**DELAYING THE DELAY ANNOUNCEMENT**

*Ring back* · *Delay announcement* · *Average time to abandon*

Abandonment

Time (seconds of delay)

reduce service level. But you have a higher value in mind: Get to as many callers as possible before they give up and hang up. For that, you'll want to consider every alternative possible.

You may also be able to reduce abandonment by adjusting the position of a second announcement. For example, if average time to abandonment is 50 seconds and the second delay announcement is set for 60 seconds, you might hang on to more callers by adjusting it to play earlier. This is psychology, pure and simple, and the purpose of the second delay announcement is to give callers who are about to abandon renewed hope that you will get to them: "We apologize for the delay; thank you for continuing to hold ..."

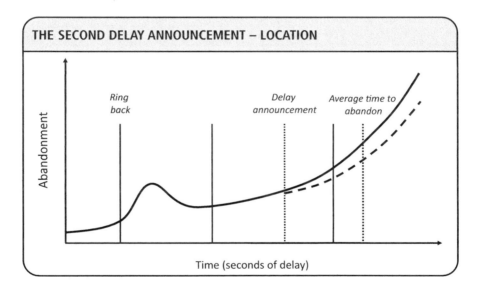

**THE SECOND DELAY ANNOUNCEMENT – LOCATION**

*Ring back*

*Delay announcement*

*Average time to abandon*

Abandonment

Time (seconds of delay)

The first and second delay announcements are valuable, but you'll need to use good judgment with repeating announcements, or they can make things worse. From a practical standpoint, customers probably have you on speakerphone or are using a headset while they catch up with other matters. (Once shunned by the general public, headsets are becoming *de rigueur* in the smartphone era). Remember, they have to mentally tune in every time the announcement is played, which can make them cynical:

"Yes, I know this call is important to you and that you'll be with me momentarily. You've told me eight times so far." Repeating announcements are repeating interruptions.

That said, if subsequent announcements are interesting and valuable, they can be helpful in minimizing abandonment. While working on this chapter, I called an airline to sort out some changes to a complex itinerary. They were backed up due to some serious weather-related disruptions in their flight network, and repeating announcements covered, in turn, baggage policies, what can be carried on, vacation packages, the airline's mobile app, updates to the frequent flyer program, and other topics. The announcements, to the time I reached an agent, were different, and (even though I'm familiar with the information) were interesting and well timed. I felt they did a good job with this approach. In short, let common sense and your company's personality and brand prevail. (See the discussion on customer access strategy, Chapter 2.)

## EXTREME ALTERNATIVES: BUSIES AND BEYOND

What if things are really rough? What if you get more calls than expected and have exhausted all other alternatives? Should you continue to let callers into the queue? The unsavory choice may be to give callers busy signals or let them enter a long queue, only to abandon anyway.

Some centers could never consider using busy signals. Emergency services are a notable example. But for others, busy signals may occasionally be an acceptable alternative. Callers who get busy signals are more likely to make immediate and repeated attempts to reach you than those who abandon.

Two reports, average speed of answer and average time to abandonment, provide useful direction. If ASA is four minutes and ATA (average time to abandonment) is two minutes, then you might begin to block some calls from getting into the queue to force ASA down. The idea is to end up with ASA and ATA in proximity.

Several technical alternatives exist that allow you to block calls from

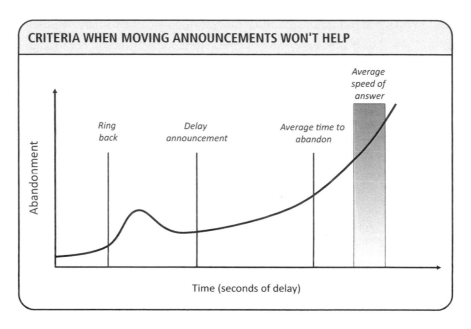

**CRITERIA WHEN MOVING ANNOUNCEMENTS WON'T HELP**

*Average speed of answer*

*Ring back*

*Delay announcement*

*Average time to abandon*

Abandonment

Time (seconds of delay)

entering the queue. With older systems, managers had to be creative. For example, they could overflow calls to "dummy" answer groups that were busied out. They could also play an "all circuits are busy" message (which is not an ideal approach because you or your callers will have to pay for the calls where toll charges apply). Today, most systems are capable of "controlled" busy signals, whereby the system blocks calls according to the thresholds you program (e.g., seconds in queue or number of calls waiting).

Matching ASA and ATA is by no means a sure-fire approach. Keep in mind, if percent abandonment is low (i.e., two or three percent), then ATA is irrelevant. When percent abandonment goes up, ATA typically goes up (and becomes more meaningful) because it includes a broader sample of callers in the calculations.

Further, ASA and ATA measure two different populations; ASA includes callers who wait until they reach agents, while ATA considers only those who abandon. Both reports tend to be moving targets, and can fluctuate widely within a few minutes. And callers who get blocked a number of times before reaching the queue tend to be more tenacious and will usually wait longer

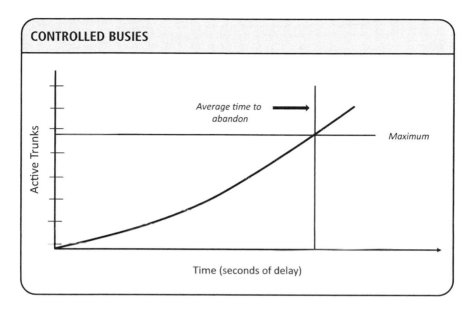

CONTROLLED BUSIES

*Average time to abandon*

Active Trunks

*Maximum*

Time (seconds of delay)

for an agent.

Consequently, this approach must be used with much discernment. Busy signals are far less common in today's contact centers, but they remain enticing to some managers because they make reports look better and take the pressure off agents. Some depend on them as a crutch for inadequate staffing. It probably goes without saying — that's poor customer service, and it defeats the mission of the contact center. This tactic should only be used in extreme or short-lived situations.

Finally, there is the option to end all options: closing the center. During precipitous declines, times of national or world crises, and other such conditions, stock exchanges will suspend trading (the very thing they're there to enable). In the world of contact centers, Zappos, which built a brand on delivering outstanding service, temporarily stopped all inbound calls and resorted to email, in order to handle the workload deluge caused by a hacking incident that forced the company to change customer passwords.

Yes, this last-resort alternative is unfortunate, untenable and completely out of alignment with the contact center's mission to provide access. But it can happen to the best. The message here is, do everything you can to prepare for the workloads you will need to handle. Then, if things go awry, deploy the options you have, scaled for the severity of the situation.

*Call Center* the Movie

© ICMI | by Greg Levin | Illustration by Gene Baikauskas

## Planning and Practice

Contact centers that do a great job of real-time management have some important things in common. They plan the escalation procedure ahead of time and define the thresholds that will determine when each tactic should be implemented. They continually review and refine their escalation plan. When the dust settles, they take the time to go back and analyze what happened, what worked and where there were problems. And they continually improve their planning process so that they are not leaving those on the floor with "mission impossible."

Real-time management takes planning, coordination and practice. It's also gratifying. One of the rewards of working in a contact center is to step up to a challenge, then be able to look back at the results ... and smile.

# Points to Remember

- Establish a good foundation ahead of time so that you are not creating many of the crises to which you are responding.
- Provide real-time information to agents and supervisors, and train them on how to interpret the information.
- Plan the escalation procedure ahead of time and define the thresholds that will determine when alternatives are deployed.
- Establish a person or a team to coordinate real-time tactics.
- Review and refine your escalation plan on an ongoing basis.
- Continually improve your planning process. Real-time management will never be an effective substitute for accurate resource planning.

# Part Four:
# Elevating Quality and Performance

## CHAPTER 12:
## Establishing the Right Measures and Objectives

## CHAPTER 13:
## Improving Contact Center and Organizationwide Performance

## CHAPTER 14:
## Boosting Individual Performance

## CHAPTER 15:
## Building a More Effective Organization

---

*The subjects of quality, performance and customer service have been reassessed with every passing management movement. But real progress in this profession is evident: High-performance contact centers have made a dramatic shift from the call processing "factories" of the past to environments marked by high agent skill levels, an incessant focus on customer experience, and organizationwide contributions to better products and services.*

---

# CHAPTER 12:
# Establishing the Right Measures and Objectives

*Not everything that can be counted counts, and not everything that counts can be counted.*

**ALBERT EINSTEIN**

Establishing the right measures and objectives is one of the most important responsibilities in leading and managing a contact center successfully. When decisions are based on solid information — and when process improvement efforts are coupled with sensible objectives and accountabilities for individuals and teams — you will be poised to create substantial value for your customers and your organization.

But there's a significant challenge from the start: Contact centers produce mounds of data. The information that hits your inbox could cover a small parking lot. Out of all the reports and data that are available, which are best for assessing and guiding your operation's performance? Are you looking at the right things? Are others? Do you agree on what's important and how to interpret results?

In this chapter, we'll look at some important definitions, then identify some of the most common measurements in use today. We'll then discuss the performance indicators that matter most and look at how every person has a role in meeting high-level measures and objectives.

# Key Definitions

There are quite a few definitions related to measures: measurement, goal, target, objective, standard, and key performance indicator (KPI), to name a few. When specifically applied, there are important distinctions in meaning. Whether a measure becomes part of, say, a performance objective or KPI depends on context, use and what you'd like to accomplish. The most important definitions include:

**MEASUREMENT:** A quantifiable unit referring to time (e.g., average handling time), an input (e.g., a call, Twitter message, email), an output, (e.g., a sale, completed contact) or a ratio expressed with a numerator and denominator (e.g., absenteeism, first-call resolution).

**GOAL:** The point of arrival. For example, if a performance objective is to cut turnover in half, and it is currently 16 percent, then 8 percent turnover is the goal.

**PERFORMANCE TARGET:** An interim improvement point at a specific point in time; a "checkpoint" to reassess progress and correct the action or work plans necessary to reach the final goal.

**STANDARD:** A quantifiable minimum level of performance; performance below or outside the standard is not acceptable.

**PERFORMANCE OBJECTIVE:** Usually stated as a quantifiable goal that must be accomplished within a given set of constraints, such as a specified period of time or by a given date (e.g., improve customer satisfaction by 10 points within one year).

**KEY PERFORMANCE INDICATOR:** A high-level measure of effectiveness. Some define KPI as the single most important measure in a department or unit, but many contact centers have multiple KPIs.

In this chapter, I refer to measures and objectives generally. But as you apply them, the context will dictate precise terms and meaning. You'll want to ensure that your team is speaking a common language, and that only the most appropriate measures become objectives (see figure).

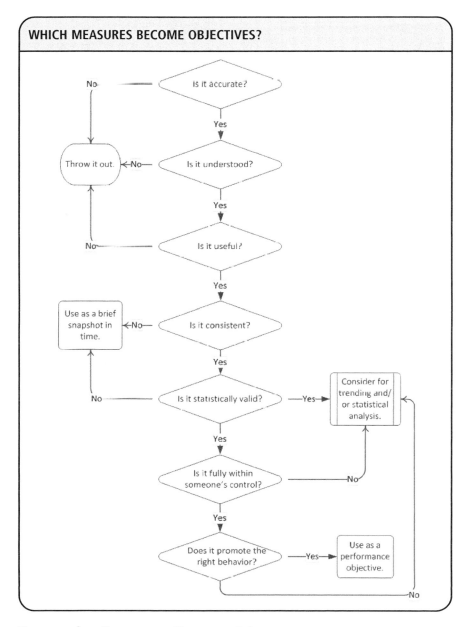

**WHICH MEASURES BECOME OBJECTIVES?**

## Example Contact Center Measures

Performance measures in contact centers can be broadly divided into a handful of categories, including:

- Quality
- Accessibility
- Operational Efficiency
- Cost Performance
- Strategic Impact

Let's take a look at common measures within each category. Stick with me here — though this chapter doesn't represent an exhaustive list, there are quite a few we'll run through. Getting a good bird's eye view of the many alternatives from which to choose is a good start to selecting measures and objectives that make sense for your organization.

Also, before we go through the summary, it's worth noting that many measures can logically fit into more than one category. Consider agent turnover. Is it a measure of efficiency (newer agents tend to be less efficient), cost performance (it is costly to replace agents), or strategic impact (experience has an impact on results)? Or how about contacts by channel, which includes the use of self-service systems? Is that a matter of accessibility, efficiency, cost performance or something else (the best answer is "all of the above")? In short, how you categorize measures is not as important as getting them on the table so that you can make sensible choices about which to use and how.

One more note (and one you're getting used to!): While many of the examples (and the terms themselves) have traditionally applied to phone calls, the underlying principles are, with the right use, applicable to any channel. If you're handling interactions through Twitter, for example, measures and objectives for quality, first contact resolution, and accessibility are just as needed and appropriate. There will be some differences in areas, such as accessibility, that need to be broken out by service level and response time (Chapters 4 and 7). And how quality is measured for a Facebook post or Twitter message versus an email or phone call will vary. Even so, the majority of quality criteria will be similar across the board, a subject we'll look at in Chapter 13.

## QUALITY

Common measures related to quality include:

**CALL (CONTACT) QUALITY:** Assigns a value to the quality of individual contacts. Criteria generally include such things as interpreting customer requirements correctly, entering data accurately, providing the

---

**PERSPECTIVE ON FIRST-CALL RESOLUTION**

First-call resolution (FCR) has become a popular performance measure in customer contact centers in recent years. And that's a good thing: Unresolved contacts are a common source of customer dissatisfaction, and the organization tends to incur many additional expenses (repeat calls, rework, etc.) when issues are not fully resolved.

However, despite clear benefits, FCR must be implemented carefully. Some important lessons have emerged:

- Learn to think critically when interpreting FCR. An exceptionally high FCR rate may point to many simple contacts that can be prevented before they happen.
- Accurate comparisons with other organizations are difficult since definitions of "resolved contact" vary widely. Focus on developing an appropriate definition for your environment, and stick to it so that you'll have a stable, baseline measure.
- Treat FCR as an organizationwide initiative. When an issue is not resolved on the first contact, the problem often may be found outside the contact center (with product or service documentation, functionality or processes, for instance).
- Track FCR at least two ways — as an internal measure, and based on whether or not customers feel that their issues were resolved on the first contact (via survey feedback). If these measures don't closely correlate, find out why.

Above all, keep your eye on the prize: business results, such as customer loyalty, profitability and market share. Remember that FCR is just a supporting indicator, not the endgame.

correct information, accurate call coding, and capturing needed and useful information (see Chapter 13). Call quality is appropriate in all environments as both a high-level indicator of trends and progress and as a specific objective for agents and supervisors, contact by contact. Data typically comes from samples via monitoring or recording contacts. Quality is discussed further in Chapters 13 and 14.

**FIRST-CALL (FIRST-CONTACT) RESOLUTION:** Studies indicate that organizations incur many additional expenses (some hidden and difficult to track) when customer issues are not fully resolved on the first contact. First-call resolution also has a great impact on customer satisfaction. There is significant value in analyzing relative increases and decreases in first-call resolution in response to changes in processes, systems and customer requirements. Consequently, first-call resolution is appropriate in all environments as a high-level objective (see sidebar). Components that lead to first-call resolution should also be built into specific quality objectives for agents — however, because not all aspects are within their control, such components must be selected carefully. First-call resolution may be tracked through quality monitoring samples, customer surveys (asking customers whether the issues were resolved), call coding based on agent judgment (supported by clear criteria), data on callbacks (e.g., from CRM systems), or a combination. I always recommend that FCR be measured both internally and externally (see sidebar).

**ERRORS AND REWORK:** As with first-call resolution, there is significant value in analyzing increases and decreases in errors and rework in response to changes in processes, systems and other factors. Measures of errors and rework are appropriate in all environments, and specific components of errors and rework are often built into quality objectives for agents (variables must be selected carefully because not all errors are within their control). Data may come from quality monitoring or recording, CRM systems, analytics capabilities, call coding or other sources. See Chapter 13.

## ACCESSIBILITY

Common measures related to accessibility include:

**CONTACTS BY CHANNEL:** These are simply measures of the number of contacts by channel: phone, chat, social, Web self-service, IVR self-service, SMS, email, etc., and when they occur. If there are customer communities associated with your products and services, it's also a good idea to assess that activity and determine how many issues are resolved within the forums versus those that require agent assistance (see Intuit case study, Chapter 2). You should also track the AHTs associated with different kinds of agent-assisted contacts so that you have a complete picture of workload by channel; this is essential data for forecasting, and is also useful as a high-level indication of relative trends and cost efficiency. AHT is available from your ACD and other routing systems, social management tools, workforce management systems (which are becoming more commonly known as "workforce optimization" systems), and related tools and systems.

**SERVICE LEVEL, RESPONSE TIME AND RESOLUTION:** Establishing service level and response time objectives is a prerequisite to the planning necessary to ensure that the organization is accessible through whatever channel customers use. Real-time reports are also necessary for tactical adjustments. If multiple exchanges are necessary, you'll also need to track overall time to resolution (common in technical support and similar environments). Service level is available directly from ACD or related routing systems, social management tools, and workforce management systems. Response time reports may come from sources such as email response management systems (ERMS), Web servers, workforce management reports, case management tools, social media systems, or, potentially, other sources. See Chapters 4 and 7.

**AVERAGE SPEED OF ANSWER (ASA):** ASA is often misinterpreted as a "typical" experience, but the average is skewed by many callers who get answered before ASA and some who wait far longer than ASA (see sidebar on this topic in Chapter 4). ASA comes from the same set of data as service level, and it is usually not necessary to have both; however, if service level data is not available, ASA can be a substitute. Also, ASA does have important operational applications; for example, it is a component of trunk load (Chapter 7). Data on ASA is available from the same systems that provide information on service level.

**ABANDONED AND BLOCKED CALLS:** Abandoned and blocked calls are generally caused by insufficient staffing or trunking resources, and should be supporting information to service level and response time reports, not primary objectives (see Chapter 4). Abandoned calls are available directly from ACD or workforce management reports or from servers handling specific types of contacts, such as chat. Reports on busy signals may come from the ACD (if using ACD-controlled busies), the local telephone company or the interexchange (long-distance) company (IXC). See Chapter 6.

**LONGEST DELAY:** Also referred to as oldest call, this figure gives you the worst case, the longest amount of time a caller had to wait before reaching an agent or abandoning. It is appropriate in all environments as supporting information to service level and response time objectives, and is available from the same sources that provide service level data.

## OPERATIONAL EFFICIENCY

Common measures related to efficiency include:

**FORECAST ACCURACY:** Forecasting the workload accurately is a high-leverage activity that is fundamental to managing a customer contact operation effectively. Forecasted call load versus actual is appropriate in all environments as a high-level objective, and, as discussed in Chapter 6, should be reported down to the interval level. It is also used for ongoing tactical adjustments. Forecasted call load is available from the system used for forecasting, such as the workforce management system, forecasting software or even customized spreadsheets. Actual call load may be tracked by your ACD, workforce management system, email management system, Web servers, social media tools, or a combination of these systems. See Chapter 6.

**SCHEDULED STAFF VERSUS ACTUAL:** This measure provides a comparison of the number of agents scheduled with the number actually in the center. It is appropriate in all environments as a high-level objective for the center and for teams. As with forecasts, reports should show each interval. The purpose of the objective is to understand and improve staff adherence and schedules. Scheduled staff is available from the system used for scheduling (the workforce management system or spreadsheets, for example). Actual staff available is reported primarily by the ACD, workforce management system, or applications associated with other contact channels. See Chapters 8 and 14.

**ADHERENCE TO SCHEDULE:** A measure of how much time and when during agents' shifts that they are taking or available to take calls. Adherence to schedule is appropriate in all environments as a high-level objective, and is also a common and recommended objective for individuals and teams. The measure is independent of whether the center actually has the staff necessary to achieve a targeted service level and/or response time; it is simply a comparison of how closely agents adhere to schedules. Data generally comes from ACD and workforce management reports. See Chapter 14.

**AVERAGE HANDLING TIME (AHT):** AHT is appropriate in all environments for forecasting, planning and process improvement activities; however, it is generally not recommended as a strict agent standard. In many centers, AHT has been increasing overall as self-service systems and customer communities proliferate and resulting agent-assisted contacts become more complex; cross-sell and upsell initiatives can also add time to calls. Relative reductions in AHT through better processes, technologies and training can create significant efficiencies. AHT is available from ACD and related routing systems as well as workforce management reports. See Chapters 6 and 13.

**OCCUPANCY, CONTACTS HANDLED, NORMALIZED CONTACTS HANDLED:** The service level that you are achieving at any given

**Confusing Objectives**

© ICMI | by Greg Levin | Illustration by Gene Baikauskas

time will dictate the resulting occupancy rate and, therefore, the number of contacts handled. Although occupancy is not within the control of an individual or group of agents, it can be "neutralized" by dividing calls handled by percent occupancy to produce a measure of "normalized contacts handled." Even so, beyond general trending purposes, these measures have limited use as indicators of productivity — see complete discussion in Chapter 14. Occupancy and calls handled are available from ACD and related routing systems, workforce management reports, and potentially from other systems and servers. See Chapters 7, 9 and 14.

**TRANSFERRED OR ESCALATED CALLS:** An excessive number of transferred or escalated calls can indicate that calls are not being routed to the right places, or that agents are not sufficiently trained, equipped or empowered to handle them. These measures are appropriate in all environments, and data is available from applicable routing systems.

## COST PERFORMANCE

Common measures related to cost performance include:

**COST PER CALL (COST PER CONTACT):** Cost per call is appropriate in all environments as a high-level objective (generally reported monthly or quarterly). However, it must be interpreted correctly; for example, a climbing cost per call can actually be a good sign (process improvements may result in fewer calls, spreading fixed costs over fewer calls and driving up cost per call). Volume of contacts requires ACD reports, and potentially other systems that track contacts. Cost data comes from several sources, such as payroll for staffing costs; budgets for equipment, building depreciation, etc.; and telecommunications reports for toll and line-usage costs.

**AVERAGE (CONTACT) CALL VALUE:** Average call value is appropriate for revenue-generating environments, such as reservation centers and catalog companies, where calls have a measurable value. It is generally reported quarterly or monthly, and sometimes more frequently. Many organizations also incorporate and track cross-sell and upsell results. Average call value is difficult to apply (and generally not recommended) in centers where the value of calls is difficult to measure (e.g., customer service centers and technical support). Revenue information comes from any report that indicates revenue generated by the contact center — sales reports, total orders, CRM system reports, etc. Volume of contacts requires reports from the ACD, workforce management or other routing systems that may be involved.

**REVENUE:** As with average call value, measures of revenue are appropriate for revenue-generating environments and can be reported quarterly, monthly, daily or for specific time periods. Results are often correlated with other variables, such as contact center costs, market conditions and revenues through other channels within the organization (e.g., retail or the direct sales force) to gauge the contact center's impact on the organization's profits. Revenue information comes from any report that indicates revenue generated by the contact center, such as sales reports, total orders, CRM system reports, etc.

**BUDGETED TO ACTUAL EXPENDITURES:** Often called variance reports, these measures illustrate the differences between projected and actual expenditures for various budget categories (see example in Chapter 10). They are appropriate in all environments as high-level objectives, assuming they are considered within the context of changing workload variables and contact center responsibilities. They are generally produced both quarterly and annually, and are available monthly in some environments. Budget versus actual information can be formulated from corporate accounting systems or customized applications.

**OBJECTIVES FOR OUTBOUND:** Outbound measures often include number or percentage of attempted calls, connected calls, contacts, decision maker contacts (reaching the right person), abandoned calls, contacts per hour, contact rate, cost per contact, cost per minute and others. These objectives are appropriate and necessary in environments that include outbound contacts. (Depending on how they are used, this genre of measures can logically fit into any of the major categories.)

**TURNOVER:** Retention is an increasingly important objective as contact centers become more complex and as agent and management skills and experience requirements escalate. Reductions in turnover typically can be translated into financial savings, overall improvements in quality and productivity, and higher levels of strategic contribution. Turnover reports are often produced monthly (calculated on an annualized basis), and should be categorized as voluntary (they decide to leave) or involuntary (they are forced to leave), as well as internal (which is often positive, e.g., for a promotion or strategic move to another area) or external (they leave the organization); we also suggest you look at when it occurs — see Chapter 14. Data is captured via entries in personnel records and/or a workforce management system, and results are typically manually calculated or reported from appropriate workforce management applications.

## STRATEGIC IMPACT

Common measures related to strategic impact include:

**EMPLOYEE SATISFACTION:** Studies have demonstrated that customer satisfaction increases as agent job satisfaction increases. Further, retention, productivity and quality often have a definable, positive correlation to agent satisfaction. Results of surveys to gauge agent satisfaction should be compared with job satisfaction levels in other parts of the organization. Data is generally captured via anonymous surveys, and can be augmented by focus groups and one-on-one interviews. See Chapters 14 and 17.

**CUSTOMER SATISFACTION AND LOYALTY:** Measuring customer satisfaction is necessary and appropriate in all environments and has greatest value when trended over time and correlated to other measures and developments (e.g., what impact do changes in policies, services and processes have on customer satisfaction?). Data can come from a variety of sources: outbound call surveys, automated post-call IVR surveys, email or mail surveys, focus groups, and other sources. Customer loyalty is usually viewed through measures of repeat business or over time, or improved wallet share, cross-sell and upsell. See Chapters 2 and 13.

**SENTIMENT TRENDING:** Sentiment analysis focuses on the nature of customer comments about a company's products, services and reputation. It is a fast-growing aspect of social customer service, and with speech and text analytics tools, can also be applied to interactions captured through virtually any channel. At a basic level, sentiment can be broadly categorized as positive, negative or neutral. Deeper levels of analysis can correlate findings to changes in services and products, competitive trends, customer demographics and other variables. In social media, a related area is identifying (and serving appropriately) the "influencers" who have large followings and can have a significant impact on the opinions and behavior of other customers and prospects.

**STRATEGIC VALUE:** Measures and objectives related to strategic value seek to identify, quantify, track, improve and communicate the contact center's return on investment (ROI) and impact on other business units. These measures are often related to:

- Customer satisfaction and loyalty
- Improved quality and innovation

- Leveraged marketing initiatives
- More focused products and services
- Efficient delivery of services
- Supporting self-service systems
- Minimizing potential legal issues
- Contributions to sales and revenue
- Improved brand reputation and word of mouth

These measures are appropriate in all environments. While revenue- and profit-related measures will not apply to non-commercial organizations (e.g., government and not-for-profit), the contact center's impact on things like innovation, quality and customer satisfaction apply in any environment. Reports are generally a synthesis of samples and analysis, and data comes from a variety of sources. See Chapters 10 and 13.

## OTHER MEASURES

There are literally hundreds of additional measures, combinations and derivatives we could add. The list is a starting point. Let your needs, objectives and imagination contribute other possibilities for consideration (see section on reporting, Chapter 10).

# Which Measures Are Right for Your Organization?

Given the sheer number of possibilities, and the constant change in the business environment, many managers are looking for clear-cut guidance on objectives and standards. Where do we stand? What are others doing? What performance is good enough? What will satisfy customers? What is "world class"?

Those are reasonable questions, and you should be asking them. But let's start with a basic truth: Ultimately, you will need to establish measures and objectives that are right for your organization. That involves learning all you can about the process of establishing contact center objectives and how variables are interrelated; developing a solid customer access strategy and tying it to your organization's overall strategic objectives; and then establishing the measures and objectives that make sense for you.

---

*The test of any policy in management ... is not whether the answer is right or wrong, but whether it works.*

**PETER F. DRUCKER**

---

"Okay," some will say. "We agree with the notion of choosing objectives that are right for our organization. Still ... help us get started. Which measures absolutely, positively must be in place?"

Fair enough. There are seven key categories of measures that should be in place in every customer contact center. They build on each other, and it helps to order them from the most elemental and tactical, to strategic. They include:

**FORECAST ACCURACY.** If you don't have an accurate prediction of the workload coming your way, it's almost impossible to deliver efficient, consistent service and achieve high levels of customer satisfaction. And that's just as true for new social interactions as it has been for phone, chat or email.

**SCHEDULE FIT AND ADHERENCE.** If you have a good handle on the workload, you can build accurate schedules that ensure the right people are in the right places at the right times. This is best managed from the bottom up, with ample buy-in, and is an important enabler to everything else you're trying to accomplish.

**SERVICE LEVEL AND RESPONSE TIME.** If customer contacts don't get to the right places at the right times, little else can happen. Establishing service level and response time objectives is a prerequisite to ensuring that the organization is accessible and part of the conversation, wherever customers choose to interact.

**QUALITY AND FIRST-CONTACT RESOLUTION.** Quality is the link between call-by-call activities and the organization's most important high-level objectives. First-contact resolution is essentially an extension of quality — a tangible result of getting quality right. Quality measures should be applied to every type of customer interaction.

**EMPLOYEE SATISFACTION.** Employee satisfaction clearly influences, even drives, customer satisfaction and is an essential measure in any environment. Further, retention, productivity and quality often have a definable, positive correlation to agent satisfaction.

**CUSTOMER SATISFACTION AND LOYALTY.** Customer satisfaction is essential in all environments and has greatest value as a relative measure and in conjunction with other objectives (e.g., what impact do changes in policies, services and processes have on customer satisfaction). Customer loyalty is usually viewed through breadth and longevity of the customer's relationship with the business.

**STRATEGIC VALUE.** What contributions does the contact center make to revenues, marketing initiatives, product innovations and other primary business objectives? Measures are often focused on samples of impact in these and related areas, fueled by listening, engaging, and learning from customer interactions. See Chapters 10 and 13.

Other measures and objectives should be driven by your organization's mission and objectives. For example, many customer service environments focus on customer satisfaction, efficiency issues and cost measures. Sales environments often base key objectives on revenue, cross-sell, upsell and customer retention activities. And encouraging the use of self-service systems and customer communities, and preventing contacts before they happen (e.g., by working with other business units to simplify features, fix glitches or improve manuals) are important objectives in many technical support environments.

As you home in on the right objectives, keep your eyes on the prize: maximum positive impact on the business, the things that really matter. As long-time industry analyst Keith Dawson put it, call-handling stats are "very comfortable" metrics. "But do they really tell a deep story of what a call center represents to an organization? No, for that you need to measure things like

**FOCUS ON WHAT REALLY MATTERS**

In recent years, there has been a lot of attention on contact center "optimization." To many, optimization is synonymous with driving costs out of the business — moving contacts to lower-cost channels (self-service, etc.), reducing human contact with the customer, and driving down handling times.

"This is all wrong," says consultant Mary Murcott in her book, *Driving Peak Sales Performance in Call Centers* (ICMI Press). "This is not optimization; this is driving a distorted view of efficiency even further down the current wayward road." According to Murcott, true optimization means optimizing business outcomes like customer loyalty and revenue. Significant performance improvement requires moving away from "ancillary measurements," such as cost per call, and instead focusing on channel profitability and loyalty.

In an era when products and services quickly become commodities, customer contact services represent significant differentiation and value-add opportunities. Do you and the rest of your team realize the potential of your services?

customer satisfaction and revenue generated. How many customer calls were turned into sales opportunities or even chances to get simple feedback on what your center is doing?"

# Building a Supporting Culture

As you establish measures, track performance and work toward achieving important objectives, it is essential that your team perceives what the measures are really saying. And that requires understanding how contact center dynamics work. For example:

- Maybe your first-call resolution rate is lower than what similar organizations say they are achieving; but you may be measuring it more rigorously and working to prevent easy-to-handle contacts at the source.

- Your center's average handling time (AHT) may be higher than that of other centers, but if you are using that time to prevent repeat calls, improve processes and capture information that can improve products and marketing, your total call load along with associated costs may, in fact, be far better than they are for other centers.

- Your service level or response time objectives may be more modest than others in your industry. But you may actually be doing better, if you hit them increment after increment, day after day.

We've seen a concerted effort in many organizations to move away from transaction-oriented measures and objectives in recent years, and instead put more focus on delivering a great customer experience. Some examples include:

- American Express tied 50 percent of the total compensation of their Vice President of Customer Experience, and 20 percent of agents' incentives, to customer feedback garnered through their voice of the customer initiative.

- Independence Blue Cross in Philadelphia removed the "average talk time" statistic from its reward and recognition program, as did Boston Coach with its "number of calls handled per shift" metric. Instead, both organizations have put more emphasis on quality and process improvements.

- Sharp Electronics tied its agents' compensation and promotions, in part, to how well they used the organization's knowledge management system.

- Aetna U.S. Healthcare went so far as to advertise its focus on first-call resolution in consumer-oriented newspapers and online ads. In these and many similar cases, organizations report better overall results when they focus on the things that matter most.

- CEO Tony Hsieh cites a Zappos phone call that went almost six hours. "We don't measure call times and we don't upsell. We just care about whether the rep goes above and beyond for every customer." (Most don't go that long, but point well taken.)

- Boden, a U.K.-based retailer recognized as one of the country's "Top 50 Call Centres for Customer Service," a popular benchmark program, has a similar philosophy. "We don't have quotas. We don't have stopwatches. And we certainly don't do the hard sell," they explain in a publication profiling winners. "All we do is go at the customers' pace, treat them like an old friend ... we know we've got it right when they smile."

It's often said, "What gets measured gets done." I believe that's an oversimplification. I've seen organizations measure lots of things, yet not make sustained improvements in those areas (see cartoon, Confusing Objectives). I am convinced that it's a matter of not only measuring the right things, but also building a culture that understands and contributes to them, removing roadblocks and conflicting objectives, and ensuring that day-to-day activities and decisions support them. And to reiterate a related observation: The contact centers that get the best results tend to have fewer performance measures; but those they have are the ones that really matter.

## Everyone Counts!

Which performance objectives are established and how they are applied tend to vary significantly from one organization to the next. However, one principle is universal: Every position — indeed, every person — plays a part in helping the contact center to achieve high-level objectives.

Unfortunately, the nature of overlapping responsibilities can leave individuals feeling like there is little connection between what they do and what the organization is trying to achieve. Nothing could be further from the truth. The following table provides a summary of the connections between roles and key objectives. While not every possible position/role is included, the summary illustrates the diverse but shared contributions those in a variety of roles make to overall results.

| Key Objectives | Responsibilities for Accomplishing Objectives |
|---|---|
| Quality | **Agents:** Have a direct impact on contact quality, which contributes to overall quality, first-call resolution, and a low rate of errors and rework.<br>**Supervisors:** Contribute to quality objectives by ensuring that individuals in their teams have the resources, coaching and feedback they need to handle each contact with quality. The experience supervisors have in handling frontline work, as well as their proximity to it, make them invaluable in quality improvement initiatives.<br>**Quality Managers:** Manage a centralized repository of quality data captured contact by contact (by the quality team or by supervisors). Analysis of this information leads to process, system, training and coaching improvements.<br>**Workforce Managers:** Affect quality by forecasting the center's workload accurately and ensuring that schedules match requirements (resulting in the right contacts going to the right places at the right times). They also are responsible for identifying the best times for people to work on quality initiatives and training.<br>**Technical Support (IT):** Enable quality by equipping the contact center with appropriate tools and technologies. For example, information systems that provide agents with accurate, real-time data on customers, products, services and policies contribute enormously to call quality and first-call resolution. Similarly, capable systems that are thoughtfully programmed ensure that the right contacts are routed to the right places at the right times.<br>**Managers/Director:** Contribute to quality and accessibility first and foremost by ensuring that agents, supervisors, planners and others have the training, skills, tools and processes that enable them to be successful in their positions. They ensure that the contact center is an inherent part of organizationwide processes (e.g., marketing and product development). They also are generally responsible for cultivating a culture that values quality from top to bottom. |

| Accessibility | **Agents:** Contribute to accessibility by being in "the right place at the right times, doing the right things." |
|---|---|
| | **Supervisors:** Contribute to accessibility by ensuring that individuals are in the right places at the right times, doing the right things. They help to resolve adherence problems and often serve as liaisons between real-time workforce managers and teams. |
| | **Quality Managers:** Are inherently close to processes that affect handling times and other key accessibility drivers. |
| | **Workforce Managers:** Accessibility is a primary workforce management responsibility. Workforce planners affect accessibility by forecasting the contact center's workload accurately and ensuring that schedules match workload requirements. |
| | **Technical Support (IT):** Enable accessibility by ensuring that systems are structured well, are responsive and support real-time call handling requirements. IT also has responsibility to ensure that systems are up and running and that technical problems are quickly resolved. |
| | **Managers/Director:** Contribute to accessibility by ensuring that the contact center's priorities and supporting operational decisions support accessibility. They see that employees have the resources they need, and that processes and systems support consistent accessibility. They ensure that departments across the organization that may affect the contact center's workload collaborate with those responsible for forecasting and scheduling. |
| Efficiency | **Agents:** Contribute to efficiency objectives, not only by how they handle contacts, but by how they code work. For example, when they use talk time, after-call work and other work modes consistently and accurately, they contribute to more stable, reliable data for forecasting, scheduling and other objectives. Agents also have a direct impact on adherence to schedule. |

*(continued next page)*

| | |
|---|---|
| **Efficiency** *(continued)* | **Supervisors:** Ensure that work is being handled as required, which leads to stable results and reliable data for planning purposes. They also usually serve as coordinators/liaisons for planning meetings and when schedules are adjusted to accommodate changing workload requirements. They have a key role in coaching agents to achieve adherence results.<br><br>**Quality Managers:** Have a responsibility not just for quality, but for associated efficiencies. For example, if it takes one agent seven screens to do the same thing another can do in three, quality specialists can drive relevant training and coaching improvements.<br><br>**Workforce Managers:** As with accessibility, objectives related to efficiency are primary workforce planning responsibilities. Accurate forecasting, staffing and scheduling, as well as competent real-time adjustments contribute enormously to efficiencies.<br><br>**Technical Support (IT):** Contribute to efficiency by ensuring that workload tracking tools are correctly programmed and that trainers and supervisors teach agents their proper use. They also have a role in providing and supporting systems that provide reports and data essential to the planning process (e.g., routing systems, reporting tools, etc.).<br><br>**Managers/Director:** Affect efficiency not only by ensuring that the center has the right tools, methods and training in place, but also by establishing a culture of collaboration, one that emphasizes the importance of accurate and comprehensive planning. And (as with accessibility) by ensuring that data, information and plans that other departments have are shared with the contact center. |
| **Cost Performance** | **Agents:** Have an indirect but significant impact on cost performance objectives. By doing the right things at the right times and handling contacts with quality, they contribute to accessibility and quality, which, in turn, have a direct bearing on cost performance. Also, in revenue-producing environments, sales skills have a significant impact on revenue results. |

| | |
|---|---|
| **Cost Performance** *(continued)* | **Supervisors:** As with agents, supervisors have a significant impact on cost performance objectives. By enabling their teams to do the right things at the right times and handle contacts with quality, they contribute to accessibility and quality, which, in turn, have a direct bearing on cost performance. Coaching and monitoring should also support overall budget and revenue objectives.<br><br>**Quality Managers:** Important aspects of quality include those things that lead to revenue and cost performance objectives (e.g., efficient processes, seeing cross-selling opportunities, etc.).<br><br>**Workforce Managers:** The accuracy of workforce planning and effectiveness in carrying out those plans affects virtually every cost performance objective. For example, forecasts and schedules that are improved by just one or two percent can translate to thousands of dollars of daily savings in medium to large centers. Appropriate schedules reduce overtime costs, and accurate planning ensures that contacts are going to the right agent groups at the right times, which has an impact on revenue and cost results.<br><br>**Technical Support (IT):** The technologies available to the contact center — their functionality and how they are programmed and used — have a significant impact on cost performance objectives. This is true for customer-facing systems (e.g., to what degree will they use self-service channels?), information systems agents use to handle contacts with quality, and reporting systems used by management to leverage efficiencies and effectiveness. Efficiency of systems, uptime, and technical support response times all contribute to cost objectives.<br><br>**Managers/Director:** Have primary responsibility for identifying budgetary requirements and ensuring that the center gets the resources necessary to fulfill its mission. They also have a significant impact on cost performance by ensuring that the right people, processes and technologies are in place and working in sync. |

| Strategic Impact | **Agents:** Contribute to customer satisfaction (and subsequent loyalty and repeat business) through their contributions to accessibility and quality on a contact-by-contact basis. But agents also have a much larger strategic impact; for example, the information captured during contacts, assuming it is complete and accurate, becomes the basis for product and service improvements and innovations, better marketing campaigns, and quality improvements (inside and outside the contact center). Agents are also key in educating customers on the availability and use of self-service and customer communities. <br><br> **Supervisors:** Contribute to the contact center's strategic impact by helping to facilitate their teams' success. Supervisors are also frequently involved in projects and initiatives to identify, measure, track, improve and communicate the center's impact on the organization (e.g., through data analysis teams and as liaisons between other groups and departments. <br><br> **Quality Managers:** Typically, quality specialists are involved in assembling information captured during contacts, analyzing it and getting it to other departments to which it would be useful. Quality specialists also are responsible for recommendations on process improvements that would contribute to higher levels of customer satisfaction and agent support. <br><br> **Workforce Managers:** Have a similar impact on both customer satisfaction and employee satisfaction. For example, when the contact center is accessible, due to accurate forecasts and schedules, customers are happier because they can reach the services they require quickly and easily. Similarly, good service levels mean occupancy levels that are not too high, giving agents breathing room between contacts and allowing them to work with callers who aren't angry from waiting in a long queue. Again, accurate planning matches the right resources with the right contacts, enabling the highest quality services and customer satisfaction. |
|---|---|

| | |
|---|---|
| **Strategic Impact** *(continued)* | **Technical Support (IT):** Technologies influence customer satisfaction first at the user interface — e.g., are customer-facing systems easy to use, and do they enable customers to accomplish what they want? Back-end systems also have a significant role — e.g., do agents have the information and support they need? Are capabilities in place to capture data from contacts that can be used to improve products, services and marketing, as well as to better understand customers? The answers to these and related questions affect customer satisfaction, employee satisfaction and the contact center's overall ROI. Technical support also has a key role in developing and maintaining disaster recovery plans. **Managers/Director:** Ensure that the culture, environment, tools and resources are in place to support a high-value environment. They also work with managers across the organization to use data captured during contacts to improve the organization's overall effectiveness in meeting the needs of customers. They ensure that employees remain focused on the vision of the organization and that behaviors are within company guidelines and support the company's brand and direction. |

In short, every role has an impact on overall results. Consequently, it is essential that you take steps to ensure that the interrelated nature of contact center objectives and responsibilities is understood at all levels.

Establishing the right measures and objectives is one of the most important and challenging responsibilities in leading and managing a contact center. However, objectives and standards will have little positive impact unless the organization is also making fundamental improvements to processes. When robust process improvement efforts are coupled with sensible objectives and accountabilities for individuals and teams, the contact center is in a position to achieve results that create real value for customers and for the organization. We'll pick up with these subjects in the next two chapters.

# Points to Remember

- Although terms such as measure, objective, goal and target are often used interchangeably, they have different meanings when specifically applied.

- Common performance measures can be broadly divided into categories that include quality, accessibility, operational efficiency, cost performance and strategic impact.

- There are literally hundreds of possible performance measures and objectives from which to choose.

- Key measures — e.g., those related to forecast accuracy, schedule adherence, service level and response time, quality and first-call resolution, employee satisfaction, customer satisfaction and strategic value — should be in place in every customer contact center.

- Other measures will be unique to your environment. You will need to establish objectives that are right for your organization, and ensure that you do not make the mistake of looking at any one in isolation.

- Each person in the contact center, whatever his or her role, has an impact on overall results. Consequently, it is essential that the interrelated nature of objectives and responsibilities be understood at all levels.

# CHAPTER 13:
# Improving Contact Center and Organizationwide Performance

*It will not suffice to have customers who are merely satisfied.*

**W. EDWARDS DEMING**

---

The ongoing need to improve quality and performance — to deliver services that are fast, better and more economical — has attracted numerous management movements over the years. Examples in recent decades include Six Sigma (popularized by Motorola in the early 1980s), excellence, management by objectives (MBO), total quality management (TQM), reengineering and Kaizen. Go back even further, and you'll find scientific management (Frederick Taylor), human relations, statistical quality control, and others.

Today's focus on a new generation of quality, collaboration, and customer experience initiatives is building on a rich history. Naturally, new ideas and other movements will follow. But boil them down to their influence on forward-thinking contact centers, and you'll find a handful of core principles that are quietly and consistently at work. I admit, it's a bit bold to condense such a vast body of management theory and work into a handful of themes. But for our purposes of cutting to the chase, I'm going to take that risk and summarize them as follows:

- Quality must be based on customer needs and expectations

**299**

- Quality and service level work together
- The process is where the leverage is
- Fix root causes to make lasting improvements
- Contact centers enable significant strategic value
- Improvements must be ongoing
- Skills, knowledge and leadership make the difference

My purpose here is both to make sense of these seven principles and (hopefully) to inspire you to see the vast opportunity that exists to innovate and improve. As you drive the right kind of change, everybody wins — your customers, your employees and your organization.

## Quality Must Be Based on Customer Needs and Expectations

The imperative to identify and address customer expectations stems from a widely accepted principle: Improvements in customer satisfaction generally lead to increased customer loyalty, better business results and a stronger brand reputation. That is why the customer access strategy must be based on the 10 customer expectations (see Chapter 2). Consider the old adage about building the best-quality horse buggy in town: It doesn't matter if no one wants it.

A lesser-known but similarly powerful principle is also at work: Meeting customer expectations often translates into higher levels of service that are delivered at proportionally lower costs. Yes, more loyal customers save the organization oodles of marketing dollars. But there's more to it than that.

Take the simple issue of being courteous (one of the 10 primary customer expectations). In today's environment, that means such things as don't make customers repeat the same information, don't transfer them around and don't make them go over their account history again. Customers don't know the extent that these guidelines require processes and systems that deliver relevant information to the right agent at the right

**AMERICAN GENERAL LIFE PUTS FEEDBACK INTO ACTION**

The American General Life Companies, which provides life, annuity and supplemental health insurance products to 13 million customers, has a three-step process for obtaining and evaluating customer and distributor feedback: listen, analyze and act.

The organization administers its satisfaction surveys via email, and avoids overwhelming its customers through careful tracking so that none are surveyed more than once in a 90-day period. Completed customer satisfaction surveys go to the company's customer feedback Web portal. The customer is then notified that the survey has been received and is awaiting review. When the survey is reviewed, AGL identifies the necessary steps for handling the feedback before reaching back out to the customer, according to Simon Leech, senior vice president, AGL Insurance Services.

When reviewing feedback, AGL uses a "critical feedback loop" model as a guide for moving both positive and negative feedback from the gathering point to the improved customer experience. The feedback loop is considered closed once the actions required by the customer's initial feedback are put into place. These actions include problem resolution, improving service quality, linkage to business or corporate initiatives, and impact validation. The process also includes "kudos alerts" back to agents. The purpose of this model to ensure critical services and quality issues are addressed and that customer loyalty is built through proactive response.

Customers are generally eager to respond to AGL's satisfaction surveys, and they appreciate the survey process and are pleased when their feedback is recognized. In some cases, customers have asked to be surveyed again after their issue has been resolved so that they can offer positive feedback about the experience. AGL continues to evolve its process by adding lost customers, potential customers and distributors to the survey mix in an effort to find out the cause of their transaction abandonment. They can then offer solutions for bringing these customers back.

AGL encourages sharing and collaboration within the organization and has established a customer feedback intranet. The site houses all satisfaction surveys, scores, stories and comments, where they can be reviewed across the company.

time. To them, it's simply a matter of courteous service.

To the organization, however, meeting this expectation almost always translates into service that is more cost effective to deliver. Being responsive, handling contacts right the first time, relaying to customers what to expect — everybody wins, including customers, employees and shareholders.

Three key questions that should always be part of your decision process are: What are your customers' expectations? Are you meeting and exceeding them? Are you using the fewest possible resources to do so? Don't guess at what your direction should be. Rather than create decisions based on what your executive team "believes" customers expect, get your information from the source. Survey them, listen to what they're saying in social channels, and, above all, take every opportunity to listen to, engage and learn from customers during interactions.

> **THREE ESSENTIAL QUESTIONS**
>
> - What are customer expectations?
> - Are you meeting/exceeding them?
> - Are you using the fewest possible resources to do so?

## Quality and Service Level Work Together

Quality and service level are inextricably associated with, and complementary to, each other. As discussed in Chapter 4, service level is an enabler. As service level deteriorates, more callers will verbalize their criticisms when calls are finally answered. Agents spend valuable time apologizing. Average handling time goes up. Morale, turnover and burnout take a hit, as can recruitment and training costs.

Further, when you consider the components of a quality contact (see insert, What is A Quality Contact?), the complementary relationship becomes clear. These items apply almost universally. Take a few minutes to study the list and think through how each item applies in your environment. What if data is not entered correctly? What if the customer doesn't

## WHAT IS A QUALITY CONTACT?

- Customer can access the contact channels desired
- Contact is necessary in the first place
- Customer is not placed in queue for too long
- Customer is not transferred around
- Customer doesn't get rushed
- Agent provides correct response
- All data entry is correct
- Customer receives correct information
- Agent captures all needed/useful information
- Customer has confidence contact was effective
- Customer doesn't feel it necessary to check-up, verify or repeat
- Customer is satisfied
- Agent has pride in workmanship
- Unsolicited marketplace feedback is detected and documented
- Others across the organization can correctly interpret and effectively use the information captured
- The organization's mission is furthered

have confidence the call was handled correctly? What if you didn't capture useful information from the interaction? These problems contribute to repeat calls, escalation of calls and complaints to higher management, and contacts through other channels. The problems often entail rework, further reducing service level.

Upshot: Quality suffers and costs go up. When service level is low because agents are overworked due to constant congestion in the queue, they work less accurately and can become less "customer-friendly." Callers tell them in no uncertain terms about the tough time they had getting through. And agents tend to make more mistakes. These errors further contribute to repeat calls, escalation of calls and diversion of agents to activities that should be unnecessary. Poor service level becomes a vicious cycle.

Just as service level and quality are linked, so, too, are quality and response time. For example, if customers don't receive a reply to an email as quickly as expected, or if they don't receive the correct or expected response, they may send another. Or, what began as an email can turn into a phone call: "I'm calling to check up on an email I sent to you. I haven't heard a reply yet and am wondering ..." If the original inquiry hasn't yet been handled, agents likely won't have the information necessary to deal with these calls without duplicating efforts for both the contact center and the customer. Even worse, customers can resort to social channels with potentially broad audiences — creating an even bigger mess for the organization. Again, costs go up.

To visualize the relationship between accessibility and quality, it's useful to view the implications through the lens of a staffing table (see figure). What portion of average talk time, average after-call work or call volume is due to repeat calls, or waste and rework? What could have been prevented?

## REVISITING SERVICE LEVEL

### Input

Average talk time (sec.) = 180
Average after-call work (sec.) = 30
Calls per half hour = 250
Service level objective (sec.) = 20

**?**

### Output

| Agents | ASA | Service Level | Agent Occupancy | Trunk Load |
|--------|-----|---------------|-----------------|------------|
| 30 | 209 | 24% | 97% | 54.0 |
| 31 | 75 | 45% | 94% | 35.4 |
| 32 | 38 | 61% | 91% | 30.2 |
| 33 | 21 | 73% | 88% | 28.0 |
| 34 | 13 | 82% | 86% | 26.8 |
| 35 | 8 | 88% | 83% | 26.1 |
| 36 | 5 | 92% | 81% | 25.7 |
| 37 | 3 | 95% | 79% | 25.4 |
| 38 | 2 | 97% | 77% | 25.3 |
| 39 | 1 | 98% | 75% | 25.2 |
| 40 | 1 | 99% | 73% | 25.1 |

How about staff — e.g., how many agents are involved in creating or fixing waste and rework? Looking at these relationships in this way can quickly dispel the notion that accessibility and quality are at odds and must be *balanced*. They work together. And driving both in the right direction often has a positive impact on costs.

**IMPACT OF REDUCING DEFECTIVE CONTACTS**

- Quality up
- Production of good contacts up
- Capacity up
- Costs lowered
- Profit improved
- Customers happier
- Agents happier

Errors and rework are part of a downward cycle. They consume valuable staff time, which can lead to insufficient staff to handle the workload. Insufficient staff then leads to a low service level/response time, high occupancy, unhappy customers and increased stress. Those things contribute to

**EXAMPLES OF COSTS WHEN QUALITY IS LACKING**

- Unnecessary service contacts
- Repeat contacts from customers
- Callbacks to customers for missing or unclear information
- Escalation of contacts and complaints to higher management
- Contacts to customer relations
- Handling product returns
- Expenses to re-ship
- Wrong problems get fixed
- Loss of revenue from cancellations
- Cancellations causing inaccurate inventory status
- Cost of closing accounts
- Negative publicity from angry customers
- Loss of referrals
- Diversion of agents to activities that should be unnecessary
- Agents "taking the heat" for mistakes made by others

errors and rework, completing the cycle. So reducing errors and rework has a positive impact on service level and response time, morale, customer satisfaction and costs!

## The Process Is Where the Leverage Is

Another basic tenet of the quality movement is continuous process improvement. The best contact centers make the effort to understand their processes and are working to improve them.

A process is a "system of causes." (Note: In the context of quality and process improvement, "system" refers to the system of causes or processes, not a technology.) The contact center itself is a process, a system of causes. It is part of the organization, which is an expansive system of causes. An agent group is a system of causes within the contact center. And each call comprises a system of causes.

The central focus of the process illustrated in the figure can be any high-level measurement or result that you're after. Note that most of the items

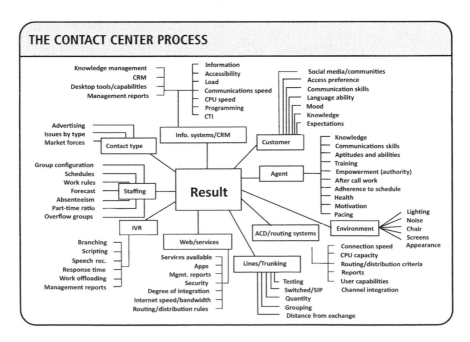

**THE CONTACT CENTER PROCESS**

are the responsibility of management, not the agents. Also notice that just about everything is interrelated, so the causes of performance problems are often difficult to isolate and measure. The diagram is only one of many ways to depict the process.

This illustration leads to a principle that is at the heart of the modern quality movement: There is little use exhorting agents to improve quality without making improvements to the system itself. Many of the things that contribute to quality are beyond their direct control, such as having good training, the right tools, accurate information and a logical work flow. The system of causes — the process — is where the leverage is. Some managers try to force change by setting strict standards for agents. But that will not improve underlying processes and is usually detrimental.

So where do you begin? One place to start is to look at the most important performance indicators (see Chapter 12), and ask some key questions. What are customers complaining about? What are customers suggesting? Where are you making mistakes? What do you want to raise or lower the level of? Where are the innovation opportunities?

But tracking results won't inherently improve them. To make improvements, you have to work on the factors that cause these outputs to be where they are. In other words, you have to work at a deeper level — the root causes.

## Fix Root Causes to Make Lasting Improvements

Without an appropriate approach and supporting tools, identifying root causes is a significant challenge. Consider a recurring problem, such as providing incomplete information to customers. Maybe the cause is insufficient information in the CRM or knowledge management systems. Or a need for more training. Or maybe a lack of coordination with marketing. Or carelessness. Or agent stress from a chronically high occupancy rate. Or a combination of any of these factors.

If the problem is to be fixed, you need to know *what* to fix. Then you can take the necessary corrective actions. The tools that the quality movement has produced and popularized over the years are helpful in understanding processes and identifying underlying causes. If you've had formal training in quality improvement, you are likely well-versed in their use. My purpose here is to illustrate some helpful ways they can be applied in the customer contact environment.

## FLOW CHART

A flow chart is a map of a process used to analyze and standardize procedures, identify root causes of problems and plan new processes. Flow charts are also excellent communication tools and can help you to visualize and understand the flow of a process.

One of the most useful applications for a flow chart is to analyze the specific types of contacts you handle. When most of us think of a "call," we think of a rather simple, singular event. Not so! Even a very simple call consists of many steps. To really understand the process of handling a contact, especially the more complex variety, it is useful to chart what happens, step by step.

If you haven't charted your contacts by type, you might try giving this task to a few of your more analytical agents. I like the low-tech approach. Put them in a conference room for a couple of hours. Give them a stack of index cards and have them write each step in a typical contact on individual cards, then lay out the cards in order on a large table. In a relatively short period of time, they will be able to tell you where there are procedure inconsistencies, information deficiencies and bottlenecks in the process. (Sticky notes on a wall also work well.) You will eventually want to invest more than a couple of hours in this activity and, possibly, use a software tool to capture the thinking; but this approach will get you started.

Sometimes a sweeping analysis of all the activities required to handle contacts is in order. With top management's support and direction, representatives from the contact center, fulfillment, marketing, billing and

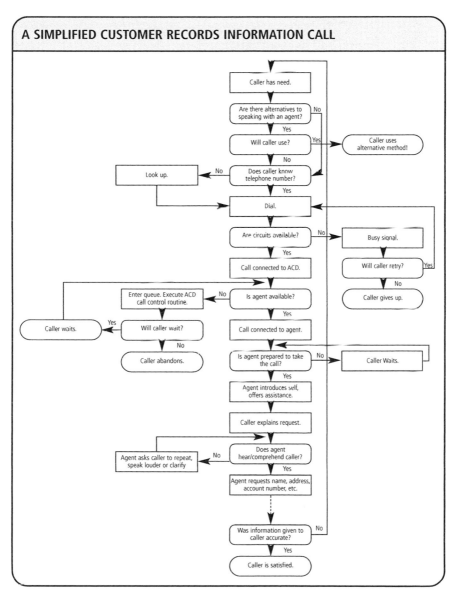

**A SIMPLIFIED CUSTOMER RECORDS INFORMATION CALL**

credit, IT and elsewhere can map out interdepartmental and interorganizational processes to identify areas that need overhaul. This is a common and necessary part of a customer experience initiative.

Here are some ideas for using flowcharts:

- Contacts, step by step
- The planning and management process
- IVR and ACD programming
- Capturing, sharing and acting on voice of the customer

## CAUSE-AND-EFFECT DIAGRAM

The cause-and-effect diagram, alternatively called a "fishbone diagram" because of its shape (or Ishikawa diagram, after its creator, Dr. Kaoru Ishikawa), is recognized and used worldwide. The chart illustrates the relationships between causes and a specific effect you want to study. Preparing a cause-and-effect diagram is an education in itself, and everyone who participates will gain a better understanding of the process. (See example, which troubleshoots an organization's high transfer rate.)

The traditional cause categories used in these diagrams are often referred to as the 4Ms: manpower, machines, methods, and materials. A variation on these categories — people, technology, methods, and materials/services — works better for contact centers. However, these labels are only suggestions; you can use any that help your group creatively focus on and think through the problem. Possible causes leading to the effect are drawn as branches off the main category. The final step is to prioritize the causes and work on the most prevalent problems first.

There is no one right way to make a cause-and-effect diagram. A good diagram is one that fits the purpose, and the shape the chart takes will depend on the group. They evolve differently every time.

A "production process classification" diagram is a variation on the traditional cause-and-effect diagram, and the cause categories follow the production process. In the transfer rate example, production categories would include: caller develops the need to call, caller dials and directs, call is routed, call is answered, need is identified by the agent, and so on.

The cause-and-effect diagram is great for analyzing problems such as:

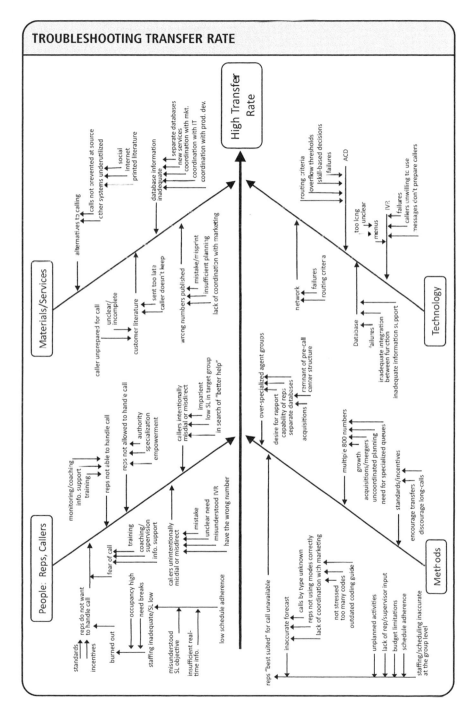

TROUBLESHOOTING TRANSFER RATE

- Long calls
- Repeat calls
- Poor adherence to schedule
- Inaccurate forecasts

## SCATTER DIAGRAM

A scatter diagram assesses the strength of the relationship between two variables, and is used to test and document possible cause and effect. The diagram of average handling time in Chapter 6, page 116, is an example.

If there is a positive correlation between the two variables, dots will appear as an upward slope. If there is a negative correlation, the dots will appear as a downward slope. The closer the pattern of dots is to a straight line, the stronger the correlation is between the two variables.

Useful (and interesting!) applications include:

- Average handling time versus experience level
- Average handling time versus revenue generated
- Service level versus error rate
- Experience level versus quality scores

## PARETO CHART

The Pareto chart, named after its creator, Italian economist Vilfredo Pareto, ranks the events you are analyzing in order of importance or frequency. For errors by type, you can create two more Pareto charts: cost to fix and time to fix. The Pareto principle (the source of the 80/20 rule) dictates that you should work first on the things that will yield the biggest improvements.

Some ideas for using a Pareto chart include:

- Contacts by type
- Errors by type
- Contacts by customer demographics
- Responses to customer surveys

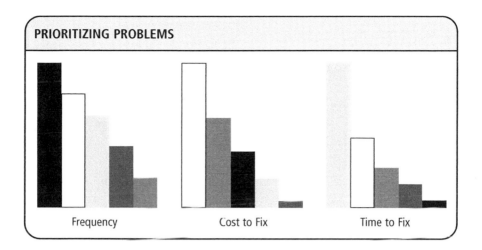

PRIORITIZING PROBLEMS

Frequency      Cost to Fix      Time to Fix

## CONTROL CHART

One of the reasons that quality problems in the contact center are challenging and often confusing is because they are a part of a complex process, and any process has variation from the ideal. A control chart provides information on variation.

There are two major types of variation: special causes and common causes. Special causes create erratic, unpredictable variation. For example, unusual calls from unexpected publicity or a computer with intermittent problems are special causes. Common causes are the rhythmic, normal variations in the system.

A control chart enables you to bring a process under statistical control by eliminating the chaos of special causes. You can then work on the common causes by improving the system and thus the whole process. Special causes show up as points outside of the upper control or lower control limits, or as points with unnatural patterns within the limits.

A control chart cannot reveal what the problems are. Instead, it reveals where and when special causes occur. Once special causes are eliminated, improving the system (the process) itself will have far more impact than focusing on individual causes. Improvements to the system of causes will move the entire process in the right direction.

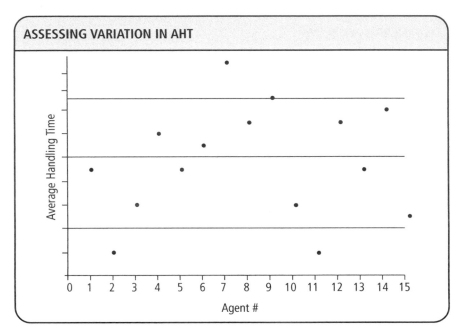

In short, control charts can help you reduce variation, prevent you from chasing the wrong problem, give early warning of changes in the process, and improve predictability and planning. This can be a pretty involved topic, and there are numerous books and seminars on statistical process control. For a more philosophical discussion of quality control and insight into the colorful life of the late W. Edwards Deming, read his pivotal work, *Out-of-the-Crisis* (Massachusetts Institute of Technology, Center for Advanced Engineering Study).

Here are some ideas for using control charts:

- Average handling time
- Percent adherence
- Percent defective calls (from monitoring)
- Requests for supervisory assistance

## BENCHMARKING

While many of these tools focus on improvements from within, the idea behind benchmarking is that breakthrough ideas often come from the outside (outside the organization and, potentially, outside your industry). Benchmarking is the process of measuring your products, services and procedures against those of other organizations.

Keep some cautions in mind: Organizations are different enough, even within a given industry, that universally accepted standards are usually not defensible. Things like labor rates, customer demographics, customer tolerances, network configurations, hours of operation and the mix of part- and full-time agents vary widely. Further, organizations often interpret performance measurements differently. What is most important is knowing how the results were achieved, not just what the results are.

With these cautions in mind, a disciplined, focused benchmarking effort can produce information that helps identify improvement opportunities in areas such as service innovation, customer satisfaction and retention, costs and revenues, management processes, measures used, new contact channels, and others. A general approach to benchmarking can be summarized as follows:

**DEFINE PROCESSES AND COLLECT PERFORMANCE DATA:** This involves getting agreements on processes to be compared and measurements to be used.

**ANALYZE COLLECTED DATA AND IDENTIFY BEST PRACTICES:** This includes normalizing the raw data for differences, such as currencies, hours of operation, etc., and then identifying the best performers from each category.

**PREPARE RECOMMENDATIONS:** This entails identifying, culling down and communicating specific recommendations based on findings.

**APPLY FINDINGS:** This involves developing a plan to implement improvements and track results.

Benchmarking, like other aspects of quality improvement, is most useful as an ongoing effort. As the industry improves, what were once cutting-edge practices become the norm. As best practices become generally

## DON'T FORGET THE OBOES

A popular trend in process improvement is the effort to correlate specific contact center activities to overall customer satisfaction. For example, some consulting organizations have been convincing clients to lower service level objectives because their scatter diagrams demonstrate minimal correlation between overall service level and customer satisfaction results.

The effort to understand how specific activities and measures influence overall results is laudable. But it can be reckless to claim that you've figured out just how much a specific variable affects customer satisfaction. The late Peter Drucker often used an orchestra analogy to remind us that a manager has the task of creating a whole that is greater than the sum of its parts. "A conductor must always hear both the orchestra and the second oboe," he said. "Can you hear the second oboe?"

There's a fine line here: We need to understand how specific activities influence overall results; but we are being irresponsible if we cut oboes or add trumpets simply because this or that study shows they have X and Y impact on customer satisfaction. As any coach, conductor or artist knows, there's more to it than that.

accepted, they can no longer be considered "best practices." (I always get a smile out of common practices identified in broad-based surveys being presented as industry best practices.)

## TOOLS ARE JUST TOOLS

With any of these tools and methods, there is a danger of getting caught up in the analysis process itself and not moving on to problem resolution. Once you identify problems to tackle, you will need to assign responsibilities, provide necessary resources and track progress.

# Contact Centers Enable Significant Strategic Value

Recall from the first chapter that customer contact centers have the potential to create value on three distinct levels: efficiency, customer satisfaction and business unit value (strategic value). Level three — working with other business units — is where you can truly begin to leverage the contact center's potential to deliver strategic value to the organization.

As a primary customer touchpoint, the contact center has enormous potential to provide other business units with valuable intelligence and support. This can include input on customers, products, services and processes — information that, when captured, identified, assimilated and turned into usable knowledge, can literally transform an organization's ability to identify and meet customer expectations and demands. John Goodman, founder and vice-chairman of TARP, a customer service research firm, puts it this way: "A strategic view perceives customer service as vital to the end-to-end customer experience, and thus to the customer relationship. This view also considers customer care to be a full-fledged member of the marketing-sales-service triumvirate."

The table Potential Contribution to Other Business Units summarizes key benefits and support that the contact center can provide to other business units. Many of these issues involve capturing, disseminating and using the information available in the course of interacting with customers.

The benefits can be significant and varied. For example, consider the impact when the contact center:

- Helps operational areas or manufacturing units pinpoint and fix quality problems, which boosts customer satisfaction and repeat purchases, reduces costs associated with warranties and repairs and prevents unnecessary contacts to the organization.
- Helps marketing develop more effective campaigns. For example, having a better understanding of what customers need and want, and ensuring that marketing efforts target best prospects can improve

**317**

response rates, reduce relative marketing costs, and even help the organization boost market share.

- Serves as an early warning system for potential legal troubles. Product defects, reactions to food or prescription drugs, security holes discovered in a company's website, inaccuracies in warranty statements or customer invoices — the list could go on for pages, and the contact center is often first to hear of these issues. Having strong, collaborative ties to other areas of the organization is a prerequisite to handling them as quickly and effectively as possible.

- Helps research and development (R&D) identify customer needs and the organization's competitive advantages and disadvantages. In many ways, focus groups, market research and traditional broad-based surveys are no match for the intelligence the contact center can capture through interactions with hundreds or even thousands of prospects and/or customers. This input can ultimately help the organization focus on providing better products and services to specific customer segments and influencers — favorably influencing costs, revenues, market share and the organization's reputation and brand.

- Enables the organization to improve self-service capabilities, based on the specific assistance the contact center provides to customers who opt out of or need help with these systems or apps. This lowers the costs of providing customer service, and can also boost customer satisfaction and ensure that the center has the capacity to focus on issues that really require or benefit from agent involvement.

In short, when the contact center has an eye on the larger implications of quality and innovation, it will have a positive impact on the entire organization's workload, productivity and quality.

| POTENTIAL CONTRIBUTION TO OTHER BUSINESS UNITS | |
|---|---|
| **Business Unit** | **The Contact Center Provides These Benefits** |
| **Sales and Marketing** | • Provides detailed information on customer demographics<br>• Tracks trends (purchases, service and support issues) and response rates<br>• Enables permission-based targeted sales and marketing<br>• Supports segmentation/branding<br>• Provides customer input on competitors<br>• Provides customer surveys and feedback |
| **Financial** | • Captures cost and revenue information by customer segment<br>• Contributes to the control of overall costs<br>• Serves as an early warning system (positive and negative)<br>• Is essential to successful mergers and acquisitions<br>• Contributes to shareholder value through strategic value contributions<br>• Is essential in establishing budgetary strategy and priorities |
| **HR/Training** | • Contributes to recruiting and hiring initiatives<br>• Contributes to skill and career path development<br>• Contributes to coaching and mentoring processes and expertise<br>• Helps foster a learning organization (e.g., through systems, processes and pooled expertise on products and customers)<br>• Contributes to training and HR expertise and processes |
| **Manufacturing/ Operations** | • Pinpoints quality and/or production problems<br>• Provides input on products' and services' usability and clarity<br>• Contributes to product documentation and procedures<br>• Highlights distribution problems and opportunities<br>• Facilitates communication related to capacity or production problems |

*(continued next page)*

| Research and Development (R&D)/Design | • Provides information on competitive direction and trends<br>• Highlights product compatibility issues and opportunities<br>• Provides customer feedback on usability<br>• Differentiates between features and benefits from the customer's perspective<br>• Identifies product and service differentiation opportunities |
|---|---|
| IT/Telecom | • Furthers organizationwide infrastructure development<br>• Furthers self-service usage and system design<br>• Provides a concentrated technology learning ground<br>• Provides the essential human bridge between diverse processes and systems<br>• Is a driver of innovation in IT/Telecom advancements |
| Legal | • Enables consistent and accurate customer communications and policies<br>• Serves as an early warning system for quality problems<br>• Identifies and addresses impending customer problems<br>• Provides a rapid response to news/media reports<br>• Contributes to internal communication<br>• Serves as a training ground for customer service policies |

Some diverse examples of organizations that have made this level of contribution a priority include:

- The GE Answer Center has been, since the mid-1980s, capturing information in the contact center and using it for everything from product improvements to targeted marketing campaigns.

- Amazon.com refers to their call centers as "R&D machines," providing information useful for continuously improving services, processes and self-service capabilities. The company "obsesses over contacts per order (CPO)," points out author and consultant Bill Price, who was Amazon's first VP of Global Customer Service. From the early days, "CPO was one of the few metrics well known to all managers and employees."

- Linksys' (a division of Cisco Systems, Inc.) contact center (a 24x7 multisite operation) works directly with engineering teams to make product improvements, based on customer feedback captured through surveys and through support interactions.

- China UnionPay is building an impressive global bankcard based on "continuous improvement and considerable service beyond expectations." Their formula is listening to customers and mining customer data to drive new products and service improvements (see sidebar, China UnionPay's Service Beyond Expectations).

- JetBlue uses phone conversations, email interactions and social channels such as Twitter, the company's website, operational data, surveys, and input directly from contact center employees to assess customer experiences and identify opportunities to improve operations. This voice of the customer information is shared (and acted on) widely — e.g., with pilots, the company's airport operations directors, the contact center and others — earning the company a net promoter score far above the industry average.

- The U.S. National Cancer Institute (NCI) is engaging customers through several social media channels, but primarily through Facebook (see example). The content team and the contact center (which heads up the posts) work closely both to address specific customer needs and to develop NCI information that can be in turn delivered to the public through social and other channels.

Even so, I believe that the contact center profession is only beginning to discover the powerful contributions that are possible. Those furthest along are the first to point out that there's a lot more potential. And the contact center's engagement through social channels is opening up even deeper levels of insight and service. In short, the processes, technologies and human know-how behind capturing, deciphering, communicating and using intelligence are works in progress.

---

### NCI ON FACEBOOK

**National Cancer Institute** via National Cancer Institute – Office of
Media Relations

> **Flexible sigmoidoscopy increases detection of colorectal cancer –
> National Cancer Institute**
> www.cancer.gov
>
> Repeated screening by flexible sigmoidoscopy increased the detection
> of colorectal cancer or advanced adenoma in women by one-fourth and
> in men by one-third, according to a study published Jan. 31 in the
> Journal of the National Cancer Institute.

Like · Comment · Share · Wednesday at 2:53pm

Lue Triplett and 4 others like this.

3 shares

 **Mark Daniels** Hemp oil cures cancer!
Wednesday at 2:55pm · Like

 **National Cancer Institute** Cancer is made up of many
diseases and no one treatment works for every cancer or
every patient. Since all cancers are different, claims that a
single compound cures all cancers should be considered very
carefully. It's important to discuss any treatment with a
doctor. The FTC has an online tool to help identify if a claim
is on the up-and-up at http://go.usa.gov/n6N.
Wednesday at 5:25pm · Like

How do you identify and leverage the potential your contact center has?
A number of key lessons have emerged:

- Seek first to understand. Develop good working relationships with the
  individuals who run other areas of the organization. Learn about their
  goals and objectives and how the contact center might best support
  their needs.
- Build an understanding of the contact center's role and potential.
  Ensure that the prevailing perspective is that the role of the center is
  to serve, not to point out flaws. While that may be obvious to those in
  the contact center, you'll want to emphasize it from the start.
- Build a team that is focused on capturing, analyzing, sharing and
  using value-added information across the organization. A suggested
  ratio is that you need one business analyst for every 30 to 50 agents.

That will depend on many factors, of course, but the right ratios and resources will become more clear once you get the ball rolling.

- Ensure that quality at the point of customer contact is given the broadest possible definition — e.g., that coaching, monitoring and objectives at the agent level support these major strategic opportunities.

- Footnote assumptions and unknowns in reports and data. Ensure that everyone understands where the data came from and what considerations are present. Strategic decisions based on misinterpreted reports can be worse than if there were no reports at all.

- Get the best tools you can. Analytics capabilities and performance management systems can help you analyze content, detect trends and causal factors, and identify improvement opportunities. Get started, even if you don't have these capabilities — but work toward acquiring and building supporting technologies, as feasible.

- Ensure the information is useful and usable, based on an ongoing commitment to understand business requirements and how to turn mounds of contact center data and "contact-center-esque" codes into actionable information.

- Don't get overwhelmed. There is an infinite amount of information that you could provide to each business unit. Instead of focusing on quantity (by trying to ensure that everything that may be valuable is shared), concentrate on providing just the information that is likely to be most useful.

Every customer contact your center handles provides implicit and/or explicit insight into processes, products, policies, services, customers and the external environment. You have the opportunity to play a central role in building a stronger organization with better services and products across the board. But it's a role that must be earned.

**CHINA UNIONPAY'S "SERVICE BEYOND EXPECTATIONS"**

Shanghai-based China UnionPay, winner of an ICMI Global Best Call Center Award (China) and other industry accolades, could be Exhibit A for building plans and services around evolving customer expectations. With more than 40 branches, 400 global member institutes, and UnionPay cards being used in over 125 countries, the organization's 180-employee contact center is committed to "continuous improvement and considerable service beyond expectations," according to Zhiyong Xiao, General Manager of UnionPay Customer Service Center.

Some of the organization's recent innovations include:

- A multichannel platform that delivers one-stop service, handling phone, short message, facsimile, email, Internet-based, social media and other customer contacts.
- New services to meet customer demands, including emergency roadside assistance, global emergency assistance, club services and a "green foods provision" for platinum cardholders.
- Evolving, customized services for specific customer segments, based on analysis of market trends, cardholder behavior, and insight picked up through data-mining and customer input.
- An internal culture of, according to Zhiyong Xiao, "improving together, growing happily" through an effective combination of employee benefits, strong technical support, a focus on positive human resources management, ongoing quality improvement, and other initiatives.

The results: Consistently high service levels, employee satisfaction scores of over 80 percent, and customer satisfaction scores above 95 percent. These successes support one of the company's most important strategic goals: growing China UnionPay into a major global bankcard brand.

## Improvements Must Be Ongoing

Remember the three levels of value; they build on each other, and the blocking and tackling of level one (efficiency) enables level two (customer loyalty) and level three (strategic value). The work doesn't end on one level as you move to the next. Making continuous innovations and improvements that lead to services that are faster, better and more cost-effective is an ongoing process that must be an inherent part of the organization's culture and outlook.

There is something powerful about consistently focusing on the things that matter most. In that spirit, the following points of advice were inspired by the well-known work of the late Dr. W. Edwards Deming and, more recently, Gordon MacPherson, Jr., now enjoying retirement. My hat is off to both of these great thinkers.

- Develop a global view of your organization's mission and principles. Identify the "big picture" in terms of the organization's mission and direction and how the contact center supports overall objectives. Then take steps to ensure that every person understands the "why" behind what they are doing, and how these principles apply to day-to-day tasks and responsibilities.

- Know your job. Analyze and understand every facet of your role and responsibilities. Then do the same for every position in the center (and the broader organization).

- Recognize that everybody's "best efforts" or just trying harder isn't enough. Look for problems and innovation opportunities in processes. Processes are where the most leverage will be.

- Fully training people to do their jobs is non-negotiable, and comes before everything else. This responsibility cannot become victim to busyness and shifting priorities.

- Use sound analytical methods to understand and improve the performance of individuals, the contact center and the organization. Don't make decisions based on assumptions — insist on having and using accurate and timely data.

- Ensure that the contact center's performance optimizes the good of the organization as a whole, not just of individual projects or departments.

325

- Remember that those who know processes and customers best are those closest to the work (agents and supervisors). Actively seek their ideas and input, and create an atmosphere of trust and open communication.

- Use performance measurements, monitoring and coaching as a means of learning and improvement at the process level (as well as for individuals). Make decisions based on data and knowledge, not just assumptions.

- As a general rule, don't wait to make sweeping changes all at once. Instead, as possible, make smaller improvements regularly and continuously.

- Encourage maximum personal development of the whole person (e.g., in terms of thinking, analysis, understanding the organization's overall objectives, etc.). This is just as important as job-specific training.

- Strive for and expect never-ending improvements. Build this perspective into the culture.

Instill the principles covered in this chapter into your organization, and stick to them, day after day, month after month, year after year. It's a never-ending journey. And an exciting one, because it prepares your organization for the unknowns ahead even as it delivers better results today.

## Skills, Knowledge and Leadership Make the Difference

What's the real secret to improving performance? (OK, it's probably not a very well kept secret.) Build the skills, knowledge and leadership in your team to make it all happen. That, along with the right culture and focus, is the secret sauce. And that is the subject of Chapters 14 and 15. Come along, my friends, onward we go …

# Points to Remember

- Quality is built around customer expectations. Since customer expectations are constantly evolving, the definition of quality must also evolve.

- Quality and service level work together. Over the long term, good quality improves service level (and response time) by reducing waste and rework. And a good service level provides an environment in which high quality can be achieved.

- The process is where the leverage is. There is little use in exhorting agents to improve quality without making improvements to the system of causes, or process.

- The tried-and-true methodologies and tools that the quality movement has produced can help find and fix root causes.

- Contact centers have enormous potential to deliver strategic value to the organization, through information and intelligence that can be shared with and applied in other business units.

- Improvements must be ongoing. This is not a once-and-done area of leadership.

- Your team is the most important source of success, now and in the future. Lasting changes require leadership and management know-how.

# CHAPTER 14:
# Boosting Individual Performance

*Leaders make things possible. Exceptional leaders make them inevitable.*
**LANCE MORROW**

Contact centers are made up of myriad personalities, backgrounds and skills. Success depends on creating an engaging environment and bringing out the best in those who are part of it. But, as many leaders have learned, some the hard way, off-the-shelf prescriptions and simplistic formulas tend to fail.

Fortunately, there are principles that don't change, that you can trust. For example, be consistent and relentlessly focused on the values that matter. Lead by example. Set the right performance expectations, at all levels. Encourage involvement and work hard to establish good channels of communication. Give people the chance to learn and grow. Expect and demand the best.

We'll look at these and related principles in this chapter. And we'll explore key performance measures for individuals; proven monitoring and coaching practices; the complementary roles of monitoring, coaching and training; and how to measure and positively manage turnover.

## Establishing an Engaging Environment

I've observed it time and again: The most successful contact centers have

**329**

environments that are motivating, and (for all the challenges of a constantly changing environment) are *fun* to be part of. How do they do it?

The subjects of motivation and engagement (the preferred term today) have been studied and addressed by thousands of successful leaders across many civilizations, and many centuries. Interestingly, there is much agreement on the core principles that enable it to flourish, such as creating a clear vision, establishing effective communication, expecting the best, and so forth. And yet, the topic continues to resonate.

One thing is certain: Leaders in organizations that maintain the highest levels of engagement take this challenge seriously. They don't leave motivation to chance. They know employees who are interested in and enthusiastic about their work predictably create great results for customers, the organization and, in turn, those who are part of it.

Johann Wolfgang Von Goethe (1749–1832), who was a German polymath (a person whose expertise spans many different subject areas ... just like most contact center managers I know) said it well: "Instruction does much, but encouragement does everything." Many recent studies bolster this view, showing a strong link between engaged employees and higher levels of productivity and profitability. (In one recent example, Gallup found that public companies ranked in the top quartile for employee engagement are 18% more productive and 12% more profitable than those in lower quartiles.)

So, what do successful contact centers, those with the most engaged employees, have in common? Here's a summary of the principles we've observed:

**PEOPLE RESPOND TO A CLEAR, COMPELLING MISSION.** A prerequisite to creating a motivating environment is to address the whats and whys. Why do the organization and the contact center exist? What are we trying to achieve? What's in it for customers? For employees? Shareholders? A clear focus, consistently reinforced by the leader, is key to pulling people in, aligning objectives and driving action (see sidebar on USAA, Chapter 17).

**IT'S WHAT YOU DO, NOT WHAT YOU SAY, THAT MATTERS.** There are countless organizations that codify and post their values, but then encourage an entirely different set of behaviors through their policies and actions. For example, building customer relationships may be the stated objective, but lack of staffing resources, or standards that stress volume-oriented production, may send conflicting messages (See cartoon, Confusing Objectives, Chapter 12). When it comes to influence, actions always win out over words.

**EFFECTIVE COMMUNICATION CULTIVATES TRUST.** Communication creates meaning and direction for people. When good communication is lacking, the symptoms are predictable: conflicting objectives, unclear values, misunderstandings, lack of coordination, confusion, low morale and employees doing the minimum required. Effective leaders are predisposed to keeping their people in the know (see Chapter 15).

**LISTENING ENCOURAGES BUY-IN AND SUPPORT.** There is a common myth that great leaders create compelling visions from gifted perspectives or inner creativity that others don't possess. But those who have studied leadership point out that, in fact, the visions of some of history's greatest leaders often came from others. Further, when people have a stake in an idea, they tend to work much harder to bring about its success.

**PEOPLE TEND TO LIVE UP TO EXPECTATIONS.** Think of your own development over the years. Those coaches, teachers or business mentors who believed in you and expected the most probably weren't the easiest on you. And they may not have been the kind to win popularity contests. But they believed in you, and you reached a little deeper to live up to their expectations.

**SINCERE RECOGNITION GOES A LONG WAY.** In study after study, participants say that personalized and sincere recognition from their managers — in other words, simply being recognized for doing a good job — is a powerful motivator. (Easier said than done, of course: You've got to really know what's going on from top to bottom to get it right ... but isn't that a part of leadership, anyway?)

**ACCURATE RESOURCE PLANNING IS ESSENTIAL.** Yep, in the time-driven contact center environment this matters a lot. We've got to have "the right people in the right place at the right times, doing the right things." When that doesn't happen, unsavory consequences begin to surface: queues build, callers get unhappy, and occupancy goes through the roof. It's stressful. And, if chronic, it zaps motivation and drains the fun out of the environment.

**WHO YOU ARE IS MORE IMPORTANT THAN ANY TECHNIQUE YOU USE.** The reality is, we trust and perform for leaders who are predictable on matters of principle, and who make their positions known. Convictions, sense of fairness, consistency of behavior and stated values, belief in the capabilities of people — these things have much more impact than any motivational approach ever could.

Let's turn to a related topic: establishing the right performance objectives and measures. We'll begin with the agent role, then look at other positions.

## Agent Performance Measures

The subject of measuring the performance of individuals has always been hotly debated. And for good reason: Performance measurements are usually tied to behavioral expectations and standards, so many issues enter the discussion (e.g., fairness; which measurements are truly under an individual's control; individual capabilities, drives and motivators; and the efficacy of the processes they are working within). Few subjects elicit such strong and varied opinions.

We've seen lots of different performance measurements and standards in play. But there are also consistent principles at work in centers that are getting the best results. Let's look at some distinct trends, and how the right performance measures and expectations encourage the right contributions.

## BEWARE CONTACTS HANDLED

There was a day when number of contacts handled (for example, calls per hour, or emails handled per day) was an almost universal productivity measurement. In fact, many managers viewed contacts handled as virtually synonymous with productivity (not something I've ever recommended, for reasons we'll discuss). While there always have been concerns about sacrificing quality for quantity, contacts handled was the usual benchmark for establishing productivity standards, comparing performance among agents and groups, and assessing the impact of changes and improvements to the center.

As a measure of performance, contacts handled has always been problematic. Yes, when overemphasized, quality can suffer. Beyond that is an unsettling reality: Many of the variables that affect contacts handled are out of agents' control. These include call arrival rate, contact types, customers' knowledge, customers' communication abilities, the accuracy of the forecast and schedule, the adherence to schedule of others in the agent group, and many more.

---

**A QUICK QUIZ**

Over which factors do agents have real control?
- ❏ Adherence to schedule (their own)
- ❏ Number of staff scheduled to answer calls
- ❏ Number of calls coming in
- ❏ Distribution of long calls and short calls
- ❏ Distribution of easy calls and difficult calls
- ❏ Callers' communication abilities

---

Several mathematical realities are also at work. As discussed in Chapter 9, small groups are less efficient (have lower occupancy) than larger groups at a given service level. Since the number of calls is changing throughout the day, so are the contacts handled averages for a group or individuals within a group. Further, as discussed in Chapter 9, when service level goes up, occupancy and calls handled go down.

| Calls In Half Hour | Service Level | Agents Required | Occupancy | Avg. Calls Per Agent |
|---|---|---|---|---|
| 50 | 80/20 | 9 | 65% | 5.6 |
| 100 | 80/20 | 15 | 78% | 6.7 |
| 500 | 80/20 | 65 | 90% | 7.7 |
| 1000 | 80/20 | 124 | 94% | 8.1 |

Assumption: Average Handle Time is 3.5 minutes

To get around the fairness problem that occupancy creates, some managers convert raw calls handled into normalized calls handled (sometimes called "true calls handled"), by dividing calls handled by percent occupancy. Using the numbers in the table, 5.6 average calls per agent divided by 65 percent occupancy (first row) is 8.6 normalized calls, as is 6.7 calls divided by 78 percent, 7.7 calls divided by 90 percent, and 8.1 calls divided by 94 percent. As an alternative, others use statistical control charts to determine whether the process is in control, what it's producing, and which agents, if any, are outside of statistical control.

But even with these efforts, contacts handled loses meaning as multiple contact channels, skills-based routing, call blending and other capabilities proliferate, resulting in increasingly sophisticated and varied types of interactions. For managers who depended on contacts handled as a performance measure, this left a vacuum. Enter the two things that truly matter: being in the right place at the right time (adherence to schedule), and doing the right things (quality).

## ADHERENCE TO SCHEDULE

Adherence to schedule is a measure of ... guess this one's obvious ...

how well agents adhere to the schedule. Many, myself included, don't particularly care for the tenor of the term. And I don't like the "big brother" interpretation I sometimes (not often, but sometimes) see in contact centers. That usually backfires.

But reality is, we're in time-driven environments. So are football players. And astronauts. And stagehands. It doesn't matter if we have the most incredible knowledge and expertise, if we're not there when customers need us.

Adherence is, first and foremost, a measure of how much time during an agent's shift he or she is handling, or available to handle, contacts. If adherence is expected to be 90 percent, each agent should be available to handle contacts .90 x 60 minutes, or 54 minutes on average, per scheduled hour.

---

*We're in time-driven environments … It doesn't matter if we have the most incredible knowledge and expertise, if we're not there when customers need us.*

---

Adherence consists of time spent in talk time, after-call work, waiting for calls to arrive, and anything else (e.g., internal contacts) associated with the work. Lunch, breaks, training, etc. are not counted and are not factored into the measurement. (Be sure to differentiate the terms "adherence to schedule" and "agent occupancy." They are two different things. In fact, when adherence to schedule goes up, service level will go up, which drives occupancy down. See Chapter 9.)

Adherence can also incorporate the issue of timing — *when* was a person available to handle contacts? This is often called "schedule compliance." The idea is to ensure that agents are ready to go when needed. (In a time-sensitive environment, staying an extra 15 minutes at the end of a shift doesn't make up for not being there at the beginning of the shift when customers were calling in droves.)

Adherence to schedule should be established at levels that are reasonable and that reflect the many things that legitimately keep agents from the work. It should also be flexible (e.g., adjustable downward) when the workload is light.

Agents cannot control how many calls are coming in, how nice or grouchy callers are (though their approach can certainly make a difference), whether marketing gave the contact center a good heads-up on their activities, and so on. But they can be in the right place at the right times. Coupled with good resource plans, that's huge.

## QUALITY

Enter quality. In successful contact centers, quality criteria — what needs to happen to handle contacts with quality — are well defined. They equate to the routine a pilot goes through in specific conditions, or the variables professional athletes play out instinctively. When well delineated, quality criteria largely define the time it will take to handle contacts well. That means not rushing contacts, of course, but also providing the essential parameters to keep them as focused (as efficient and effective) as possible.

Adherence and quality make a powerful pair. When in place, other measures — e.g., average handling time, number of contacts handled, percent of time spent in talk or after-call work, and others — take care of themselves. Case in point: If you want to increase the number of contacts agents are handling, you've got two options. You can increase their *availability* to take contacts, and/or you can work on the *way they handle* contacts. (Remember that average handling time is not something they do; it's simply a clock.)

Establishing adherence to schedule and quality as primary areas of focus enables agents to concentrate on the two things they can control: *being in the right place at the right times* and *doing the right things*. Note the consistency between individual objectives and the two themes that run throughout contact center management, beginning with the definition that we introduced

**KEEP IT SIMPLE**

I am seeing a trend in recent years to streamline and simplify agent performance standards. In many cases, they had become too complex — weighted averages, percent time in this and that mode, formulas that would take a mathematician to figure out.

Yes, if I'm one of your agents, give me some objectives on being in the right place at the right times (schedule adherence), and doing the right things (quality). Beyond that, give me an understanding of your business, the unique environment I'm part of, and the importance of my contribution. I'll produce good numbers and, more importantly, I'll produce good business results.

As Dee Hock, founder and former CEO of Visa, once put it, "Simple, clear purpose and principles give rise to complex and intelligent behavior; complex rules and regulations give rise to simple and stupid behavior."

in Chapter 1: *service level* and *quality*.

Of course, focusing on adherence and quality is not feasible if these measurements are vague and indeterminate. They must be implemented fairly, and with foresight and care. With that in mind, let's look at each in more detail.

# Using Adherence Measurements

As introduced above, adherence to schedule is a general term that can refer to either (or both) of the following:

1. *The amount of time* in the course of a shift that agents were available to handle contacts. Alternative terms include "availability" and "plugged-in time."
2. *When* agents were available, during their shift. Alternative terms include "schedule compliance" or just "adherence." (I use the term adherence interchangeably with adherence to schedule, in a general sense.)

Most centers with adherence to schedule objectives track the amount of time agents are available. Many also incorporate the issue of timing. There's certainly latitude for using different variables or activities that qualify as adherent. Putting your approach in place should be a team effort that includes those who will be assessed by it.

Average adherence should be determined individually and for each agent group. Sometimes individuals need specific coaching or training that is not necessary for the whole group. And tracking adherence as an average for the group reveals how well management is doing in creating an environment in which objectives can be achieved.

(Be sure to count after-call work as a part of adherence, along with talk time and the time agents spend waiting for contacts to arrive. After-call work, when defined appropriately, is a legitimate part of handling time — see Chapter 6. Putting a ceiling on it can be detrimental to quality. If you feel it is too high, you can investigate what is causing it to be where it is, and make appropriate process improvements, or adjustments to training.)

Real-time adherence monitoring capabilities are available in many workforce management systems. The thresholds are yours to set, and you can really drill down if you'd like. For example, if an agent is supposed to be back from break at 10:15, and you set a 3-minute threshold, your screen will highlight that person's name at 10:18 if they aren't buckled up and ready to go. You could, then, call them out on it ... but guess how well that usually goes over?

I am not suggesting that you shouldn't use adherence monitoring capabilities. But at a tactical level, they work best as information tools for agents themselves, and for team leaders who have good perspective on what's happening within their groups. The alternative is strict mandates, which puts supervisors in the role of filling out "exception reports" as things come up. Ensure your approach is supporting the culture you want to establish. Here are some suggestions for getting the best results:

1. Educate each person on how much impact he or she has on the queue, and therefore, the importance of adherence to schedule (see Chapter 9).

2. Establish concrete service level and response time objectives that everybody knows and understands (see Chapter 4).

3. Educate agents on the basic steps involved in resource planning so that they understand how schedules are produced, where they come from.

4. Develop appropriate priorities for the wide range of tasks that your agents handle, and guidelines for how to respond to real-time conditions.

5. Provide real-time service level information to agents, but be sure to back it up with training on how to interpret it, and how to respond at the team and individual levels (see Chapter 11).

6. Manage schedule adherence as locally as possible, e.g., by individuals themselves and within their supervisory teams. It should be tracked for trending and planning purposes (next point), but a bottom-up approach works best.

7. Adherence results and trends for agent groups and the contact center itself are valuable for planning and to assess how well the management approach and supporting processes are working.

In sum, adherence to schedule is an important objective. But apply it carefully, get involvement from the ground up, and back it up with the right education on why timing matters so much.

## Quality Monitoring and Coaching

Monitoring and coaching go hand in hand. Monitoring is an evaluation process that appraises the qualitative aspects of handling customer interactions. Coaching, (usually) through one-on-one discussions, encourages employees to continue positive behavior and provides constructive feedback and guidance on areas of improvement.

The usual objectives of a monitoring and coaching initiative are many, and often include:

- Provides the basis for organizationwide quality improvement and innovation
- Measures the quality of interactions and accuracy of information provided
- Measures the effectiveness of and adherence to processes
- Provides data for trend analysis to look for patterns of effectiveness across contact types, teams and centers
- Supports coaching by providing specific information that can be used for feedback
- Identifies additional training needs for individual agents
- Evaluates the effectiveness of training
- Identifies customer needs and expectations
- Helps assess customer satisfaction
- Contributes to hiring and training by highlighting needed skills and competencies
- Ensures legal compliance and mitigates liability
- Ensures the organization's policies are followed and provides input on how they can be improved

With so much at stake, it's important to design an effective approach and establish supporting performance criteria that you can confidently use to set a baseline and assess progress. Here's a summary of the most important steps in developing a monitoring and coaching program:

- **Identify your goals and objectives for the program**, which often include agent improvement, consistency, process improvement, identifying training needs, and providing the basis for coaching.
- **Determine program requirements**, including the types of monitoring you will use (record and review, silent, side-by-side, etc.), how often

## ICMI'S RECOMMENDED MONITORING PRACTICES

- Communicate to job candidates the monitoring process and how it's used to improve individual, contact center, and organizationwide performance.
- Cover the monitoring program in detail during agent orientation; allow new-hires to monitor and assess contacts themselves using the monitoring form.
- Clearly inform agents about the purpose of monitoring, how it is conducted and how the results are used. Post the organization's written monitoring policy for all employees to see, and have them sign off on it when they are hired.
- Determine whether or not to tell agents when they are being monitored, according to their individual preferences.
- Advise agents that the organization's business lines will be monitored, and where to find unmonitored lines for personal calls.
- Permit only qualified personnel to monitor for quality or to evaluate the results of monitoring.
- Do not publically provide monitoring results by name or other data that could identify an individual.
- Do not single out an individual agent for unsatisfactory performance detected by monitoring when the issues are common to the group.
- Use standardized and consistently applied evaluation forms and monitoring techniques.
- Use objective criteria in evaluation forms and techniques.
- Monitor across all contact channels and types. As much as possible, use consistent criteria, adjusting for the unique requirements of individual channels and contact types.
- Monitor all agents periodically to determine where the performance level of the group is centered. This level is management's responsibility. New-hires, agents whose performance indicates a need for more training and coaching, and agents who request it can be monitored more frequently.
- Give feedback promptly.

*(continued next page)*

- Conduct regular calibration sessions to ensure consistency and fairness.
- Permit only personnel with a legitimate business need to monitor contacts for orientation purposes. Examples are: new employees who will be handling interactions, consultants working on improvements and visitors approved by management who are studying the center's operations.

representatives will be monitored, what systems and technologies are required, and how results will be used.

- **Create standards for performance**, which may be divided into base requirements (behaviors that represent the minimum acceptable level of performance) and those that can be continually refined and improved.
- **Create the scoring system**, which includes forms, criteria, and a scoring approach. Important components include records (typically, electronic) of each monitored contact, standards of performance, basic identification information (agent name, call ID, date, time), notes for observations, checklists, and the rating system.
- **Develop an ongoing calibration process**, which helps ensure that supervisors, quality analysts or others who do the monitoring rate agent interactions consistently and fairly.
- **Develop an approach for coaching**, which involves deciding who will have responsibility for coaching activities (generally, the individual who monitors the interaction provides coaching and feedback), identifying standards for coaching, and anticipating when coaching will happen and how it will be scheduled.
- **Communicate program details to employees**, informing them of the purpose of monitoring, how it will be conducted, and how results will be used; and, providing written monitoring policies, the criteria on which they will be monitored, and applicable forms and scorecards.

## STANDARDS AND SCORING

The cornerstone of an effective monitoring process is documenting specific, observable behaviors and tailoring agent coaching accordingly. There are many types of monitoring forms and evaluation methods, and many possible scoring systems. Your monitoring form should incorporate those approaches that best address the skills you are evaluating.

An effective way to consider performance standards is to categorize them as either "foundation" or "finesse." Foundation standards measure *whether* something was done, and can be assessed with a simple yes or no. For example, the agent uses his name in the greeting. He verifies the customer's account number. He uses spell check in email or social interactions. He went through the three-step closing process. Yes or no — these things either happened or they didn't. Foundation standards are objective, consistent, and accomplished the same way by every agent. They are, as a rule, easy to understand and easy to score.

Finesse standards, on the other hand, measure *how* something was done. They are more subjective, allow for style and individuality, and provide — require, really — room for interpretation. For example, the agent listens carefully and effectively probes the customer for relevant input. She demonstrates professional courtesy. She upsells or cross-sells appropriately. She guides the customer to convenient online resources. She captures needed and useful information for product, process or service improvements. These standards require clear guidance on what is expected, but performance happens in degrees.

Accordingly, common scoring approaches can be categorized as either yes/no or as a numerical range. The yes/no approach (alternately indicated by 1/0, Y/N, checkboxes) best fits foundation standards. Overall results for foundation standards related to an interaction may be expressed by the number of yes's and no's (e.g., 9 Y and 1 N), a fraction (9/10) or a percentage (90%).

## SAMPLE MONITORING FORM

Agent Name: A.C. Dee
Caller ID#: 272-A

### I. FOUNDATION SKILLS

> 1 = Yes, achieves foundation skill
> 0 = No, does not meet foundation skill
> N/A = No opportunity to demonstrate skill

**OPENING**  Coach's Notes:

| | |
|---|---|
| Thanks customer for calling, identifies company/group | (Yes)  No |
| States name, offers assistance | (Yes)  No |
| Gathers and verifies customer account and identity | (Yes)  No |

**DATA QUALITY**

| | |
|---|---|
| Asks for and verifies required information | (Yes)  No |
| Provides accurate and appropriate information | (Yes)  No |
| Accurately codes call | Yes  (No) |

*Please review new coding categories*

**PROFESSIONAL ETIQUETTE**

| | |
|---|---|
| Uses please, thank you, caller's name | (Yes)  No |
| Uses appropriate hold steps | Yes  No  (N/A) |
| Follows warm transfer procedure | Yes  No  (N/A) |

**CONCLUSION**

| | |
|---|---|
| Offers further assistance | (Yes)  No |
| Summarizes next steps/agreements | Yes  (No) |
| Uses close procedure | (Yes)  No |

*Improves caller FCR, data accuracy*

**Foundation Skills Achieved:** 8/10 = 80%

### II. FINESSE SKILLS

> 1 = Below Average
> 2 = Average
> 3 = Above Average
> N/A = No opportunity to demonstrate skill

**CUSTOMER RESPONSIVENESS**  Coach's Notes:

| | | | | |
|---|---|---|---|---|
| Demonstrates sincerity, helpfulness, patience | 1 | 2 | (3) | N/A |
| Acknowledges customer's issue | 1 | 2 | (3) | N/A |
| Takes steps to further relationship | 1 | 2 | (3) | N/A |

*Took tangible, well-received steps to further relationship!*

**CALL MANAGEMENT**

| | | | | |
|---|---|---|---|---|
| Asks directed questions | 1 | 2 | (3) | N/A |
| Guides call flow / attempts call objective | 1 | 2 | (3) | N/A |
| Handles objections/gains customer's commitment | 1 | 2 | (3) | N/A |

**LISTENING/VOC**

| | | | | |
|---|---|---|---|---|
| Checks & restates for understanding | 1 | 2 | (3) | N/A |
| Captures needed and useful information | 1 | (2) | 3 | N/A |
| Educates customer on multiple solutions | 1 | (2) | 3 | N/A |

*Opportunity to capture caller's ideas for feature improvements. Mention our new mobile app*

**KNOWLEDGE**

| | | | | |
|---|---|---|---|---|
| Uses systems effectively | 1 | (2) | 3 | N/A |
| Demonstrates industry and product expertise | 1 | 2 | (3) | N/A |
| Further knowledge management | 1 | (2) | 3 | N/A |

*Use KM system (helps us build database for self-serve FAQs and other purposes)*

**Finesse Skills Achieved:** 32/36 = 89%

| | | |
|---|---|---|
| Foundation Skills | 80% x .5 = | 40% |
| Finesse Skills | 89% x .5 = | 45% |
| **TOTAL SCORE** | | **85%** |

| Total Score: | |
|---|---|
| 90-100% | Exceeds Expectations |
| 80-89% | Meets Expectations |
| 70-79% | Needs Improvement |
| Below 69% | Unacceptable |

NOTE: This is a simplified illustration adapted from an example provided by ICMI. Forms and criteria should reflect your mission and brand, and criteria should be supported by detailed descriptions, training, coaching and calibration to ensure clear expectations and consistency.

Numerical scoring generally presents a range (e.g., 1 to 5) of possibilities, which scorers can use to rate finesse standards, the agent's proficiency in applying the skill. The wider variation of scores possible with a numerical scoring method reveal subtle skill improvements; for example, an employee may have improved a skill but not achieved full mastery.

Many variations or combinations in scoring are possible. You might choose to indicate N/A (not applicable) or exempt specific skills during certain types of calls (where N/As are either counted as yes's or another agreed-upon score, or are not counted at all). You might give certain foundation or finesse criteria more weight in scoring, e.g., providing accurate information might be more important than addressing the caller by name. Your mission and most important objectives should dictate what you stress.

When looking at the sample monitoring form, page 344, remember that forms and criteria vary widely and yours should reflect your organization's unique mission and brand. As noted, criteria should be backed up by detailed descriptions, training, coaching and ongoing calibration to ensure all who are involved understand expectations and can deliver the essential components of service consistently (while allowing for differences in personalities and individual communication styles to flourish). In short, your approach should fit your needs.

Before you implement a scoring system, consider the following recommendations, which come from ICMI's monitoring and coaching courses:

- The scoring system should be easy to use.
- A scoring system should emphasize the award of points for positively demonstrated skills, rather than deductions for negative behaviors.
- Managers, supervisors and agents should thoroughly understand how the scoring system works.
- Advise management and agents to keep scores in context. Specific feedback and coaching is the most essential part of the monitoring and coaching process and is what ultimately improves quality. Don't overemphasize scores.

- Resist the temptation to coach to scores. Scores don't improve the quality of an interaction; specific feedback and coaching to behaviors do. Some contact centers do not share scores with agents until after the coaching session.
- The scoring system should directly reflect contact center objectives, objectives for interactions, and the behaviors you want to encourage. A flawed system may underemphasize critical behaviors and overemphasize non-essential skills.
- Confirm the mathematical validity of the scoring system, especially if a total score is compiled or the system is weighted.
- Establish the validity of the system by testing it before it can have an impact on individuals (e.g., before scores are included as part of performance-based pay).
- Understand that agents become very interested in scoring systems if they are tied to bonuses, performance evaluations and salary reviews. Be prepared to handle their questions and concerns.
- When possible, define variations in specific behaviors associated with a skill and the corresponding scores (e.g., what behaviors earn a 1 or a 3 or a 5?).

## CALIBRATION

In a contact center, calibration is the process in which variations in the way performance criteria are interpreted from person to person are minimized. When high levels of calibration are achieved, it will not matter who did the monitoring and scoring; the outcome will be the same. For a monitoring process to succeed, it is essential to integrate calibration into the planning, implementation and ongoing maintenance of your monitoring program.

Calibration is one of the key ways to move contact center quality in the right direction. A number of the quality tools discussed in Chapter 13 can be helpful. For example, flow charts enable end-to-end mapping of

## USING AGENT-LEVEL CUSTOMER FEEDBACK

Unbeknownst to them, customers are becoming very effective coaches. While, historically, contact centers have relied solely on supervisors and/or quality assurance specialists to rate contacts and provide agents with feedback, Hilton Reservations, Wells Fargo Banker Connection and others are going straight to the source to find out just how a particular agent performed on a call, email, chat or other type of contact.

Gathering agent-level customer feedback typically involves a brief survey of several questions that focus on a specific interaction that took place between an agent and a customer, and that seeks to find out how satisfied the customer was with that contact and agent. These surveys typically include questions that are related to the key criteria also included on the center's monitoring form. Common survey methods include short post call IVR surveys or email surveys.

One of the main reasons why such feedback is a hit in contact centers is that it is a hit with agents. Most find it much easier to accept an assessment of their performance that includes feedback from the person who was directly involved in the contact rather than from a third-party observer alone. And the more palatable and trusted a performance assessment is, the more likely an agent is to accept it and to strive to improve.

Terri McMillan, a senior vice president with Wells Fargo Banker Connection, points to the connection between customer feedback and a stronger QA program overall. "The management benefit of tying customer surveys directly to QA evaluations is the enhanced calibration between the customer experience and QA, and the added confidence it gives our specialists in the QA program," she says. "The real bonus is in sharing customer survey scores and verbatim comments with specialists to reinforce coaching, incorporate into performance measurements and spotlight specialists through recognition!"

interactions and provide specific guidance on how assessments should be made. Cause-and-effect diagrams can help troubleshoot inconsistencies in monitoring and calibration sessions. And scatter diagrams can correlate scores to individuals doing the monitoring, to assess inconsistencies across scorers.

Proper calibration provides consistency, reduces the likelihood of agents questioning fairness, and is a means for continuously developing and assessing monitoring criteria. It eliminates perceived biases by ensuring consistent application of standards and scoring. And it allows the coaching process to focus on recognizing achievements and identifying opportunities for improvement, instead of whether a particular score is accurate.

## Getting the Most from Quality Monitoring

Chances are your contact center has made significant investments in quality monitoring. You have probably spent hundreds of combined hours and tens of thousands of dollars developing monitoring criteria and forms, investigating legal requirements, and orienting agents and supervisors to the program. And it's likely that monitoring and related coaching activities take more combined time than any other activity beyond handling the customer workload.

Are you getting the results you should? As discussed in the previous chapter, there's far more to handling customer contacts than improving the satisfaction of those customers, as important as that is. As a primary customer touchpoint, the contact center has significant potential to provide other business units with invaluable intelligence and insight. Organizations that get the most leverage out of these efforts share some common characteristics:

**THEY ALIGN QUALITY MONITORING WITH KEY BUSINESS OBJECTIVES.** There's a common understanding within the organization that the contact center has a larger mission than just handling customer interactions well. So it makes sense that effective quality monitoring programs — whether they employ low-tech listening, recordings or high-tech call analytics — are expected and designed to do much more than assist with individual training and development. They also focus on leveraging the knowledge gathered from contacts into better systems, processes and

## CMPA BREAKS QUALITY OUT OF THE VACUUM

The Canadian Medical Protective Association (CMPA) operates in a demanding environment. Each day, CMPA's 26 agents talk to the organization's 81,000 physician-members, giving them advice and legal assistance and risk management education. As you can imagine, CMPA's quality assurance program is critical — and it gets a lot of focus, both for the customer experience and the bottom line.

"Best-in-class quality is an attainable goal for all organizations. It is derived from focusing on the right behaviors and can only be delivered by employees who are highly engaged and accountable for improvements and results," says Michelle Jousselin, director of Membership and Contact Centre Services for the Ottawa, Ontario-based organization. "Improving quality will lower costs and significantly improve resolution and customer satisfaction." CMPA's successful efforts to improve its quality program secured the center ICMI's inaugural Silver Award for quality in the Global Call Center of the Year Awards.

In 2010, CMPA embarked on a major project to assess and reconstruct its quality audit program and form. The team consisted of dedicated and contributing resources, as well as four frontline agents from the Membership and Contact Centre Services department.

CMPA established weighting for each category as part of the review and determined that a basic met/not met bonus structure was their preferred approach. The team created a quality standards document with scoring criteria and concrete examples for each of the established categories. Finally, calibration sessions were organized and maintained on an ongoing basis to ensure consistent application of the standard, and to identify new and upcoming training needs.

"As long as the direction is clear and we have the team's buy-in, we will continue to produce quality and member satisfaction results in the mid to high 90s," says James Watson, who manages CMPA's Contact Centre Services division. In addition to strong overall quality scores, CMPA produces strong first call resolution results that are trended through multiple tracking points. First-call resolution is a key metric within the new quality audit form.

services across the organization. In short, the most effective centers identify issues that are beyond the center's jurisdiction but need to be fixed.

**THEY INCORPORATE QUALITY CRITERIA THAT SUPPORT BROAD IMPROVEMENTS.** These commonly include capturing needed and useful information; detecting and documenting unsolicited marketplace feedback; assessing whether contacts could have been prevented; and encouraging and noting customer insight that helps design better products and services. (They recognize that many aspects of accomplishing these objectives are not within the direct control of those handling interactions and must be addressed across the organization; but they have to be identified at the point of contact.)

**THEY CORRELATE MONITORING TO OTHER KEY RESULTS.** For example, how do monitoring results compare to customer satisfaction, social sentiment and trending, employee satisfaction, service levels, revenues and costs? Are there correlations and how strong are they? Better understanding the interrelated nature of the organization's mission, contact center results, and day-by-day, contact-by-contact activities will lead to improvements and innovations of the highest order.

**THEY REGULARLY CALIBRATE FOR FAIRNESS AND CONSISTENCY.** Does your monitoring program reflect, in a consistent and unbiased way, what is really happening? To quickly find out, conduct a simple experiment. Have those who do the evaluations independently score 5 to 10 recorded interactions. Then, compare the results. If the scores are significantly different, take the system back to the shop for a tune-up or overhaul (see discussion on calibration, above). Until you do, you'll be getting mixed results and wasting time and effort. Or worse, you'll be alienating agents who don't trust the results and who aren't getting the recognition and help they need.

**THEY INVOLVE AGENTS IN ROOT CAUSE ANALYSIS.** It's become a recognized (and true!) tenet of the quality movement that those closest to the work know and understand it best. Your agents are in an ideal position to help define what constitutes a quality experience for customers, and how processes, training, systems and interdepartmental coordination can be improved. And agent involvement encourages ownership and engagement, and pays off handsomely in job satisfaction

---

**ALTERNATIVES TO MONITORING**

Here are some of the alternatives that can supplement monitoring efforts:

- Provide name at the beginning of the conversation, establishing a sense of accountability and ownership.
- Provide opportunity for customers to take short IVR surveys (if they call) or to provide feedback and input through email, SMS, social or other channels that apply.
- Managers walk the floor and observe the agent side of interactions. With phone, this may give only one side of the conversation, but does provide a feel for what is happening.
- Agents simulate interactions and role-play situations in training.
- Incentives are provided for survey results at the team level, making each agent accountable to others in the group.
- "Mystery shoppers" from outside firms initiate interactions and provide a report on their experiences.
- New-hires or agents who are struggling are seated next to top performers.

---

## THE COMPLEMENTARY ROLES OF HIRING, TRAINING AND COACHING

As is often pointed out, the best contact centers do a great job of hiring, training and coaching. But the point that is sometimes understated is the degree to which these processes depend on and benefit each other.

Consider hiring. An effective recruiting and hiring process ensures that your contact center will have the right people for the job. Without it, you'll be placing a huge burden on training and coaching — and those processes will, most likely, be focused on the bare essentials. With it, you'll be assembling a team that, with the right training and support, can work together effectively, support and further the organization's culture, and

## BOOSTING TRAINING ROI

There are countless potential benefits from training — increased performance, improved motivation, higher customer and employee satisfaction, increased organization success, to name a few. "Potential" is the key word, because some critical ingredients are necessary. Training has the best chance of success, and will deliver the highest ROI, when:

1. Training is, in fact, the right solution. Training can't "fix people."
2. The reason for training has been communicated to the target audience. Do participants know what the training is about and why they are there?
3. You've done some pre-planning. It's powerful to have someone come to training with a checklist or summary of goals, and especially so when they create it with their manager around a shared set of objectives.
4. You reinforce training after it happens. Training can facilitate learning new skills, and knowledge, but without practice and reinforcement, it won't stick.
5. You deliver refresher training as needed. (Example: Training new agents on adherence and other performance metrics is great, but they will need a refresher as they settle in.)
6. Training is relevant to the job, the center, the customer and the organization.
7. The trainer/facilitator understands (as much as reasonably possible) the goals and objectives for the training as well as the target audience.
8. The training delivery method matches the need: The method (e.g., formal, informal, online, classroom, e-learning, etc.) is appropriate for the learning objectives.
9. The workforce management team has built training into staffing plans, and, with leadership, established appropriate guidelines that determine if and when training gets moved based on real-time circumstances.
10. You remember that time is currency, and how you spend it sends a strong message about what is important.

By Rose Polchin, Senior Consultant, ICMI

adapt and change as the customer contact environment evolves.

Some underlying trends have resulted in training becoming increasingly important. One is that the environment is becoming more complex, requiring robust training that provides a strong and effective base of know-how for employees. A more subtle trend is that many managers are placing greater emphasis on finding agents who support and further the culture of the organization and then training them on appropriate skills, rather than finding those with the right skills but who may not fit as well into the culture and environment.

Effective coaching is in-the-trenches, hands-on activity and is directly focused on specific problems, solutions and opportunities. There's no hiding from the details, no glossing over the issues at this level. Coaching provides valuable insight into the hiring process by helping to identify the traits and makeup of employees who perform best. And it can and must be a primary feeder of training — identifying improvement opportunities, gaps that must be addressed, practical lessons learned, and other issues that are leveraged when they are addressed at the group (not just individual) level.

In short, hiring, training and coaching are interrelated aspects of an overall effort. They work best when they are viewed and managed as such.

## Assessing Performance for Other Job Roles

What about assessing performance for those in other positions, such as analysts, trainers and managers? How does the reality of overlapping responsibilities (discussed in Chapter 12) translate into performance standards for individuals and teams? Every person has a bearing on contact center performance objectives. But is it fair to set performance standards on things that are outside the direct control of an individual?

In principle — and in practice — the answers are fairly simple. Managers are inherently responsible for achieving results through other people. Consequently, senior-level managers and directors are generally

| EXAMPLE EXPECTATIONS BY JOB ROLE |
|---|
| **Agents**<br>• Adherence to schedule<br>• Quality (contact by contact), including:<br>  • Identify and handle customer inquiries<br>  • Apply customer service policies<br>  • Perform business retention activities<br>  • Resolve customer problems<br>  • Educate customers on products and services offered<br>  • Match product benefits with customer needs<br>  • Enter coding and tracking information completely and accurately |
| **Supervisors**<br>• Team adherence to schedule<br>• Quality of the team<br>  • Ensure team meets quality objectives<br>  • Provide monitoring and coaching to individuals<br>  • Work with management to identify systemic quality problems<br>• Effectiveness of performance reviews and team meetings<br>• Performing the work of the agents during peak periods (as applicable)<br>• Representing the team on special projects/initiatives |
| **Quality Analysts/Managers**<br>• Leading and managing monitoring processes<br>• Ensuring consistent calibration<br>• Synthesizing monitoring input and preparing timely reports<br>• Identifying individual and process improvement opportunities<br>• Tracking and analyzing monitoring results vs. customer satisfaction measures |
| **Workforce Analysts/Managers**<br>• Creating accurate workload forecasts<br>• Organizing schedules that fit well for workload and agent requirements<br>• Assessing budgetary needs and implications of resource requirements<br>• Taking the initiative to coordinate plans with other departments<br>• Ensuring proper use of work modes (after-call work, auxiliary modes, etc.)<br>• Presenting key performance results to executive management |

---

**Technical Support Managers**
- Maintaining existing systems with minimum downtime
- Addressing usability issues (e.g., configuration, programming, etc.)
- Updating routing tables and systems as required
- Troubleshooting technical problems
- Recommending system improvement opportunities

---

**Managers and Directors**
- Ensuring that the contact center meets key objectives related to:
  - Quality
  - Accessibility
  - Efficiency
  - Cost performance
  - Strategic impact
- Establishing clear objectives for employees
- Maintaining morale
- Preparing budgets, illustrating budgetary tradeoffs
- Overseeing hiring and training efforts
- Aligning contact center objectives with organization and customer objectives
- Maximizing returns on investments (ROI)

---

held responsible for the full repertoire of performance objectives that the organization establishes. Of course, they shouldn't be held accountable for objectives that are in conflict or that are mutually exclusive. And they can only accomplish what is possible within the context of the resources they have to work with. But, by nature, they answer for overall results.

Managers and analysts in supporting roles are in a similar situation; however, with more specific responsibilities, accountabilities are generally associated with the areas in which they have primary responsibility. For example, the workforce manager in charge of forecasting and scheduling is generally accountable for the accuracy of the forecast (among other things) even though it is influenced by many variables, people and departments outside of their immediate control. Even so, if the forecast is way off the mark, they need to have answers as to why, and recommendations on how it can be improved.

Given overlapping responsibilities, successful centers put much more emphasis on processwide improvements than on strict output quotas. They work hard to educate everyone on the interrelated nature of processes and the impact each person has on results. They also establish key areas of accountability.

As you establish accountabilities (see table), keep your eye on the prize. What is the contact center's mission? Which activities best support the mission? How can you best align expectations to drive the right activities and, in turn, further your mission and strategy?

## Understanding and Managing Turnover

Turnover (attrition) is a fact of life in any organization. Some contact centers operate with annual rates of less than 5 percent, while others see rates exceeding 30 percent (and in some cases, far more).

Excessive turnover costs an organization in many ways: Higher recruiting and training costs; a lower average experience level leading to higher handling times, more transferred calls and lower service levels/response times; the need for more coaching and supervision; and the impact on everyone's morale when key people leave.

But some types of turnover can also bring benefits. Take internal agent attrition, for example: If employees leave for other positions within the organization, the contact center will have experienced advocates in other departments. And turnover can create the means for the center to bring in additional employees with needed skills and fresh insights.

The causes and costs/benefits will vary by type of turnover. For example, voluntary external turnover is more of a detriment to the organization than planned internal turnover. For better or worse, turnover will have an impact on your center. Since the cost of low quality and productivity can be significant, it is important to track and manage turnover as aggressively as other important performance indicators.

## CALCULATING YOUR TURNOVER RATE

To measure turnover correctly, you'll need to calculate an annualized turnover rate, which provides a consistent basis for comparison and trending. An annualized number does not require 12 months' worth of data. The calculation is as follows:

---

**EXAMPLE: INPUT FOR TURNOVER CALCULATION**

| | Number of agents exiting the job during the month | Average number of agents on staff during the month* |
|---|---|---|
| January | 2 | 104 |
| February | 1 | 103 |
| March | 4 | 101 |
| April | 0 | 101 |
| May | 3 | 109 |
| June | 5 | 106 |
| July | 2 | 105 |
| August | 3 | 103 |
| **Total/Average** | **20** | **104** |

* The average number of agents on staff during the month is often calculated by taking an average of the counts at the end of each week of the month. Alternatively, an average can be taken of the trained staff count at the beginning and end of the month.

---

Turnover = (number of agents exiting the job ÷ average number of agents during the period) x (12 ÷ number of months in the period)

Using the data from this example, the calculation yields the following: (20 ÷ 104) x (12 ÷ 8) = 28.8%. So, the center has an annualized turnover rate of about 29 percent.

While an overall annualized turnover rate is a useful number, it is of more value to further break down the number into internal/external, and voluntary/involuntary categories. Internal turnover refers to employees who leave the contact center but stay within the organization. External turnover refers to employees who leave the organization entirely. Since the causes are usually different than those for internal or involuntary turnover, the manager can prepare an action plan accordingly.

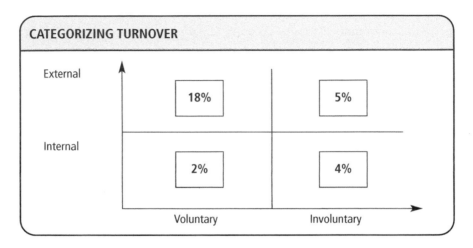

To take your analysis one step further, determine when each kind of turnover happens, e.g., within 30 days, 60 days, 90 days, 6 months, 12 months, etc. You can also analyze attrition by skill set, supervisor, shift hours and other factors. "I slice and dice it as many ways as I can because sometimes the root cause is hidden," says consultant Laura Grimes. "That almost always leads to clues about root causes and factors you can address."

## WORKING ON ROOT CAUSES

The best contact centers continually work on the root causes of turnover. Problems are often by-products of a poor planning process, so they assess and address resource issues. They are also broadening the responsibilities that agents have and their opportunities to learn, grow and advance (see discussion on career paths, Chapter 15).

I've also noticed a shift in perspective on internal turnover (people leaving the contact center for other opportunities within the organization). In

**COMMON CAUSES OF TURNOVER**

(Not listed in any specific order)

- Better opportunities within or outside the organization
- Insufficient development opportunities
- Pace of effort required
- Frustration with supervisor/manager
- Repetition
- Over-regimentation
- Sense of powerlessness to make a difference
- Frustration of not being allowed to do a good job
- Unrelenting attention necessary
- Being "tied to a desk"
- Feeling of being excessively monitored
- Feeling of not being appreciated
- Handling complaints or problems all day
- Odd work hours
- Insufficient pay
- Lack of proper tools and training
- The demand for increased skills from agents who do not want to perform those skills or who are not equipped to perform them

many ways, it's a good thing. The time people spend on the front lines with customers gives them a healthy perspective that they carry into other departments. But there has to be a balance. Losing people too soon can cost the contact center, and the organization, dearly.

Consequently, a growing number of contact center managers are working to expand the time agents spend in the center before moving elsewhere (e.g., they are working with their colleagues in other parts of the organization to encourage agents to stay longer). They are also helping agents to see the enormous impact the center can have on the organization and customer base, as well as the exciting future ahead as communications change and trends such as social media services enter the picture.

In the next chapter, we'll explore some topics closely related to those we've looked at here. They include organizational structure, job roles, career paths, and effective communication — each complementary to establishing an effective and engaging organization.

# Points to Remember

- Creating an engaging environment is key to success.
- Adherence to schedule and qualitative measurements can effectively replace other measurements (such as contacts handled) that are merely after-the-fact outputs.
- Qualitative measurements have become more focused, as they've become more important in today's environment.
- Performance standards can be broadly categorized as "foundation" (whether something was done) and "finesse" (how something was done), and scoring should match the type of criteria established.
- For the best results, involve agents in establishing and maintaining the monitoring and coaching program. And build your initiatives with strategic contributions to the organization in mind.
- Given shared responsibilities for achieving many contact center results, it's important to establish the right accountabilities, both for those in individual job roles and for the overall team.
- Don't leave turnover to chance — track it, manage it, and take steps to fix it. Create paths for your people to grow and develop.

# CHAPTER 15:
# Building a More Effective Organization

*Every organized human activity — from the making of pots to the placing of a man on the moon — gives rise to two fundamental and opposing requirements: the division of labor into various tasks to be performed, and the coordination of those tasks to accomplish the activity.*

**HENRY MINTZBERG**

---

Like the road network in a metropolitan area or the design of the hull on a boat, the forces of organizational design are constantly at work. A well-designed organization will enable the contact center to be flexible, effective and efficient. When structured poorly, it will hamper communication, create barriers to performance and lead to unpredictable and inefficient workarounds.

In this chapter, we'll look at some of the most important aspects of building an organization, including:

- The principles of effective structure
- Job roles and responsibilities
- Establishing career and skill paths
- Spans of control (i.e., agent to supervisor ratios)
- Cultivating good communication

An important theme runs through these subjects: Successful organizations design their structures to fit their unique and evolving situations.

**361**

Don't let your organizational structure become stagnant. It can and must change as your services develop.

## The Principles of Effective Structure

There is a paradox at work in many organizations, related to organizational structure. On one hand, the organizational design is constantly exerting its forces as it channels communications, shapes protocol and establishes lines of authority. It is one of the most influential and "visible" aspects of any enterprise. Most managers can draw their organizational charts in their sleep. And yet it is an issue that, in the daily hubbub, somehow becomes assumed — almost outside the realm of managerial consciousness.

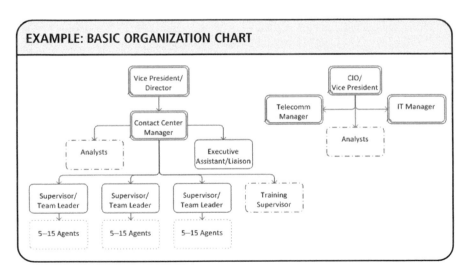

**EXAMPLE: BASIC ORGANIZATION CHART**

While any center is undergoing constant change at the agent group level as the organization evolves to meet variable workload demands and new content requirements, a bigger question remains. Stop and think: Is your organization working for you?

Although some aspects of organizational design are similar from one contact center to the next — e.g., the basic components illustrated in the

## THE IMPACT OF ORGANIZATIONAL DESIGN

Organizational structure (also called organizational design) provides the alignment of roles and responsibilities for business units, departments and individuals. There are many reasonable definitions of organizational structure, but almost all refer to both the division of labor and the coordination of responsibilities and tasks. Major issues defined or affected by organizational design include:

- The contact center's position in the larger organization
- The contact center's role in relation to other channels of service delivery (such as retail locations or field sales and service operations)
- The contact center's overall mission and responsibilities
- Specific job roles and accountabilities
- Lines of communication and authority
- Political protocol
- Agent group structure
- Analyst and support positions
- Ratios (e.g., staff to supervisor)
- Number of sites and level of integration
- Process, technology and facility requirements
- The role of self-service
- Budget allocations

figure are present in most organizations — there are about as many unique structures as there are organizations. Even so, there are some consistent principles at work behind any effective design. These include the following:

**THE ORGANIZATION'S MISSION, VISION AND STRATEGY DRIVE THE STRUCTURE.** Organizational design is a strategy to help the organization reach its objectives; design helps translate strategy into operations. Answers to major questions, such as the contact center's role, to whom the center reports and how the center will be positioned vis-à-vis other service delivery methods (e.g., the sales force, retail operations and online services), must flow from the highest levels of strategy. In a common example of how strategy drives structure, many contact centers are handling an increasingly wide range of customer contacts (e.g., social channels, email, Web-initiated, support calls related to self-service systems, etc.) as organizations focus on consolidating related services in order to provide timely and consistent service.

The culture and environment of the organization play a large role in determining structure. For example, more formal, bureaucratic organizations often have more formal structures, while less formal organizations tend to choose flatter structures with dispersed responsibilities.

**INFORMAL AND FORMAL STRUCTURES ARE WELL-ALIGNED.** The formal structure is the one defined by organizational charts and in position and process descriptions. The informal structure is how things *really* function. I've run into a number of cases over the years where contact centers had grown their own ad hoc training and technology support functions (e.g., "Hey, Christine can do that ... let's ask her") because they weren't getting timely support from those areas. That's a symptom that it's time to sit down across these functions and revisit requirements, accountabilities, and approach.

Organizations are complex, and there will always be some degree of informal communication and workflow. But if an informal structure grows topsy-turvy, it's important to address the root causes. Just as great sports teams define positions around natural talent and abilities (e.g., quarterback, kicker, running back), formal structures should reflect efficient flows, natural lines of authority and earned responsibilities.

**AGENT GROUPS FORM THE FOUNDATION OF CONTACT CENTER STRUCTURE.** Once the contact center's place in the larger organization is defined, it should be built from agent groups upward. (Recall from Chapter 6 that agent groups share a common set of skills and knowledge, handle a specified mix of contacts and can comprise hundreds of agents across multiple sites. Supervisory groups and teams are often subsets of agent groups.)

## ARE YOUR AGENT GROUPS TOO POOLED? TOO SPECIALIZED?

There is no formula for deciding how pooled or specialized agent groups should be. However, the symptoms of groups that are too pooled or too specialized are usually evident.

**Symptoms of over-specialized agent groups:**

- Small groups with low occupancy and/or erratic service level/response time results
- An overly complicated planning process
- Many contacts are not handled by the intended group (e.g., due to overflow or reassigned agents)
- Agents become frustrated with narrow responsibilities

**Symptoms of over-generalized agent groups:**

- Customer interactions have a higher handling time than necessary as agents grapple with a broad range of issues
- There is a high number of transferred or escalated contacts
- Training time is relatively long
- Quality often suffers
- Agents are frustrated with "too much to know"

The ideal agent group is one in which each person is equally proficient at handling every type of contact, through any channel, speaks all required languages, and can maintain the company's branding and image for every customer segment. That, of course, is not realistic in most environments — thus the tiered groups, network configurations, overflow parameters, skills-based routing and other alternatives that many use to get the right contact to the right place at the right time.

Here's the point: Everything — hiring, training programs, supervisory and management responsibilities, analyst activities, quality standards, workforce planning, you name it — is based on agent group structure. But as agent group requirements evolve, the larger organization built on those groups can become obsolete. This is an issue that requires constant review. Has the superstructure become obsolete even as agent group requirements have moved on? Think through those agent groups. Redefine the responsibilities of that expanding analyst area. Bring supervisor ratios into sensible alignment. And rethink, as feasible, your training programs.

**DIVISIONS AND RATIOS ARE SUPPORTED BY THE HIGHEST PRIORITIES.** Any team, agent group, functional area or location (unless networked seamlessly to other sites) is defined by dividing lines, and divisions should be justified by the highest priorities. It's important to constantly review any divisions.

For example, after much discussion and analysis, a governmental organization decided to combine dozens of small, localized contact centers into a few larger regionalized centers. They determined that overall service to constituents was a higher priority than satisfying the interests pushing to keep the jobs in each local community. In another case, a high-tech company with 24x7 technical support combined several daytime groups into a pooled group at night equipped to handle a broad range of interactions; although handling time moved higher, quality remained consistent with daytime service. The organization decided that the ability to reach a capable agent — albeit one who may need a bit more time handling the contact — wisely wins out over maintaining small, specialized groups in the wee hours of the morning.

**REPORTING ARRANGEMENTS ASSIGN APPROPRIATE ACCOUNTABILITIES.** There are situations in which the contact center is dependent on people who report to other areas that have different or even competing interests. Yes, everybody is ultimately on the same team. But when contact centers are being judged on their ability to handle a changing workload, the IT/telecom department is intent on operating within a reconfigured budget, and marketing is being assessed on response rates ... that can be a recipe for problems.

The answer? Sit down with colleagues across these areas and identify objectives and accountabilities that could be in conflict. Maybe training needs to report to the same area as the contact center, or to the contact center. Maybe some expenditures that are spread across IT, marketing and

## STRATEGY DRIVES STRUCTURE

Many contact centers have been through consolidations or restructurings that are really just cleanup efforts for lack of having or using an effective customer access strategy. For example, I recall helping an insurance company with agent group "consolidation." Their sales team would sell an account to a major client and, if pressed by the prospect, would agree to provide a dedicated agent group. In all cases, they promised agents trained on the characteristics of the clients' accounts (e.g., small business, large business, government agencies, etc.). After each sale, the organization would roll out dedicated telephone numbers and the contact center would then be left to figure out how to best support the account.

The center pooled agent groups whenever possible, but they eventually reached the point where they were faced with the near-impossible task of managing numerous agent groups, routing plans, overflow contingencies and access numbers. The purpose of the consolidation plan was to get a handle on all of the available access numbers and routing plans, and then combine and simplify agent groups and accounts as possible. It was a painful effort necessitated by decisions that were being made in the absence of an overall plan. They are now taking steps to ensure that the contact center and sales teams work from a common plan.

customer service budgets should be combined. Perhaps some support functions (e.g., components of hiring, training, technical support or others) ought to be brought under the contact center umbrella. Answers begin to emerge given an open and honest look at needs.

**SUPPORT POSITIONS ARE ENABLERS.** Roles geared around ensuring compliance, establishing rules and creating exception reports are often counterproductive. Alternatively, creating better processes, facilitating collaboration and, in general, supporting and enabling the contact center's highest values are support responsibilities that will contribute to overall success. Those in support roles must find a good balance between burdensome control and an organization so loosely managed that it loses effectiveness.

367

## SHOULD YOU CONSIDER HOME AGENTS?

As of this writing, an estimated half or more of all U.S. contact centers (with similar strong uptake in many other regions of the world) are sending at least some of their people home to work, and for very good reasons. Numerous studies have illustrated the benefits of working from home (the following statistics are based on U.S. figures and come from The Telework Research Network and statistics from the U.S. government), including:

- Increased productivity. The average productivity increase for home workers was 27%, and two thirds of companies surveyed reported an increase in productivity.
- Increased agent satisfaction. Agents commonly cite a better work/life balance, improved time management, decreased costs of working (see next point), the feeling of being trusted, and better health.
- Compensation benefits. Working from home effectively provides a significant raise without spending more on staffing costs. The estimated average annual savings to an employee working from home in the U.S. is $8,517.
- Reduced costs. Average annual savings to U.S. companies, per employee, on electrical and real estate costs alone is an estimated $3,000.
- Better employee retention. About 80% of employees say they'd like to work from home; and a third of employees would choose working from home over a pay raise. Additionally, 85% of employers say the working from home option increases retention.
- Easier recruitment. Many organizations report advantages in recruiting, including a wider reach to potential employees and more mature employees interested in working from home. (In a related statistic, two thirds of employees say they would take another job to ease their commutes.)
- Decreased environmental impact. Carbon emissions in the United States could be reduced by an estimated three tons annually, with an estimated 95,000 fewer traffic injuries annually, and a reduction in the need for energy imports.
- Increased adherence and attendance. Companies benefit from an

estimated 63% reduction in unscheduled absences.

- Business continuity. Home agents can minimize companies' reliance on outside vendors, lessen the costs of establishing remote sites for business continuity, and ensure a smoother transition during events that could lead to service disruptions.

While results vary from one organization to the next, many sources report other benefits as well: possible reduced starting pay for home agents, tax advantages to companies and employees, improved scheduling flexibility, increased sales conversions, reduced support and benefit costs (in part due to part-time versus full-time employment), and improved revenue per hour. All of these can translate into more efficient and effective service delivery.

And what about the effect on customers of teleworking employees? Michele Rowan, CEO of At Home Customer Contacts, reports that customer satisfaction scores were equal to or greater than those of organizations using only on-site agents.

Technical and data security hurdles have been largely resolved, and most ACD systems today provide remote agent capability. (If you're planning on acquiring a new contact center system, make sure that home agent capabilities are available.) In fact, many organizations report that the greatest remaining barrier to establishing home agent programs is organizational culture. Be sure to develop a solid business case for home agents, as well as an implementation plan that encompasses necessary employee participation, clear eligibility requirements, and a tangible plan for supporting home-based agents.

By Jean Bave Kerwin, JBK Consulting and ICMI Senior Certified Associate

**THE STRUCTURE FACILITATES BRANDING.** The organization's desired image, how it wishes to define and serve customer segments, and the specific requirements of individual customers should comprise objectives that span the organization's marketing efforts, the products and services it provides, and the contributions of the contact center. While that doesn't necessarily mean that separate divisions or agent groups within the center are required to serve different customer segments, it does mean that divisions, groups and responsibilities should further rather than hinder branding requirements. (Example: Many organizations are currently implementing customer experience initiatives designed to break down historical silos and provide a unified focus on customer needs; a common and important aspect of these efforts is consolidation and better coordination across functional areas.)

**THE ORGANIZATION IS DESIGNED TO BE NIMBLE.** Finally, in a theme that runs throughout this book, the contact center should be designed and managed to be as scalable and flexible as possible. There are many considerations covered in prior chapters that go into creating a nimble organization: having a thoughtful and current customer access strategy (Chapter 2); establishing an accurate planning and management process (Part 2); ensuring that everyone understands important contact center dynamics (Chapter 9); building budgets that match requirements (Chapter 10); implementing an appropriate approach to real-time management (Chapter 11); establishing the right objectives and metrics (Chapters 12 and 14), and an ongoing approach for understanding and improving quality (Chapter 13).

## Job Roles — Emerging, Evolving

An important part of developing an effective organization is to identify the positions you'll need, and the responsibilities that will go along with each. The table below provides a look at how job titles and responsibilities can be defined in a larger contact center. (Large centers tend to have more specialized roles and provide good illustrations of how specific responsibilities can become. Smaller centers often combine some or many areas of responsibility when creating positions. In some of the smallest centers, the manager may wear every hat — and yes, still serve as an agent at least part of the time.)

A glance through these roles and responsibilities underscores an important trend in recent years: From supervisors on up, management-level job roles are becoming increasingly specialized. Consider workforce management, which is seeing the emergence of forecasting, scheduling and real-time management expertise. Similarly, quality monitoring depends on monitoring and coaching, program design, calibration and data analysis. Technology can also lead to specialization, such as specific positions dedicated to managing or supporting speech or IVR, desktops, analytics, networks, quality monitoring systems, social or sentiment tools, or workforce management applications. If you manage or support a small center, you may assume many of these responsibilities, but they are more specialized than in the past.

---

*Clearly, running a successful contact center is, more than ever, a team sport.*

---

Interestingly, at the agent level, job requirements are often becoming more generalized. Agents must increasingly understand the access channels customers use, the interrelated nature of services the organization provides, and the breadth of needs and expectations that customers have, e.g., to identify cross-sell and upsell opportunities. (And by the way, maybe we shouldn't refer to them as "front-line" agents. "'Ambassadors' is a more fitting term," says ICMI Strategic Training Director Linda Riggs. "It's not a military conflict — these are opportunities to build relationships.")

Clearly, running a successful contact center is, more than ever, a team sport. The most successful centers cultivate training and development programs at all levels that deliver specific skills and knowledge while reinforcing overall objectives. And the best leaders encourage collaboration and an appreciation for the diverse responsibilities the center requires while keeping everyone focused on the business results that matter most.

| EXAMPLE JOB ROLES AND RESPONSIBILITIES (LARGE CONTACT CENTER) | |
|---|---|
| **Job Role** | **Typical Responsibilities** |
| **Agent** | • Identify and handle customer inquiries<br>• Apply customer service policies<br>• Perform business retention activities<br>• Resolve customer problems<br>• Educate customers on products and services offered<br>• Match product benefits with customer needs<br>• Enter coding and tracking information completely and accurately<br>• Serve as ambassador for the company and further customer relationships |
| **Team Leader/ Supervisor** | • Resolve agent and customer issues<br>• Participate in new-hire interviews<br>• Conduct performance reviews and team meetings<br>• Help to handle the workload, if and when feasible and appropriate<br>• Conduct monitoring and coaching sessions<br>• Coordinate with training and quality assurance to identify systemic quality improvement opportunities<br>• Represent the team on special projects/initiatives |
| **Technical Support** | • Maintain existing software/hardware<br>• Recommend technology solutions<br>• Install technology systems and upgrades<br>• Provide technical assistance to operations<br>• Help to update contact-routing tables and systems as needed<br>• Troubleshoot technical problems<br>• Plan and schedule system backup/outages to minimize customer impact |
| **Workforce Manager** | • Spearhead the contact center planning process<br>• Ensure key planning concepts are understood by the entire organization<br>• Ensure contact center and staffing models include accurate, updated information |

| | |
|---|---|
| **Workforce Manager** *(continued)* | • Conduct meetings with relevant departments regarding forecast and workload requirements<br>• Research and recommend vendor and software for forecasting and scheduling activities<br>• Train team leaders, managers and trainers on the use of workforce planning tools (e.g., work modes, schedule adherence, etc.)<br>• Provide executive management with reports on workload trends and staffing requirements |
| **Workforce Analyst** | • Develop reports on daily workload<br>• Participate in forecasting meetings with relevant departments; develop accurate short- and long-term workload forecasts<br>• Control master systems files with schedule information and shift preferences<br>• Serve as initial contact point for all issues regarding schedules<br>• Process day-off requests and update systems<br>• Determine workforce requirements to meet service level and response time objectives<br>• Determine agent schedules to meet contact center objectives |
| **Workforce Real-Time Analyst** | • Provide intraday monitoring and reporting<br>• Recommend real-time schedule changes and identify efficiency opportunities<br>• Adjust schedules based on workload/forecast shifts<br>• Update systems with real-time shift adjustment information<br>• Develop and distribute real-time summary reports to management team |
| **Training Manager** | • Work with operations and HR to determine new-hire and ongoing training needs<br>• Develop or buy appropriate training courses; implement programs<br>• Determine best methods of delivery<br>• Create effectiveness evaluations and update/improve training accordingly<br>• Partner with operations and QA to identify gaps, calibration requirements and training resources required |

| Quality Assurance Manager | • Recommend, implement and direct monitoring program (e.g., record and review, side-by-side, silent, etc.)<br>• Work with managers, supervisors/team leaders, and training to calibrate monitoring processes and results<br>• Research and recommend vendors for automated processes<br>• Gather and distribute results<br>• Align internal monitoring with external customer feedback |
|---|---|
| Contact Center Manager | • Implement contact center strategies and tactics<br>• Establish agent and team objectives<br>• Work with the workforce management team to ensure accurate staffing and scheduling<br>• Work with supervisors/team leaders, analysts and support positions to establish and manage priorities<br>• Coordinate with VP/director and other managers to monitor budget requirements and compliance<br>• Conduct supervisor/team leader performance reviews and administer rewards<br>• Provide on-the-job training and mentoring<br>• Oversee recruiting, hiring and training processes<br>• Ensure that leaders in other parts of the organization understand the role and strategic value of the contact center |
| Vice President/ Director | • Collaborate with senior-level management to determine the strategic direction of the contact center<br>• Align contact center objectives with the organization and customer objectives<br>• Oversee implementation of strategies<br>• Develop and manage budgets; secure required resources<br>• Maximize and communicate the contact center's return on investment<br>• Oversee recruiting, hiring and training of managerial staff<br>• Conduct performance reviews of managers and administer rewards<br>• Champion the contact center throughout internal and external channels |

# Establishing Career and Skill Paths

The root causes of turnover put a spotlight on the importance of devel-

---

**INVESTMENT IN PEOPLE AT AMERICAN EXPRESS**

Credit card giant American Express has set its sights on becoming the world's most respected service brand. As part of this initiative, the business has invested a large sum in creating career paths for its employees.

A case in point is AMEX's vice president of customer service for United Kingdom operations, Jose Vasquez-Mendez, who started out with the company as a call center agent in Mexico City. "This gives our leaders real knowledge of the job our front-line teams do and is a great example of our commitment to personal development across the company. We have a strong culture of personal development and helping employees be the best they can be — to realize their potential" says Vasquez-Mendez, referring to the company's robust internal development program.

Vasquez-Mendez was a beneficiary of AMEX's development culture, and he used what he learned to build and hone his own skills and put them to work for the brand that nurtured him. One aspect of his development was industry certification. "Working toward and obtaining the CIAC-Certified Strategic Leader certification has not only helped validate many of the practices employed by my team and me, but more importantly, it has helped me gain deeper insight into how I should be deploying my management skills when developing call center strategies. The experience has served to broaden my understanding of practices within the industry and given me a wider scope of knowledge to draw from when dealing with the dynamics of a call center," he says.

Vasquez-Mendez is hardly a one-off story: AMEX uses investment in professional development as a reward for leaders who perform well against the brand's goals for becoming the world's most respected service brand. And it's a virtuous cycle — those leaders who gain this investment level turn their newfound skills around to work for continuous improvement in AMEX contact centers.

---

oping opportunities for agents to learn, grow and advance. There are two general options for formal employee advancement: career paths and skill paths.

A typical career path model requires the development of job families, which comprise a number of jobs arranged in a hierarchy by grade, pay and responsibility, e.g., agent, team leader, supervisor, manager, senior manager, director. The career path then indicates the requirements for each job within the family, e.g., education, experience, tenure, knowledge, skills, behavioral competencies, etc.

Because the historical corporate ladder approach to staff development can be limited for contact centers (due to the finite number of supervisory and management positions available), a more effective approach may be the skill path model. Skill paths focus on an individual's acquisition of skill sets. Individuals often receive more recognition, responsibility and (in many cases) compensation as they achieve new skill levels within their position.

Contact centers require more diverse skills than perhaps any other part of the organization. Customer behavior, information systems and technologies, queuing theory, forecasting, statistics, human resources management, training, written and verbal communication skills, reporting, real-time management and strategy are all an inherent part of the environment. Developing attractive career and skill paths remains a significant opportunity.

## Span of Control

Though it sounds a bit dated and hierarchical, span of control is a widely used term in business management that refers to the number of individuals a manager supervises. A large span of control means that the manager supervises many people. A small span of control means the manager supervisors fewer people. Span of control tends to decrease as the complexity and variability of the conditions in the environment increase.

## AGENT-TO-SUPERVISOR RATIOS

In contact centers, the agent-to-supervisor ratio is an especially important consideration. Effective ratios are dependent on the tasks, standards and responsibilities of both agents and supervisors. Many centers today have between 8 and 12 staff per supervisor.

However, there are notable differences by industry. For example, financial and insurance companies tend to be on the low end of that spectrum (with more supervisors managing fewer agents), while catalog companies and telecommunications providers tend to be on the high end. Further, there can be significant exceptions; e.g., some reservations centers have a relatively large span of control, approaching or exceeding 20 staff per supervisor. And technical support centers and other complex environments can have as few as five staff per supervisor. Even within an industry, there can be a wide variance (one well-known catalog company has 40 agents per supervisor — not a number I recommend — while another has 10).

Hours of operation can also be a significant factor. For example, many organizations maintain a minimum number of supervisors, even during off-hour shifts that require proportionally fewer agents.

In short, be careful about drawing quick conclusions based on these figures or industry benchmarks. There are no simple answers along the lines of, "If you are a such-and-such type of contact center, you ought to have X staff per supervisor."

Some of today's trends are working to drive the span of control up, including:

**GROWING WORKLOADS:** In some sectors, contact center workloads have consistently increased. In those centers that struggle to keep up with growth, the span of control tends to increase.

**BUDGET CONSTRAINTS:** As organizations go through restructurings and/or budget cutbacks, they often must reduce the relative number of supervisors (increase spans of control). Many managers admit that a downward adjustment of span of control would be ideal but insist that funds simply are not available for more supervisor/manager positions.

**GROWTH OF TEAMS:** A positive development has been the growth of team-based environments, which has challenged the traditional role of supervisors. Contact centers have largely moved away from production-oriented "factories" toward organizations that are flatter and more team-oriented. In many cases, team leaders are assuming functions that traditionally have been in the domain of managers and supervisors.

**LOWER TURNOVER:** Another positive development is that a growing number of centers are directly and successfully reducing turnover. As the average experience level of agents moves upward, less supervision is generally required.

Other developments in today's environment tend to drive span of control down, including:

**THE GROWING COMPLEXITY OF CONTACTS:** As better-applied technologies offload routine contacts and as new contact channels proliferate, agents are handling interactions that require more human savvy and know-how. The growing complexity of the work tends to inherently require more coaching and feedback.

**MORE MONITORING AND COACHING, MORE EXTENSIVELY:** Many contact centers are employing more robust monitoring approaches and taking larger samples for coaching and development than in the past (see Chapter 14). Monitoring, feedback and coaching take a significant amount of time.

**MORE SMALL CONTACT CENTERS:** This may be the biggest reason that the average ratio across the industry has moved down — there are simply more small groups in the sample. For example, if a new contact center has only seven or eight agents, it will still likely have a supervisor even though that person will be able to supervise more people as the center grows.

There are potentially other factors that can confuse the issue of ratios. For example, the tasks of supervisors vary widely from one organization to the next. Some lean more toward "lead agent" responsibilities, in which they lead a team but also help to handle the workload, while others are much more involved in management responsibilities. Further, the time that supervisors spend monitoring and coaching (the most time-consuming activity beyond handling calls, in most centers) can vary by many multiples. And some organizations have set up internal help desks to field inquiries from agents who need help — a responsibility traditionally handled by supervisors.

Recommendations in general business literature vary from the "train them, empower them, and get out of the way" school of thought on one end of the spectrum to a more structured approach on the other. In their classic book, *Executive Leadership*, authors Elliot Jacques and Stephen D. Clement mince no words: "There is more nonsense centering around the topic of span of control than around nearly any other subject in the whole field of organization and management." They go on to criticize managers who search for "easy-to-apply rules of thumb that need no thought." This is applicable to the contact center environment, as well. While somewhere between 8 and 12 agents per supervisor makes sense in many centers, a 5:1 or 20:1 ratio may be equally justifiable.

### SUPERVISOR-TO-MANAGER RATIOS

In terms of supervisor-to-management spans of control, ratios of between 5:1 and 12:1 are typical. Given the higher level and more complex interactions that must take place between managers and supervisors, spans of control are usually smaller than those between agents and supervisors. This underscores a principle generally true in most organizations: The higher up in the organization, the smaller the spans of control.

## Cultivating Effective Communication

Effective communication results in a shared understanding of what's most important. When people are aligned behind a set of compelling values, enthusiasm, commitment and significant productivity tend to follow.

In that sense, effective communication is inseparable from effective leadership ... leaders are only as effective as their ability to communicate.

Communication creates meaning and direction for people. When good communication is lacking, the symptoms are predictable: conflicting objectives, unclear values, misunderstandings, lack of coordination, confusion, low morale and people doing the bare minimum required.

Although cultures and communication styles vary, there are predictable and notable commonalities among successful contact centers. Among the most important are:

**COMMIT TO KEEPING PEOPLE IN THE KNOW.** Leaders of high-performance organizations are predisposed to keeping their people in the know. They actively share both good news and bad. This minimizes the rumor mill, which hinders effective, accurate communication. It also contributes to an environment of trust. It sounds simple, but just making a commitment is the first step. I know of a manager who decided to make great communication a top priority. She literally includes it as an item on her daily task list — and her commitment is working wonders for productivity and clarity in the organization.

**CULTIVATE A SUPPORTING CULTURE.** One of the most distinguishable aspects of a positive culture is that the contact center's vision, mission and impact on the rest of the organization are well known and understood. Why does the center exist? What is it working to achieve? What's in it for customers and for the organization? What's in it for employees? Take steps to build employee commitment to the vision. Get their input as it's being developed, then publish it, live by it. Use it to guide tactical, day-to-day decisions. (See Chapter 17 for more on culture.)

**ESTABLISH APPROPRIATE COMMUNICATION TOOLS.** A prerequisite to an environment in which communication thrives is that individuals and teams have compatible and capable communications technologies. The usual channels apply — instant messaging, internal collaboration and conferencing tools, email, phone, conferencing capabilities, and other tools offer enormous potential if they are available and compatible across the organization. Further — and this is so simple but so effective — have easy-to-access online directories for your contact center and cross-functional teams. This provides necessary information, and it creates symbolism that reinforces communication and camaraderie.

**DEVELOP FORMAL AND INFORMAL CHANNELS OF COMMUNICATION.** Effective leaders cultivate both formal and informal channels of communication. But the mission and values being communicated remain consistent. The communication formats can include newsletters, meetings, visual displays, email, voicemail, posters, wikis and internal forums, and informal "hallway meetings." One of the formal means of communication between frontline workers and management is employee satisfaction surveys. As part of the process, the best contact centers involve agents in addressing problems, and they close the loop by consistently communicating progress toward resolving issues.

**ENSURE THAT STRUCTURE AND POLICIES SUPPORT COMMUNICATION.** In general, flatter, more collaborative organizations help to foster an environment in which trust and communication flourish. Policies and procedures can also influence trust and communication. For example, monitoring and coaching programs that truly contribute to the growth and well-being of individuals and the organization help to build trust and encourage communication.

**LISTEN ACTIVELY AND REGULARLY.** Listening encourages diverse perspectives, enables individuals to grow, and creates community within the organization. Active listening enables a culture that brings out the best in people. Further, many studies on the subjects of leadership and strategy have shown the visions of some of history's greatest leaders actually came from others in their circles. The leaders may have selected the best vision to focus on, then shaped it and communicated it to others in a compelling way, but they rarely originated the vision.

**DON'T OVERDO IT.** Experienced leaders are aware of an interesting

## SUCCESSFULLY LEADING DISTRIBUTED TEAMS

Information and communications technologies have spawned organizations that span geography and time. Multisite environments, cross-functional teams, and extended-hour or 24x7 operations are common contact center examples. If you are a manager or director, you likely have the responsibility of getting results from those who work in different locations, who don't report to you or who don't work the same hours.

Unfortunately, technology hasn't eliminated the natural barriers that exist between people who work in distributed environments. Those who work in different places and/or at different times often have trouble seeing themselves as an integral part of a larger team.

Like leadership in general, there's no specific recipe for building a cohesive virtual team. There are, however, tried-and-true steps you can take that will significantly increase your chances for success:

- Create a clear vision for the contact center.
- Create opportunities for the people in the distributed environment to get to know each other. (For example, I know of a manager who set up an internal website page profiling the members of a multisite team, and occasionally gives everyone a short quiz on the interests and backgrounds of the other members. Others are tapping video-based meetings, internal social communities, and other ways to bring people together.)
- Look for ways to keep everyone involved. Often, some amount of expediency must be traded for the sake of fostering a collaborative environment.
- Take steps to ensure that everyone gets key information at the same time.
- Spend a disproportionate amount of time tending to the needs and relationships of the more "distant" members of the group. (Distant may mean the members who work the night shift, or those who are in a site thousands of miles away.)
- Look for ways to scrap or, at least, minimize the impact of unnecessary hierarchies and cumbersome bureaucracies, which tend to wreak havoc on distributed teams.
- Consistently communicate progress. It's important to keep the group

updated and on the same track.

The challenges of leading a distributed team are real and ongoing, but being part of an environment in which people successfully work together across distance and time is one of the most rewarding professional experiences you can have. In today's world, it is also one of the most necessary.

paradox: too much communicating inhibits effective communication. There is an optimal level of communication beyond which more communication becomes counterproductive. Too many meetings, memos, conferences, email messages and on-the-fly discussions may be symptoms of weaknesses in plans and processes. With better tools, more focused training and appropriate levels of empowerment, the need for excessive real-time communicating can be avoided — because the communication is built into individual understanding and established processes.

Meg Whitman, former CEO of eBay, reportedly required her leadership team to turn off mobile devices during meetings. I'm convinced she was onto something that goes beyond just the ability to focus on a meeting.

---

*Too many meetings, memos, conferences, email messages and on-the-fly discussions may be symptoms of weaknesses in plans and processes.*

---

One of the highest forms of leadership is to build an organization or team that runs smoothly without your constant involvement. If you're perpetually glued to your computer or mobile, there's probably opportunity to clarify responsibilities and improve processes and training. The alternative consists of ongoing interruptions that hamper your concentration and perpetuate dependencies. Can you go on vacation without checking in? That's a sign that you've probably built a team or an organization that's working. (And you deserve that vacation!)

# Points to Remember

- Your organizational structure should be unique and fit your specific environment. It can and must change as your services evolve.

- Even though organizational structures are unique from one organization to the next, there are dependable, consistent principles that lead to effective design.

- An important part of developing an effective organization is to identify the positions you'll need and the responsibilities that will go along with each — and then keep them up to date.

- Developing attractive career and skill paths that keep employees interested, engaged and productive is an important leadership responsibility.

- Sensible agent-to-supervisor ratios are dependent on the tasks, standards and responsibilities of both agents and supervisors.

- Good communication results in a shared understanding of what's most important. When everyone is aligned behind a set of compelling values, enthusiasm, commitment and productivity will follow.

# Part Five:
# Leadership in the New Era of Customer Relationships

## CHAPTER 16:
## Enabling Technologies, New Possibilities

## CHAPTER 17:
## Characteristics of the Best-Managed Contact Centers

---

*Improved management techniques, enabling technologies, and an emerging focus on creating higher levels of strategic value are changing contact centers dramatically. Forward-thinking leaders recognize the opportunities — and challenges — that these changes bring. They are moving forward with foresight and optimism, and are creating cultures in which positive change is welcomed.*

---

# CHAPTER 16:
# Enabling Technologies, New Possibilities

*We think we invent technology, but technology also invents us.*

**RICHARD FARSON**

New management techniques coupled with emerging technologies are changing contact centers dramatically. A notable example is the emergence of environments characterized by proliferating contact channels, high levels of skill, and a strong focus on customer experiences. The opportunities for better serving customers and delivering more value to the organization are there for the taking.

But the changes that bring opportunities for those organizations that lead can rather quickly morph into competitive pressures for others to keep up. Customer expectations seem to evolve overnight. The convergence of social, mobile, broadband, smartphones, and other tools and developments is becoming a catalyst for progress. Customers are better informed and better connected — and organizations must upgrade their service delivery capabilities or risk dissatisfying, disillusioning or driving them away.

And there's a related challenge: New technologies almost always present new management and process requirements. To get anticipated results, they must be viewed in terms of how they can support and further the organization's mission and strategy, and be implemented and managed with foresight.

387

Here, we'll look at some of the major technology developments changing today's environment. We'll summarize important underlying trends. And we'll identify the key leadership responsibilities required to make it all work.

## Infrastructure: Change from the Ground Up

To get a sense of context, go back with me for just a moment to 1858. This was a decade and a half after Samuel B. Morse introduced the telegraph (Chapter 1). After more than a year of enduring

**SOME OF TODAY'S COMPETITIVE PRESSURES**

- Address more complex issues
- Handle growing and increasingly varied workloads
- Improve customer satisfaction and loyalty
- Deepen customer engagement
- Accelerate service delivery
- Boost revenues
- Reduce costs
- Improve cross-sell and upsell
- Improve consistency in service delivery
- Provide more personalized services
- Offer customers greater choices and control
- Provide the right access alternatives
- Increase hours of operation
- Deliver exceptional customer experiences

storms, sickness and failures on the high seas, the crew of the HMS *Agamemnon* had just completed running the first transatlantic telegraph cable. Investors on both sides of the Atlantic had provided the funding, and hopes for the beginnings of a new communications era were high.

Unfortunately, the signals that trickled through the cable were so weak that it took 16 and a half hours and the most sensitive equipment available to decipher the first message of just 90 words sent by Queen Victoria. Worse, the cable's insulation failed several days later, and it never worked again. For onlookers, investors and especially the crew, this was a heartbreaking, bitter end to an immense and bold undertaking. But the project

— though viewed as a failure at the time — helped to firmly establish a vision of a more connected world.

---

*"A plate of silver and one of zinc are taken into the mouth, the one above, the other below the tongue. They are then placed in contact with the wire, and words issuing from the mouth are conveyed by the wire."*

**1854 NEWSPAPER, DESCRIBING HOW THE**

**YET-TO-BE-INVENTED TELEPHONE MIGHT WORK**

---

It wasn't until almost a century later, in 1956, that the first transatlantic telephone cable, running between the British Isles and Newfoundland, Canada, was inaugurated. The crew and investors of 1858 would be amazed to see what has transpired since. High-capacity fiber optic cables crisscross oceans and continents, and satellites reach the most remote parts of the globe; this network reaches into your business and home, and with almost five billion subscriptions, wireless services provide virtually ubiquitous connectivity across the rest of the map. (As I write, I'm in Lima, Peru — but

### Prehistoric IVR
© ICMI | by Greg Levin | Illustration by Gene Baikauskas

could be in Liverpool, the Leeward Islands, or L.A. When I land, I turn on my mobile and it *works*.) Let's call this worldwide connectivity *phase one*; it was a century and a half in the making.

Of course, the development of our global communications network has led to more than just the ability to connect. A key part of the equation is the *way* information and services are digitally represented and transported. Consider a familiar example, digital photography: You can snap a picture on your camera or mobile phone, post it to Facebook, email a link to Grandma, even use it as the home screen image on your phone. Similarly, music can be downloaded, edited, transferred to a portable player, used as the ringtone on your mobile device, and played through your car radio. Pictures, music, phone calls, messaging, video, television, movies, games (you name it) have been forever freed from the rigid technical confines of the past. Everything becomes digital — let's call that *phase two*.

If it all comes down to 1s and 0s, if it's all digital, then any of these media can be integrated to create new services. That phone call from Lima? Let's make it a video connection and show Grandma the neighborhood we're in. Let's put a few things to Peruvian music and share it with the rest of the family ... it will just take a moment. Let's refer to this integration of digital media and services as *phase three*. (Do you remember the sitcom, *The Jetsons*, which ran through the 1980s? How much has come to pass!)

Speaking of Peru, someone mentioned a fascinating documentary that contrasts the very different cultures of the Andes Mountains and the adjacent Amazon Basin. I could go online and buy the Blu-ray Disc. It will be waiting when we get home. Or ... wait, I can stream it *now* for a modest rental fee, and save the cost, shipping and storage. Let's take a look. And while I'm on, it really is a bad idea to have all these priceless pictures in one place; let me back them up to the server. Now we're getting a glimpse at what we can refer to as *phase four*: cloud-based or hosted services.

We've seen a similar progression in contact centers. Telephone and, later, data networks came into existence over many years. Toll-free "800 service" was introduced in 1967 and the automatic call distributor (ACD) came along in 1973. These and related developments provided the basic capabilities contact centers depend on today: identify and corral customer contacts and match them up with agents who are cross-trained and ready to respond as real-time needs dictate.

In later years, other significant developments would follow. For example, integrated services came along in the form of computer telephony integration (CTI), introduced in the late 1980s. In the years since, great strides have been made in CTI applications, which, through standards, middleware and (traditionally) lots of programming, can integrate the computer and telephony worlds. CTI can enable screen pops (simultaneous voice and data delivery), database-driven call-routing, integrated performance reporting and a host of other capabilities. But CTI is transitional and will fade in meaning as "computer" and "telephony" lose distinction.

Early CTI applications were just a taste of things to come. The migration of the voice-switching infrastructure from traditional circuit-switching based on TDM (time-division multiplexing) to packet-switching based on IP (Internet Protocol) networks is bringing fundamental change to customer contact centers. What were essentially two sets of technologies in contact centers — one for voice, one for data — are now being integrated. The advantages over the separate voice and data architectures of the past are many, including:

- **MULTIMEDIA CONTACTS.** All contacts (e.g., voice, chat, text, video, social) can be handled by a common routing and reporting system.
- **MULTISITE OPERATIONS.** Anyone who is part of the organization's network — including agents in satellite offices, home agents or colleagues in other departments — can be part of the contact center, whether routinely or on an ad hoc basis.
- **COST EFFICIENCIES.** All things equal, the costs to purchase, use and maintain IP-based systems are often lower than for TDM-based systems.

- **SIMPLIFIED MANAGEMENT.** Moving to IP architecture often results in fewer systems, licenses and maintenance agreements to manage.
- **SCALABLE.** Adding or reducing agents is simple and cost-effective, with minimal technology impact.
- **INTEGRATED REPORTS.** With activities consolidated in one architecture, reports can provide a more holistic perspective of contacts and customers across sites and media.
- **DISASTER BACKUP.** If harnessed appropriately, IP-based architecture can provide the redundancies inherent in Internet-based services.
- **OPEN STANDARDS.** Systems based on open, common standards are more readily integrated.

With IP-based architecture, creative applications are proliferating; and empowered by a common, integrated platform, organizations are increasingly designing unique customer applications for their specific environments. Reports that give deeper meaning to what customers do and experience are becoming more common. Databases that include information on customers, products and services are becoming more involved in handling contacts — e.g., in how and where they are routed, the people and information that are involved, and how insight from them is captured and reported. And increasingly, thinking of computers and telephones as separate technologies is beginning to fade.

For all the advantages, though, making the switch from TDM to IP requires some serious consideration. Changing out systems can be costly, and what you have may be working just fine. Your network has to be ready or you'll run into quality problems. You'll need to look at all of the systems capabilities you have now, and consider how or even whether they can make the transition to the new environment. You'll want to revisit the technology strategy for the larger organization — being part of an overall transition plan usually makes the most sense. Reliability and voice quality are essential in the contact center environment, and you'll need to prepare accordingly. And yes, you'll need to take stock of your organization's readi-

## BLUECROSS BLUESHIELD OF SOUTH CAROLINA ADOPTS CLICK-TO-TALK

BlueCross BlueShield (BCBS) of South Carolina is an early adopter of VoIP capabilities. In 2004, BCBS of S.C. implemented an application they call STATchat both to offer health care providers an effective and efficient support option and to gradually wean them from the more expensive traditional phone channel.

In the event that a provider's agents fail to find the answers they seek on the provider portal of BCBS of S.C.'s website, they can click on the STATchat button (next to the button are the words "Click here to speak to the next available agent"). A box then pops up and says, "initializing," and then "dialing." Soon thereafter, "connected" appears in the box, and the provider hears a live agent through his or her computer: "Hello, this is [agent's name]. Thank you for calling BlueCross BlueShield of South Carolina. How may I help you?"

The center uses priority queuing to give Web callers quicker service, and the majority of provider inquiries come in through the click-to-talk application. With so many providers moving online, BCBS of S.C.'s savings have been substantial. "Those who call using STATchat cost our center a fraction of what traditional callers do," explains David Boucher, assistant vice president of Health Care Services.

Boucher was confident that the organization could steer providers to the Web by promoting the fact that they'd be able to speak to a live agent online with little to no wait and no IVR hassle. He also knew that many providers, once on the website, would at least try to get the information they were seeking without live assistance — thus freeing agents to handle only the most complex provider inquiries.

BCBS of S.C. initially began trials with a small set of subscribers. After working out a few technical glitches (e.g., screens not populating with claims data and poor audio) and receiving much provider praise, the contact center rolled out STATchat to all provider organizations already registered to use BCBS of S.C.'s interactive website services.

ness — in terms of IT support, vendor relationships, budgets, growth plans and culture — to embark on what will amount to a pretty dramatic change.

In short, you'll need a sensible migration strategy that considers your current situation, where you want to go, and how best to get there in coming months and years.

Enter a next phase of development, one made possible by IP-enabled services: hosted or cloud-based services. (In contact centers, you'll hear the terms cloud-based contact center, hosted contact center, virtual contact

## HOSTED/CLOUD-BASED CONTACT CENTERS

Imagine two farmers, Farmer Brown and Farmer McGregor, need new wells. Farmer Brown elects to drill a new well and pump, while Farmer McGregor enters into an agreement with the local water utility for water. Both farmers now have enough water for their crops. While Farmer Brown does not have to pay for the water, he is responsible for the entire water production. Farmer McGregor is responsible for his infrastructure and pays for what water he uses.

This story is an allegory of two call center delivery models: Farmer Brown's water system is an on-premise system and Farmer McGregor's water supply is a hosted service. When enterprises elect to use hosted call center services, they delegate some of the call distribution and routing responsibility to a hosted call center service provider. The hardware and software used to route interactions, schedule agents or store customer data, is not located within the enterprise's technical infrastructure but is located in a data center or data centers managed by the service provider.

Over the past decade or so, as the hosted call center services market has grown rapidly, the available services have also become more numerous. Hosted call centers started with hosted IVRs and expanded into hosted ACDs. With the maturity of IP communication and Session Initiated Protocol (SIP), the functionality available to businesses through hosted services is almost equal to that available through on-premise solutions, including CRM, multimodal interactions, workforce management, quality assurance and recording, and predictive dialers.

Excerpted from the 2011 ICMI whitepaper "Cloud Cover for the Call Center."

center, software as a service or SaaS, on-demand contact center, and others.) Virtually any capability available in premise-based equipment and software can be "rented" and delivered through the cloud, leaving much of the development and maintenance activities to the supplier.

In short, these ground-up (or cloud-down?) developments have opened up lots of opportunity for organizations of virtually any size to build contact centers that are feature-rich, scalable, and cost-effective. When you think about capabilities that were once available to only the largest organizations now being accessible to a 5- or 10-person contact center, the competitive implications become evident. And that puts a premium on harnessing these technologies in a way that helps you further your mission and create real value for your customers and organization.

## Routing: Getting the Right Contacts to the Right Places

The efficiencies contact centers can bring to an organization have always stemmed largely from how customer contacts are routed and distributed. Prior to call centers, the "clientele approach" was prevalent. Customers tended to ask for and talk to the same representatives, whom they reached through a switchboard operator or by dialing a direct number. It was not very efficient. When automatic call distributors (ACDs) came along in the early 1970s, they challenged existing thinking. Rather than send calls to individuals, the idea was that they could be automatically connected to a group of agents cross-trained to handle a variety of contacts. Shared computer systems and information also played important roles in enabling pooled groups of agents. In short, the powerful pooling principle became — and still is — the essential core of contact center efficiency (see Chapter 9).

The pooling principle is only powerful if agents are truly cross-trained to handle the variety of contacts that come their way. Most organizations have more than one agent group — sometimes many — geared around specific types of interactions, channels or areas of specialized expertise. In

## IDENTIFYING CUSTOMERS AND WHAT THEY NEED

To implement customized routing and contact-handling routines (e.g., skills-based routing), you'll need to know who your customers are and/or (especially) what they need when they contact the organization (see Chapter 7). Common identification methods include:

- Caller-entered information (e.g., into an IVR or speech system), which can be matched to services desired or specific customer records.
- ANI (automatic number identification), the billing number the call originated from, which can often be matched to customer records in a database.
- DNIS (dialed number identification services), the telephone number the caller dials, which can indicate the reason for the call, language preferred, etc.
- Email addressed to, subject line, sender's address or customer-entered data, which can be matched to services desired or customer records.
- Web URL, cookies or customer-entered data, which can be matched to services desired or customer records.

the early days of ACDs, agent groups and other parameters were rigidly defined. You might have been able to move an agent from one group to another based on keyboard command, or make various other changes (e.g., to overflow parameters), but the systems themselves didn't do much to help. Then along came "dynamic reconfiguration" in the late 1970s, which enabled ACDs to automatically change system thresholds based on real-time circumstances (the term was coined by designers at Rolm, later acquired by Siemens). It was a precursor to the intelligent routing capabilities we have now, which go far beyond these pioneering efforts.

Today, routing and distribution software is based on if-then programming logic, which has enabled system managers to design flexible and sophisticated contact handling routines: "If the queue is backed up beyond 120 seconds in group A, then ..." You can specify routing, priority, announcements and information-access alternatives for each interaction, based on many criteria. And skills-based routing, which entered the market in the early 1990s, makes it possible to route individual contacts to specific agents on a call-by-call basis (see Chapter 7).

Advanced network and cloud-based services can extend routing, distribution and other call-handling variables to distributed contact centers that include sites across the globe or to home-based agents. Customer information, agent availability, workload conditions and many other parameters can be part of routing and distribution criteria. Further, tools that enable organizations to monitor, assess and, as appropriate, route social interactions to agents for handling are becoming part of the mix. The vision many have is for one routing application to handle all types of interactions and channels across the contact center's operations.

A single routing engine does not mean that you must use universal agents (sometimes called "super agents") to handle everything — that's for you to decide. Instead, criteria you define dictate how contacts are delivered and handled. The degree to which your center is pooled or specialized depends on the business rules you establish. Applied well, these capabilities can deliver quicker, more effective service for customers, and efficiencies for the organization.

## Boosting Productivity and Quality

In recent years, there have been many developments in systems that can improve contact center performance. Again, the underlying themes include architecture based on open standards, ready integration with other systems, flexibility and maximum user control. Examples include:

**QUALITY MONITORING SYSTEMS.** At a basic level, quality monitoring systems record interactions and enable review for quality improvement purposes. Many systems can be set up either to record all interactions or to take samples. Return on investment is usually defined in terms of reductions in errors and rework, improved first-call resolution and the time that is saved by being able to quickly find and review any contact.

**397**

But the benefits can go far beyond those associated with recording and reviewing calls. Both voice and screen activities can be recorded in many cases, and, increasingly, all contact channels can be included. Supervisors can insert voice annotations into original recordings for training purposes and managers can include specific contacts in reports that go to others, e.g., for VOC (voice of the customer) purposes.

Integration with other systems can provide rich, three-dimensional reports on activities, help with coaching and training, and even link to technology-based training modules that are geared around individual performance evaluations. And reports that reflect information picked up in the QA process can be used across the organization for improving products, services and processes.

**WORKFORCE OPTIMIZATION TOOLS.** At a basic level, workforce management systems can provide automated tools for forecasting, staff calculations, schedules and tracking/reporting. In recent years, applications have become ever better at handling these core processes. For example, forecasting and scheduling for the full range of contact channels, skills-based scheduling and user-defined reports that integrate with other systems have paralleled the needs created by the emerging multichannel environment.

Further, real-time adherence monitoring software can highlight discrepancies between actual and planned schedules (see Chapter 14) and account for a wide range of activities. Administration tools have become much friendlier, enabling everything from automated shift-swaps and vacation approvals to integration with payroll and financial systems. And one of the most useful developments has been improvements in modules that enable what-if analysis for budgeting and resource decisions.

Integration with quality monitoring systems and training tools is becoming robust, enabling seamless forecasting, scheduling and real-time management of virtually any kind of contact center activity. This can include those that are not immediately related to handling customer interactions.

**CUSTOMER RELATIONSHIP CAPABILITIES.** There are many tools that can help you establish and build better relationships with customers. For example, contact management technologies enable you to log contacts, view customer profiles and access a consolidated history of all contacts customers have had with the organization through any media — face-to-face, phone, email, Web, social and others.

Sales automation tools enable you to track contacts and leads with prospects or existing customers, provide scripts, schedule follow-up contacts and, in general, manage interactions. Fulfillment tools can manage the delivery of products, services and materials. Help desk capabilities or support systems can assist you in tracking and managing incidents that require support or problem resolution.

Other tools enable you to access account histories, as well as information on billing, shipping, services delivered and related activities. Product suites and open systems can help you pull together the pieces that make the most sense for your organization and customers, and business rules enable you to define how it's all going to work.

**ANALYTICS, SOCIAL TOOLS, PERFORMANCE MANAGEMENT.** Many organizations are realizing that their data is the proverbial gold mine, and are turning to increasingly sophisticated tools for gathering, storing, analyzing and reporting.

Data analytics tools can help you find, pull together and analyze information from many sources — e.g., who's buying what, what are the trends, where are the opportunities, and what are the secrets to high performance among the most successful agents? Speech analytics systems can explore the content of recorded calls, search for key phrases or expressions (e.g., competitor names, or red flags such as "cancel"), and even detect and provide insight into caller emotions.

Relatively new social listening and sentiment analysis tools enable you to observe what's being said across social sites. And they can identify influencers — those who have the greatest impact on your reputation and brand given the nature or size of their audiences.

And performance management tools — sometimes referred to as dashboards or scorecards — can integrate data from many systems with goals and objectives, to help guide decisions at many levels of the organization.

**KNOWLEDGE MANAGEMENT TOOLS.** Knowledge management systems enable you to cultivate and benefit from the knowledge gained through handling customer interactions and supporting the organization's processes, products and services. The main objective of knowledge management is to create, leverage and reuse resources so people will not spend time "reinventing the wheel." Whether homegrown or off-the-shelf, these systems can be a boon to first-contact resolution, efficient handling times and heightened customer satisfaction.

---

*There must be an app for that.*
**TODAY'S MOST COMMON REFRAIN WHEN DISCUSSING
TOUGH BUSINESS CHALLENGES**

---

**DESKTOP CAPABILITIES AND RELATED TOOLS.** The agent desktop has been a major area of development in recent years, providing access to systems, information and media through a familiar browser-based interface. Document imaging and on-screen retrieval can boost FCR. The ability to send real-time information on contact center performance to the desktop helps agents stay abreast of trends and developments.

Auto-greetings allow agents to prerecord their introductions and provide them in digital clarity at the beginning of calls — starting every contact with the right greeting and a chipper voice. Communications tools such as instant messaging (IM) and internal collaboration capabilities can help agents — or virtually anyone across the organization — access information and assistance when and as needed.

Telephony features themselves provide increasingly customizable work states, call coding options and call handling capabilities (e.g., one-click transfers or requests for assistance, etc.). These features can be provided on a telephone (TDM or IP) or through a "softphone," a virtual phone on the computer desktop.

**IVR AND SPEECH CAPABILITIES.** The proliferation of interactive voice response (IVR) technology and its impact on contact centers for self-service and call-routing has been nothing less than phenomenal. When coupled with databases and routing systems, IVR systems enable callers to provide and access information through keypad input or speech recognition. For callers, IVR systems have become a way of life, along the lines of bank ATMs.

Speech recognition, a high-end IVR capability that has become widely used, has improved dramatically in recent years. By enabling a more natural interface, well-designed systems greatly extend application opportunities (it's a lot easier to say "Rancho Cucamonga, California" than to try to enter it on a keypad). And personalized applications (see Chapter 2) tend to attract customers who would not otherwise successfully complete self-service transactions. Speech engines and algorithms have become increasingly robust, recognizing accents, colloquialisms and expansive vocabularies. Some organizations are using caller-specific speech identification technology for security purposes.

IVR technologies have also provided other performance-boosting goodies, such as post-call surveys that can prompt callers through questions that capture information that can be tied back to specific transactions and agents. And development standards have enabled speech systems to leverage and use Web-based architectures and programming, attracting a broad base of programmers working on new applications.

**WEB-BASED SERVICES AND MOBILE APPS.** The Internet continues to open up new ways for organizations to deliver services, add value and communicate with customers and suppliers. From the simple FAQs (frequently asked questions) that became common a decade ago to today's powerful multimedia applications that enable everything from financial trading to real-time flight tracking, the Web and mobile apps are changing the way we work and live.

In many cases, these capabilities enable both customers and agents to tap into the same tools and information, improving the consistency and cohesiveness of services. And the important role of search capabilities — which cannot be overstated — has turned a vast unnavigable universe of content into a source of immediately accessible information, content and solutions.

Web-based and mobile apps have created an interesting shift in customer attitudes, creating a large percentage of customers who choose to use them whenever possible, and who have developed loyalties and expectations of them.

## Customer Capabilities

When discussing today's technologies, it's easy to focus on contact center technologies *per se*. Indeed, the most significant developments to date have been on the organization's end: The invention of 800 number (toll-free) service and ACD routing systems in the late 1960s and early 1970s; the introduction of workforce management capabilities and computer telephony integration in the 1980s; Web browsers and Internet-based services in the 1990s; and more recently, the amazing developments in multimedia, cloud-based capabilities, analytics and so much more.

We are now, however, seeing a major and fundamental shift: For the first time, developments on the customers' end — the meteoric rise of smartphones, social media, broadband and mobility — are the most significant factors driving customer expectations and services. Given what is happening, I'm convinced we'll see more change in the next five years than we've seen in the past two decades. We can harness and leverage the trends to our benefit, or get tumbled by them.

As communication hubs, contact centers can accommodate the many

**iCONTACT TRANSFORMS SOCIAL MEDIA
INTO A CUSTOMER ACCESS CHANNEL**

The contact center at iContact Corp. — a provider of email and social media marketing to small and midsized companies and causes — is a trailblazer when it comes to structuring and operationalizing social media as a customer service channel. The support center's mastery of channel integration, aided by the organization's management support and investment, contributes to consistently high customer satisfaction scores.

Building on its strengths, iContact (which garnered an ICMI Global Call Center of the Year Award for the small-to-medium category), is succeeding at operationalizing the social channel's inclusion in its customer access points, which serve the company's more than 7,000 users. Resources are provisioned to meet real-time requirements through forecasts and schedules that match the channel's growing volume.

While iContact's marketing department is currently the primary owner of social customer care, marketers (and others) escalate direct and indirect social media contacts to the contact center's Tier 3 support team. The center's initial response time objective was 30 minutes, says Sarah Stealey, senior vice president of customer support. "Our goal is to shorten that by always having Tier 3 support personnel scheduled for this channel." Stealey expects ongoing improvements as the support center continues to deepen its integration of social media within the organization's customer relationship strategy and approach.

ways customers want to interact and access expertise and information. It's no small feat, but forward-looking organizations are turning this challenge into a competitive opportunity.

## Seven Key Trends

What do we make of these advances? What should we — rather, must we — prepare for? While there are many trends that have emerged, I believe that the following are especially important. These are not predictions —

**SEVEN KEY TRENDS**

1. Customers are better informed and have higher expectations
2. You'll always need agents — but for different reasons
3. Agent-assisted services are being prioritized
4. Contact center employees require increasingly high levels of skill
5. Organizational structures are being redefined
6. Yet-to-be imagined services will emerge
7. Clear business thinking is more important than ever

they have been set in motion and are changing the customer contact landscape significantly.

## CUSTOMERS ARE BETTER INFORMED AND HAVE HIGHER EXPECTATIONS

The proliferation of search, social communities, mobile apps, self-service capabilities, a vast range of information resources, and ever-changing cultural expectations have created a better-informed, more empowered and more savvy customer base. As industry pioneer (and my former business partner at ICMI) Gordon MacPherson Jr. could foresee almost two decades ago, "A new breed of technology-sophisticated consumers is demanding a choice of how they will be served. They often know what the choices could be, and they will become increasingly critical if you do not offer the choices they think you should offer." It's up to you to open up and develop the alternatives as technologies and expectations evolve.

You also must make access choices clear to customers. "I can't find the support number on your website." "I got trapped in the system." "I can't seem to figure out how to reach a real person." These complaints are indicative of a fundamental misunderstanding of the value of customer relationships and of the contact center's potential to contribute strategic value (see Chapters 12 and 13).

All channels have a place. An agent won't suffice when you want to review feedback from a diverse social community. Speech recognition doesn't illustrate a graph of movement in a financial market. Web-based services don't come close to matching the proficiency of an experienced technical support rep, nor can they cross-sell and upsell in the personalized manner of a seasoned sales representative. Your customers and their specific situations will dictate the best channels to use in each case.

Heightened customer expectations also add a sense of context, even urgency, to the quality- and performance-boosting technologies that are becoming available. The contacts that require agent assistance have to go well — you can and must deliver value on all three levels — efficiency, customer loyalty and business unit contributions (see Chapters 1 and 13).

## YOU'LL ALWAYS NEED AGENTS — BUT FOR DIFFERENT REASONS

I recall having a lunch meeting some years ago with an executive of a company based in New York City. After a discussion in his office that morning, we walked to a restaurant for lunch — about four short city blocks away. It was high noon, and there was a throng of people on the sidewalks and crossing intersections — literally hundreds at each corner. I found myself fixated on just how many people were either talking on their mobile

"In Case of Unexpected Call Spike, Break Glass"

Contingency Plan

© ICMI | by Greg Levin | Illustration by Gene Baikauskas

phones or typing away on tiny keypads. (I've since found myself making the same observation in cities around the world; it's a strange pastime, I admit, but it puts faces — lots of them — on industry stats).

After lunch, we continued our discussion. "Our plans are for customer calls to go away," he told me. "Any interaction we can get onto the Web is going to be cheaper for us and better for them [the organization's customers]." I pondered the contrast between this strategic initiative and what we had just seen on the street below. "You mean the masses of people we just saw making calls and sending messages are all going to hang up and use self-service when they contact your company?" That led to a deeper and more useful (and detailed) assessment of the interactions that would benefit from agent involvement.

Quite a few industry pundits predicted that self-service capabilities would dramatically reduce reliance on agent-assisted services. Some were convinced that we would need fewer agents, period. Yet, there are more agents working in more contact centers across the globe than at any time in prior history. More recently, I'm hearing similar predictions from some observers who are looking at developments in mobile apps and social communities. But the variable missing in much of the analysis is that communications capabilities help create new kinds of services and needs.

"There has to be a person in there somewhere," write Don Peppers and Martha Rogers in *Rules to Break & Laws to Follow*. "At some point, human judgment will always have to be accommodated in your customer-facing processes. It's impossible to serve customers well without it, and generally the more important decisions are the ones that require the most judgment."

Many organizations are finding that total contact workload often — not always, but often — increases as new customer access channels are added. And that's true in general — the widespread use of collaboration tools and social networks, for example, has not yet led to a commensurate drop in phone calls or in-person travel; at best, these developments have slowed the growth of agent-assisted channels.

## THE CONTACT CENTER'S ROLE IN BUILDING SELF-SERVICE CHANNELS

Many organizations are learning firsthand that contact centers can play a central role in encouraging and supporting low-cost access channels. For example, the contact center can provide a wealth of information on which contacts can be automated (or handled in customer communities), and what can be done to improve customer acceptance. Further — and paradoxically — providing agent assistance when and as needed encourages customer confidence in these alternatives.

Here are some things you can do to further the contact center's opportunity to build self-service channels:

- Equip agents to educate customers on self-service options. Agents should be trained on the advantages and use of these alternatives so that they can encourage customers to use these options when appropriate.
- Collect and analyze data about contacts currently handled in the center. Look for opportunities to provide self-service features or build communities that customers will want to use (see Intuit case study, Chapter 2). Improved speed of access and around-the-clock availability are often at the top of the list.
- Observe agents handling contacts, step-by-step. Your best agents really know how to serve customers; watching them work can present many opportunities for developing and improving self-service systems. In many ways, self-service systems can be modeled after effective agent practices.
- Involve agents in system design. Your agents should actively serve on project teams responsible for building self-service systems. They can also help monitor and test systems and interpret customer behavior and feedback.
- Integrate self-service and contact center systems and developments. Integrated systems can enable agents to use the information captured in self-service applications when assisting customers.
- Capture customer feedback about self-service systems. The nature of

*(continued next page)*

407

input is that you'll get a lot more of it when things go wrong than when they go right. Even so, customers who share their dissatisfaction represent the tip of the iceberg; in most cases, there will be many more who were dissatisfied but who did not bother to tell you. This information is essential to improving system design.

- Enable customers to easily reach agents. If callers can't reach an agent when necessary, they will often resent the need to use self-service systems. Support may take many forms, such as:
  - A clearly identified way to exit an IVR application
  - Prominently displayed telephone numbers on your website
  - Text-chat, click-to-talk or co-browsing capabilities
  - Email addresses and Web templates for questions, comments and other input
  - Posting access numbers and alternatives in relevant social communities.
- Track data from all support modes and analyze it for improvement opportunities; specifically, why do customer contacts happen? Which do you want to encourage and which do you want to prevent (as possible)?

Self-service systems must be an integrated part of your customer access strategy. If they are perceived primarily as replacements for agents rather than complementary access channels that free agents to do more high-value work, then employees will be less enthusiastic about helping to improve them and encourage their use. But by keeping the focus on cultivating better ways to serve customers, self-service systems become an essential part of building valuable, cost-effective services.

By opening access alternatives and improving services, we seem to be encouraging customers to contact us more often. Contacts will happen — and that puts a premium on ensuring that we squeeze maximum strategic value out of them (Chapter 13). Get used to that reality now, and you'll be better positioned to open all forms of channels and encourage — not force, encourage — optimum use of search, social options, and self-service systems.

## AGENT-ASSISTED SERVICES ARE BEING PRIORITIZED

Here's the tricky part of predicting that you'll always need agents: Many of the contacts still being handled today can be, will be and should be handled by self-service channels and other options in coming years. Consider the travel sector. Every time a long-established airline closes a reservation center somewhere, journalists jump on the story — "Is the call center industry in decline? Is this representative of what's happening across the board?" (The fact that they even care is indicative of the kind of employment numbers contact centers post.) Short answer: No. Those interactions needed to be automated. Most of us are simply not calling airlines as much as we used to — we're seeing the advantages of booking online and checking in by Web, mobile app or kiosk.

Historically, that kind of displacement has been going on for decades. For example, when telephone companies automated switching centers, there were marches on the streets to protest the hundreds of thousands of lost operator jobs. The fear was that there would simply not be enough jobs to go around. That was over a half-century ago.

Forward-thinking organizations are taking tangible steps to establish self-service alternatives and encourage customers to use them. And leading contact centers are taking a proactive role in this effort (see box, The Contact Center's Role in Building Self-Service Channels). They are ensuring that their highly trained, highly paid agents are handling interactions that truly benefit from the human touch.

## CONTACT CENTER EMPLOYEES REQUIRE INCREASINGLY HIGH LEVELS OF SKILL

Agents face a number of challenges as search, online resources, social communities and self-service technologies offload relatively simple or well-defined contacts, and as products and services grow increasingly diverse and complex. In addition to handling more difficult interactions, they must serve increasingly well-informed and varied customers; adjust to rapid changes in products, services and technologies; operate in a time-sensitive, multimedia environment; communicate quickly and accurately in both verbal and written form; and understand technology-based services and be able to help customers use those alternatives.

At the management level, the traditional "jack-of-all-trades" manager role is being divided among specialists doing everything from data analysis to scheduling, quality monitoring and coaching. Evolving technologies are powerful and enormously flexible, but they are contributing to the emergence of technology managers who require specialized expertise to understand, manage and maintain them.

And an undeniable trend fueling further complexity is the addition of new channels, including the untamed territory of social media. While the core principles of effective management are timeless and universal, the operational specifics vary from one channel to another — e.g., staffing for Twitter is in notable ways different from staffing for chat, email, or phone (see Chapter 7). And requirements at the agent level vary, even though the products and services being supported from one channel to the next are similar.

## ORGANIZATION STRUCTURES ARE BEING REDEFINED

Many organizations are restructuring so that all channels of contact with customers are under the same management umbrella (see Chapter 15). This is causing enormous internal structural change that involves IT, marketing, HR and virtually every other department. Whatever the final structure, all contact channels must be planned and operated cohesively — each has impacts on the others (see Part 2).

Many centers are also becoming more distributed. Multisite centers and agents based at home, in other departments or even in other organizations have proliferated rapidly in recent years (see Chapters 8 and 15). Virtually any place with up-to-spec communications technology and a skilled and flexible labor force is a candidate for regional, national or international-oriented contact centers.

Job roles are changing along with organizational structures. As discussed in Chapters 13 through 15, it will be increasingly important for contact center managers to cultivate and broaden the skills of agents and supervisors, and for organizations to provide attractive skill and career paths for them.

## YET-TO-BE-IMAGINED SERVICES WILL EMERGE

As advanced as technologies have become, many are still in their infancy. Multimedia will prevail and the distinctions between phone, chat, browsing, dialog through social channels, and video will blur — they'll just be interactions. The single-channel, monomedia environment will continue to fade as richer forms of communication that combine all of these elements emerge.

Multimedia appeals to the way we are wired up. We communicate best when our senses work together. Think about these ingredients, and ponder ways they can be combined:

- Mobile
- Social
- Virtual
- Telephone
- Video
- Broadband
- Software
- Computer
- Interactive
- Information
- Multimedia
- Network
- Community
- Application

In coming months, these components will be mixed and harnessed in numerous, yet-to-be-imagined ways. And the latest technology won't be on customers' minds. They just want things to work, to be easy. If they're browsing your website and need further help, they want a knowledgeable agent a click away — or perhaps another customer, or a community of users. And if they end up in a queue — queues will still happen — they'll expect a reasonably short wait time. They want processes to be transparent and thoughtful. And they will expect to reach professional, competent agents. In short, they want services that are reliable, intuitive, accessible — even enjoyable — to use.

## CLEAR THINKING IS MORE IMPORTANT THAN EVER

New technologies are not passive — to get good results, they must be implemented with foresight and good planning. Take, for example, skills-based routing. Remember how it was supposed to solve scheduling and staffing problems? And yet, many contact centers have taken a few steps back from the most involved types of skills-based routing, having been unable to achieve the efficiency and effectiveness they had with pools of cross-trained agents. It turns out that it's like hot pepper sauce — a little bit goes a long way, and the use and context must be precise.

Similarly, today's open and highly customizable systems offer wonderful flexibility, but (stating the obvious here) they need to be programmed to do what you want them to do. Clarification and definition of the underlying business rules is an ongoing challenge for any organization. And that has a lot more to do with clear business thinking than a specific technology capability. The late Peter Drucker contended that the most important impact of information technology is not the capabilities of the technologies themselves, but that these systems force you to organize processes and information more logically.

Author Emily Yellin summarizes the opportunity this way: "Our billions of everyday transactions are both simpler and more complicated than they appear," she writes in *Your Call Is (Not That) Important to Us.* "But while the infrastructure that supports them are continually in flux, the intangibles at the heart of each positive encounter remain constant on all sides: trust, respect, empathy, caring, and even some fun — within companies, and between companies and their customers."

## Leadership Is Essential

Effective leadership in this environment requires a multifaceted approach, and a few important recommendations come to mind:

1. Keep your eyes on the prize: The purpose of any new technology should be to support the governing principles and mission of your organization. Keep it simple — don't over-complicate applications to the point that they are ineffective or unmanageable. When complexity begins to throw things off course, go back to the basics. Stay focused on what really matters.

© 2003 Ted Goff

"This plan will be much easier not to implement than the last plan we didn't implement."

Reprinted with permission.

2. Remember that new capabilities both depend on and dramatically affect training, policies, planning, budgeting, other systems and many other issues. Those who take a systemic approach to planning and implementing systems, and who put adequate thought into process- and people-

**THE BUSINESS CASE**

A helpful way to consider the business case for contact center technologies is to broadly categorize the benefits in the four areas.

**Foundational**, required to support the contact center's mission and strategy. Example: ACDs and related multichannel routing systems that enable the organization to identify and deliver the full range of customer interactions to agents.

**Legal**, necessary to comply with requirements or minimize liability. Example: Recording systems that enable interactions to be captured and stored for security purposes.

**Return on investment**, where potential benefits exceed costs based on the organization's accepted ROI approach (payback time, return on capital, or others). Example: Desktop capabilities that enable agents to access needed information more quickly, reducing handling times and boosting first-contact resolution.

**Intangible**, providing benefits that are more difficult to quantify but are believed to be worth more than the cost. Example: Improvements to facilities that create a more pleasing work environment. (Note that in many cases, these investments can be estimated by looking at factors related to performance, turnover and others.)

related issues earn the highest returns on technology investments.

3. Recognize that just about any technology can be viewed as the proverbial double-edged sword. For example, quality monitoring capabilities can be great sources of stress for agents. Or they can be used to identify improvement opportunities and coach agents to higher levels of performance. Similarly, collaboration and reporting tools that give colleagues across the organization access to contact center information may bring unwanted attention. Or they may be a boon to the interest level and support the contact center receives. Ensuring that others have an understanding of technologies and how they will be used is key.

4. It's essential to develop a sound customer access strategy and use it to guide decisions (see Chapter 2). As you view technology possibilities

though the lens of your customer access strategy, some key questions will likely surface, such as ... Which technologies best support your plans and direction? How will processes need to change? What impact will the technology have on agent requirements, both in staffing numbers and skills required? What impact will it have on your cost structure — expenses and revenues? How will overall service be improved? How technologies are implemented, supported and used is as important as the capabilities of the technologies themselves. The answers to these and related questions will help you make wise investments, and ensure that technology is being led by your mission and direction — not the other way around.

5. In a theme that has run throughout the book: If you want it, you'll need to show the return on investment. Contact center leaders have the responsibility to evaluate how technology can add value to the organization and build that into their business case. What impact will new capabilities have on customers, employees, or business units? What are the benefits, and returns on those benefits?

6. Inaction is the worst action you can take. Given the pace of change, it's important to begin planning your contact center's migration into the next era now.

# Points to Remember

- Advanced contact center technologies are creating enormous opportunities for better serving customers, empowering agents and increasing efficiencies and effectiveness.
- New technologies are not passive, and they are changing caller behavior, leading to significant reallocations of resources, and having an impact on the responsibilities of agents and managers.
- New capabilities must be implemented with foresight and care, and must support the organization's mission.
- The key trends that have been set in motion provide a framework for

**415**

understanding the changes taking place and preparing your contact center for tomorrow's environment.

- New capabilities both depend on and have dramatic impact on training, policies, planning, budgeting and many other issues. Effective leadership is essential to getting the most out of your technology investments.

# CHAPTER 17:
# Characteristics of the Best-Managed Contact Centers

*A vision without a task is but a dream; a task without a vision is drudgery; a vision and a task is the hope of the world.*

**CHURCH INSCRIPTION, SUSSEX, ENGLAND 1730**

In some organizations, you can feel the energy as soon as you walk in the door. It takes many forms: pride of workmanship, a feeling of community, good planning, coordination and the willingness to make the "extra

---

**CHARACTERISTICS OF THE BEST-MANAGED CALL CENTERS**

1. They produce high levels of value.
2. They have a supporting culture.
3. They know that their people are the key to success.
4. They build plans and services around evolving customer expectations.
5. They have an established, collaborative planning process.
6. They leverage the key statistics.
7. They view the contact center as a total process.
8. They leverage technology to support and further their mission.
9. They get the budget and support they need.
10. They build an effective organization.
11. They are willing to experiment.
12. They see the possibilities.

---

effort." Everybody knows what the mission is and everybody is pulling in the same direction. The contact center "clicks."

While there are a myriad of factors that go into creating this sort of environment, I have observed 12 overarching and interrelated characteristics that emerge in contact centers that consistently outperform others.

# 1. They Produce High Levels of Value

Great contact centers have an incessant focus on creating high levels of value for their organizations and customers. Far too many organizations are still focused primarily on one level or one dimension of value — e.g., to deliver services efficiently, improve revenues, or boost customer satisfaction. While those are fundamental goals, the best have their sites set

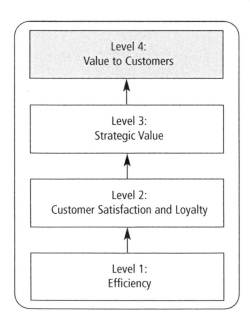

even higher. They align their resources, strategy and culture to deliver maximum value on all three levels (see Chapters 1 and 13): efficiency, customer satisfaction and loyalty, and strategic value.

By doing so, they create a fourth level of value, one that could never be sufficiently measured, but is as real as any of the others: the ultimate value these services provide to customers. What really happens when customers can access the services they need and want — seamlessly, easily? What is the impact on their economic situation? Their peace of mind? Their families? The economy? The things we value most in our communities? Because they are central to the delivery of services that so many organizations provide, contact centers — and all who are part of them — really can make a difference.

## 2. They Have a Supporting Culture

Culture — the inveterate principles or values of the organization — tends to guide behavior, and can either support and further or, as some

---

**USAA'S "SECRET SAUCE"**

San Antonio-based USAA is a member-owned financial and insurance company that serves U.S. military members and their families, and is consistently — year after year — one of the top-rated organizations for customer service and loyalty. How do they do it? "Our 22,000 employees are all focused on the same thing all the time. That's our secret sauce," said Len Hambrick, vice president of Contact Center Management, to attendees of a recent ICMI conference.

The mission of the association is "to facilitate the financial security of its members, associates and their families through provision of a full range of highly competitive financial products and services. In doing so, USAA seeks to be the provider of choice for the military community." USAA supports the mission from day one, with an orientation that is provided to every new employee, coming in at any level of the organization. "The first thing they teach you, the first day, the first 10 minutes, is our mission," says Hambrick. Beyond that, "every meeting we have, we start with the mission."

According to Hambrick, 5,000 of the organization's employees are part of the contact center. "You could go to any one of our employees and ask them what the mission is and how they internalize it in terms of how to serve folks who are calling in." USAA does not stress handle time, but instead maps out call flows to understand what's required to meet the mission and the correlations among services delivered, customer satisfaction and first-call resolution. Every decision, every metric, every call is gauged by the mission. As an organization, "We need to empower you and set you free to serve the member."

---

have learned the hard way, ruin the best-laid plans for organizational change. While there is no guaranteed formula for creating a supporting culture, many seasoned managers agree that shaping culture — or, more correctly, enabling it to flourish — is a primary leadership responsibility. As a result, they devote a significant amount of time to understanding the organization and the people who are part of it.

How do leading contact centers create high-performance cultures? How do they communicate their mission and values in a way that gets buy-in and alignment? There are some notable characteristics that stand out:

- They have a people-first perspective (see next characteristic).
- They are committed to effective communication (see Chapter 15).
- They have — and use — an up-to-date customer access strategy, which ensures that everyone is "on the same page" (Chapter 2).
- They cultivate a collaborative planning process so that their operations run smoothly, enabling them to focus on higher-level issues that matter most (see the fifth characteristic).
- They ensure that everyone across the contact center and larger organization has an understanding of their contribution to the organization and its customers (see the first characteristic).

## 3. They Know that Their People Are the Key to Success

Cultures vary dramatically from one organization to the next. You'd likely notice some hairstyles that you don't see every day at Virgin Mobile's Customer Care center. Nintendo has a break room (yes, with video games) that puts most others to shame. Wells Fargo Banker Connection (see insert) has a somewhat more formal, polished atmosphere — expected and fitting in the banking environment. But in each case, a people-first philosophy is evident.

Nancy Tichbon, vice president of Customer Care, Virgin Mobile Canada

## FIRST AND LASTING IMPRESSIONS
## AT WELLS FARGO BANKER CONNECTION

Vanita Vik-Ohlgren describes how Wells Fargo Banker Connection, a multisite center with locations in Fargo, ND and Billings, MT, welcomes new hires on their first day. Banker Connection is a past recipient of ICMI's Global Call Center of the Year award.

*"First impressions are lasting, and we didn't want new-hires to perceive that we (or their new jobs) were going to be dull and boring. So we made an effort to transition from a lackluster and unwelcoming environment to one where our new team members would go home at the end of the day and say, 'I made a great choice when I accepted their offer.' How did we do that? Here are some of the ways:*

- *A welcome sign is signed by the management team prior to day one and hung on the new team member's cube.*
- *A welcome to the team greeting card is signed by every team member on the new person's team, and is mailed to them before they even start.*
- *The hiring manager greets the new-hire(s) at the front door.*
- *A welcome gift kit is presented to each new-hire on day one.*
- *We provide a welcome to Banker Connection manager tour.*
- *The team member is welcomed by a senior manager.*
- *We review our vision/values, Wells Fargo and Banker Connection history, and an overview of our business and community involvement*
- *We conduct a getting to know you exercise.*
- *Lunch is on us!"*

Besides the welcoming atmosphere, the organization developed a buddy program, where new-hires are paired with seasoned team members through training over the initial weeks, and a connection activities program, which includes weekly interaction and activities designed to build relationships between new-hires and their managers. "Once we've attracted talented employees, we work hard to keep them."

421

and Bell Mobility/Bell Residential Service, put it this way: "It just makes sense to us: If our people are happy and motivated, our customers are going to have a great experience. And it goes without saying that if our customers are satisfied, our shareholders will be delighted. Thus, if we live by this value ... ultimately, everyone wins."

The most important implication of the trends discussed throughout the book, and particularly in Part Four (Chapters 12 through 15), is clear: Your people are the key to success.

## 4. They Build Plans and Services around Evolving Customer Expectations

One of the most critical — and difficult — aspects of managing a contact center in coming months and years will be to provide services that satisfy changing consumer demands. Those who fall behind will pay a brutal price: dissatisfied customers, insufficient support from the organization and low morale in the contact center. But those who stay ahead of the curve will enjoy strong customer loyalty and the many benefits that come with it. The stakes are high.

Most organizations have discovered firsthand a basic reality of customer psychology. When you improve your service, customers rather quickly progress through four distinct stages:

1. They appreciate it.
2. They get used to it.
3. They expect it.
4. They demand it.

Consequently, continually improving services to meet evolving customer expectations is a mandate in today's environment. In leading contact centers, the 10 customer expectations (see Chapter 2) are an important part of the organization's development and culture. The list is sometimes plastered to the wall — literally — and works its way into everything from strategy to process design to day-to-day planning and coaching activities.

In short, the best-managed centers have an incessant focus on evolving customer needs and expectations. They are continually redefining plans and reshaping services around those expectations (see Chapter 13, China UnionPay's Service Beyond Expectations). They know that what worked yesterday will not necessarily work tomorrow.

## 5. They Have an Established, Collaborative Planning Process

Effective planning is a central theme in Part Two and Part Three of this book. A major objective of good planning is to get the right number of skilled people and supporting resources in place at the right times, doing the right things.

But systematic planning accomplishes more than that. It also improves communication and culture in the following ways: creating a body of information that wouldn't otherwise be available; forcing people to look into the future and see their work in the context of a large framework; and necessitating communication about values — issues such as resource allocations, budgeting and workload priorities.

Perhaps most important, systematic planning necessitates communication about values on issues such as resource allocations, budgeting and workload priorities. It forces the kind of communication that the contact center requires.

Largely due to effective planning, great contact centers work so well that they are almost transparent. The teams concentrate on delivering the organization's services and on building the organization's value and brand — not on running the contact center *per se*. The center just works. As a result, higher levels of value are possible.

## 6. They Leverage the Key Statistics

As discussed in Chapters 12 through 14, measurements are plentiful and it's easy to get buried in information. The contact centers that get the best results from using their reports and information have several things in common:

- They focus on a relatively small number of measures and objectives that support their mission and direction. They know that trying to focus on too many things is counterproductive.
- They ensure that measurements are as accurate, complete and unbiased as possible. They are aware of how easily statistics can be misinterpreted. They view reports in light of how they relate to each other. They know that a single report, outside the context of the others, can lead to erroneous conclusions.
- They understand that simply tracking high-level measurements won't inherently improve results. Instead, they work on the factors — the root causes — that cause these outputs to be where they are (see next characteristic).

## 7. They View the Contact Center as a Total Process

Contact centers that consistently get the best results view the operation as a total process. That has been a major theme in this book, and it takes many forms:

- Ensure that everyone in the contact center, and those with key supporting roles outside the center, have a basic understanding of how contact centers operate (encourage them to read Chapters 9 and 10!).
- Recognize the process to be where most quality problems occur — and also where the opportunities for improvement in services and

reductions in costs reside (Chapter 13).

- Develop an effective, collaborative planning and management process.
- Take the initiative in coordinating with other departments.
- Be prepared to respond to changing conditions.
- Understand how the contact center supports the organization's direction.

The days of the contact center existing as an island unto itself — "That's our customer contact center, and they handle sales and customer service" — are gone. The reality is that the contact center is an important part of a much bigger process.

# 8. They Leverage Technology to Support and Further Their Mission

As discussed in Chapter 16, new technologies are not passive — they are changing customer expectations, causing reallocations of resources, creating power shifts in organizations, and changing the responsibilities of agents and managers. The best contact centers identify the technologies that further the mission of the organization, and they implement them with the necessary foresight, planning and training.

They also recognize that an important (according to the late Peter Drucker, the most important) impact of technology is not the capabilities of the technologies themselves, but that they require you to organize your processes and information more logically. Their systems are supported by processes that ensure that information on customers, products, processes and services is current and accurate.

For example, their knowledge management systems work because they make entering and updating knowledge a priority at the point of contact. Their quality monitoring systems are valuable because they have clearly defined quality and what needs to happen to support the organization's

**425**

highest-level objectives. Their reporting systems provide essential support for making sound business decisions because they produce accurate information on the right things, delivered to the right people at the right times. Their workforce management systems work well for them because they understand and apply sound underlying principles of planning and management.

In short, they respect what technology can do but they know that it's of little use without supporting processes and a clear direction. Some have the latest capabilities, others don't — but what they have, they use to support their mission and most important objectives.

## 9. They Get the Budget and Support They Need

Far too many contact centers are operating under the auspices of, "OK, here are the resources we're willing to give you, and here's what we want you to achieve ..." That is the proverbial cart before the horse.

Consider an analogy. Airlines couldn't possibly operate a flight without a tangible connection between the results they want to achieve and the supporting resources they need. They start with an objective — fly 300 people from Washington to London. The objective is not a wishful goal, but is a specific predetermined outcome supported by carefully calculated resources.

Similarly, the best contact centers first decide on the objectives they want to achieve. They then allocate the resources necessary to support those objectives, through informed calculations and disciplined planning (as discussed in Chapters 4 through 10).

## 10. They Build an Effective Organization

Successful contact center leaders design an organizational structure that facilitates collaboration among and across job roles and business units. They tap into the principles of good organizational design (covered in

Chapter 15) and revisit their structure often. They continually work on identifying positions they need and defining the responsibilities that go along with each. They gauge whether agent-to-supervisor and supervisor-to-manager ratios are working as they should, and adjust them as needed.

Above all, successful leaders know that communication is the glue that holds the whole thing together. They work hard to maintain effective communication, including across distributed teams. They understand how communication creates meaning and direction for people, and they are committed to keeping a common vision at the forefront of the culture and daily activities.

## 11. They Are Willing to Experiment

The most successful contact center teams continually review and reassess how they do things and the results they are achieving. What can be improved? What should be scrapped? What assumptions no longer make sense? What can be done differently? They would agree with the advice of management consultant Dr. Ichak Adizes, who reminds us, "You don't know what you don't know until you know it ... The right solution is a continuous search for the right solution."

---

*An idealist believes that the short run doesn't count. A cynic believes the long run doesn't matter. A realist believes that what is done or left undone in the short run determines the long run.*

**SIDNEY J. HARRIS**

---

## 12. They See the Possibilities

The contact center profession has come a long way in recent years. Customer expectations are high, and for good reason. For the most part, contact centers have learned how to deliver. Collectively, they have invested billions in equipment, networks and software. They have spent untold hours training and equipping people. They have learned the nuances of forecasting, staffing and the behavior of queues. They continue to improve processes and find new and better ways to get things done. And, they have identified evolving customer needs, and are constantly changing to meet those needs.

But things are changing fast, and some in our industry are understandably viewing the future with at least some apprehension. They fear the impact and uncertainties that new channels of communication (such as those through social media) bring. They are concerned about ever-heightening competition. They contemplate the increasingly diverse interactions their centers will handle. They wonder how they're going to keep up in an environment that changes so quickly, so persistently.

It's important to remember, though, that the very things that are bringing uncertainties are also bringing the most relevant opportunities. More than ever, organizations need professionals who can help them sort through these changes and make sound business decisions. By virtually any measure, there's a shortage of leaders who really understand the unique contact center environment and how to deliver great business results.

---

*In many ways, we are all pioneers in creating the next generation of services — services our customers will come to expect, our organizations will depend on and our economy will require.*

---

## Where to from Here?

Clearly, customer contact operations are becoming increasingly complex to operate. Choices, mobility, social interactions, search tools, new multimedia services, and other developments are leading to better-informed and savvier customers. Self-service, online resources and social communities are offloading the more straightforward contacts of the past, leaving contact centers with more complex (and more important) work. I firmly believe that if you know and practice the principles covered in this book, you will have a big head start.

We have become a communication-oriented economy. In many ways, we are all pioneers in creating the next generation of services — services our customers will come to expect, our organizations will depend on and our economy will require. We've got more opportunity right now than at any time in the history and growth of this profession to shape services that have a positive impact.

And for all the developments that have transpired in recent years, I think we're just getting started. The opportunities are there for the taking — this is *the new era of customer relationships.*

Thank you for joining me on this journey!

# Notes

## CHAPTER 1

First telegraph transmission, Annie Ellsworth, Henry Ellsworth, source: *The Connecticut Magazine: An Illustrated Monthly,* Volume 8, 1904, page 22.

Numbers reference: Numbers 23:23, King James Version.

Puvis de Chavannes quote, source: John Brooks, *Telephone, the First Hundred Years,* Harper and Row, 1976, page 118.

John Brooks quote, source: John Brooks, *Telephone, the First Hundred Years,* Harper and Row, 1976, page 117.

Contact center management, definition, source: ICMI's management seminar, *Essential Skills and Knowledge for Effective Contact Center Management,* 2012.

Planning steps, source: ICMI's management seminar, *Essential Skills and Knowledge for Effective Contact Center Management,* 2012.

## CHAPTER 2

Contact center definition, source: ICMI's management seminar, *Contact Center Strategy: A Planning Workshop,* 2012.

Customer access strategy, definition: ICMI's management seminar, *Contact Center Strategy: A Planning Workshop,* 2012.

Kip Wetzel, Bill Gerth quotes: Video profiling Comcast's social service, posted to YouTube, "Salesforce + Comcast = Like," uploaded by Salesforce.com on Nov 22, 2011.

BlueCross BlueShield of South Carolina, source: *Call Center Management on Fast Forward,* second edition.

National Cancer Institute, source: Facebook.com/cancer.gov and author interviews with Deborah Pearson, February 3, 2012.

USAA mobile app, source: Nathan Conz, "USAA Launches RDC app for iPhone," *Bank Systems and Technology,* August 13, 2009.

Intuit sidebar, sources: Presentation at ACCE 2010, New Orleans, by Todd Hixson, Derrick Moore and Michael Pivinski, Intuit. Also, author interviews with Todd Hixson, January 19, 2012.

Ten customer expectations, source: ICMI's management seminar, *Essential Skills and Knowledge for Effective Contact Center Management,* 2012.

Steve Jobs' advice, source: Walter Isaacson, *Steve Jobs,* Simon & Schuster, 2011, drawn from chapters 27, 30, and 34.

## CHAPTER 3

Three driving forces (random call arrival, visible and invisible queue, and seven factors of caller tolerance), source: ICMI's management course, *Essential Skills and Knowledge for Effective Contact Center Management*, 2012.

Three types of traffic arrival, source: J. Jewett, J. Shrago, J. Gilliland, B. Yomtov. *Traffic Engineering Tables: The Complete Practical Encyclopedia*, Telephony Publishing Corporation, 1980.

WordPerfect and Microsoft references, source: *Call Center Management on Fast Forward*, first edition.

British Airways case study, source: *Call Center Management on Fast Forward*, first and second editions.

Virtual queuing, source: Virtual Hold Technology customer case studies, www.virtualhold.com. Also see lucyphone.com and fonolo.com.

## CHAPTER 4

Dialog with Zappos Customer Loyalty Team representative Derek Flores, source: Author's blog, bradcleveland.com/blog, June 12, 2009.

Service level and response time examples, source: ICMI surveys.

ASA and delay calculations, source: ICMI's QueueView staffing program, based on Erlang C.

Service level calculations, source: Cheryl Odee Helm, from *Call Center Management on Fast Forward*, first edition.

Laura Grimes, quote, source: Author interview with Laura Grimes, February 5, 2012.

Incremental Revenue (Value) Analysis, source: ICMI.

Comcast sidebar, sources: "Cable Rage Pushes Granny Over the Edge," ABC's *Good Morning America*, transcript posted October 19, 2007. Also, video profiling Comcast's social service, posted to YouTube, "Salesforce + Comcast = Like," uploaded by Salesforce.com on Nov 22, 2011.

## CHAPTER 5

Georgia Power, Mountain America Credit Union, and Eddie Bauer examples, source: *Call Center Management on Fast Forward*, second edition.

Capital One example, source: Video profiling Capital One's "Voice of the Customer" initiative, winner of ACCE 2011 video contest.

Hot Topic's "Daily Huddle", source: Hot Topic, Inc., video profiling best practices, winner of ACCE 2010 video contest.

## CHAPTER 6

Breaking down a forecast, source: ICMI management course, *Essential Skills and Knowledge for Effective Contact Center Management*, 2012.

Worksheets used throughout chapter, source: ICMI.

Armstrong, J.S. (Editor). *Principles of Forecasting — A Handbook for Researchers and Practitioners*, Springer, 2001.

Forecasting study (10 common problems), source: ICMI.

Gina Szabo sidebar, source: Author interview with and written story by Gina Szabo, submitted for *Call Center Management on Fast Forward*, third edition, February 20, 2012.

## CHAPTER 7

W. Edwards Deming quote, source: W. Edwards Deming, *Out of the Crisis*, Massachusetts Institute of Technology, 1986.

Staffing and delay examples, source: ICMI's QueueView staffing program.

Variations on Erlang C, source: Interviews with Mike Hills for *Call Center Management on Fast Forward*, first edition. Also, HTML Technologies and Pipkins, Inc.

Skills-based routing case, source: Original example produced by Martin A. Prunty.

Web chat examples, source: ICMI Consulting Division; original examples produced by Jay Minnucci for *Call Center Management on Fast Forward*, second edition.

Traffic Engineering Tables and Formulas, source: J. Jewett, J. Shrago, J. Gilliland, B. Yomtov. *Traffic Engineering Tables: The Complete Practical Encyclopedia*, Telephony Publishing Corporation, 1980.

## CHAPTER 8

Rostered staff factor (shrink factor) illustrations, source: ICMI's management course, *Essential Skills and Knowledge for Effective Contact Center Management*, 2012.

Vanguard and MetLife examples, source: *Call Center Management on Fast Forward*, first edition.

People's United Bank, AMVESCAP, Day Timer and Accor partnership, source: From *Call Center Management on Fast Forward*, second edition.

John Deere and American Girl, source: Hannah Clark, "In-Sourcing," *Forbes.com*, April 21, 2006.

Vegas.com example and Rob Cate quote, source: From video profiling Vegas.com service, by Interactive Intelligence (inin.com), posted to YouTube, December 28, 2009.

JetBlue, American Express, Wyndam International examples, source: author interviews and experiences with these companies.

Service level graphs, source: ICMI management course, *Essential Skills and Knowledge for Effective Contact Center Management*, 2012.

## CHAPTER 9

Immutable laws, graphs, tables and examples, source: ICMI management course, *Essential Skills and Knowledge for Effective Contact Center Management*, 2012.

## CHAPTER 10

In the section on what senior-level managers should understand, some points are adapted from a booklet by Gordon MacPherson, Jr., *What Senior Management Needs to Know About Incoming Call Centers*, ICMI, 1996.

BT Global, source: *Call Center Management on Fast Forward*, second edition.

Staffing budget example, source: ICMI's Consulting Division; original examples prepared by Jay Minnucci and Dan Rickwalder for *Call Center Management on Fast Forward*, second edition.

Stephanie Winston quote, source: Stephanie Winston, *The Organized Executive: The Classic Program for Productivity — New Ways to Manage Time, Paper, People and the Electronic Office, Revised Edition* (Paperback), Warner Business Books, 2001.

Variance, Total Expenses, source: ICMI's management course, *Contact Center Strategy: A Planning Workshop*, 2012.

## CHAPTER 11

"Due to our inability to staff..." (cartoon), source: Kathleen Peterson, quote, from first edition of book.

Igor Stravinsky quote, source: *Bartlett's Roget's Thesaurus*, Little, Brown and Company Inc., 1996, page 718.

Reacting in advance tables, source: Drawn from ICMI management course, *Essential Skills and Knowledge for Effective Contact Center Management*, 2012. Original examples created by Tim Montgomery.

Real-time management graphs and examples, source: ICMI management course, *Essential Skills and Knowledge for Effective Contact Center Management*, 2012.

Apple Inc., source: *Call Center Management on Fast Forward*, second edition.

## CHAPTER 12

Which measures become objectives, flow chart, source: ICMI's management course, *Contact Center Strategy: A Planning Workshop*, 2012.

Mary Murcott quote, source: *Call Center Management on Fast Forward*, second edition.

Keith Dawson quote, source: *Call Center Management on Fast Forward*, second edition.

Peter Drucker quote, source: Peter F. Drucker, *The Daily Drucker*, Collins, 2004.

Independence Blue Cross (Philadelphia), Boston Coach, Sharp Electronics, Aetna U.S. Healthcare, source: *Call Center Management on Fast Forward*, second edition.

American Express compensation example, source: This was originally publicized in *1to1 Magazine*; Mila D'Antonio, "Can American Express Lead the Charge in Service," *1to1 Magazine*, July/August 2008.

Boden example, source: "Top 50 U.K. Call Centres," 2011 program publication for ICMI/Call Centre Focus, by Raconteur Media Publications, page 9.

Zappos example, source: Tony Hsieh, *Delivering Happiness*, Business Plus, 2010, page 145.

## CHAPTER 13

What is a quality contact, source: ICMI management course, *Essential Skills and Knowledge for Effective Contact Center Management*, 2012.

Costs When Quality is Lacking, source: ICMI management course, *Essential Skills and Knowledge for Effective Contact Center Management*, 2012.

American General Life, source: Written by Layne Holley, based on the ICMI webinar "Customer Feedback in Action: Turning the Voice of the Customer into Results," November 23, 2010.

Peter Drucker quote, source: Peter F. Drucker, *The Daily Drucker*, Collins, 2004.

Quality tools, examples: ICMI

John Goodman, quote, source: John A. Goodman. *Strategic Customer Service*, Amacom, 2009, page 2.

W. Edwards Deming quote, source: W. Edwards Deming, *Out of the Crisis*, Massachusetts Institute of Technology, 1986.

Amazon example, source: Bill Price and David Jaffe, *The Best Service is No Service*, Jossey-Bass, 2008, page 43.

Linksys example, source: *Call Center Management on Fast Forward*, second edition.

China UnionPay, source: Author interview with and written submission by Zhiyong Xiao, January 31, 2012. Translated by Stella Yang, ICMI China.

JetBlue example, source: Ginger Conlon, "JetBlue's 4 Keys to Voice of the Customer," *1to1 Magazine*, May 30, 2011.

NCI example, source: Facebook.com/cancer.gov and author interviews with Deborah Pearson, February 3, 2012.

## CHAPTER 14

Johann Wolfgang Von Goethe quote, source: Widely cited to a letter written to A. F. Oeser, November 9, 1768.

Gallup statistics, source: Jennifer Robison, "The Economic Crisis: A Leadership Challenge," *Gallup Management Journal*, May 12, 2009.

Dee Hock quote, source: Douglas DeCarlo, *eXtreme Project Management: Using Leadership, Principles, and Tools to Deliver Value in the Face of Volatility*, Jossey-Bass, 2004, p. 28.

Recommended monitoring practices, source: ICMI.

Sample monitoring form, source: Adapted from examples used in ICMI's monitoring and coaching seminars, 2012. Original example prepared by Rebecca Gibson.

Wells Fargo using agent-level feedback and Terri McMillan quote, source: *Call Center Management on Fast Forward*, second edition.

Canadian Medical Protective Association, source: Written by Layne Holley, based on "Call Center Spotlight: The Canadian Medical Protective Association," ICMI.com, July 14, 2011.

Rose Polchin, sidebar, source: Written for *Call Center Management on Fast Forward*, third edition, February 17, 2012, based on series originally appearing in ICMI's blog, icmi.com/blog.

Laura Grimes, quote, source: Author interview with Laura Grimes, February 5, 2012.

## CHAPTER 15

ICMI reports on staffing and retention, source: ICMI.

Should You Consider Home Agents?, sidebar, source: Jean Bave Kerwin, submitted for *Call Center Management on Fast Forward*, third edition, March 19, 2012.

Linda Riggs, quote, source: Author interview with Linda Riggs, March 24, 2012.

Investment in People at American Express, sidebar, source: Layne Holley, based on in-person interviews and ICMI's webinar "Driving Success for the Agent, the Contact Center and the Company," October 6, 2010.

Elliot Jacques and Stephen D. Clement quote, source: Elliot Jacques and Stephen D. Clement, *Executive Leadership*, Blackwell Publishing, Inc., reprint edition May 1994.

## CHAPTER 16

HMS *Agamemnon*, source: W.H. Russell, *The Atlantic Telegraph*, Nonsuch Publishing, 2005.

"Plate of silver  " reference, source: John Brooks, *Telephone, the First Hundred Years*, Harper and Row, 1976, p. 36.

BlueCross BlueShield of South Carolina example, source: *Call Center Management on Fast Forward*, second edition.

Hosted/Cloud-Based Contact Centers, sidebar, source: Excerpted from "Cloud Cover for the Contact Center," ICMI whitepaper, 2011.

iContact Transforms Social Media into a Customer Access Channel, sidebar, source: by Layne Holley, based on Social Customer Service Panel, Dreamforce 2011, September 1, 2011.

Don Peppers and Martha Rogers quote, source: Don Peppers and Martha Rogers, *Rules to Break and Laws to Follow*, John Wiley & Sons, Inc., 2008, page 113.

Gordon F. MacPherson Jr. quote, source: Gordon F. MacPherson Jr. "The New Forces of Change," *Best of Service Level Newsletter* — Volume 4, 1997, p. 460.

Emily Yellin quote, source: Emily Yellin, *Your Call Is (Not That) Important to Us*, Free Press, 2009, page 261.


## CHAPTER 17

USAA's "Secret Sauce," source: Presentation at ACCE 2010, New Orleans, by Len Hambrick.

Virgin Mobile, source: *Call Center Management on Fast Forward*, second edition.

Wells Fargo Banker Connection, source: *Call Center Management on Fast Forward*, second edition.

Dr. Ichak Adizes quote, source: Dr. Ichak, as quoted in *Manage*, Jan 1993, p. 14.

Sidney J. Harris, source: widely quoted. Sidney J. Harris (1917-1986) wrote the syndicated column, "Strictly Personal," from 1944-1986.

# Acronyms

| | |
|---|---|
| ACD | Automatic Call Distributor |
| ACW | After-Call Work |
| AHT | Average Handling Time or Average Holding Time on Trunks |
| ANI | Automatic Number Identification |
| ASA | Average Speed of Answer |
| ASP | Application Service Provider |
| ASR | Automatic Speech Recognition |
| ATA | Average Time to Abandonment |
| ATB | All Trunks Busy |
| CCR | Customer-Controlled Routing |
| CCS | Centum Call Seconds |
| CDR | Call Detail Recording |
| CED | Caller-Entered Digits or Customer-Entered Digits |
| CIS | Customer Information System |
| CLEC | Competitive Local Exchange Carrier |
| CLI | Calling Line Identity |
| CLID | Calling Line Identification |
| CMS | Call Management System or Contact Management System |
| CO | Central Office |
| CPE | Customer Premises Equipment |
| CPU | Central Processing Unit |
| CRM | Customer Relationship Management |
| CSR | Customer Service Representative |
| CTI | Computer Telephony Integration |
| DID | Direct Inward Dialing |
| DN | Dialed Number |
| DNIS | Dialed-Number Identification Service |
| DTMF | Dual-Tone Multifrequency |

| | |
|---|---|
| ERMS | Email Response Management System |
| ERP | Enterprise Resource Planning |
| EWT | Expected Wait Time |
| FCR | First-Call Resolution or First-Contact Resolution |
| FIFO | First In First Out |
| FTE | Full-Time Equivalent |
| FX | Foreign Exchange Line |
| GOS | Grade of Service |
| HTML | Hyper-Text Markup Language |
| HTTP | Hypertext Transport Protocol |
| IM | Instant Messaging |
| IBC | In-Between Contacts |
| IP | Internet Protocol |
| IS | Information Systems |
| ISDN | Integrated Services Digital Network |
| ISP | Internet Service Provider |
| IT | Information Technology |
| IVR | Interactive Voice Response |
| IWR | Interactive Web Response |
| IXC | Interexchange Carrier |
| KM | Knowledge Management |
| KPI | Key Performance Indicator |
| LAN | Local Area Network |
| LEC | Local Exchange Carrier |
| LWOP | Leave Without Pay |
| MIS | Management Information System |
| MM | Multimedia |
| NCC | Network Control Center |
| NOC | Network Operations Center |

| NPA | Numbering Plan Area |
|---|---|
| OJT | On-the-Job Training |
| OPA | Off-Phone Activity |
| PABX | Private Automatic Branch Exchange |
| PBX | Private Branch Exchange |
| PCP | Post-Call Processing |
| PDA | Personal Digital Assistant |
| PRI | Primary Rate Interface |
| PSN | Public Switched Network |
| PSTN | Public Switched Telephone Network |
| PTT | Postal Telephone & Telegraph |
| QA | Quality Analysis or Quality Assurance |
| QM | Quality Monitoring |
| QOS | Quality of Service |
| RFI | Request for Information |
| RFID | Radio-Frequency Identification |
| RFP | Request for Proposal |
| RFQ | Request for Quote |
| RNA | Ring No Answer |
| ROI | Return on Investment |
| RSF | Rostered Staff Factor |
| SaaS | Software as a Service |
| SBR | Skills-Based Routing |
| SCRM | Supply Chain Risk Management |
| SFA | Sales Force Automation |
| SIP | Session Initiation Protocol |
| SL | Service Level |
| SLA | Service Level Agreement |
| SMS | Short Message Service |

| | |
|---|---|
| SOHO | Small Office Home Office |
| TCP/IP | Transmission Control Protocol/Internet Protocol |
| TDM | Time-Division Multiplexing |
| TQM | Total Quality Management |
| TSF | Telephone Service Factor |
| TSR | Telephone Sales or Service Representative |
| TTS | Text-to-Speech |
| UCD | Uniform Call Distributor |
| URL | Uniform Resource Locator |
| VDT | Video Display Terminal |
| VOC | Voice of the Customer |
| VoIP | Voice Over Internet Protocol |
| VPN | Virtual Private Network |
| VRU | Voice Response Unit |
| VXML | Voice Extensible Markup Language |
| WAN | Wide Area Network |
| WFMS | Workforce Management System |
| WWW | World Wide Web |
| XHTML | Extensible Hypertext Markup Language |
| XML | Extensible Markup Language |

# Glossary

**Abandoned Call (Inbound).** Also called a lost call. The caller hangs up before reaching an agent. Related terms: Abandoned Rate (Outbound), Caller Tolerance, Service Level.

**Abandoned Rate (Outbound).** In a predictive dialing mode, this is the percentage of calls connected to a live person that are never delivered to an agent. Related terms: Abandoned Call (Inbound), Caller Tolerance, Dialer.

**Activity Codes.** See Wrap-up Codes.

**Adherence to Schedule.** A general term that refers to how well agents adhere to their schedules. The two terms most often associated with adherence include availability (the amount of time agents were available) and compliance (when they were available to handle contacts).

**After-Call Work (ACW).** Also called wrap-up, post-call processing, average work time or not ready. Work that is necessitated by and immediately follows an inbound call. Related terms: Average Handling Time, Talk Time.

**Agent.** The person who handles incoming or outgoing contacts. Also referred to as customer service representative (CSR), customer care representative, telephone sales or service representative (TSR), rep, associate, consultant, engineer, operator, technician, account executive, team member, customer service professional, staff member, attendant or specialist.

**Agent Group.** Also called split, gate, queue or skills group. An agent group shares a common set of skills and knowledge, handles a specified mix of contacts (e.g., service, sales, billing or technical support) and can comprise hundreds of agents across multiple sites. Supervisory groups and teams are often subsets of agent groups.

**Agent Out Call.** An outbound call placed by an agent.

**Agent Performance Report.** An ACD report that provides statistics for individual agents (e.g., on talk time, after-call work and unavailable time).

**Agent Status.** The mode an agent is in (e.g., talk time, after-call work, unavailable, etc.). See Work State.

**All Trunks Busy (ATB).** When all trunks are busy in a specified trunk group. Generally, ATB reports indicate how many times all trunks were busy (how many times the last trunk available was seized), and how much total time all trunks were busy. They don't reveal how many callers got busy signals when all trunks were busy. Related Terms: Erlang B, Trunk Load.

**Analog.** Telephone transmission or switching that is not digital. Signals are analogous to the original signal.

**Analytics.** Broadly refers to data analysis and reporting tools that enable the organization to analyze disparate data to uncover correlations and better understand customer trends and business activities. Related terms: Speech Analytics, Text Analytics.

**Announcement.** A recorded message played to callers. See Delay Announcement.

**Answer Supervision.** The signal sent by the ACD or other device to the local or long-distance carrier to accept a call. This is when billing for either the caller or the contact center will begin, if long-distance charges apply.

**Answered Call.** When referring to an agent group, a call is counted as answered when it reaches an agent. Related terms: Handled Call, Offered Call, Received Call.

**App.** A commonly-used abbreviation for application, e.g., a "mobile app."

**Application Service Provider (ASP).** An outsourcing business that enables other organizations to access and use technologies or services for a fee.

**Application-Based Routing and Reporting.** An ACD capability that enables the system to route and track transactions by type of call, or application (e.g., sales, service, etc.), versus the traditional method of routing and tracking by trunk group and agent group.

**Architecture.** The basic design of a system. Determines how the components work together, system capacity, ability to upgrade and ability to integrate with other systems.

**Attendant.** A person who works at a company switchboard, often called a receptionist or operator. See Agent.

**Audio Response Unit (ARU).** See Interactive Voice Response.

**Audiotex.** A voice processing capability that enables callers to automatically access prerecorded announcements. Related terms: Interactive Voice Response.

**Auto-Available.** An ACD feature whereby the ACD is programmed to automatically put agents into available after they finish talk time and disconnect calls. If they need to go into after-call work, they have to manually put themselves there. Related terms: Auto Wrap-Up, Manual Available.

**Auto Wrap-Up.** An ACD feature whereby the ACD is programmed to automatically put agents into after-call work after they finish talk time and disconnect calls. When they have completed any after-call work required, they put themselves back into available. See Auto-Available.

**Automated Attendant.** A voice processing capability that automates the attendant (operator or receptionist) function. The system prompts callers to respond to choices (e.g., press one for this, two for that ...) and then coordinates with the ACD or related routing system to send callers to specific destinations. See Interactive Voice Response.

**Automated Greeting.** An agent's pre-recorded greeting that plays automatically when a call arrives at his or her station.

**Automated Reply.** A system-generated email that is automatically sent to a customer acknowledging that his or her email was received. See Response Time.

**Automatic Answer.** See Call-Forcing.

**Automatic Call Distributor (ACD).** The specialized system — or more specifically, a software application — that is used to route, manage and report on customer contacts. Basic ACD capabilities include: route calls (contacts); sequence calls; queue calls; encourage callers to wait (by playing delay announcements and, in some cases, predicting and announcing wait times); distribute calls among agents; capture planning and performance data, both real-time and historical; and integrate with other systems.

**Automatic Call Sequencer (ACS).** A simple system that is less sophisticated than an ACD, but provides some ACD-like functionality. See Automatic Call Distributor.

**Automatic Number Identification (ANI).** A telecommunications network feature that passes the number of the phone the caller is using to the contact center in real-time. ANI is an American term; Calling Line Identity (CLI) is an alternative term used in many other countries. Related terms: Computer Telephony Integration, Dialed Number Identification Service.

**Automatic Speech Recognition (ASR).** An IVR capability that enables customers to interact with computers using spoken language.

**Auxiliary Work State.** An agent work state that is typically not associated with handling telephone calls. When agents are in an auxiliary mode, they will not receive inbound calls.

**Availability.** The time agents spend handling calls or waiting for calls to arrive. See Adherence to Schedule.

**Available State.** The work state of agents who are signed on to the ACD and are waiting for calls to arrive. See Occupancy.

**Available Time.** The total time that an agent or agent group waits for calls to arrive, for a given time period.

**Average Call Value.** A measure common in revenue-producing call centers. It is total revenue divided by total number of calls for a given period of time.

**Average Delay.** See Average Speed of Answer.

**Average Delay to Abandon.** See Average Time to Abandonment.

**Average Handling Time (AHT).** The sum of average talk time plus average after-call work. Related terms: Talk Time, After-Call Work.

**Average Holding Time on Trunks (AHT).** The average time inbound transactions occupy the trunks.

**Average Speed of Answer (ASA).** A measure that reflects the average delay of all calls, including those that receive an immediate answer. Also called average delay.

**Average Time to Abandonment (ATA).** Also called average delay to abandon. The average time that callers wait in queue before abandoning. The calculation considers only the calls that abandon. Related term: Caller Tolerance.

**Average Work Time (AWT).** See After-Call Work.

**Back Office.** Business applications and functions that are "behind the scenes" to a customer, e.g., accounting, finance, inventory control, fulfillment, productions and human resources. See Front Office.

**Bandwidth.** The transmission capacity of a communications line.

**Barge In.** An ACD feature that allows a supervisor or manager to join or "barge in" on a call being handled by an agent.

**Base Staff.** Also called seated agents. The minimum number of agents required to achieve service level and response time objectives for a given period of time. Related term: Rostered Staff Factor.

**Beep Tone.** An audible notification that a call has arrived. Beep tone can also refer to the audible notification that a call is being monitored. Also called zip tone. Related terms: Automated Greeting, Call-Forcing.

**Benchmarking.** In quality terms, benchmarking is comparing products, services and processes with those of other organizations to identify new ideas and improvement opportunities.

**Blended Agent.** An agent who handles both inbound and outbound calls, or who handles contacts from different channels (e.g., email and phone). See Call Blending.

**Blockage.** Callers blocked from entering a queue. See Blocked Call.

**Blocked Call.** A call that cannot be connected immediately because: A) no circuit is available at the time the call arrives, or B) the ACD is programmed to block calls from entering the queue when the queue backs up beyond a defined threshold. See Controlled Busies.

**Blog.** An article or personal journal published on the Web. Blog can also be a verb, e.g., "to blog" about a topic. Related terms: Facebook, LinkedIn, Search, Social Media, Twitter.

**Business Rules.** A phrase used to refer to various software (or manual) controls that manage contact routing, handling and follow-up. At a basic level, business rules are a sequence of "if-then" statements. Often used interchangeably with workflow.

**Business to Business (B-to-B).** Refers to business or interactions between businesses. See Business to Consumer.

**Business to Consumer (B-to-C).** Refers to business or interactions between a business and consumers. See Business to Business.

**Busy.** In use, or "off hook."

**Busy Hour.** A telephone traffic engineering term, referring to the hour of time in which a trunk group carries the most traffic during the day.

**Busy Season.** The busiest time of a year for a contact center.

**Calibration.** In a contact center, calibration is the process in which variations in the way performance criteria are interpreted from person to person are minimized. See Monitoring.

**Call.** Also called contact, interaction or transaction. Although it most often refers to a telephone call, call can also refer to a video call, a Web call and other types of customer contacts.

**Call Blending.** Traditionally, the ability to dynamically allocate contact center agents to both inbound and outbound calling based on conditions in the center and programmed parameters. More recently, call blending is also used to refer to blending calls with non-phone work or handling contacts from different channels (e.g., email, SMS, chat, social, and phone). See Blended Agent.

**Call-By-Call Routing.** See Contact-by-Contact Routing.

**Call Center (Contact Center).** ICMI defines call center (contact center) as "A coordinated system of people, processes, technologies and strategies that provides access to information, resources, and expertise, through appropriate channels of communication, enabling interactions that create value for the customer and organization." Call center is an umbrella term that generally refers to cross-trained groups of agents handling customer service, sales, technical support or other types of contacts. Call center and contact center are often used interchangeably, although some make a distinction. Alternative terms include contact center, interaction center, customer care center, customer support center, technical support center, help desk, resource center, information line, and others. See Contact Center.

**Call Center-Initiated Assistance.** Typically, this refers to a text-chat session initiated by the agent, rather than the customer.

**Call Center Management (Contact Center Management).** ICMI's definition is: "The art of having the right number of properly skilled people and supporting resources in place at the right times to handle an accurately forecasted workload, at service level and with quality."

**Call Control Variables.** The set of criteria the ACD uses to process calls. Examples include routing criteria, overflow parameters, recorded announcements and timing thresholds.

**Call Detail Recording (CDR).** A telephone system feature that allows the system to record the details of incoming and outgoing calls (e.g., when they occur, how long they last and which extensions they go to). Also called station message detail recording.

**Call-Forcing.** An ACD feature that automatically delivers calls to agents who are available and ready to take calls. Sometimes called automatic answer. Related terms: Manual Answer, Auto-Available, Auto Wrap-up.

**Call Load.** Also called workload. Call load is volume multiplied by average handling time, for a given period of time. See Workload.

**Call (Contact) Management System (CMS).** Another term for an ACD reporting system.

**Call Quality (Contact Quality).** Typically, a measure that assigns a value to the quality of individual contacts.

**Call Recording.** A type of monitoring in which the supervisor or automated system records a sampling of calls (contacts). The person conducting the monitoring then randomly selects calls for evaluation of agent performance.

**Callback Messaging.** A feature that enables callers waiting in queue to leave a message or to enter their telephone numbers for later callback from an agent.

**Contact-by-Contact Routing.** The process of routing each call (contact) to the optimum destination according to real-time conditions. Related terms: Network, Network Interflow, Percent Allocation.

**Caller-Entered Digits or Customer-Entered Digits (CED).** The digits a customer enters on his or her communications devices. Usually used for auto attendant, voice response and CTI applications. Also referred to as prompted digits.

**Caller ID.** See Automatic Number Identification.

**Caller Tolerance.** How patient callers will be when they encounter queues or experience busy signals. Related terms: Abandoned Call, Delay Announcements.

**Calling Line Identity (CLI).** See Automatic Number Identification.

**Calls in Queue (Contacts in Queue).** A real-time report that refers to the number of calls (contacts) received by the ACD system but not yet connected to an agent. Related term: Contacts in Queue.

**Career Path.** Career paths guide individual employee development through structured advancement opportunities within the contact center and/or organization. A typical career path model requires the development of job families, which comprise a number of jobs arranged in a hierarchy by grade, pay and responsibility (e.g., agent, team leader, supervisor, manager, senior manager and director). See Skill Path.

**Carrier.** A company that provides telecommunications circuits. Carriers include both local telephone companies, also called local exchange carriers (LECs), and long-distance providers, also called interexchange carriers (IXCs).

**Cause-and-Effect Diagram.** A chart that illustrates the relationships between causes and a specific effect you want to study.

**Central Office (CO).** Can refer to either a telephone company switching center or the type of telephone switch used in a telephone company switching center. The local central office receives calls from within the local area and either routes them locally or passes them to an interexchange carrier (IXC). On the receiving end, the local central office receives calls that originated in other areas from the IXC.

**Centum Call Seconds (CCS).** A unit of telephone traffic measurement referring to 100 call seconds. The first C represents the Roman numeral for 100. 1 hour of telephone traffic=1 Erlang=60 minutes=36 CCS. Related terms: Erlang, Erlang B, Erlang C.

**Channel Hopping.** See Channel Switching.

**Channel Switching (also, Channel Hopping).** When customers switch to a different access alternative, e.g., they use the Web instead of waiting on hold. The term can also refer to customers who use the same channel but try different routing alternatives (e.g., they dial alternative phone numbers or try different selections in an IVR menu). Related term: Simultaneous Contact.

**Chat.** Enables customers visiting the company's website to have real-time, text-based conversations with live agents. Also called Text Chat or Web Chat.

**Chatter.** A communication and collaboration tool from Salesforce.com. See Collaboration Tools.

**Circuit Switching.** The traditional method of establishing dedicated, end-to-end connections for voice conversations.

**Circuit.** A transmission path between two points in a network.

**Client/Server Architecture.** A network of computers that share capabilities and devices.

**Cloud-Based Services.** Refers to software or services delivered "on-demand" through shared services, over a network — akin to a utility delivering services to subscribers. For contact centers, many features once available only in premise-based systems can now be delivered through the cloud, e.g., contact routing, reporting, quality and workforce management, collaboration capabilities, social media management tools, and others. Similar terms include Software as a Service (SaaS), Hosted Call Center, Virtual Call Center, Cloud-Based Call Center, and others.

**Close-out.** In chat, the moment in time when the session is considered to be complete. Related terms: Customer Response Time, Exchange, Exchange Handle Time, Exchange Response Time, Session, Session Handle Time, Session Response Time, Session Transaction Time.

**Co-Browsing.** A term that refers to the capability of both an agent and customer to see a Web page simultaneously and share navigation and data entry.

**Collaboration Tools.** Broadly refers to social media tools that enable a group of users to communicate and share information.

**Collateral Duties.** Non-phone tasks (e.g., data entry) that are flexible and can be scheduled for periods when call load is slow. Related term: Schedule.

**Completed Call.** A general term that refers to an inbound contact that successfully reaches and is handled by an agent. Can also refer to an outbound call that successfully reaches a live person (or answering machine, if leaving a message is acceptable). In an outbound context, also called connected call.

**Compliance.** See Adherence to Schedule.

**Computer-Based Training (CBT).** Training programs delivered through software applications without the need for a facilitator.

**Computer Simulation.** A computer-based simulator program that predicts the outcome of various events in the future, given many variables.

**Computer Telephony Integration (CTI).** The software, hardware and programming necessary to integrate computer systems and telephone systems so they can work together seamlessly and intelligently.

**Concentrated Shift.** A scheduling technique that requires agents to work more hours in a day, but fewer days in a week. "Four-by-10" shifts (four days on for 10 hours each, with three days off) are particularly popular with many agents.

**Conditional Routing.** The capability of the ACD to route calls based on real-time criteria (e.g., calls in queue, time of day and type of call). It is based on "if-then" programming statements. For example, "if the number of calls in agent group one exceeds 10 and there are at least two available agents in group two, then route the calls to group two."

**Conversation.** In a contact center, conversation can refer generally to social media (i.e., "join the conversation" — listen to what's being discussed in social networks and respond when and as appropriate), or to a specific interaction through a communications channel, e.g., having a dialog or "conversation" through Twitter or by phone.

**Contact Center.** A term often used interchangeably with call center, although some make a distinction when referring to centers that handle a greater variety of contact channels (beyond phone calls), or that have progressed on a maturity continuum. Currently, the popular business and consumer press widely use the term call center, while many inside the industry prefer contact center or other alternatives. See Call Center.

**Contacts Handled (Calls Per Agent).** The number of contacts an agent handles in a given period of time. Related terms: Occupancy, True Calls Per Agent.

**Contacts in Queue.** See Calls in Queue.

**Contacts Per Hour.** An outbound term that refers to the number of contacts divided by agent hours on the dialer. See Contacts.

**Control Chart.** A quality tool that provides information on variation in a process.

**Controlled Busies.** The capability of the ACD to generate busy signals when the queue backs up beyond a programmable threshold. See Blocked Call.

**Conventional Shift.** A traditional five-day-a-week shift during "normal business hours" (e.g., 9 a.m. to 5 p.m., Monday through Friday).

**Cookie.** A small file that identifies a user or provides user-related information to Web servers.

**Cost of Delay.** The money you pay to queue callers, assuming you have toll-free service.

**Cost Per Call.** Total costs (fixed and variable) divided by total calls for a given period of time.

**Cross-Sell.** A suggestive selling technique that offers additional products or services to current customers, usually based on relationships established between the customer's profile and the attributes of customers who have already purchased the products or services being cross-sold. See Upsell.

**Cross-Train.** To train agents to handle more than one defined mix of calls (e.g., to train technical support agents handling laptop calls to also handle tablet computer issues).

**Customer Access Strategy.** The overall strategy that defines how customers will interact with the organization. Specifically, "a set of standards, guidelines and processes describing the means by which customers and the organization can interact and are enabled to access the information, services and expertise needed."

**Customer Contact.** See Call.

**Customer Controlled Routing (CCR).** A vendor-specific term (originated by Nortel) that refers to a call routing application that enables calls to be handled (e.g., routed, queued, distributed) based on user-defined criteria.

**Customer Expectations.** The expectations customers have of a product, service or organization.

**Customer Experience.** The totality of an experience the customer has with an organization, including with products, customer service, processes, policies, branding, and other factors. See Voice of the Customer.

**Customer Information System (CIS).** An information system that provides data on customers, e.g., what they have purchased, prior contacts, and other customer related information.

**Customer Lifetime Value.** Expresses the value of a customer to the organization over the entire probable time period that the customer will interact with the organization.

**Customer Loyalty.** Typically defined in terms of the customer's repurchase behavior, intent to purchase again or intent to recommend the organization.

**Customer Premises Equipment (CPE).** A telecommunications term referring to equipment installed on the customer's premises and connected to the telecommunications network.

**Customer Relationship Management (CRM).** The process of holistically developing the customer's relationship with the organization. It takes into account their history as a customer, the depth and breadth of their business with the organization, as well as other factors.

**Customer Response Time.** In chat, the time it takes the customer to read an agent's reply and send a response. Related terms: Close-Out, Exchange, Exchange Handle Time, Exchange Response Time, Session, Session Handle Time, Session Response Time, Session Transaction Time.

**Customer Satisfaction.** The level of satisfaction customers have with the organization and the organization's products and services. See Customer Loyalty.

**Customer Segmentation.** The process of grouping customers based on what you know about them, in order to apply differentiated marketing, relationship and contact treatment strategies.

**Customer Service Representative (CSR).** See Agent.

**Data Mining.** Generally refers to the use of analytics capabilities to analyze data, e.g., to identify trends and causal factors. See Analytics.

**Day-of-Week Routing.** A network service that routes calls to alternate locations, based on the day of week. There are also options for day-of-year and time-of-day routing.

**Delay.** Also called queue time. The time a caller spends in queue waiting for an agent to become available. Average delay is the same thing as average speed of answer. Related term: Average Speed of Answer.

**Delay Announcements.** Recorded announcements that encourage callers to wait for an agent to become available, remind them to have their account number ready, and provide information on access alternatives.

**Delayed Call.** A call that cannot be answered immediately and is placed in queue.

**Dialed Number (DN).** The number that the caller dialed to initiate the call.

**Dialed Number Identification Service (DNIS).** A string of digits that the telephone network passes to the ACD, IVR or other device to indicate which telephone number the caller dialed. One trunk group can have many DNIS numbers. See Automatic Number Identification.

**Dialer.** Dialers are technologies (hardware/software) for automating the process of making outbound calls. Dialers may also provide campaign management and scripting functionality, and provide detailed real-time and historical reporting. Predictive dialing is an application that instructs the switch to dial multiple simultaneous calls from a preloaded list of phone numbers, then matches completed calls with agents. Related terms: Abandoned Rate (Outbound), Completed Call.

**Digital.** The use of a binary code — 1s and 0s — to represent information.

**Direct Call Processing.** See Talk Time.

**Disaster Recovery Plan.** A plan that enables managers to avoid or recover expediently from an interruption in the center's operation. Comprehensive plans should include an approved set of arrangements and procedures for facilities, networks, people and service levels.

**Display Board.** See Readerboard.

**Distributed Call Center.** See Virtual Call Center.

**Dual-Tone Multifrequency (DTMF).** A signaling system that sends pairs of audio frequencies to represent digits on a telephone keypad. It is often used interchangeably with the term Touchtone (an AT&T trademark).

**Dynamic Answer.** An ACD feature that automatically reconfigures the number of rings before the system answers calls, based on real-time queue information. Since costs don't begin until the ACD answers calls, this feature can save callers or the contact center money on long-distance charges.

**Email Response Management System (ERMS).** A system that tracks and manages email contacts, similar to how an ACD tracks and manages inbound calls.

**Enterprise Resource Planning (ERP).** Generally refers to a system that manages back office functions.

**Envelope Strategy.** A scheduling approach whereby enough agents are scheduled for the day or week to handle both the inbound call load and other types of work. Priorities are based on the inbound call load. When call load is heavy, all agents handle calls, but when it is light, some agents are reassigned to work that is not as time-sensitive.

**Erlang.** One hour of telephone traffic in an hour of time. For example, if circuits carry 120 minutes of traffic in an hour, that's two Erlangs. Related terms: Erlang B, Erlang C, A.K. Erlang (listed as Frlang, A.K.), Queue Dynamics.

**Erlang B.** A formula developed by A.K. Erlang, widely used to determine the number of circuits or ports required to handle a known calling load during a one-hour period. The formula assumes that if callers get busy signals, they go away forever, never to retry ("lost calls cleared"). Since some callers retry, Erlang B can underestimate requirements. However, Erlang B is generally accurate in situations with few busy signals.

**Erlang C.** Calculates predicted waiting times (delay) based on three things: the number of servers (agents); the number of people waiting to be served (callers); and the average amount of time it takes to serve each person. It can also predict the resources required to keep waiting times within targeted limits. Erlang C assumes no lost calls or busy signals, so it has a tendency to overestimate staff required.

**Erlang, A.K.** A Danish engineer who worked for the Copenhagen Telephone Company in the early 1900s and developed Erlang B, Erlang C and other telephone traffic engineering formulas.

**Error Rate.** The number or percentage of defective (e.g., incomplete) transactions or the number or percentage of defective steps in a transaction.

**Errors and Rework.** As a measurement, the percent (and types) of errors and rework that are occurring.

**Escalation Plan.** A plan that specifies actions to be taken when the queue begins to build beyond acceptable levels. See Real-Time Management.

**Exchange.** In chat, a part of a session that begins with an inquiry from the customer and concludes with a response from the agent. Related terms: Close-Out, Customer Response Time, Exchange Handle Time, Exchange Response Time, Session, Session Handle Time, Session Response Time, Session Transaction Time.

**Exchange Handle Time.** In chat, the time it takes for the agent to prepare and deliver a response during an exchange. Related terms: Close-Out, Customer Response Time, Exchange, Exchange Response Time, Session, Session Handle Time, Session Response Time, Session Transaction Time.

**Exchange Line.** See Trunk.

**Explanatory Forecasting.** See Forecasting Methodologies.

**Exchange Response Time.** In chat, the time that elapses between the customer sending a question or comment and the delivery of the agent's response. Related terms: Close-Out, Customer Response Time, Exchange, Exchange Handle Time, Session, Session Handle Time, Session Response Time, Session Transaction Time.

**Facebook.** A popular social site that enables people to connect and communicate with friends, interest groups and organizations. Related terms: Blog, LinkedIn, Search Engine, Social Media, Twitter.

**Fast Clear-Down.** A caller who hangs up immediately after hearing a delay announcement. Related term: Delay Announcement.

**Fiber Optics.** Thin filaments of transparent glass or plastic that use light to transmit voice, video or data signals.

**First-Call Resolution (First-Contact Resolution).** The percentage of calls (contacts) that do not require any further contacts to address the customer's reason for calling. The customer does not need to contact the organization again to seek resolution, nor does anyone within the organization need to follow up. Related term: Errors and Rework.

**First-Contact Resolution.** See First-Call Resolution.

**Flex-Time Scheduling.** Several weeks in advance, agents are promised schedules within a window of time (e.g., only Tuesdays through Saturdays or from 8 a.m. to 8 p.m. any day of the week), according to their personal availability. Then, specific work hours, and in some cases, days worked, are determined from week to week as forecasted staff requirements are refined. This approach may involve the entire staff, but usually includes only a subset of employees.

**Flow Chart.** A map of a process that is used to analyze and standardize procedures, identify root causes of problems and plan new processes.

**Flushing out the Queue.** A real-time management term that refers to changing system thresholds so that calls waiting for an agent group are redirected to another group with a shorter queue or more available agents. Related term: Real-Time Management.

**Forecasted Call Load vs. Actual.** A performance objective that reflects the percent variance between the call load forecasted and the call load actually received. Related term: Forecasting Methodologies.

**Forecasting.** The process of predicting contact center workload and other activities. See Forecasted Call Load vs. Actual and Forecasting Methodologies.

**Forecasting Methodologies.** General methods used to predict future events, such as the amount of workload that will come into a contact center in future time periods. Methodologies are broadly categorized into quantitative and judgmental approaches. Quantitative forecasts include: time-series forecasts, which assume past data will reflect trends that continue into the future; and explanatory forecasting, which essentially attempts to reveal a linkage between two or more variables. Driver-based and event-driven forecasting approaches are variations of explanatory forecasting. Judgmental forecasts go beyond purely statistical techniques. They involve intuition, interdepartmental committees, market research and executive opinion. See Forecasting.

**Front Office.** Generally refers to customer-facing applications used in customer interactions. Related term: Back Office.

**Full-Time Equivalent (FTE).** A term used in scheduling and budgeting, whereby the number of scheduled hours is divided by the hours in a full work week. The hours of several part time agents may add up to one FTE.

**Gate.** See Agent Group.

**Gateway.** A server dedicated to providing access to a network.

**Grade of Service (GOS).** The probability that a call will not be connected to a system because all trunks are busy. Grade of service is often expressed as a probability, e.g., p.01, meaning 1 percent of calls will be blocked. Sometimes, grade of service is used interchangeably with service level, but the two terms have different meanings. Related terms: Erlang B, Service Level, Trunk Load.

**Graphical User Interface (GUI).** A computer interface that is graphical in nature, and uses menus, icons and a mouse or touchscreen to enable the user to interact with the system. Web browsers and the Windows and Apple operating systems are examples of GUIs.

**Handled Call.** A call that is received and handled by an agent or peripheral equipment. Related terms: Answered Call, Offered Call, Received Call.

**Handling Time.** For a phone call, the time an agent spends in talk time and after-call work handling an interaction. Handling time can also refer to the average time it takes for an agent to handle any kind of contact (SMS, social, email, etc.) or the time it takes for a machine to process a transaction. See Average Handling Time.

**Hashtag.** In Twitter, a word or phrase used to find, sort or identify groups or topics.

**Headset.** A device that consists of an earpiece and a microphone, and replaces a telephone handset. Headsets are designed to fit comfortably on the user's head, freeing both hands.

**Help Desk.** A term that generally refers to a call center (contact center) that provides technical support (e.g., queries about product installation, usage or problems). The term is most often used in the context of computer software and hardware support centers. See Call Center.

**Historical Forecasting.** Any method of call volume forecasting that relies solely on past call volume to determine future projections. See Forecasting Methodologies.

**Historical Report.** A report that tracks contact center and agent performance over a period of time. See Real-Time Report.

**Hosted Services (Hosted Call Center).** See Cloud-Based Services.

**Idle Time.** The inverse of occupancy. The time agents are available and waiting for contacts to arrive. See Occupancy.

**Imaging.** A process whereby documents are scanned into a system and stored electronically.

**Immutable Law.** A law of nature that is fundamental and not changeable (e.g., the law of gravity). In an inbound contact center, the fact that occupancy goes up when service level goes down is an immutable law.

**Incremental Revenue (Value) Analysis.** A methodology that estimates the value (cost and revenue) of adding or subtracting an agent.

**Increments.** Also called intervals. In contact centers, increments are the timeframes used for staffing and reporting. Given the variation in workload throughout the day, staff requirements must be calculated at specific increments (which are generally the smallest units of time reflected in the forecast).

**Index Factor.** In forecasting, a proportion used as a multiplier to adjust another number.

**Influencer.** In social media, refers generally to those who influence the opinions or behaviors of others. The term is often used to describe people who have large followings or above-normal sway in social communities or with a company's prospects or customers. Related terms: Sentiment Aggregator, Sentiment Analysis, Social Media.

**Information Systems (IS).** A generic term for systems that perform data processing.

**Information Technology (IT).** A generic term that refers either to computer and/or communications systems and technologies, or the profession that develops and manages these systems.

**Instant Messaging (IM).** A type of text-chat between two or more Internet users.

**Integrated Services Digital Network (ISDN).** A set of international standards for digital telephone transmission.

**Intelligent Routing.** The use of information about the caller, current conditions or other parameters to route calls to the appropriate group, individual, automated system, etc.

**Interexchange Carrier (IXC).** A long-distance telephone company.

**Interactive Voice Response (IVR).** An IVR system responds to caller-entered digits or speech recognition in much the same way that a conventional computer responds to keystrokes or clicks of a mouse. When the IVR is integrated with database computers, callers can interact with databases to check current information (e.g., account balances) and complete transactions (e.g. make transfers between accounts). Related terms: Automated Attendant, Automatic Speech Recognition.

**Interflow.** See Overflow.

**Interval.** See Increment.

**Internet Protocol (IP).** The set of communication standards that control communications activity on the Internet. An IP address is assigned to every computer on the Internet.

**Intraday Forecast.** A short-term forecast that assumes activities early in the day will reflect how the rest of the day will go.

**Intraflow.** See Overflow.

**Intraweek Forecast.** A short-term forecast that assumes activities early in the week will reflect how the rest of the week will go.

**Invisible Queue.** When callers do not know how long the queue is or how quickly it is moving. Related terms: Queue, Visible Queue.

**Job Role.** The function or responsibilities related to a specific position in an organization.

**Judgmental Forecasting.** Goes beyond purely statistical techniques and encompasses what people believe is going to happen. It is in the realm of intuition, interdepartmental committees, market research and executive opinion. See Forecasting Methodologies.

**Key Performance Indicator (KPI).** A high-level measure of contact center performance. Note, some interpret KPI as the single most important measure in a department or unit; however, in common usage, most centers have multiple KPIs. See Performance Objective.

**Law of Diminishing Returns.** The declining marginal improvements in service level that can be attributed to each additional agent, as successive agents are added.

**Lean Six Sigma.** A disciplined variation of Six Sigma that focuses on the elimination of different kinds of waste in production and service delivery. Related terms: System of Causes, Process, Six Sigma.

**LinkedIn.** A popular social networking site that enables users to network, communicate and share information. Related terms: Blog, Facebook, Search Engine, Social Media, Twitter.

**Load Balancing.** Balancing traffic between two or more destinations.

**Local Area Network (LAN).** The connection of multiple computers within a building so that they can share information, applications and peripherals. Related term: Wide Area Network.

**Local Exchange Carrier (LEC).** Telephone companies responsible for providing local connections and services.

**Long Call.** For staffing calculations and traffic engineering purposes, calls that approach or exceed 30 minutes.

**Longest-Available Agent.** Also referred to as most-idle agent. A method of distributing calls to the agent who has been sitting idle the longest. With a queue, longest-available agent becomes next available agent. Related term: Next Available Agent.

**Longest Delay (Oldest Call).** The longest time a caller has waited in queue, before abandoning or reaching an agent.

**Look-Ahead Queuing.** The ability for a system or network to examine a secondary queue and evaluate the conditions before overflowing calls from the primary queue.

**Look-Back Queuing.** The ability for a system or network to look back to the primary queue after the call has been overflowed to a secondary queue and evaluate the conditions. If the congestion clears, the call can be sent back to the initial queue.

**Lost Call.** See Abandoned Call.

**Make Busy.** To make a circuit or terminal unavailable.

**Manual Answer.** The ACD system is set up so that agents must manually answer calls. See Call-Forcing.

**Manual Available.** The ACD system is set up so that agents must put themselves back into the available mode after completing any after-call work. See Auto-Available.

**Measurement.** A quantifiable unit.

**Metrics.** Another word for measurements or, sometimes in usage, objectives. Related terms: Key Performance Indicator, Performance Objective.

**Middleware.** Software that mediates between different types of hardware and software on a network, so that they can function together.

**Mobile App.** See App.

**Monitoring.** Monitoring is a call (contact) evaluation process that appraises the qualitative aspects of call handling (contact handling). Monitoring programs include the tracking and analysis of data to identify individual agent and overall contact center performance trends, anticipated problems, and training and coaching needs. There are several ways to monitor agents' performance; e.g., silent monitoring, call recording, side-by-side monitoring, peer monitoring, and mystery shoppers. Monitoring is also called position monitoring, quality monitoring or service observing. Related terms: Calibration, Call Quality.

**Multimedia.** Combining multiple forms of media in the communication of information (e.g., a traditional phone call is "monomedia," and a video call is "multimedia").

**Multimedia Routing and Queuing.** Systems and processes that handle contacts across media — including voice, text-based and Web transactions — based on business rules that define how any transaction, inquiry or problem is processed.

**Mystery Shopper.** A type of monitoring in which a person acts as a customer, initiates a call to the center and monitors the skills of the agent. See Monitoring.

**Network.** In the contact center profession, the term network is typically used to describe the interexchange (IXC) services that route calls (contacts) into a center or among several centers. The network is the "pipe" between the customer and the contact center, or among contact centers. Related terms: Call-by-Call Routing, Network Control Center, Network Interflow, Percent Allocation.

**Network Control Center (NCC).** Also called traffic control center. In a networked contact center environment, where people and equipment monitor real-time conditions across sites, change routing thresholds as necessary, and coordinate events that will impact base staffing levels. Related terms: Network, Network Management System.

**Network Interflow.** A technology used in multisite contact center environments to create a more efficient distribution of calls between sites. Related terms: Call-by-Call Routing, Network, Percent Allocation.

**Next Available Agent.** A call (contact) distribution method that sends contacts to the next agent who becomes available. The method seeks to maintain an equal load across skill groups or services. When there is no queue, next available agent reverts to longest-available agent. Related term: Longest-Available Agent.

**Non ACD In Calls.** Inbound calls that are directed to an agent's extension rather than to a general group. These may be personal calls or calls from customers who dial the agents' extension numbers.

**Normalized Calls Per Agent.** See True Calls Per Agent.

**Number Portability.** A shared database among network providers that enables contact centers to keep the same telephone numbers if they change carriers.

**Occupancy.** Also referred to as agent utilization or percent utilization. The percentage of time agents handle calls (contacts) versus wait for calls to arrive; the inverse of occupancy is idle time. Related terms: Adherence to Schedule, Idle Time.

**Offered Call.** Offered calls include all of the attempts callers make to reach the contact center. There are three possibilities for offered calls: 1) They can get busy signals; 2) they can be answered by the system, but hang up before reaching an agent; or 3) they can be answered by an agent. Offered call reports in ACDs usually refer only to the calls that the ACD receives. Related terms: Answered Call, Handled Call, Received Call.

**Off-Peak.** Periods of time other than the contact center's busiest periods. Also a term to describe periods of time when long-distance carriers provide lower rates.

**On-the-Job Training (OJT).** A method of training that exposes the employee to realistic job situations through observation, guided practice and while working on the job.

**Open Ticket.** A customer contact (transaction) that has not been completed or resolved (closed). Related terms: First-Call Resolution, Response Time.

**Outsourcing.** Contracting some or all contact center services and/or technology to an outside company. The company is generally referred to as an outsourcer, service partner, or service bureau.

**Overflow.** Calls that flow from one group or site to another. More specifically, intraflow happens when calls flow between agent groups and interflow is when calls flow out of the ACD to another site.

**Overlay.** See Rostered Staff Factor.

**Overstaffing.** A scheduling term that refers to situations when the contact center has more staff than is required to handle the workload.

**Overtime.** Time beyond an established limit (e.g., working hours in addition to those of a regular schedule or full work week).

**Pareto Chart.** Created by economist Vilfredo Pareto, a Pareto chart is a bar chart that ranks events in order of importance or frequency.

**Payback Period.** A capital budgeting method that calculates the length of time required to recover an initial investment.

**PBX/ACD.** A private branch exchange (PBX) that is equipped with ACD functionality. See Private Branch Exchange and Automatic Call Distributor.

**Peaked Call Arrival.** A surge of traffic beyond random variation. It is a spike within a short period of time. There are two types of peaked traffic — the type you can plan for, and incidents that are impossible to predict. Related term: Increment.

**Peer Monitoring.** Call center agents monitor peers' calls and provide feedback on their performance. See Monitoring.

**Percent Allocation.** A call routing strategy sometimes used in multisite call center environments. Calls received in the network are allocated across sites based on user defined percentages. Related terms: Call-by-Call Routing, Network, Network Interflow.

**Performance Driver.** A suspect performance driver that has been validated through statistically sound analysis.

**Performance Objective.** Usually stated as a quantifiable goal that must be accomplished within a given set of constraints, a specified period of time, or by a given date (e.g., reduce turnover by 20 percent within one year).

**Performance Target.** An interim improvement point at a specific point in time, when striving to attain a new level of performance. Related terms: Key Performance Indicator, Performance Objective.

**Personal Digital Assistant (PDA).** A small palmtop computer often used for personal organization tasks (e.g., calendar, database, calculator and note-taking functions) and communications (e.g., email, mobile apps, wireless Internet access and wireless telephone). Related terms: Tablet Computer, Mobile App.

**Poisson.** A formula sometimes used for calculating trunks. Assumes that if callers get busy signals, they keep trying until they successfully get through. Since some callers won't keep retrying, Poisson can overestimate trunks required. Related terms: Erlang B, Retrial Tables, Trunk Load.

**Pooling Principle.** The powerful pooling principle states: Any movement in the direction of consolidation of resources will result in improved traffic-carrying efficiency. Conversely, any movement away from consolidation of resources will result in reduced traffic-carrying efficiency. A common contact center application is that if you take several small, specialized agent groups, effectively cross-train them and put them into a single group, you'll have a more efficient environment (assuming all other things are equal). Related terms: Agent Group, Queue Dynamics, Skills-Based Routing.

**Position Monitoring.** See Monitoring.

**Post-Call Processing (PCP).** See After-Call Work.

**Predictive Dialer.** See Dialer.

**Priority Queuing Application.** Programming that recognizes and "bumps" higher-value customers up in the queue to ensure that they receive the most efficient service possible.

**Private Automatic Branch Exchange (PABX).** See Private Branch Exchange.

**Private Branch Exchange (PBX).** Also called private automatic branch exchange (PABX). A telephone system located at the contact center's site that handles incoming and outgoing calls. ACD software can provide PBXs with ACD functionality. Many refer to a PBX as a "switch."

**Private Network.** A network made up of circuits for the exclusive use of an organization or group of affiliated organizations. Can be regional, national or international in scope and are common in large organizations.

**Process.** A system of causes. See System of Causes.

**Qualitative Analysis.** Analysis that interprets descriptive data, and is usually expressed as text. Related term: Quantitative Analysis.

**Quantitative Analysis.** Analysis that focuses on numerical, mathematical or statistical data. Related term: Qualitative Analysis.

**Quantitative Forecasting.** Using statistical techniques to forecast future events. Related terms: Forecasting Methodologies, Judgmental Forecasting.

**Queue.** Queue literally means "line of waiting people." Holds callers until an agent becomes available. Queue can also refer to a line or list of items in a system waiting to be processed (e.g., email messages).

**Queue Display.** See Readerboard.

**Queue Dynamics.** Queue dynamics refer to how queues behave; e.g., when service level goes up, occupancy goes down. Related terms: Agent Group, Average Speed of Answer, Occupancy, Service Level, Trunk Load.

**Queue Time.** See Delay. Random Call Arrival. The normal, random variation in how incoming calls arrive.

**Readerboard.** Also called display board, queue display, wallboard or electronic display. A visual display, usually mounted on the wall or ceiling of a contact center, that provides real-time and historical information on queue conditions, agent status and contact center performance.

**Real-Time Adherence Software.** A function of workforce management software that tracks how closely agents conform to their schedules. See Adherence to Schedule.

**Real-Time Management.** Making adjustments to staffing and thresholds in the systems and network in response to current queue conditions. Related terms: Queue Dynamics, Real-Time Report, Service Level.

**Real-Time Report.** Information on current conditions.

**Real-Time Threshold.** A marker that is identified in advance (e.g., number of calls in queue, longest in queue, etc.) that automatically initiates a certain response in a contact center. For example, at a given time, a contact center may not react to a queue unless it reaches 25 calls or more.

**Received Call.** A call detected and seized by a trunk. Received calls will either abandon or be answered by an agent. Related terms: Answered Call, Handled Call, Offered Call.

**Recorded Announcement.** A general reference to announcements callers hear while waiting in queue. Recorded announcements may remind callers to have certain information ready for the call, include general information about products or services, or provide contact alternatives (e.g., "Visit our website at..."), etc. See Delay Announcement.

**Recorded Announcement Route (RAN).** See Delay Announcement.

**Response Time.** Expressed as "100 percent of contacts handled within N days/hours/minutes" (e.g., all email will be handled within 24 hours). It is the preferred objective for contacts that do not have to be handled when they arrive. See Service Level.

**Retention.** The opposite of turnover; keeping employees in the contact center. See Turnover.

**Retrial Tables.** Sometimes used to calculate trunks and other system resources required. They assume that some callers will make additional attempts to reach the contact center if they get busy signals. Related terms: Erlang B, Poisson.

**Retrial.** Also called redial. When a person tries again to complete a call after encountering a busy signal.

**Ring Delay.** Also called delay before answer. An ACD feature that enables the system to adjust the number of rings before the system automatically answers a call.

**Root Cause.** A primary cause of a problem or outcome. See System of Causes.

**Rostered Staff Factor (RSF).** Alternatively called overlay, shrink factor or shrinkage. RSF is a numerical factor that leads to the minimum staff needed on schedule over and above base staff required to achieve your service level and response time objectives. It is calculated after base staffing is determined and before schedules are organized, and accounts for things like breaks, absenteeism and ongoing training. Related term: Base Staff.

**Round-Robin Distribution.** A method of distributing calls to agents according to a predetermined list. Related terms: Next Available Agent, Longest-Available Agent.

**Sales Force Automation (SFA).** The use of computer and communications systems to support and boost the productivity of salespeople.

**Scatter Diagram.** A quality tool that assesses the strength of the relationship between two variables. Is used to test and document possible cause-and-effect scenarios. See System of Causes.

**Schedule.** A plan that specifies when employees will be on duty, and which may indicate specific activities that they are to handle at specific times. A schedule includes the days worked, start times and stop times, breaks, paid and unpaid status, etc.

**Schedule Compliance.** See Adherence to Schedule.

**Schedule Exception.** An activity not planned in an employee's schedule that becomes an "exception" to the plan. Related terms: Adherence to Schedule, Schedule.

**Schedule Horizon.** How far in advance schedules are determined.

**Schedule Preference.** A description of the times and days that an employee prefers to work. Related terms: Schedule, Schedule Horizon.

**Schedule Trade.** When agents are allowed to trade or "swap" schedules.

**Scheduled Callback.** A specified time that the contact center will call a customer, usually based on the customer's preferences.

**Scheduled Staff vs. Actual.** A performance measure that is a comparison of the number of agents scheduled versus the number actually in the center, involved in the activities specified by the schedule. Related term: Adherence to Schedule.

**Screen Monitoring.** A system capability that enables a supervisor or manager to remotely monitor the activity on agents' computer terminals. See Monitoring.

**Screen Pop.** A CTI application that delivers an incoming call to an agent, along with the data screen pertaining to that call or caller. See Computer Telephony Integration.

**Screen Refresh.** The rate at which real-time information is updated on a display (e.g., every five to 15 seconds). Screen refresh does not correlate with the timeframe used for real-time calculations.

**Search Engine.** Tools that enable customers to find information on the Web. Related terms: Blog, Facebook, LinkedIn, Social Media, Twitter.

**Seated Agents.** See Base Staff.

**Self-Service System.** A system that enables customers to access the information or services they need without interacting with an agent.

**Sentiment Aggregator.** Tools (engines) and/or methodologies that browse the Web, social networks, and feedback sites to collect and assess customer sentiment, opinions and conversations on companies, products, services or virtually any topic of discussion. Related terms: Influencer, Sentiment Analysis, Social Media.

**Sentiment Analysis.** Tools and methodologies used to assess the nature of customer sentiment and comments about a company's products, services and reputation. It is a fast-growing aspect of social customer service, and with speech and text analytics tools, can also be applied to interactions captured through virtually any channel. At a basic level, sentiment can be broadly categorized as positive, negative or neutral. Deeper levels of analysis can correlate findings to changes in services and products, competitive trends, customer demographics and other variables. In social media, a related area is identifying (and serving appropriately) the "influencers" who have large or pertinent followings and can significantly impact the opinions and behavior of other customers and prospects. Related terms: Analytics, Influencer, Sentiment Aggregator, Social Media.

**Service Bureau.** A service bureau, sometimes referred to as an outsourcer, is a company hired to handle some or all of another organization's contacts. See Outsourcing.

**Service Level.** Also called telephone service factor (TSF). Service level is expressed as: "X percent of contacts answered in Y seconds"; e.g., 90 percent answered in 20 seconds. Contacts that must be handled when they arrive require a service level objective, and those that can be handled at a later time require a response time objective. Related Terms: Response Time, Service Level Agreement.

**Service Level Agreement (SLA).** An agreement — usually between a client organization and an outsourcer (although they increasingly exist between departments within an organization) — which defines performance objectives and expectations.

**Service Observing.** See Monitoring.

**Session.** The whole of an interaction by chat, from hello to goodbye. Related terms: Close-Out, Customer Response Time, Exchange, Exchange Handle Time, Exchange Response Time, Session Handle Time, Session Response Time, Session Transaction Time.

**Session Handle Time.** In chat, the cumulative total of the exchange handle times for the session. Related terms: Close-Out, Customer Response Time, Exchange, Exchange Handle Time, Exchange Response Time, Session, Session Response Time, Session Transaction Time.

**Session Response Time.** In chat, the time it takes the organization to respond to the initial request for a session from the customer. Related terms: Close-Out, Customer Response Time, Exchange, Exchange Handle Time, Exchange Response Time, Session, Session Handle Time, Session Transaction Time.

**Session Transaction Time.** In chat, the time elapsed from the beginning of the initial exchange to close-out. Related terms: Close-Out, Customer Response Time, Exchange, Exchange Handle Time, Exchange Response Time, Session, Session Handle Time, Session Response Time.

**Shrink Factor.** See Rostered Staff Factor.

**Shrinkage.** See Rostered Staff Factor.

**Silent Monitoring.** See Monitoring.

**Simultaneous Contact.** When customers contact the organization through multiple channels, e.g., they send an email, text message and call, in an an attempt to see which alternative results in the fastest or most desirable response. Related term: Channel Switching.

**Site Selection.** The process of choosing a contact center location that best meets the needs of the organization.

**Six Sigma.** Originally developed by Motorola, Six Sigma is a disciplined process that focuses on developing and delivering near-perfect products and services. Sigma is a statistical term that measures process variation. Lean Six Sigma is a variation of Six Sigma that focuses on the elimination of waste. See System of Causes.

**Skill Group.** See Agent Group.

**Skill Path.** Skill paths focus on the development of specific skills rather than the progression of positions through the contact center and/or organization. Skill paths can move laterally (e.g., a printer technical support agent can be cross-trained to handle technical support on laptops, as well) or upward (e.g., an agent can acquire leadership and coaching skills to add peer coaching responsibilities to his or her current position). See Career Path.

**Skills-Based Routing.** An ACD capability that matches a caller's specific needs with an agent that has the skills to handle that call, on a real-time basis. Related terms: Agent Group, Pooling Principle.

**Smooth Call Arrival.** Calls that arrive evenly across a period of time. Virtually non-existent in incoming contact center environments.

**Social Media.** Web-based or mobile technologies that enable user-generated content and/or communication between and among people who are part of a social network. Related terms: Blog, Collaboration Tools, Facebook, Influencer, LinkedIn, Search Engine, Sentiment Aggregator, Sentiment Analysis, Social Media, Twitter.

**Software as a Service.** See Cloud-Based Services.

**Span of Control.** The number of individuals a manager supervises. A large span of control means that the manager supervises many people. A small span of control means he or she supervisors fewer people.

**Speech Analytics.** Broadly refers to analytics applied to speech content, e.g., to call recordings. Related terms: Analytics, Text Analytics.

**Speech Recognition.** Speech recognition enables IVR systems to interact with databases using spoken language, rather than the telephone keypad. There are two major types of speech recognition used in call centers today: 1) directed dialogue or structured language, which is prompting that coaches the caller through the selections; and 2) natural language, which uses a more open-ended prompt, recognizing what the caller says without as much coaching. See Interactive Voice Response.

**Split.** See Agent Group.

**Split Shifts.** Shifts in which agents work a partial shift, take part of the day off, then return later to finish their shift. Related term: Schedule.

**Staff Sharing.** A staff-sharing relationship is when two or more organizations (or different units of an organization) share a common pool of employees, typically to meet seasonal demands. Related term: Schedule.

**Staggered Shifts.** Shifts that begin and end at different times. For example, one shift begins at 7 a.m., the next at 7:30 a.m., the next at 8 a.m., until the center is fully staffed for the busy midmorning traffic. Related term: Schedule.

**Standard.** A quantifiable minimum level of performance; performance below or outside the standard is not acceptable.

**Super Agent.** See Universal Agent.

**Supervisor Monitor.** Computer monitors that enable supervisors to monitor the contact handling statistics of their supervisory groups or teams.

**Supervisor.** The person who has frontline responsibility for a group of agents. Generally, supervisors are equipped with special telephones and computer terminals that enable them to monitor agent activities. Related terms: Job Role, Monitoring, Span of Control.

**SWAT Team.** The term some companies use for a team of non-contact center employees that act as "reservists" to quickly be assigned to call handling duties if the call load soars. Related term: Schedule.

**System of Causes.** The variables that are part of a process. A contact center is a process or system of causes.

**Tablet.** A common reference to a tablet computer, a flat, mobile computer that is designed to be operated through a touch screen rather than a keyboard.

**Talk Time.** Everything from "hello" to "goodbye" in a phone call. In other words, it's the time callers are connected with agents. Anything that happens during talk time, such as placing customers on hold to confer with supervisors, should be included in this measurement. Also called Direct Call Processing. Related terms: After-Call Work, Average Handling Time, Call Load.

**Telemarketing.** Generally refers to outbound calls for the purpose of selling products or services, or placing informational calls to customers, prospective customers or constituents.

**Telephone Sales or Service Representative (TSR).** See Agent.

**Telephone Service Factor (TSF).** See Service Level.

**Text Analytics.** Broadly refers to analytics applied to text content, e.g., email or calls that have been converted into text documents. Related terms: Analytics, Speech Analytics.

**Text-Chat.** See Chat.

**Threshold.** The point at which an action, change or process takes place.

**Toll-Free Service.** Enables callers to reach a contact center out of the local calling area without incurring charges.

**Touchtone.** A trademark of AT&T. See Dual-Tone Multifrequency.

**Trouble Ticket.** The report of a customer's problem with a particular device or system, which is tracked through the workflow process.

**True Calls Per Agent.** Also called normalized calls per agent. It is actual calls (contacts) an individual or group handled divided by occupancy for that period of time. Related terms: Adherence to Schedule, Call Quality, Contacts Handled (Calls Per Agent).

**Trunk.** Also called a line, exchange line or circuit. A telephone circuit linking two switching systems. See Trunk Load.

**Trunk Group.** A collection of trunks associated with a single peripheral and usually used for a common purpose. Related terms: Trunk, Trunk Group.

**Trunk Load.** The load that trunks carry. Includes both delay and talk time.

**Turnover.** When a person leaves the contact center. Turnover can be categorized as voluntary (when the employee decides to leave the organization or position) or involuntary (when management makes the decision to end the employment relationship).

**Twitter.** A popular social microblogging site, based on messages (called tweets) of 140 characters or fewer.

**Unavailable Work State.** An agent work state used to identify a mode not associated with handling telephone calls.

**Unified Reporting.** When data from different channels and systems are included on one reporting tool. This supports better analysis and decision-making in the organization.

**Uniform Call Distributor (UCD).** A simple system that distributes calls to a group of agents and provides some reports.

**Uniform Resource Locator (URL).** The address for a Web page that is translated to an IP address.

**Universal Agent.** Also known as super agent. Refers to either: A) an agent who can handle all types of issues, or B) an agent who can handle all channels of contact (e.g., inbound calls, outbound calls, email, text-chat, social interactions, etc.).

**Upsell.** A suggestive selling technique of offering more expensive products or services to current customers during the sales decision. See Cross-sell.

**Variance Report.** A report illustrating budget/cost objectives that looks at the difference between projected and actual expenditures for various budget categories.

**Virtual Call Center (Virtual Contact Center).** A distributed call center (contact center) that acts as a single site for call handling and reporting purposes.

**Visible Queue.** When callers know how long the queue that they just entered is, and how quickly it is moving (e.g., they hear a system announcement that relays the expected wait time). Related terms: Invisible Queue, Queue.

**Voice of the Customer.** Broadly refers to tools, methods and collaboration that capture customers' input and perceptions, seek to understand customer needs and wants, and use captured data to improve products, services and processes. In contact centers, voice-of-the-customer initiatives seek to harness the potential the organization has to better understand customers and shape products, services and customer service so that the overall customer experience is improved. See Customer Experience.

**Wallboard.** See Readerboard.

**Web Callback.** By clicking on a button, the customer lets the company know that he/she wants to be called back either immediately or at a designated time.

**Web Call-Through.** Using voice over Internet (VoIP) technology, the customer clicks on a button that establishes a voice line directly to the contact center.

**Web Chat.** See Chat.

**Web Collaboration.** A broad term referring to the ability for an agent and customer to share content by pushing/pulling Web pages and/or whiteboarding and page markup.

**Web Self-Service Tools.** Tools that enable customers to receive information and answers to questions, place orders and view order status directly from the corporate website without agent assistance. See Self-Service System.

**Wide Area Network (WAN).** The connection of multiple computers across a wide area.

**Work State.** An ACD-produced indicator of the status of a contact center agent's activity or status. See Agent Status.

**Workforce Management System (WFMS).** Software systems that, depending on available modules, forecast call load, calculate staff requirements, organize schedules and track real-time performance of individuals and groups. Related terms: Computer Simulation, Erlang B, Erlang C, Forecasting Methodologies, Queue Dynamics.

**Workforce Optimization.** A broad description of the latest generation of advanced workforce management and quality systems, which include features such as multichannel forecasting and scheduling, quality monitoring and recording, scoring and coaching tools, analytics capabilities, e-learning integration, customer and employee surveys, advanced reporting capabilities, and others.

**Workload.** Often used interchangeably with Call Load. Workload can also refer to non-call activities.

**Wrap-Up Codes.** Codes that agents enter on their phones to identify the types of calls they are handling. The ACD can then generate reports on call types by handling time, time of day, etc. See After-Call Work.

**Zip Tone.** See Beep Tone.

# Index

# Other Books from ICMI ...

*Call Center Technology Demystified: The No-Nonsense Guide to Bridging Customer Contact Technology, Operations and Strategy*

*Driving Peak Sales Performance in Call Centers*

*Survey Pain Relief: Transforming Customer Insights into Action*

*ICMI's Call Center Management Dictionary*

Find these titles and more at www.icmi.com/Resources/Books

## About ICMI

The International Customer Management Institute (ICMI) is the leading global provider of comprehensive resources for customer management professionals — from agents to executives — who wish to improve the customer experience and increase efficiencies at every level of the contact center. Since 1985, ICMI has helped tens of thousands of organizations in 167 countries through training, events, certification, consulting, and informational resources. ICMI's experienced and dedicated team of industry insiders, trainers, and consultants are committed to helping you raise the strategic value of your contact center, optimize your operations and improve your customer service. For more information, visit www.icmi.com.

ICMI is a part of UBM (www.ubm.com), a global live media and B2B communications, marketing service and data provider.

# How to Reach ICMI Press

We would love to hear from you! You can reach us at:

| | |
|---|---|
| Mailing Address: | ICMI Press |
| | 121 South Tejon Street, Suite 1100 |
| | Colorado Springs, CO 80903 |
| Telephone: | 719-268-0328, 800-672-6177 |
| Fax: | 719-268-0184 |
| Email: | icmi@icmi.com |
| Website: | www.icmi.com |

# Connect with Brad

To follow Brad's blog or newsletter, or to arrange a visit to your organization or event, see:

Website: bradcleveland.com

Blog: bradcleveland.com/blog

Twitter: @bradcleveland

Facebook: bradcleveland.com/faccbook

Email: info@bradcleveland.com

Visit the website for *Call Center Management on Fast Forward* to meet the author, see videos, interact, ask questions and learn more about the book! **www.icmi.com/fastforward**